# sappi tree spotting

## BUSHVELD
### INCLUDING PILANESBERG & MAGALIESBERG

**TREE IDENTIFICATION MADE EASY**

Wild-pear Dombeya
*Dombeya rotundifolia*

Rina Grant and Val Thomas
Illustrations by Joan van Gogh

Jacana

# Acknowledgements

**Sappi Tree Spotting Bushveld** has taken two years of intensive research and testing to reach publication. Jacana is grateful to all the people from many different fields who contributed their time and commitment to produce this superb publication. We would like specifically to thank the following individuals and organisations for their dedication, time and expertise during the project.

We sincerely thank Professor Kader Asmal, Minister of Education, for his support and for writing the foreword.

The research and development of **Sappi Tree Spotting Bushveld** was carried out by the Jacana Team, primarily Val Thomas and Dr Rina Grant. This would not have been possible without the assistance of the following scientists and researchers: Hugo Bezuidenhout; Duan Biggs; Bruce Brockett; Jutta von Breytenbach, Yvette Coetzee; Linden Estes; Mike Peel; Gerhard Strydom and Riëtte Smit (Dendrological Society); Neels van Tonder (Bonsai Friend); Guin Zambatis.

Many people gave generously of their time and we thank them for their invaluable assistance, particularly Hugo Bezuidenhout; Bruce Brockett; John Rushworth; Jutta von Breytenbach and Guin Zambatis for their contributions to the editing of the book; and the rangers and staff at Pilanesberg National Park, especially Gus van Dyk and George Phiri for their involvement.

Our special thanks to Joan van Gogh for the beautiful artwork which will assist tree spotters to discover and identify trees of the Bushveld. We would also like to acknowledge and thank Sally MacLarty for her contributions to the line-artwork.

We sincerely thank the following for their photographs: Michael Brett, Riëtte Smit, Gary van der Merwe and the Jacana Team (Dr Rina Grant, Peter Thomas and Val Thomas).

We would like to thank the various companies and individuals for their expert help in the production of the maps: Michael Brett; Gordon Lumby (Cartographics) for layout and DTP; The National Botanical Institute for the use of data from the Herbarium, Pretoria (PRE) Computerised Information Systems (PRECIS), in particular Hannelie Snyman, Trevor Arnold, Hugh Glen and Marie Jordaan (NBI), and Jutta von Breytenbach (The Dendrological Society) for the Tree Distribution Maps.

The polished surfaces of the wood samples were photographed by André Pretorius and Gary van der Merwe, by courtesy of Stephanie Dyer, Division of Water Environment and Forestry Technology (Environmentek) CSIR, Timber Utilisation Programme, Forestek. The wood ornaments were donated to Pretoria University by the late WEC van Wyk and photographed by courtesy of Magda Nel and Professor AE van Wyk (Department of Botany).

The book was designed by Jacana, and the cover by David Selfe Designs. The Desktop Publishing was carried out by Jacana.

We are proud to acknowledge the work of the entire Jacana Team who have contributed in their specialised fields to produce **Sappi Tree Spotting Bushveld**: Janet Bartlet, Debbie Benjamin, Carol Broomhall, Ryan Francois, Tracey Fisher, Liz Godfrey, Dr Rina Grant, Joanne Mallet, Andrea Meeson, Obed Molobe, Debbie Munro, Fortune Ncube, Davidson Ndebele, Jannett Ndebele, David Ngwenya, Sue Nel, Bambi Nunes, Karen Pereira, Jenny Prangley, Zamila Rayman, Joan Sibiya, Mariette Strydom, Amanda Thoane, Camilla Thomas, Peter Thomas, Val Thomas, Pamela Thompson, Gary van der Merwe, Rika van Rooyen and Bridget Walters.

Finally we would like to thank Sappi Limited for their vision and commitment in helping to fund the research and development of a book that we believe will significantly add towards helping South Africans and our visitors to be aware of, care for, protect and enjoy our magnificent Bushveld trees.

# Foreword

Perhaps of all of our natural systems, it is the Bushveld that many South Africans find particularly evocative, as it is widely associated with the big game of our national parks and nature reserves. It has intrigued me that there are people who are genuine experts on our large mammals, or on our birds, but who know very little about the systems that support them.

One might speculate on a fairly typical evolution in an interest in ecology, where the big game is the initial lure, and our glorious abundance of bird species the bait. Sadly, many people stop there, and fail to develop an understanding of how these species have adapted to their environment, and their part in the dynamics of those environments. It is a plausible contention that one of the reasons why so many people fail to capitalise on their initial interest in nature is the dearth of appropriate literature on the integrated functioning of our natural systems.

It is relatively easy to elicit excitement in fierce predators, or to be captivated by the liquid eyes and luscious eyelashes of antelope; awesomely colourful birds are sure attention-grabbers; and the spiders and snakes provoke primordial passion in most of us. But trees and grasses, and the soils and water regimes, require a far greater skill to sell to your average nature-lover.

It is with this perspective in mind that I recommend this latest book in the magnificent **Sappi Tree Spotting** series. The Bushveld Trees book is a marvellous companion to the acclaimed books on the trees of the Lowveld, Highveld and KwaZulu-Natal. What makes them special, to my mind, is the way in which they entice us into the intricacies and inter-relationships of Nature, through the perspective of trees.

I wrote the forewords to the previous books in my former capacity as Minister of Water Affairs and Forestry. I am delighted to write this foreword in my capacity as Minister of Education. I am delighted for two reasons. Firstly, these **Sappi Tree Spotting** books are exceptional educational aids, and deserve recognition as such. Secondly, I have publicly announced my intention to make environmental education a central focus of my tenure as Minister of Education, and delight in being able to signal this intention by having this as the first book that I endorse in my new portfolio.

But old habits die hard, and I must close with something that concerned me as Minister of Water Affairs and Forestry, and continues to concern me as an educationalist: the thorny subject of invading alien plants that spread without control, and take over our natural ecosystems. There is no greater threat to our biological diversity than the invasion of alien species. This wonderful book is thus also a reminder of what it is that we have to lose, should we not take control of these invading species.

I would like to wish Sappi and Jacana well in the distribution of this book, and the others in the series. We are all richer for their publications.

**Professor Kader Asmal, MP**
**Minister of Education**

Red Ivorywood,
page 342

# sappi

The Bushveld is a huge area of northern South Africa, much of which remains in a pristine state, suffering little impact from agriculture or industry. It is an area of open savannah grassland, dotted with large trees. The five major hill and mountain ranges of the Magaliesberg, Pilanesberg, Waterberg, Soutpansberg and the Drakensberg punctuate the Plains with special and exciting blends of rocks, kloofs, waterfalls, escarpments and valleys that are home to unique fauna and flora. Believe it or not, some tree inhabitants in these areas have ancestry that pre-dates the land mammals on Earth.

The Bushveld, being close to metropolitan areas, has long provided many South Africans with opportunities for outdoor pursuits, whether it be hiking, walking, fishing or camping. The discovery of Birding as a pastime has increased South Africans' pleasure in the Bushveld. Tree Spotting in the Bushveld, even in identifying and learning about a few of the most common trees, indigenous to the area, will lift the Bushveld experience to a new high.

The pastime of "spotting trees" has not kept pace with "watching birds", largely because trees show markedly individual variations, even when they are actually identical species. Every Hadeda in the country looks exactly like its cousins and in-laws, but confusingly, no single Paperbark Acacia is identical to any other! Until the easy-to-use and understandable **Sappi Tree Spotting** series was published, tree identification always appeared complicated, and only for the scientific community.

With the **Sappi Tree Spotting** series has come three major breakthroughs in enjoying tree spotting:

- It de-mystifies tree spotting talk into everyday language.
- It identifies the specific area covered by the information (using a scientific base).
- It highlights likely trees (and their striking features) that can be found in each area.

Beause of this, tree spotting has become the preserve of the beginner and tree enthusiast alike.

Tree spotting adds a new dimension to the outdoor experience, and has become a passionate hobby for a new breed of nature lovers who are chasing the incredible total of 1 200 South African woody species. Sappi is proud to have been a part of this exciting outdoor pursuit.

We hope you enjoy **Sappi Tree Spotting – Bushveld**, our fourth in the series of **Sappi Tree Spotting** books.

*The Sappi Portfolio: John Meyer – The Northern Bushveld*

# The National Botanical Institute (NBI)

*The mission of the National Botanical Institute is to promote the sustainable use, conservation, appreciation and enjoyment of the exceptionally rich plant life of South Africa, for the benefit of all its people.*

The NBI is an autonomous, state-supported, statutory organisation, which has its head office in the Kirstenbosch National Botanical Garden. It has physical resources such as the eight National Botanical Gardens, three Herbaria and two Research Units. In addition, it boasts the human resources of many highly qualified scientists, horticulturists, academics and support staff.

## National Botanical Gardens

The eight National Botanical Gardens propagate and display the unique wealth and diversity of South African flora. Our National Botanical Gardens are situated throughout the country and specialise in local flora.

## Herbaria

The combined collections of dried plant material of the three NBI herbaria, in Pretoria, Cape Town and Durban, contain over 1,5 million specimens of mainly Southern African plant material. They are an invaluable resource to researchers throughout the African continent, as well as internationally.

## Education

Environmental Education, both within the National Botanical Gardens and working with communities on greening projects country-wide, is a major priority of the National Botanical Institute.

## Research

The Conservation Biology Research Programme focuses on conservation of plant diversity and plant resources in Southern Africa.

Many plants could prove invaluable to humans in terms of new food crops or medicinally as cures for diseases for which, at present, there are no cures. However, many are being eradicated before their potential has been investigated.

The Stress Ecology Research Programme focuses on responses of vegetation to environmental stress and global change. These are crucial questions facing mankind to which answers must be found before it is too late.

## Botanical Society membership

Members of the public who are interested in the work of the NBI can join their nearest branch of the Botanical Society, or can visit their local National Botanical Garden.

## NBI and Sappi Tree Spotting

As a sheer coincidence of positive energy the early phase of planning the Tree Spotting series overlapped with the NBI publication of the *Low and Rebelo Vegetation Map of South Africa* (see page 4).

Defining the boundaries of each Tree Spotting book, and the zones within each boundary, was automatically facilitated by this essential piece of scientific work. It is services and relationships such as these that make the NBI an unique and invaluable asset to South Africa. As part of the information about each tree, there are mini maps of their South African distribution. The information for each of these maps was supplied by the NBI from data collected throughout the country.

# Botanical Society of South Africa

*The Botanical Society aims to support the National Botanical Institute and to promote the conservation, cultivation, study and wise use of the indigenous plants of Southern Africa for the benefit of all.*

The Botanical Society is a non-governmental organisation with 12 branches throughout the country. Most of these support the National Botanical Gardens.

## Botanical Society Branches' Membership

Information and application forms are obtainable from the various National Botanical Gardens, Botanical Society head office or branches.

### Head office: Kirstenbosch

Tel: (021) 797-2090 Fax: (021) 797-2376
e-mail: botsocsa@gem.co.za
Private Bag X10, Newlands, 7725
New members are welcome.
Members enjoy the following benefits:

- The privilege of visiting any of South Africa's National Botanical Gardens free of charge.
- The opportunity to create an indigenous garden from your annual allocation of free seed.
- First hand experience can be gained of our magnificent indigenous plants on organised hikes and outings.
- The opportunity to increase your knowledge by attending demonstrations and lectures.
- The pleasure of receiving Veld & Flora, our quarterly magazine full of interesting articles, free of charge.
- A discount of 10% on plants and books purchased at Kirstenbosch Gardens, Cape Town and at the Witwatersrand National Botanical Garden, Roodepoort.
- The opportunity to support and participate in plant conservation and environmental education projects and to assist with development projects for the National Botanical Institute.

## Botanical Society Branches and Botanical Gardens

### Botanical Society Branches

| | |
|---|---|
| Albany Branch | (046) 636-1370 |
| Bankenveld Branch | (011) 954-2890 |
| Bredasdorp / Napier Branch | (02842) 42082 |
| Durban Branch | (031) 260-2416 |
| Free State Branch | (051) 436-3612 |
| Garden Route Branch | (0441) 877-1360 |
| Johannesburg Branch | (011) 716-4012 |
| Kirstenbosch Branch | (021) 671-5468 |
| Kogelberg Branch | (028) 272-9404 |
| Lowveld Branch | (013) 744-0241 |
| Pietermaritzburg Branch | (0331) 43-1386 |
| Pretoria Branch | (012) 333-4629 |
| Villiersdorp Branch | (028) 840-2244 (pm) |

### Botanical Gardens

| | |
|---|---|
| Free State National Botanical Garden | (051) 436-3612 |
| Harold Porter National Botanical Garden | (028) 272-9311 |
| Karoo National Botanical Garden | (023) 347-0785 |
| Kirstenbosch National Botanical Garden | (021) 762-9120 |
| Lowveld National Botanical Garden | (013) 752-5531 |
| Natal National Botanical Garden | (033) 344-3585 |
| Pretoria National Botanical Garden | (012) 804-3166 |
| Witwatersrand National Botanical Garden | (011) 958-1750/1 |

# Dendrological Society

*Arborum silvarumque conservatio salus mundi est. – The conservation of trees and forests is the salvation of the world.*

## The Dendrological Foundation

When the Dendrological Foundation was formed in 1979 by Dr F. von Breitenbach, the terms "Dendrology" and "Dendrologist" were fairly unknown in South Africa. The Foundation was created as an independent, non-profit, non-racial association aimed at the promotion of the knowledge of trees. This was with particular emphasis on the protection, planting and preservation of indigenous tree-dominated ecosystems.

Early projects were carried out:
- to standardise the common English and Afrikaans tree names, and species' numbers
- to standardise the ethnic names
- to create a "Big Tree Register" of the biggest trees of any species in South Africa
- to publish the "*Dendron*" newsletter

"*Dendron*" has been published ever since 1979 on a more or less regular basis. In 1981 the first issue of the Journal of Dendrology appeared containing more scientific essays on all aspects of dendrology.

## Dendrological Society

In 1980 the Dendrological Society was formed. The aims of the Society were similar to those of the earlier Foundation, focusing on conservation and education.

Tree conservation cannot succeed without the active participation of both city dwellers and country people. In order to preserve trees, people have to love and respect them and to do this, they at least have to know their names or their families.
Many of the Society's activities support this basic philosophy.

- The Society runs correspondence Tree Knowledge Courses which aim to spread the joy of trees through information.
- The Society provides a Tree Identification Service for members who submit specimens for identification.
- Tree Number Plates are available from the Society. They are made in a high-quality ABS-material with the National tree number, and the botanical and common names in Afrikaans and English. They are also available with an ethnic common name in place of Afrikaans. Contact Jutta von Breitenbach for further information.

### Publications of the Dendrological Society
- "National List of Indigenous Trees" (1995) in its third, revised edition
- "National List of Introduced Trees" (1984) in its second, revised edition
- The first volume of the "Tree Atlas of Southern Africa" (1992) which is to be followed by another 22 volumes

### Branches
Branches around the country are named after a tree species or a significant geographical feature.
- "Magalies" – Pretoria
  (012) 567-4009 Jutta von Breitenbach
- "Umdoni" – Durban
- "Celtis" – Pietermaritzburg
- "Kameeldoring" – Potgietersrus
- "Erythrina"– Pietersburg
- "Atalaya" – Port Elizabeth
- "Wolkberg" – Tzaneen
- "Tafelberg" – Cape Town
- "Witwatersrand" – Johannesburg
- "Boekenhout" – Witbank
- "Langeberg" – Swellendam
- "Manketti" – Ellisras
- "Olienhout" – Groot Marico
- "Soutpansberg" – Louis Trichardt
- "Outeniqua" – Knysna
- "Vaal" – Meyerton
- "Kwambonambi" – Zululand

The Society is growing annually and looks forward to new members.

# Tree Society

*The Tree Society of Southern Africa has been actively involved in promoting an interest in our natural heritage since 1946.*

Our members are enthusiasts from all walks of life, including professional botanists, who will gladly assist you to extend your knowledge of the environment. Discussions on walks extend beyond trees to cover geology, general flora, fauna and history.

## Tree Society outings

Enjoy the opportunity to walk in undisturbed areas, of natural history interest, not accessible to the public.

- Day outings are arranged to local areas of particular botanical interest within reasonable driving distance of Johannesburg and Pretoria.
- Weekend and long weekend outings are when visits are organised to areas in our neighbouring provinces, including KwaZulu-Natal.
- A prime objective of these outings is to compile vegetation checklists for the landowners, and to alert them to any particularly rare species or to advise them on noxious invaders which need to be controlled. Specimens are sometimes collected for the Gauteng herbaria.

## Education

- The Tree Society has been instrumental in establishing three prizes for excellence in the field of Plant Systematics at the University of the Witwatersrand.
- Funds being available, the Society will assist deserving students to further their studies in the field of botany.
- The Tree Society collaborates with the C.E. Moss Herbarium of the Department of Animal, Plant and Environmental Sciences in offering courses on tree identification to the public. These courses involve lectures, laboratory practicals and field work.
- On request courses and lectures can be arranged for specific groups such as students or local conservation organisations.

## Tree Society publications

- *"Trees in South Africa"* – The Society journal has been published since 1949 and back numbers of many issues are still available. The articles published are of general and botanical interest.
- *"Peltophorum"* – The Society Newsletter is issued twice a year to provide outing details and commentary on Society activities plus items of general interest to members.

Of the other works published by the Society over the years, copies of two monographs are still available as are two works by J.D. Carr. These are:

- Some Observations on the Genus Commiphora in South and South West Africa by B. de Winter
- The Wild Figs of Southern Africa by J. von Breitenbach
- Combretaceae in Southern Africa by J.D. Carr
- The Propagation and Cultivation of Indigenous Trees and Shrubs on the Highveld by J.D. Carr

## Society membership

Membership entitles you to participate in the activities of the Society and to the Journal and Newsletter. Details may be obtained from:

The Tree Society of Southern Africa
P.O. Box 70720, Bryanston, 2021

Tel / Fax: (011) 465-6045     Walter Barker
e-mail: walterb@icon.co.za

Tel:     (011) 316-1426     Cheryl Dehning
Fax:    (011) 316-1095
e-mail: dehning@mweb.co.za

### WITS courses

For information on these courses contact Reneé Reddy or Kevin Balkwill on
Tel: (011) 717-6467
or e-mail: kevinb@gecko.biol.wits.ac.za

# Trees for Africa

*Trees for Africa (TFA) encourages South Africans to celebrate trees. TFA's mission is to contribute to a healthy and sustainable quality of life for all South Africans through environmental awareness and greening programmes.*

TFA's objectives are two-fold:
- To involve at least 10% of the population in greening projects by the year 2000.
- Secondly to create an awareness of the benefits of environmental upliftment activities amongst all communities of southern Africa.

TFA, established in 1990, has quickly evolved into the only national, non-governmental, non-profit, greening organisation in South Africa. It is currently involved in diverse projects ranging from urban greening, permaculture, environmental awareness and education to township nurseries. Over 1,2 million trees have been distributed to thousands of disadvantaged, community-based organisations.

## Some achievements include the following:
- The creation of an indigenous forest at Nelson Mandela's property in Qunu, Transkei.
- The facilitation of eight community nurseries – some of the first ever township nurseries.
- Ten large permaculture gardens established with pensioners, women, ex-convicts and unemployed community members.
- Numerous schools' permaculture projects developed nationally. A number of schools are now growing enough fruit and vegetables to feed all the pupils, and some even have surplus to sell to their communities.
- "Introduction to Permaculture" Workshops run for hundreds of teachers in all provinces to encourage participation in the EduPlant Competition, encouraging schools to create a sustainable food producing environment.
- Working with 20 municipalities and local greening authorities to develop urban greening programmes.
- Contributing to the National Forestry Action Programme and co-writing the first ever South African Urban Forestry guidelines to this programme.
- Three newsletters are produced and distributed locally and internationally to over 4 500 organisations and individuals.

## Membership – per annum
- R35,00 – individual membership; receiving the quarterly newsletter, *Newsleaf*; outside S.A. add on R13,00 postage.
- R100,00 – family membership per year; receiving certificate in the family name; three newsletters quarterly.
- R40,00 – subscription to *Forestry for a Small Planet* (FFASP) and *Permaculture Villager* (PV), two informative, networking newsletters, produced quarterly; outside S.A. add on R13,00 postage.
- Company membership – negotiable; TFA links companies with meaningful community upliftment programmes; receiving a personalised certificate; coverage in TFA's newsletters and Annual Review and subscription to all three newsletters; Media exposure and additional publicity can be organised with larger company sponsors, on request.

## For more information contact:
**Trees for Africa**
P O Box 2035
Gallo Manor 2052
Fax: (011) 803-9604
Tel: (011) 803-9750
Email: trees@cis.co.za
Website: www.trees.co.za
       www.Eduplant.org.za

# Contents

## HOW SAPPI TREE SPOTTING WORKS

| | |
|---|---|
| How Sappi Tree Spotting works | 4 |
| How the pages help you find trees | 10 |
| The Bushveld | 20 |
| Ecozone Tree Lists | 46 |

The tree groups in the contents have been graded from easy-to-spot (palest colour) to the most difficult-to-spot (darkest colour). The colours of the tabs on the side of each page cross-correlate with the contents. These colours have nothing to do with the Ecozones.

## TREES GREET YOU

**Distinctive Striking Features**

| | |
|---|---|
| Flowers | 58 |
| Bean pods | 61 |
| Unusual pods | 62 |
| Unusual pods and fruit | 63 |
| Plums and berries | 64 |
| Leaves | 65 |
| Families | 74 |
| Bark | 80 |

**Unique Trees**

| | |
|---|---|
| Baobab *Adansonia digitata* | 86 |
| Eastern Sesame-bush *Sesamothamnus lugardii* | 90 |
| Ladies Cabbage-tree *Cussonia spicata* | 94 |
| Naboom Euphorbia *Euphorbia ingens* | 98 |
| Squat Star-chestnut *Sterculia rogersii* | 102 |

**Seasonally Striking Trees**

| | |
|---|---|
| Brittlewood Nuxia *Nuxia congesta* | 108 |
| Bushveld Bead-bean *Maerua angolensis* | 112 |
| Flame-pod Acacia *Acacia ataxacantha* | 116 |
| Hairy-leaved Monkey-orange *Strychnos madagascariensis* | 120 |
| Kooboo-berry *Cassine aethiopica* | 124 |
| Large-fruited Bushwillow *Combretum zeyheri* | 128 |
| Large Sourplum *Ximenia caffra* | 132 |
| Peeling-bark Ochna *Ochna pulchra* | 136 |
| Red Bushwillow *Combretum apiculatum* | 140 |
| Russet Bushwillow *Combretum hereroense* | 144 |
| Sacred Coral-tree *Erythrina lysistemon* | 148 |
| White Cats-whiskers *Clerodendrum glabrum* | 152 |
| Wild-pear Dombeya *Dombeya rotundifolia* | 156 |

**Common Spikethorn**
*Gymnosporia buxifolia (Maytenus heterophylla)*
SA Tree no 399
  This tree is very common throughout the Bushveld. It is a single-stemmed, low-branching tree with an angular, untidy outline formed by haphazardly upward-growing branches. Leaves are elliptic, shallowly toothed in upper two thirds and clustered to form sleeves. Flowers are white and star-shaped (February to June) and berry-like fruit is three-celled, densely clustered and ripens May to January.

# You find trees by Ecozone and Habitat

**Ecozone Specialists**

Big-leaf Fever-tree
   *Anthocleista grandiflora*     162

Kiaat Bloodwood
   *Pterocarpus angolensis*     166

Mobola-plum
   *Parinari curatellifolia*     170

Paperbark Acacia
   *Acacia sieberiana*     174

Paperbark Albizia
   *Albizia tanganyicensis*     178

**Bushveld Generalists**

African Olive
   *Olea europaea*     184

Buffalo-thorn Jujube
   *Ziziphus mucronata*     188

Bushveld Shepherds-tree
   *Boscia foetida*     192

Common Wild Fig
   *Ficus burkei*     196

Shepherds-tree
   *Boscia albitrunca*     200

Small-leaved Guarri
   *Euclea undulata*     204

Sweet-thorn Acacia
   *Acacia karroo*     208

**Plains – Large Trees**

African Weeping-wattle
   *Peltophorum africanum*     214

Black-monkey Acacia
   *Acacia burkei*     218

Knob-thorn Acacia
   *Acacia nigrescens*     222

Leadwood
   *Combretum imberbe*     226

Marula
   *Sclerocarya birrea*     230

**Plains – Sandy Areas**

Bukea
   *Burkea africana*     236

Camel-thorn Acacia
   *Acacia erioloba*     240

Silver Cluster-leaf
   *Terminalia sericea*     244

**Plains – Trees in Groups**

Black-thorn Acacia
   *Acacia mellifera*     250

Scented-pod Acacia
   *Acacia nilotica*     254

Sickle-bush
   *Dichrostachys cinerea*     258

Umbrella Acacia
   *Acacia tortilis*     262

**Forest Lavender-tree**
*Heteropyxis canescens*
SA Tree no 454
This is one of South Africa's most beautiful and rarest trees. It can only be found in the forests and wooded kloofs in the mountains near Barberton and Nelspruit. It often grows along streams, where it can reach 12 metres. It has an exceptional peachy-brown underbark which is exposed in unusual concentric rings when circles of darker bark flake off. The leaves are very similar to those of the Weeping Lavender-tree (Heteropyxis natalensis), page 354, but are larger and hairy on the under-surface.

### Rocky Areas

Hornpod-tree
 *Diplorhynchus condylocarpon*   268
Jacket-plum
 *Pappea capensis*   272
Large-leaved Rock Fig
 *Ficus abutilifolia*   276
Lavender Croton
 *Croton gratissimus*   280
Mountain Kirkia
 *Kirkia wilmsii*   284
Red-leaved Fig
 *Ficus ingens*   288
Rock Tree-nettle
 *Obetia tenax*   292
Stamvrug Milkplum
 *Englerophytum magalismontanum*   296
Tall Firethorn Corkwood
 *Commiphora glandulosa*   300
Velvet Bushwillow
 *Combretum molle*   304
White Kirkia
 *Kirkia acuminata*   308

### Mountains

Bushveld Resin-tree
 *Ozoroa paniculosa*   314
Common Hook-thorn Acacia
 *Acacia caffra*   318
Highveld Protea
 *Protea caffra*   322
Highveld Silver-oak
 *Brachylaena rotundata*   326
Live-long Lannea
 *Lannea discolor*   330
Moepel Red-milkwood
 *Mimusops zeyheri*   334
Pipe-stem Fingerleaf
 *Vitex rehmannii*   338
Red Ivorywood
 *Berchemia zeyheri*   342
Silver Raisin
 *Grewia monticola*   346
Weeping Faurea
 *Faurea saligna*   350
Weeping Lavender-tree
 *Heteropyxis natalensis*   354

### Rivers and Kloofs

African White-stinkwood
 *Celtis africana*   360
Broom-cluster Fig
 *Ficus sur*   364
Karree
 *Rhus lancea*   368
Red Currant-rhus
 *Rhus chirindensis*   372
River Bushwillow
 *Combretum erythrophyllum*   376
Robust Acacia
 *Acacia robusta*   380
Small Knobwood
 *Zanthoxylum capense*   384
Tamboti
 *Spirostachys africana*   388
Umdoni Waterberry
 *Syzigium cordatum*   392

**Lover's Cheesewood**
*Pittosporum viridiflorum* SA Tree no 139
This tree can easily be identified by the yellow-green flowers that grow in the leaf-rosettes at the tips of twigs (September to December). Posy-like bunches of yellow-brown fruit burst open to expose shiny, sticky, brilliant-red seeds (November to April). The simple leaves have an intricate net-vein pattern that can be seen clearly when the leaf is held against the sun.

### REFERENCES

Enjoy tree spotting   398
Information grids   400
Bushveld maps   410
Family features   416
Index   421
Book references   428

# How Sappi Tree Spotting works

This section lays the foundation for understanding the Sappi Tree Spotting method. It is enjoyable reading, and will help you to find trees faster.

| | |
|---|---|
| How Sappi Tree Spotting works | p. 4 |
| How the pages help you find trees | p. 10 |
| The Bushveld | p. 20 |
| Ecozone Tree Lists | p. 46 |

Goro Game Reserve in the Soutpansberg, Northern Mountains (N), offers an unusual combination of luxury, beauty, large game and magnificent trees. Here an early morning sun warms the rocks of a steep riverbed.

# How Sappi Tree Spotting works

The main aim of this book is to introduce outdoor enthusiasts to the exciting hobby of tree spotting, and through this to promote recreational tree spotting in South Africa. It is also written to offer experts a new interpretation of trees according to where they grow naturally. The ground-breaking difference between **Sappi Tree Spotting** and other tree books is that the reader is helped to find certain trees according to where they grow. The book, in general, is not designed to answer the question "What tree is that?"

The Bushveld, as defined for this book, is a huge area, with a number of Mountain ranges, interspersed with vast, flattish plains. It has a range of altitude from about 1 000 metres along Mountain and Highveld escarpments, to about 300 metres at the western edge of the Lowveld. It has an average annual rainfall between 350 mm in the west, to over 1 500 mm near the escarpment in the east. This ensures you can look for a wide variety of trees. Some of these are the common-place South African favourites, like Marula (page 230) and Sweet-thorn Acacia (page 208). Others are truly unique, and even breathtaking, and are found only in very limited geographical and/or Habitat ranges. These include the Paperbark Albizia (page 178) and Eastern Sesame-bush (page 90). You are going to have fun tree spotting in the Bushveld!

## WHY SAPPI TREE SPOTTING IS DIFFERENT

**Sappi Tree Spotting** is a creative new way to make the most of the outdoors. It is designed to do for trees what Roberts and Newman have done for birds. Eight years of intensive, scientific field and market research have gone into fine-tuning a simple and innovative method of getting to know trees in their natural environments. Until recently trees have remained inaccessible to all but the most devoted, botanically minded, tree-key followers.

With **Sappi Tree Spotting** this changes in four ways.

1. **Innovative methods of linking real trees to book theory**
   In most other field guides, for either animals or plants, the system is based on:
   - seeing a species in the wild
   - looking it up in the guidebook to identify it, and to gain further information
   In some circumstances this method does work in this series. This is covered in the section **"Trees greet you"** where, because some feature of the tree is so Unique or Seasonally Striking, you cannot fail to identify it. However there are a number of other ways that **"You can find trees"** using this book, and all of them are based on the fact that virtually every tree only thrives successfully in certain Habitats. This means you need to look for the right tree in the right place.

2. **Creation of Search Images to help you look for the right trees**
   Whichever area you are in, and whichever trees you are setting out to find, you need to build up a series of Search Images of those trees. The whole layout and philosophy of this series is to make that as easy as possible.

3. **Simple language**
   All the text is easy to follow in simple English. The average recreational tree spotter will never use 'pubescent' when 'hairy' will do! Learning to know and love trees need not only be for the botanically trained.

4. **Summarised information**
   The book helps the reader by means of accessible, easy-to-use information like: height and shade density icons; grids indicating seasonal changes; maps and information blocks that direct you to the most convenient park, lodge or game reserve. It also gives information on modern and traditional uses for trees, and their gardening possibilities.

As a main summary the book is divided into two methods: Trees greet you and You find trees.

# TREES GREET YOU – YOU IDENTIFY A SPECIFIC TREE THAT YOU ARE LOOKING AT

There are a number of Bushveld trees that you can identify easily. None of these trees need a complex system of 'keying', because they are instantly recognisable, in many instances even from a distance. There are three ways, using this book, to find the names of these trees.

## Distinctive Striking Features

On pages 58 - 83 you will find a series of visual summaries of striking leaves, flowers, fruit and bark, as well as comparisons of a number of families. Using these pages you could well come across a **Distinctive Striking Feature** on a tree in the wild, and look it up here, and be able to identify it immediately.

*Fruit of Peeling-bark Ochna, page 136*

## Unique Trees

On pages 86 - 105 are the **Unique Trees** that are so unusual in their growth form that, after you have browsed through the book once or twice, you will not fail to recognise them if you see them in the wild.

*Ladies Cabbage-tree in Sour Bushveld, page 94*

## Seasonally Striking Trees

On pages 108 - 159 are the trees that have very striking flowers or fruit, in certain seasons, **and** they are difficult to identify without these features. The recommendation is that if you want instant recognition, you first look for these trees in the specified season. This is made easier by the Seasonal Grid on the last page of each tree's description.

*Flowers of the Wild-pear Dombeya, page 156*

5

# You find trees — you identify a specific tree by creating a Search Image

Essentially this is what makes the **Sappi Tree Spotting** series so different. You are encouraged to spend a few minutes working out which trees you should be looking for in your area, creating a Search Image for them, and then setting out to find them.

There are two ways that "**You can find trees**":
- You could look for a specific tree from the detailed information given for that tree.
- You could find a specific tree by its Ecozone and/or Habitat. You will be in one or other of the five Ecozones, and could recognise the specific Habitat like Rocky Areas. You could use the book to decide which three or four trees to look for.

In either case you need to create a Search Image first.

## Create a Search Image using Striking Features

Finding a tree that you do not know is like looking for a stranger in a crowded room. You need to have a clear Search Image of certain Striking Features that you can visualise. For example, you might be looking for a grey-haired, elderly man, smoking a pipe.

Most tree species covered in this book have a specific shape and pattern that will help you find them. This pattern is so strongly encoded that it is repeated to a greater or lesser degree in each individual tree. As you get to know these patterns of growth, you will learn to recognise many trees at a glance. For example, your Search Image could be for a large, single-trunked tree, with rough-bark, and small, simple, toothed leaves.

To create a Search Image you should have a clear idea about a number of important things. After reading the description of the tree, visualise at least some of the following:
- the tree's likely size
- the trunk form
- how this trunk splits up into branches, branchlets and twigs
- the form and density of the canopy
- the shape, size and colour of the leaves, flowers, fruit or pods

See the example of the Shepherds-tree below.

*Shepherds-tree Search Image; about 5 m tall, single-trunked with pale bark; branches profusely; has a dense V-shaped to semi-circular canopy (see page 200).*

# THINK OF A TREE THAT YOU HAVE HEARD OF THAT YOU WOULD LIKE TO FIND

This could be a tree that you would like to know because it is medicinally interesting, has beautiful flowers, or a special historical interest. A good example of this is the Marula which meets all these criteria.

Marula, page 230

Read **"Where you'll find this tree easily"** on the first page of the tree. The profile drawing, shown below, summarises this information in a visual picture.

- This symbol tells you where the Marula is easiest to find first.
- This symbol tells you where else the Marula is easy to find.

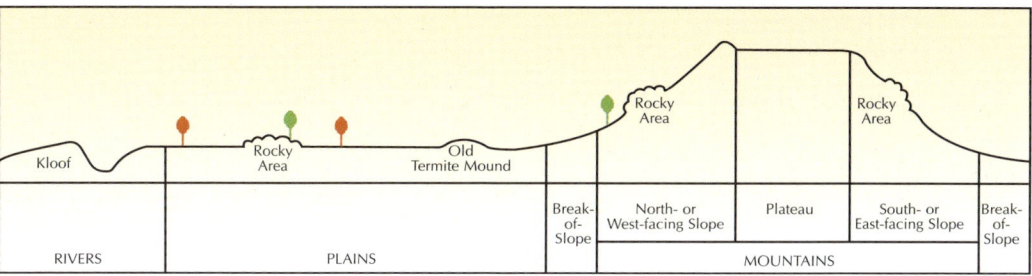

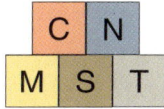

These blocks tell you where else you could look for the Marula. The colours and the letters in these blocks lead you to different Ecozones. How to do this is summarised on the next two pages.

# Find a tree by Ecozone or Habitat – a seven step guide

Further on in the book is a full description of the five Ecozones and four major Habitats of the Bushveld (pages 22 - 45). Below are the steps you should follow every time you want to find a tree. It will soon become second nature.

### Decide where you are. In which Ecozone is this?

To identify specific trees you must first work out where you are. Turn to the Maps on pages 410 - 415, and note the Ecozone you are in.
**Example: Ecozone M – Mixed Bushveld**

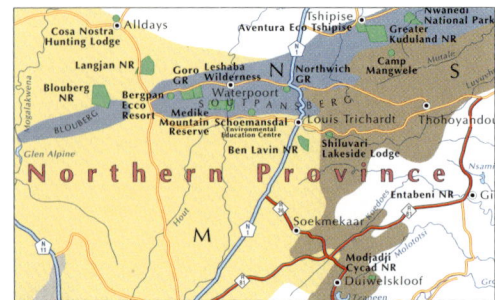

### In which Habitat are you?

The descriptions on pages 22 - 39 give details of the Ecozones and their Habitats. Decide which of these applies to you.
**Example: Plains, Pilanesberg**

### Which trees can you find in your Ecozone and Habitat?

On pages 46 - 55, you will find the Tree List for your Ecozone. Read this and make a note of the three or four trees you are most likely to find, and mark their pages.
**Example: Marula, pages 230 - 233**

#### Ecozone M – Mixed Bushveld

##### Plains

| Tree | Page | | |
|---|---|---|---|
| **Baobab** | 86 | Silver Raisin | 346 |
| **Buffalo-thorn Jujube** | 188 | Robust Acacia | 380 |
| **Burkea** | 236 | Sweet-thorn Acacia | 208 |
| **Camel-thorn Acacia** | 240 | Tamboti | 388 |
| **Leadwood** | 226 | Bushy Three-hook Acacia | 63 |
| **Marula** | 230 | Wild-pear Dombeya | 156 |
| African Weeping-wattle | 214 | Worm-cure Albizia | 61 |
| Black-monkey Acacia | 218 | | |
| Hairy-leaved Monkey-orange | 120 | | |

### Create Search Images for these trees

Look at the pictures and read the Striking Features of each of these trees. In the same way as you would create a mental picture of a blonde child, with a green shirt eating an ice-cream, imagine the Striking Features of the trees you are hoping to find.

#### Striking features

- It is a single-trunked tree, dividing high up into a few bare branches and a semi-circular canopy.
- **The bark often peels in conspicuous, characteristic rounded depressions, revealing smooth, pink-brown under-bark.**
- In summer blue-green, compound leaves hang, crowded towards the end of thickened twigs; in winter the bare twigs stand out like stubby fingers.
- Unripe green and ripe yellow fruit are often seen on the ground under the female trees (January to March).

## Match your Search Images to nearby trees
Look at the larger, mature trees nearby, and see if you can find one that has similar Striking Features to any of your Search Images.

## Check the details
When you find a tree, check the details more carefully. Check all the Striking Features, then read the details about the leaf, flower, pod and bark. If you have any problems with any of the terms in the text, read **"How to meet a tree"**, pages 14 - 19.

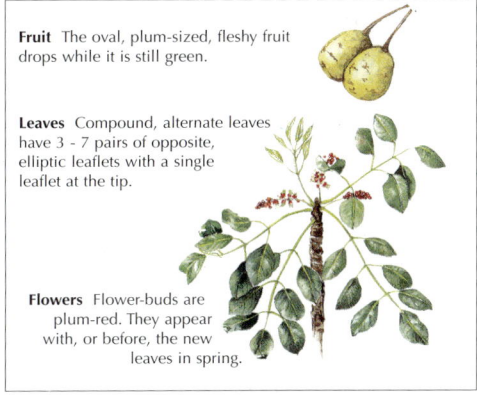

**Fruit** The oval, plum-sized, fleshy fruit drops while it is still green.

**Leaves** Compound, alternate leaves have 3 - 7 pairs of opposite, elliptic leaflets with a single leaflet at the tip.

**Flowers** Flower-buds are plum-red. They appear with, or before, the new leaves in spring.

## How successful were you?

### Successful?
That's great! Remember the key to enjoyable, long-term tree spotting is to focus on all the Striking Features – not only on one conspicuous pod or flower that is seasonal. One of the excitements and satisfactions of learning about trees is that they are not like birds. Once you know a bird it is the same wherever you go. Trees even vary at different ages, from Habitat to Habitat, or Ecozone to Ecozone, and vary greatly in different parts of the country.

### Not sure?
Look around. Are there any other similar trees you could check? If not, move on and find another tree to help you confirm your identification.

### Unsuccessful?
Don't lose heart. Think of how often you saw one of the Big Five disappear into the bush as you rounded the corner. The joy of tree spotting is that trees in the wild are everywhere you look, all year round, and they don't fly or run away when you approach. Simply try another spot and another tree.

# How the pages help you find trees

### English name/Scientific species name/Scientific family name
### English family name/Other South African names
These identify the specific tree. The majority of the names in different South African languages were compiled by the Dendrological Society in 9 of our 11 languages. There is further information about Recommended English tree names on page 399.

### Where you'll find this tree easily
As with the cross-section diagram below, the **red tree icon** shows the easiest place to find the tree. The **green tree icon** shows the other Habitats where the tree is likely to be found.

### Ecozone blocks
**The blocks that are coloured show the Ecozones in which you can find this tree easily.**
The colours and their letters are the same ones you will find on the Maps – pages 410 - 415.

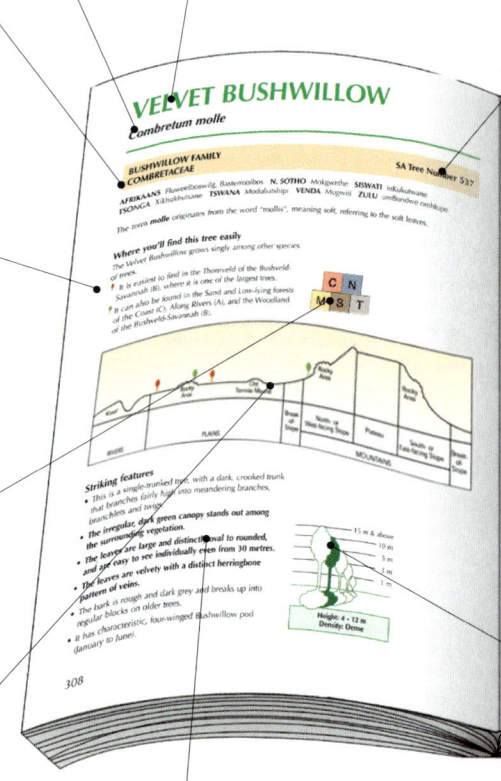

### Cross-section diagram of the Bushveld
The **red tree icons** show the Habitat where it is easiest to find the tree. The **green tree icons** show the Habitat to look in as second choice. Note that the icons of trees are proportionately too large for the scale of the landscape.

### Striking Features of mature trees
These are features of mature trees which will help you find an example of the tree with the greatest ease.
**The bold items are those Striking Features which are the most important in helping you with positive identification.**

## South African tree number
The numbers are according to the National List of Indigenous Trees, compiled by National Botanical Institute.

## Line drawing
This drawing will indicate the most important Striking Feature that will help you to differentiate the tree from any others.

## Artwork of the tree
Trees vary greatly and no single photograph or illustration can represent every tree you will find. However this artwork gives an overall impression of the size and the common form of mature trees, which are easiest to find. It emphasises the Striking Features listed on the opposite page.

## Identification tab
For easy reference the colour-coded tabs indicate **Sappi Tree Spotting** groups, as well as the specific tree. These same groups are colour-coded in the Contents (pages xi - 1). The green colour-codes are purely to separate sections of the book – they have no correlation to Ecozones.

## Dendrological Society record tree
This information is from the society's register indicating the largest tree of this species currently registered. The location of the tree is also given. See further information on the Grids (Record breaking trees) page 400.

## Density and height icon
This will help you form a more accurate Search Image.
**The tree which is coloured** gives an idea of the average height of mature trees you will find easiest to identify in the Bushveld, in comparison with other common trees. The height is given in metres.
**The density of the colour** indicates the average summer density of the leaves and branches, as well as the resultant density of the shade.

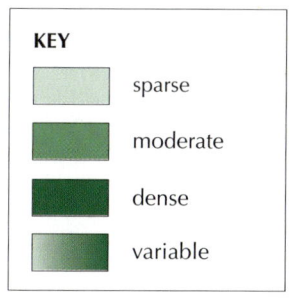

KEY
- sparse
- moderate
- dense
- variable

# How the pages help you find trees (continued)

### Wood samples and ornaments
Many South African trees have beautiful wood that is workable for carving, turning or furniture. Where possible a picture of the polished wood, as well as a finished product, are included to show the texture and the colour. Not all the workable timbers are included in the book.
These pictures should help with the appreciation of the value, beauty and diversity of South Africa's indigenous woods, and should encourage sustainable usage. Wasteful chopping and burning of our rarer trees is leading to a number of them becoming "endangered" in the wild, although none of these trees are covered here. The photographs of these wood samples were taken courtesy of the CSIR, Pretoria. Sets of wood samples and technical details of different woods can be obtained from CSIR (Environmentek). The photographs of the ornaments were taken courtesy of Prof A E van Wyk, University of Pretoria.

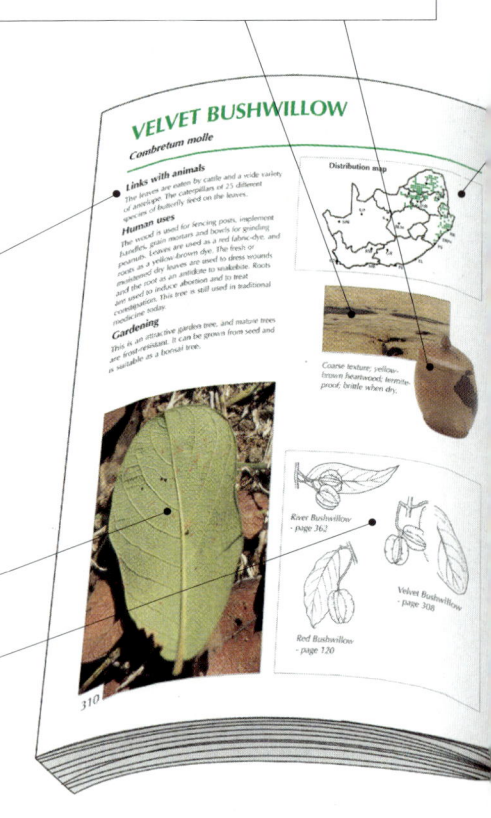

### General information and usages
Details of interest about the tree, in relation to people and to animals, as well as gardening, are given here.

### Photographs/Look-alikes
These are **photographs** of the tree, or its features, chosen to increase either your information or your pleasure!
In some trees there is a **diagram** and/or text which covers look-alike trees.

## Map of South Africa

This is an adaptation from maps supplied by the National Botanical Institute in Pretoria, and the Dendrological Society.

**Abbreviations:**

| | | | | | |
|---|---|---|---|---|---|
| BLM: | Bloemfontein | GR: | Graaff Reinet | PE: | Port Elizabeth |
| BW: | Beaufort West | JHB: | Johannesburg | PS: | Port Shepstone |
| CT: | Cape Town | K: | Kimberley | RB: | Richard's Bay |
| DBN: | Durban | MB: | Mossel Bay | SC: | Sun City |
| EL: | East London | N: | Nelspruit | SPR: | Springbok |
| | | P: | Pietersburg | UP: | Upington |

## Growth details

These details will help you to check your identification. They build up a wider Search Image so you can find the same tree elsewhere. For each specific tree the size of the leaves, flowers, fruit and/or pods are shown in relation to one another. However this size relationship does not carry through proportionately from one species to another.

## Seasonal changes

This grid is to help you find trees at different times of the year. However, Bushveld Habitats offer varying protection, therefore it is an average guide only.

- The information will vary from year to year depending on temperature and rainfall.
- The information also varies from Ecozone to Ecozone and within Habitats.
- The colours represent the months during which the leaves, flowers, fruit / pods are most likely to be seen.
- The colours themselves are a very rough guide only. You should refer to the artwork for more accurate colours.
- Pale yellow is used for inconspicuous flowers or pods.
- Whether a pod has seeds or not, it is shown on the grid, while it is still visible on the tree.

# HOW TO MEET A TREE – SAPPI TREE SPOTTING TERMS

Finding a tree that you do not know, is like looking for a stranger in a crowded room. You need to have a clear Search Image of certain Striking Features that you can visualise easily. For example, when looking for a specific person, you may think of a tall, red-haired woman with glasses. Most trees covered in this book have a specific form and look about them that will help you find them.

Look at a number of different trees carefully and you will see many patterns. The fascinating part is that most species do have their own pattern so strongly encoded that it is repeated to a greater or lesser degree in each individual tree. As you learn these patterns of growth you will learn to recognise many trees at a glance.

**Sappi Tree Spotting** descibes these patterns in this order:
- Main branches splitting off the trunk/stem.
- Branchlets splitting off the branches, then splitting into twigs.
- Leaf-stalks attaching the leaves to the twigs, or in a few trees the leaves to the branchlets.

Main branches always leave the main trunk (or stem) in a generally upward or horizontal direction.
However, branchlets and twigs can tend to be in an upward, horizontal or downward pattern, or they can be a mixture.

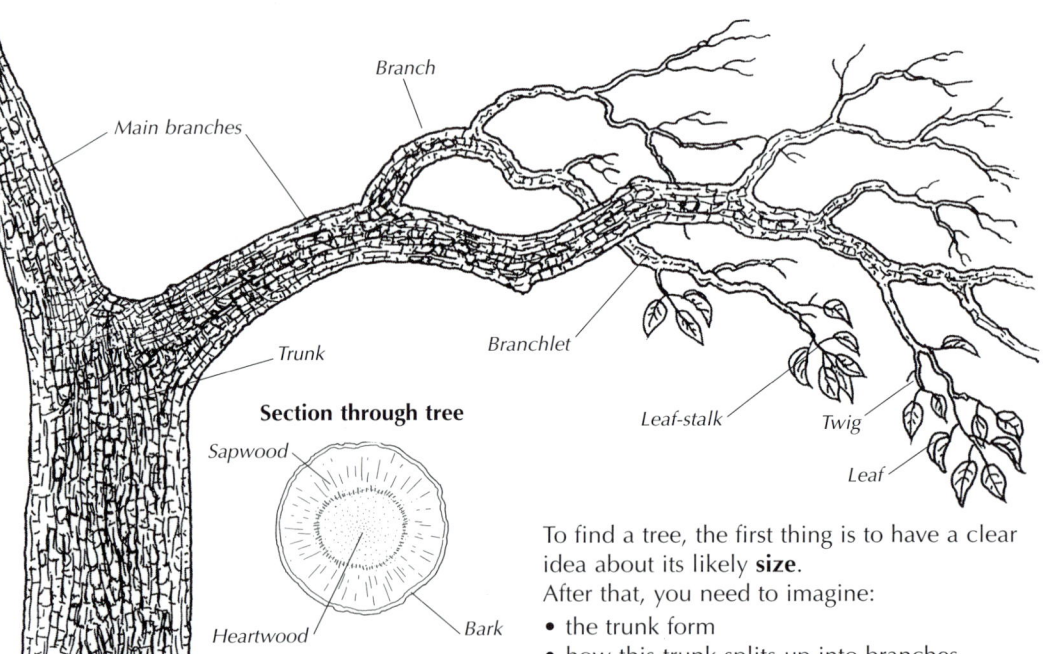

**Thorns and spines**
They are both sharp. **Thorns** are protuberances not covered in bark. **Spines** are bark-covered twigs that may carry leaves.

To find a tree, the first thing is to have a clear idea about its likely **size**.
After that, you need to imagine:
- the trunk form
- how this trunk splits up into branches, branchlets and twigs
- the form and density of the canopy

Finally the shape, size and colour of the leaves, flowers, fruit or pods will help you with a positive identification.
On the following pages you will find the terms used in **Sappi Tree Spotting**. These will help you to create your Search Images.

## TRUNKS AND STEMS

"Trunk" is used for larger trees and "stems" for smaller and multi-stemmed trees.

**Multi-stemmed**
eg. Sickle-bush
- p. 258

**Single-trunked, low-branching**
eg. Red-leaved Fig - p. 288

**Single-trunked, high-branching**
eg. Burkea
- p. 236

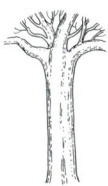

**Straight trunk**
eg. Big-leaf Fever-tree
- p. 162

**Crooked trunk**
eg. Velvet Bushwillow
- p. 304

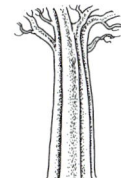

**Fluted trunk**
eg. African Olive
- p. 184

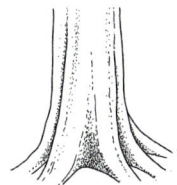

**Buttressed trunk**
eg. Broom-cluster Fig
- p. 364

## CANOPIES

The canopy is the upper area of a tree, formed by the branches and the leaves.

**Round**
eg. Sacred Coral-tree
- p. 148

**Semi-circular**
eg. Marula
- p. 230

**Umbrella**
eg. Umbrella Acacia
- p. 262

**Wide spreading**
eg. River Bushwillow
- p. 376

**V-shaped**
eg. Bushveld Shepherds-tree
- p. 192

**Narrow**
eg. Tamboti
- p. 388

**Irregular**
eg. Fever Croton
- p. 44

# LEAVES

A leaf grows on a leaf-stalk that attaches the leaf to the twig or branchlet. It snaps off the twig or branchlet relatively easily at the leaf-bud (auxillary bud). You can often see this bud as a swelling at the base of the leaf-stalk.

**All leaves are described as simple or compound.**
Sometimes it is not easy to tell the difference between a simple and a compound leaf. Some of the ways are:
- Look for the position of the leaf-bud.
- Compound leaves look organised on their leaf-stalk. Most simple leaves that are grouped close together look irregular on the twig.
- The leaflet of a compound leaf tends to tear off the leaf-stalk – it does not snap off neatly, the way the leaf itself usually snaps off the twig at the leaf-bud. Please note this is not true for all species, nor at all times of the year.

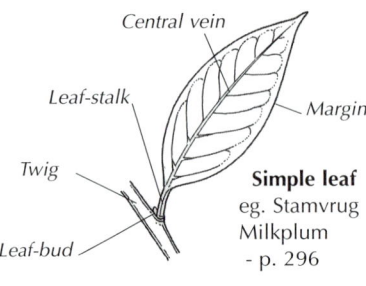

**Simple leaf**
eg. Stamvrug Milkplum
- p. 296

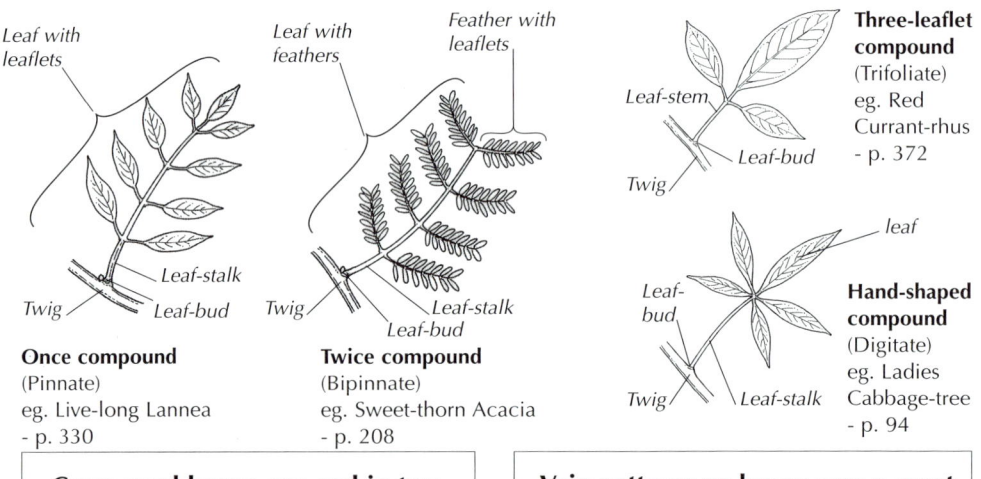

**Once compound**
(Pinnate)
eg. Live-long Lannea
- p. 330

**Twice compound**
(Bipinnate)
eg. Sweet-thorn Acacia
- p. 208

**Three-leaflet compound**
(Trifoliate)
eg. Red Currant-rhus
- p. 372

**Hand-shaped compound**
(Digitate)
eg. Ladies Cabbage-tree
- p. 94

**Compound leaves can end in two ways:**

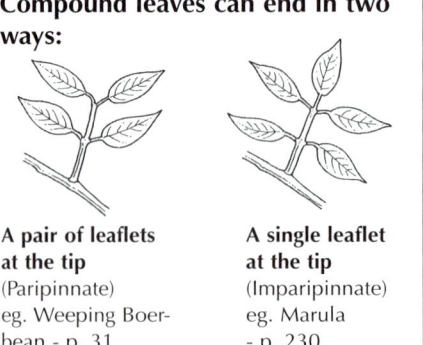

**A pair of leaflets at the tip**
(Paripinnate)
eg. Weeping Boer-bean - p. 31

**A single leaflet at the tip**
(Imparipinnate)
eg. Marula
- p. 230

**Vein patterns on leaves vary a great deal. Two distinctive patterns are:**

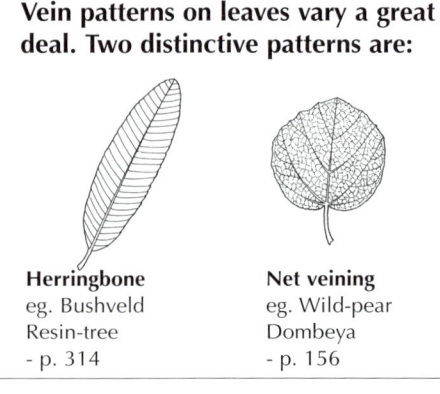

**Herringbone**
eg. Bushveld Resin-tree
- p. 314

**Net veining**
eg. Wild-pear Dombeya
- p. 156

## LEAF ATTACHMENTS TO TWIGS OR BRANCHLETS

Leaf-stalks can attach to the twigs in a number of ways and these tend to be predictable, species by species. Sometimes, however, you will find a variety of attachments on a single tree – this is done simply to confuse you and to make traditional keying methods difficult to follow! Attachments of the leaves to the twig or branchlet can be:

**Opposite**
eg. River Bushwillow
- p. 376

**Alternate**
eg. Buffalo-thorn Jujube - p. 188

**Spiral**
eg. Red-leaved Fig - p. 288

**Clustered**
eg. Hairy-leaved Monkey-orange
- p. 120

**Winged**
Bushveld Red-balloon
-p. 37

## LEAF OR LEAFLET SHAPE

There are many varieties of leaf shape. As a basis for all descriptions this book refers to them as:

    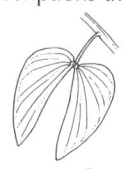 

**Round**
eg. Wild-pear Dombeya
- p. 156

**Heart-shaped**
eg. Sacred Coral-tree
- p. 148

**Narrow elliptic**
eg. Weeping Faurea
- p. 350

**Broad elliptic**
eg. Broom-cluster Fig
- p. 364

**Butterfly**
Mopane
- p. 28

**Needle**
eg. Broad-leaved Yellowwood
- p. 33

**Triangular**
eg. Pigeonwood
- p. 66

## LEAF MARGINS

The edge of the leaf can be:

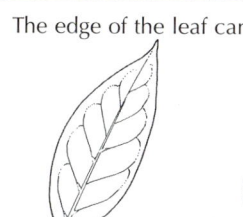 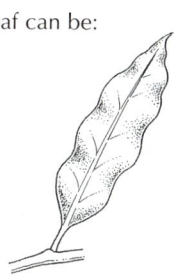 

**Smooth**
eg. Red Bushwillow
- p. 140

**Wavy**
eg. Small-leaved Guarri
- p. 204

**Toothed**
eg. Tamboti
- p. 388

## FLOWER PARTS

All flowers are made up of these parts:

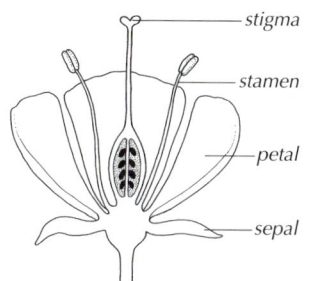

- stigma
- stamen
- petal
- sepal

17

## BARK

The bark texture, and/or colour, is often characteristic of a tree. However, it often differs between trunk and branches, older and younger trunks, and older and younger branches. Thinner and younger branches mostly have smoother and paler bark.

   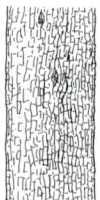 

**Smooth**
eg. African White-stinkwood
- p. 360

**Coarse**
eg. Highveld Protea
- p. 322

**Fissured or grooved**
eg. Highveld Silver-oak
- p. 326

**Blocky**
eg. Tamboti
- p. 388

**Flaking, peeling**
eg. Peeling-bark Ochna
- p. 136

## FLOWERS

Plants, including trees, are scientifically classified and named according to their flower shape. Looking carefully at flower-shapes can help with family identification, but this is often very technical and not easy to see.

Most species within a family, however, share general flower-shapes (pages 398 - 401). Some flowers have a unique shape, eg. Baobab, page 86, or are inconspicuous, eg. Tall Firethorn Corkwood, page 300. These are described in detail in the specific texts.

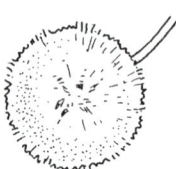 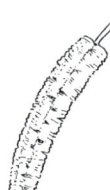 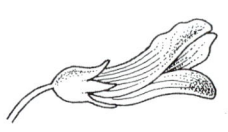 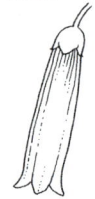

**Ball**
eg. Sweet-thorn Acacia - p. 208

**Spike**
eg. Sickle-bush
- p. 258

**Pea-like**
eg. Round-leaved Bloodwood
- p. 29

**Trumpet**
eg. White Cats-whiskers - p. 152

 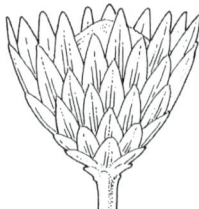 

**Star**
eg. Silver Raisin
- p. 346

**Protea**
eg. Highveld Protea
- p. 322

**Pincushion**
Paperbark Albizia
- p. 178

## FRUIT

Fruit has a fleshy pulp covering the seed/s. The pulp may be oily, watery or dry, and must be removed before the seeds can germinate. Birds and animals are attracted to the fruit and help distribute the seeds.

**Berry – small, single**
eg. African White-stinkwood
- p. 360

**Grape – small, in bunches**
eg. Red Currant-rhus
- p. 372

**Plum – larger, single**
eg. Large Sourplum
- p. 132

## PODS

Pods are hard envelopes covering a seed, or more often, several seeds.

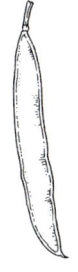

**Flat bean**
eg. Black-monkey Acacia
- p. 218

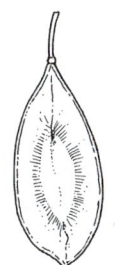

**Broad bean**
eg. Paperbark Albizia
- p. 178

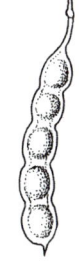

**Bumpy bean**
eg. Bushveld Bead-bean
- p. 112

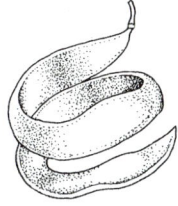

**Coiled**
eg. Umbrella Acacia
- p. 262

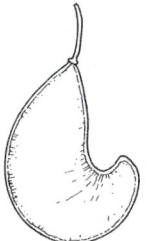

**Sickle/kidney**
eg. Camel-thorn Acacia
- p. 240

**Capsule**
eg. White Kirkia
- p. 308

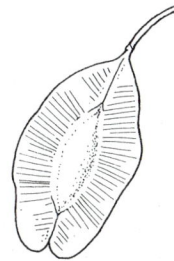

**Two-winged**
eg. Silver Cluster-leaf
- p. 244

**Four-winged**
eg. Large-fruited Bushwillow - p. 128

# The Bushveld

The **Sappi Tree Spotting** series helps you find trees by Ecozone and Habitat. The fundamental definition of the Ecozones is based on the detailed vegetation map by Rebelo and Low published by the National Botanical Institute in 1996. This map was adapted by Jacana to create the five Ecozones that are one of the foundations of this book.

The area covered is artificially limited in the north and west by the South African political boundaries with Botswana and Zimbabwe. The southern boundary is one of altitude. Along the line where the Bushveld rises to above 1 000 metres, it is influenced by the rigors of Highveld frost and fire. As this boundary swings eastwards, the Highveld's flat grassland Plains give way to the steep escarpment of the Drakensberg. Here massive mountain buttresses, deep ravines and spectacular cliffs are home to Highveld species as well as the more tropical species of Kwazulu-Natal. **Sappi Tree Spotting Bushveld** covers the species that thrive on the lower slopes and foothills, as well as in the ravines that are winding their way to the Lowveld.

Most of the Bushveld falls south of the Tropics, but the very northern limits are influenced by an increasing tropical position. This area also runs along the massive Limpopo River which alters the variety of trees.

*The Bushveld has many Habitats, each one with its own particular combination of trees; Soutpansberg*

# PATTERNS OF TREE DISTRIBUTION

The patterns that influence which trees grow where, and how they grow, have been simplified in this book. However the fundamentals that govern any inland area, and its patterns of trees, are the same all over the world. These are primarily the altitude, the latitude and the climate.

Information on this page is for those readers who wish to confirm data presented throughout the book. You do not need to study, remember or understand the details of these maps to enjoy Bushveld trees.

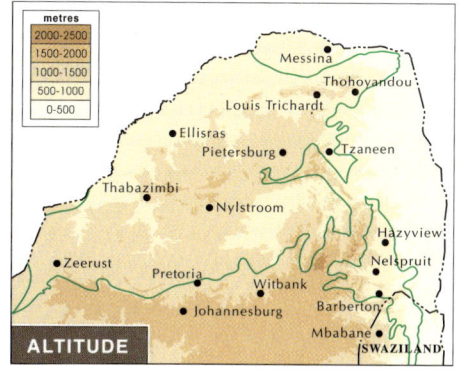

### Altitude
Altitude varies from 300 to 2 000 m on the tops of the Mountains, but most of the Bushveld lies between 600 and 1 000 m.

### Rainfall
This is a summer rainfall area. The average annual rainfall varies from 350 mm in the west, to over 1 500 mm on the Escarpment in the east.

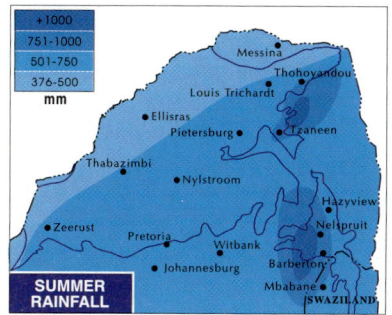
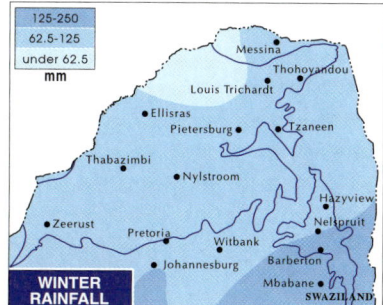

### Temperature
The summers are hot over most of the Bushveld with temperatures up to 40°C. The mild winters have temperatures that very seldom drop below 0°C, except on the high Plateaus of the larger Mountains.

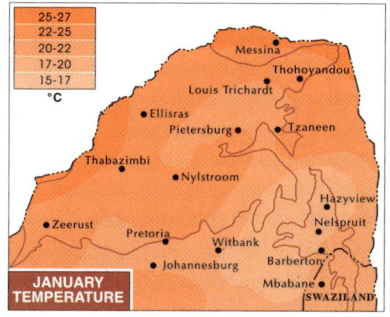
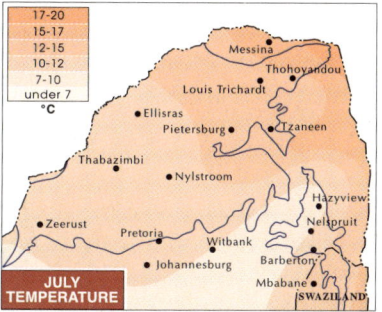

# YOU FIND TREES BY HABITAT

The Bushveld covered in this book is a vast area of land with five large Ecozones, each made up, in varying combinations, of four major Habitats. Habitats are smaller areas influenced locally by conditions of soil, shade, heat and moisture, as well as immediate landscape features like incline, water and aspect (North-, South-, East- or West-facing).

The Habitats and their subdivisions that are used throughout **Sappi Tree Spotting Bushveld** will help you find trees easily. They are described as follows:

- **Mountains**
    - Hot, sunny, drier Slopes – usually North- and/or West-facing (page 26)
    - Cool, moister Slopes – usually South- and/or East-facing (page 27)
    - Plateaus – the mountain tops often too high for Bushveld trees (page 34)
    - Break-of-Slope – the zone where hills or Mountains meet the Plains (page 23)

- **Plains**
    - Deep Sandy Soils (page 29)
    - Clay and Turf Soils (page 30)
    - Old Termite Mounds (page 31)

- **Rocky Areas on Plains and on Mountain Slopes (page 35)**

- **Rivers, Streams and Kloofs (pages 32 - 33)**

## Habitat profile

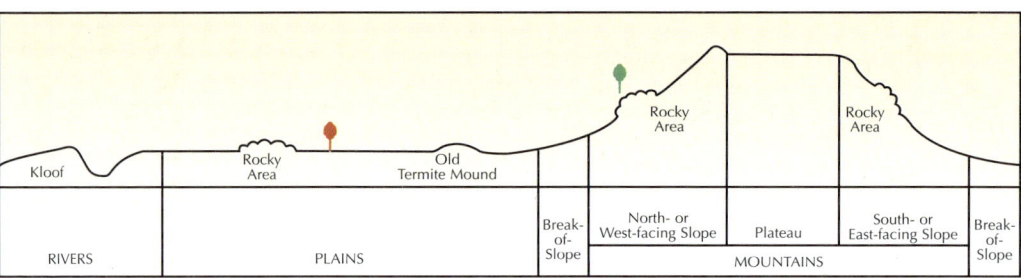

This profile of Habitats is used throughout the book to indicate where you are **most likely to find each tree easily**. It cross-references with the Ecozone Tree Lists, (pages 46 to 55) which indicate where trees are likely to occur by Ecozone and by Habitat.

The profile is an over-simplification of the many complex Habitats that you will find in reality. However it is a very useful visual aid to help you look for the right trees in the right places.

🔴 The red trees tie in with the text "**Where you'll find this tree easily**", and indicate the best Habitats in which to look for this tree **first** – if that is possible!

🟢 The green trees tie in with the same text, and are the next best Habitats in which to look for the tree.

# Mountains, Plains and Rivers

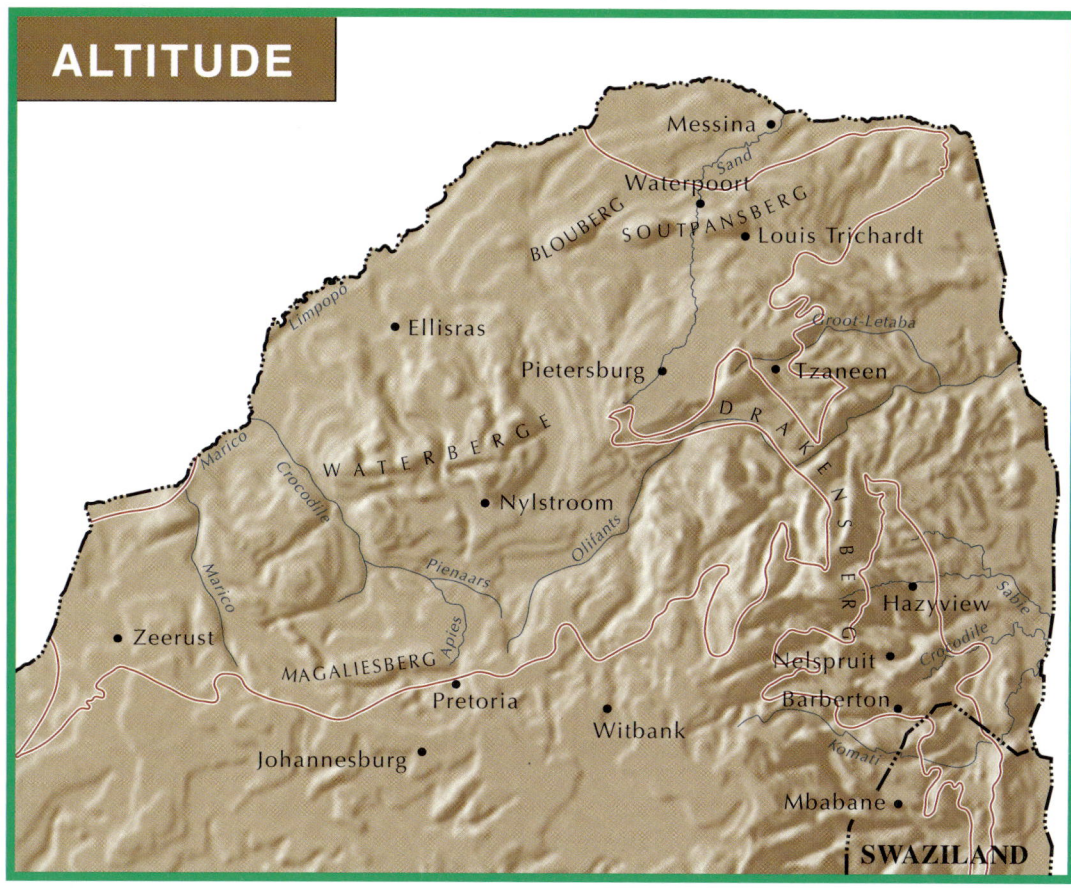

## ALTITUDE

## Mountains

Mountains in the Bushveld are variable, but the profile on the previous page gives you a starting point to work from. The tops of high mountains – the **Plateaus** – are higher areas above 1 000 metres that will probably have Highveld trees. You can learn about these in **Sappi Tree Spotting Highveld.**

**Break-of-Slope** are areas where a Mountain, or even a hill, meet the flatter Plains below. Here you are in a crossover zone, and many different elements, such as more available water, will change the types and density of trees that you will find. Break-of-Slope is not a good place to start if you are a beginner. The guidelines for the rest of the book are on how to interpret the **Mid-slopes of Mountains**. These guidelines do not necessarily apply to Break-of-Slope, or the high Plateaus.

Trees that grow on the Mid-slopes of Mountains can be roughly divided into those that really thrive on hot, drier Slopes (North- and West-facing), and trees that thrive best on cooler, more shaded, moister Slopes (South- and East-facing). The next few pages will describe how to work out these directions easily.

# Mountain Slopes – North-, South-, East- or West-facing

As a generalisation, you can start with some knowledge that could well change the way you watch the scenery go by throughout sub-tropical South Africa, ie south of the Tropic of Capricorn. By knowing very roughly which way a Slope faces, you can anticipate the trees to look for.

**On most relatively pristine Slopes you can rely on the following:**
- If the Slope you are looking at faces more or less north or west, it will be hot and dry, and will generally have fewer trees, further apart. The types of trees that grow here will tend to be those trees that enjoy hot, dry conditions.
- Across the valley, or over the hill, the Slope will be facing more or less south or east, and you will usually find more trees closer together. The types of trees that grow here will tend to be those trees that thrive in cooler, moister surroundings.

The following exceptions will alter this sub-tropical Southern Hemisphere rule, and lead to fewer or more trees than you expected:
- The amount of fire, grazing and agriculture that the Slope has experienced over the past 100 or even 1 000 years.
- The proximity of other Mountains close by that offer unusual protection to a certain Slope. This is common in the circular mountain pattern found in the Pilanesberg (pages 36 - 37).
- Unusual soils on a Slope will alter the tree distribution, again common in Pilanesberg.

With this in mind, once you know roughly the direction the Slope faces, it will be easy to know which trees to look for. Listed here are four ways of finding out which way the Slope faces. Determining the aspect can add to the general enjoyment of your outing.

## 1 Look at a map, compass or GPS

If you have any of these available, this is the easiest way. Simply work out which way the relevant Slope runs. There is more information on GPS on page 398.

*June; steep, cool, moist, South-facing Slope; Lajuma Lodge; Soutpansberg*

## 2 Follow the path of the sun

**In the early morning and late afternoon see where the sun rises and sets**
Slopes that face the early morning sun face east, while those facing the later afternoon sun, face west.

**From mid-morning to mid-afternoon look at the direction of the shadows of the trees**
Throughout the sub-tropical area of the Southern Hemisphere, Slopes with tree shadows falling more or less **downhill** are South-facing. Slopes with shadows that fall more or less **uphill** are North-facing.

## 3 Use your watch as a compass

Follow the steps below to find a rough direction for north.

i  Hold a grass-stalk or small stick vertically upright on the 12 on your watch.

ii Turn your arm so that the shadow of the stick crosses the middle of your watch and the 6.

iii Halve the distance between 12 and the hour arm of your watch. This direction is very roughly north.

This method gives an approximate reading for north. It will change according to the season of the year and the longitude at which you take the reading. However for tree spotting purposes your reading will be accurate enough.

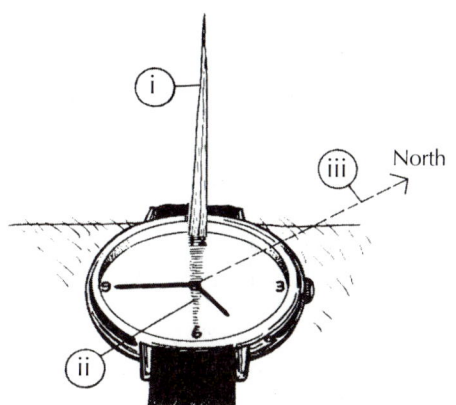

## 4 Look at the types of trees

This sounds impossible for beginners who are trying to get to know their trees! However a simple check is whether the most dominant groups of trees on the Slope are broad-leaved or fine-leaved. Remember not to look at the trees on the Break-of-Slope, as other types of trees are often found here. In the Bushveld area the following is a simple summary.

- If the the trees are mostly broad-leaved, there are likely to be some Red Bushwillows amongst them (page 136). This is then probably a hot and sunny, North- or West-facing Slope.

- If the trees are mainly fine-leaved, it is likely that there are some Common Hook-thorn Acacias amongst them (page 314). This is then probably a South- or East-facing Slope.

**Broad-leaved**
Red Bushwillow

**Fine-leaved**
Common Hook-thorn Acacia

These two trees, Red Bushwillow and Common Hook-thorn Acacia, are so specific in their Habitat preferences that when they occur in large numbers they can usually be used to indicate whether a Slope is hot and sunny, or cool and shaded.

### More or less wooded?

From what you have just read you will **not** expect regular patches of dense woodland on a North-facing, hot, dry Slope. However when you find this exception and you are on a North-facing, heavily wooded Slope, the trees will still usually be the trees that are lovers of hot, dry conditions.

Equally you do **not** expect South/East-facing Slopes to have only scattered trees. Again when this exception occurs, you can still rely on the lists in this book to tell you what kind of trees these lovers of cool, moist conditions are likely to be.

The full details of the two different Slopes are covered on pages 26 to 27.

# MOUNTAINS – Hot, dry, North- or West-facing Slopes

North-facing Slopes are hotter and drier because they are exposed to more direct sun rays throughout the day, all year round. West-facing Slopes are hotter and drier because temperatures are already high when the sun's rays strike the Slopes directly, in the afternoon. These direct rays, on already hot Slopes, dry the soils out.

Only plants that thrive under hot, sunny conditions, and do not need much water, are common on these Slopes. Because of the limited availability of water, there tend to be fewer trees overall, and as a result these Slopes are often not densely wooded. However, even on these hot, dry Slopes, where the soil is deep or very fertile, or where water accumulates such as on Rocky Areas, trees grow in denser stands. Species that are common on hot, dry slopes are Red Bushwillow (page 140), Live-Long Lannea (page 330) and Bushveld Resin-tree (page 314).

*June; hot, dry, West-facing Slope, Soutpansberg*

**Velvet-leaved Sweetberry**
*Bridelia mollis* SA Tree no 325
This single-trunked, small tree can be found on the lower Slopes where it often grows among rocks. It branches low down into many smaller, low-hanging branches, forming a rather spreading, irregular canopy. The large, simple, alternate leaves are soft and velvety, and covered by hairs on both surfaces. They have a distinct herringbone vein pattern, visible on both surfaces. The small greenish-yellow flowers and small, round berries grow in the angles of the leaves. See also page 66.

# MOUNTAINS — Cool, moist, South- or East-facing Slopes

South-facing Slopes are relatively more shaded, and are only exposed to hot, fairly direct sun rays in the middle of summer. Eastern Slopes are only exposed to more direct sun in the morning, when the soil is still cool, and the sun has less of a drying out effect. These Slopes therefore have higher moisture levels, and trees that thrive with high soil moisture and shade are most common here. Because more moisture is available, trees may often form dense stands.

Many tall-growing grass species also thrive under these higher moisture conditions.

In areas that are exposed to regular veld fires these Slopes may appear less densely wooded because of the suppressing effect that fire has had on tree growth.

When these Slopes are also fairly high, such as the South-facing Slopes of the Soutpansberg, the height of the mountains above tends to lead to an increase of local rainfall, which adds to the cool, moist conditions.

Common trees are Common Hook-thorn Acacia (page 318), Highveld Protea (page 322) and Weeping Lavender-tree (page 354).

*February; cool, moist, East-facing Slope; Elands Valley, Sour Bushveld*

**Pride-of-De Kaap Bauhinia**
*Bauhinia galpinii* SA Tree no 208.2
This tree is easiest to recognise by the simple, butterfly-like leaves and the brick-red flowers that often cover the tree in summer (November to January). It is climber-like and multi-stemmed, and has long, thin branches that lean on the surrounding vegetation. It is mostly found along watercourses, or on cool, shady Slopes of the Sour Bushveld. The long, flat bean pods have pointed tips and are hard and woody (March to July). See also page 65.

# Plains

These large, flat areas are found between the Mountain ranges, and can vary from a few square kilometres to vast areas like the Springbok Flats of the Thorny Bushveld (T). Due to the erosion of the surrounding Mountains, soils on the Plains are often high in nutrients, and these areas are mostly intensely cultivated.

Vegetation here is determined by climate, especially rainfall, but mostly by soil type.

The three soil types that are easiest to differentiate are Deep Sandy Soils, Clay or Turf Soils, and nutrient-rich, aerated soils of Old Termite Mounds. These three soil types are discussed in more detail on the following pages.

*May; Plains viewed from Rocky ridge; Mixed Bushveld, near Thabazimbi*

**Mopane**
*Colophospermum mopane SA Tree no 198*
*This tree may be large and single-stemmed, or small and multi-stemmed. It grows in vast uniform stands in the north-western area of the Bushveld. It is easy to identify by the butterfly-shaped, compound leaves. The pods are flattened and slightly kidney-shaped, and turn light brown when ripe from April to June. The leaves turn yellow-gold during autumn.*

# Plains – Deep Sandy soils

Deep Sandy Soils are more common in the west, mostly in the Mixed Bushveld (M), and are often red. Water penetrates the sand easily, and filters through very fast, washing out nutrients. As a result plants have to absorb large amounts of water to obtain sufficient food. To remove the excess water the majority of these trees tend to have broad leaves to help the water evaporate. Specialised species that can be found on these sandy soils are the Round-leaved Bloodwood, described below, and the trees covered in the section "Plains – Sandy Areas" (pages 236 - 247).

*November; Camel-thorn Acacia at Sangiro's homestead ruins (pages 240 and 400); near Brits; deep sandy soil; Mixed Bushveld*

## Round-leaved Bloodwood
*Pterocarpus rotundifolius  SA Tree no 237*
This tree is often small and multi-stemmed. The round leaflets are large and very shiny, and have a distinct herringbone pattern. The leaves are once compound with one or two pairs of alternate leaflets and a larger end leaflet. The pea-like flowers are yellow, and grow in sprays from September to February. Bunches of winged pods ripen to dark brown in autumn.

## Plains – Clay and Turf Soils

These are the soils of the Thorny Bushveld, Ecozone (T), and they are very fertile. Although they hold water for extended periods, this water is tied to particles of clay, and is not easy for roots to absorb. However, even by absorbing small amounts of water, trees get plenty of nutrients. These trees need to conserve water so they tend to have small leaves to restrict the water lost through transpiration. Sweet-thorn Acacia (page 208) and Black-thorn Acacia (page 250), that form very dense stands in these areas, are good examples of such trees, as is the Purple-pod Cluster-leaf discussed below.

The fact that these soils are so rich in nutrients, make them sought after for agriculture. Large areas of natural vegetation have therefore been replaced by agricultural lands. Where these areas are ploughed up, the difference in the colour of the soil can be seen. These are either red, due to the presence of weathered minerals such as iron oxides, or black (more common in low-lying areas).

*Sweet-thorn Acacia next to agriculture fields; Springbok flats; Thorny Bushveld*

### Purple-pod Cluster-leaf
*Terminalia prunioides  SA Tree no 550*
This tree can be easily identified by the striking, oval, flat, purple to wine-red, winged pods that cover the canopy from February to August. It has drooping foliage, with small, simple leaves. They are spirally arranged in clusters around the ends of branchlets and twigs that end in spines. The white flower-spikes have a pungent smell, and cover the tree in spring and early summer.

# Plains – Old Termite Mounds

Throughout the Plains of all Ecozones of the Bushveld, Old Termite Mounds form patches of well-aerated and better-drained soils.

Old Termite Mounds are more common in areas with sandy soils, and these mounds form nutrient-rich islands in these poorer soils. They are made more porous by the tunnels in the mounds, and are high in nutrients because of the fungi and plant seeds deposited there by the termites.

Some of the grass seeds germinate on the surface of the Mound, and are very attractive fodder for grazers. Clumps of taller trees can often be found on these patches. Buffalo-thorn Jujube (page 188), Jacket-plum (page 272) and African Olive (page 184) are often easy to find here.

Some trees that normally only grow along Rivers can be also found on these Old Mounds, such as the Weeping Boer-bean, described below.

Sandy Plain; clump of trees on Old Termite Mound

## Weeping Boer-bean
*Schotia brachypetala  SA Tree no 202*
*This single-trunked tree often grows on Old Termite Mounds and along Rivers at lower altitudes. It has a dense, dark green canopy. The once compound leaves have four pairs of roundish leaflets with a pair at the tip. Conspicuous, dense sprays of crimson flowers grow on the old branches from August to November. The brown, broad bean pods burst open on the tree from January to August.*

# RIVERS AND STREAMS

Because of the increased availability of water and the high level of nutrients, a wide variety of trees grow here, often forming dense forest patches. Most riverine trees are evergreen, and grow very tall, standing out from the surrounding vegetation.

Many of the larger trees tend to develop buttressed roots to anchor themselves more securely in times of heavy flow and flood. This is true of Big-leaf Fever-tree (page 162), African White-stinkwood (page 360) and River Bushwillow (page 376). The River Bushwillow, growing on the edge of permanent Rivers and Streams, is one of the more common trees leaning over river banks. Along smaller Rivers, and in drier drainage valleys, Sweet-thorn Acacia (page 208) is often the dominant tree, growing in dense groups.

Many Rivers open up to form a large, flat, valley floor. This is where groups of Tamboti (page 388) are easy to find. Where these areas have been previously ploughed, dense stands of Black-thorn Acacia (page 250) and Umbrella Acacia (page 262) may be common. Where the floors have deep sand, mini-forests of Silver Cluster-leaf (page 244) are spectacular.

*June; Sand River; Sour Bushveld*

**Eastern Rapanea**
*Rapanea melanophloeos*
SA Tree no 578
This is a forest tree often growing in the understory in kloofs. The stems of the younger trees and branches are pale grey and covered with small knobs resembling ostrich skin (page 80). The simple leaves typically have dark purple leaf-stalks and are clustered at the ends of the thick branchlets and twigs. The fruit and flowers grow close to the stalk under the leaves, leaving permanent scars when they drop.

# KLOOFS

Valleys and Kloofs carved out in Mountain ranges are often well shaded, and a wide variety of shade- and moisture-loving trees can be found here. The African White-stinkwood (page 360) is one of the larger, common and spectacular trees.

There are many other trees associated with forests, such as the Eastern Rapanea and the Broad- and Small-leaved Yellowwoods described on these two pages. Because of the very unusual Habitat, these Kloofs are not easy places for beginners to tree spot. The trees grow very closely together, and the species themselves differ from the more common trees in the surrounding areas.

Heavily-wooded Kloof

Both species of Yellowwoods can grow to over 30 metres, and look similar from a distance.

### Broad-leaved Yellowwood
*Podocarpus latifolius  SA Tree no 18*
These trees grows very tall in the Kloof forests. The leaves are long and are spirally arranged at the tips of the branchlets, and tend to hang down forming a uniform, dense, green canopy. The thin grey- to khaki-coloured bark has shallow lengthways grooves, and peels in long, thin strips.

### Small-leaved Yellowwood
*Podocarpus falcatus  SA Tree no 16*
This tree has dark chocolate-coloured bark that peels in large, irregular, circular flakes. The leaves are thin and often sickle-shaped, and grow in rounded, separated clumps around the main branches.

# HIGHER ALTITUDE PLAINS AND PLATEAUS

Although most of the Bushveld is fairly low lying, four large Mountain ranges fall within or just outside its boundaries. Because of the height of the Drakensberg, Soutpansberg, Blouberg and Waterberg, some exposed, high-lying Plateaus that are typical of Highveld, are found in the Bushveld. The tops of these Mountains are covered by grassy plains with small groups of trees like Ouhout (described below) and Highveld Protea (page 322). These trees and their Habitats are covered in detail in **Sappi Tree Spotting Highveld.**

On the Slopes of these Mountains, or between minor peaks, flat, plain-like areas are found. These higher altitude "Plains" often have more grass cover than the Slopes themselves, and trees may grow denser and taller here because the soils are deeper. Trees that are found on these areas are typical Bushveld trees, mostly the same as those on the Slopes. They often include Weeping Faurea (page 350) and Weeping Lavender-tree (page 354).

*January; high altitude Plateaus; near Blyde River, Sour Bushveld*

### Ouhout
*Leucosidea sericea  SA Tree no 145*
Ouhout often grows in groups in open grassland on Plateaus above 1 100 metres, and is also common along Rivers. A small tree, with gnarled trunk, it is covered by red-brown bark that peels in long, thick, flaking strips. Characteristic leaves are once compound with four pairs of leaflets, deeply and sharply toothed. The veins are visibly sunken on the upper-surface and stand out below. Leaflets are covered by silky, silver hairs, with the under-surface more densely covered and whiter than the dark green upper-surface.

# ROCKY AREAS

Rocky Areas are usually very well drained and are high in nutrients. More water can be available in the patches of soil between the rocks even though temperatures are often very high.

Lavender Croton (page 280) thrives in these Rocky Areas, both on the Plains and on Mountain Slopes. Rock Figs (pages 276 and 288) need very little soil, their roots obtaining nutrients from the small pockets of sand in the cracks between the rocks. Over decades, as the roots grow in between cracks, the rocks often split further and pieces of rock may even break off.

Some trees are very strongly associated with specific nutrients that can only be obtained from particular rock formations. Bushveld Red-balloon (page 37), for example, is only found in the Pilanesberg area, and Paperbark Albizia (page 178) only in the Northern Mountains.

July; dense stands of trees; Rocky Areas, Soutpansberg

**Golden-haired Rock Fig**
*Ficus glumosa* SA Tree no 64
This Rock Fig is often found along dry watercourses. The bark is pale yellow-grey and flaking. The broadly elliptic to round leaves are spirally arranged around the branchlets. Young leaves and leaf-stalks are covered by long, golden hairs, and mature leaves are thick, shiny, and dark green above. The small figs are hairy and reddish when ripe (August to March).

# PILANESBERG

The Pilanesberg area is an old volcano, and as a result the Pilanesberg Mountains form a circle. The vegetation patterns here are more complex than in the rest of the Bushveld, for four reasons. Firstly the unusual circular shape of the Mountains makes the normal "interpretation" of north, south, east and west quite complex. Secondly because the circle gives protection in different ways, the actual tree distribution patterns change. Thirdly, the soils, that result from the volcanic action 1 300 million years ago, are very fertile, and also influence tree growth. Finally, again because of the usually beneficial landscape, humans have utilised the area literally over tens of thousands of years. This means that human fires, grazing of stock and even cultivation have changed many "natural" patterns.

As is true for all South African Mountain ranges, the Slopes that are exposed to the afternoon sun from the west, or face north and the equator, are hotter. They have longer periods when sun-rays strike the soil directly, and cause the Slope to dry out (page 26). Red Bushwillow (page 140), Live-long Lannea (page 330) and Lavender Croton (page 280) are characteristic trees of these Slopes. However, where these Slopes are protected by other Mountains or Slopes, they become more wooded and denser than you would expect.

Generally South- and East-facing Slopes are only exposed to the morning sun and are cooler and wetter. Common Hook-thorn Acacia (page 318), Weeping Faurea (page 350) and Highveld Protea (page 322) are characteristic of these Slopes.

Tamboti thickets (page 388) are often found on the foot Slopes of the hills, where the soils have more clay. In the eroded streambeds, and in areas that were once heavily overgrazed, Black-thorn Acacia (page 250) form dense groups, while Scented-pod Acacia (page 254) are the most common trees of the valley floors. Sweet-thorn Acacia (page 208) and Karree (page 368) are easy to find growing along watercourses.

*February; view over Mankwe Lake; Pilanesberg*

*December; view across the Plains to the circle of Mountains; Pilanesberg*

**Bushveld Red-balloon**
*Erythrophysa transvaalensis*
SA Tree no 436.2
This tree is quite rare, and can be found on the red syenite koppies in Pilanesberg. It is easiest to recognise by the balloon-like, three-angled, fruit capsules that turn red when ripe (October to February). The tree is sparsely branched with a moderate canopy. Once compound leaves have 7 pairs of leaflets with one at the tip, and a winged leaf-stalk. The unusual and attractive flowers appear before the new leaves in spring.

# MAGALIESBERG

The Magaliesberg run east-west and form part of the southern boundary of the Mixed Bushveld (M) (page 44). This Mountain range rises to a height of 1 600 - 1 800 metres and the Plateaus are mainly grasslands. Tree species vary according to the way the Slope faces, the soil depth and rainfall. Steeper, more protected, cooler Slopes face the south, and less steep, hotter, drier Slopes face north (pages 24 to 27).

Rivers such as the Apies, Sand and Pienaars Rivers cut through the Mountain range to form Kloofs where forest species such as Eastern Rapanea (page 32) thrive.

The water running off the Mountains accumulates at the Break-of-Slopes, and very dense stands of trees grow here. Although very attractive, these are difficult areas in which to start tree spotting.

In summer the radiant yellow flowers of the Peeling-bark Ochna (page 136) and the white flowers of the Wild-pear Dombeya (page 156) transform the cooler Slopes into a mass of colour.

As the vegetation changes from Bushveld to Highveld, species such as Quilted Buddleja and Olive Buddleja, both described below, can be found on cooler Slopes and in Kloofs. Other Highveld trees such as Ouhout (page 34) can be found on the highest Plateaus.

*Ridges of the Magaliesberg running east to west*

### Quilted Buddleja
*Buddleja salviifolia* SA Tree no 637
This is a densely branched, multi-stemmed tree. It can be easily recognised by dense sprays of pink to purple, sweet-scented flowers from May to October. The long, simple leaves are characteristic, and are wavy and deeply indented by an intricate network pattern of veins that resembles quilting.

# Mpumalanga Heritage Millenium Forest

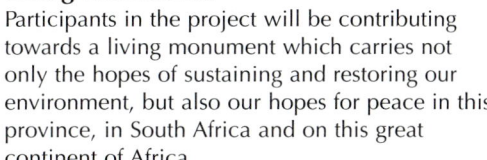

Mpumalanga Tourism Authority has marked the new millennium with the establishment of a "living monument" in celebration of the province's natural splendour. This is a forest, in recognition of the organisation's millennium theme, "In Celebration of Life", emphasising hope and growth.

The forest is being established on the lip of the Blyde River Canyon, and aims to conserve the Blyde River Canyon Nature Reserve and its fauna and flora, in perpetuity. The existing rainforest at God's Window is being incorporated into the Millennium Forest. As a heritage site the Blyde River Canyon is irreplaceable. Aeons ago, Gondwana tore apart, freeing Africa from Asia, and setting it on its path to the diverse species richness that we see in the forest today. Over centuries, the Blyde River has cut its way through more than 1 000 metres of the quartzite and dolomite rocks of the Drakensberg, creating immense canyons and kloofs, and unusual Habitats. A number of the trees covered in this book occur in the forest. However, because it is a unique phenomenon, many other species can also be found that are not typical Bushveld.

Interested parties and organisations, tourists, ambassadors and heads of states are being approached to be part of the project. Participants will have an option of either buying a new tree, or adopting an existing tree. New trees can actually be planted by donors if they choose! A list of trees up for "adoption" is available.

The projects fund raising phase ran from 2 000 hours before the first sunrise of the year 2000, and will finish 2 000 hours after the first sunrise of the year 2001. All sponsors will be acknowledged by a black and white, limited edition, exhibition-quality photograph of a stunning Blyde River Canyon view from the escarpment, as well as their name on a commemorative wall.

## Millennium Trust Fund
All donations will be payable to the Millennium Trust Fund and will become part of a trust securing the future of this forest in perpetuity.

## Living Monument
Participants in the project will be contributing towards a living monument which carries not only the hopes of sustaining and restoring our environment, but also our hopes for peace in this province, in South Africa and on this great continent of Africa.

For more information please contact Mpumalanga Tourism Authority:

**Tel: (013) 752-7001/2**
**Fax: (013) 759-5441**
**e-mail: mtanlpsa@cis.co.za**

**Olive Buddleja**
*Buddleja saligna  SA Tree no 636*
*This densely branched tree has creamy to dark brown bark which is deeply fissured lengthways. Cream-coloured flowers grow in dense sprays from August to January. Leaves are simple and bicoloured with distinct veining on the under-surface.*

# YOU FIND TREES BY ECOZONE

The five Ecozones used in this book have been adapted and re-named from those published by the National Botanical Institute (NBI) in 1996. Below is a summary of the five zones and their NBI origins.

**S** — The **Sour Bushveld** (NBI Zone 21) encompasses the area from the loosely-defined boundaries of the Lowveld, up to the Drakensberg escarpment. It includes many of the scenic walks along the escarpment in Mpumalanga.

**M** — Those areas of the North West and Northern Provinces that have always been loosely termed "Bushveld" form most of the **Mixed Bushveld** (NBI Zones 17 & 18). This area is relatively flat, with scattered Rocky Areas, and includes the Pilanesberg and Magaliesberg mountain ranges.

**T** — The **Thorny Bushveld** (NBI Zone 14) is formed by the large Springbok Flats and surrounding Plains, as well as other flat Plains areas, that are characterised by clay and turf soils

**C** — This is formed by the **Central Mountains** (NBI Zone 12), and consists mainly of the Waterberg Mountains.

**N** — This is formed by the **Northern Mountains** (NBI Zone 11), and consists of the Soutpansberg and Blouberg Mountains.

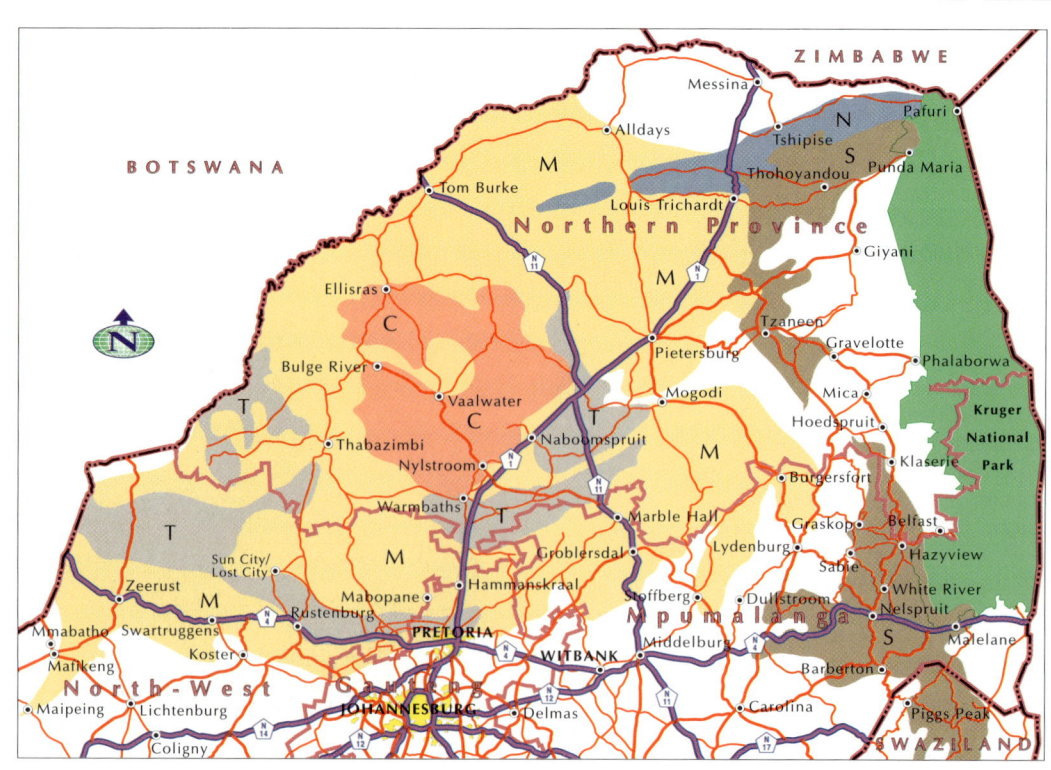

# Sour Bushveld (s)

Altitude: 550 - 800 m; Rainfall 600 - 1 000 mm, increasing from the lower to higher altitudes. Mist in the mist-belt zone along the escarpments of the Mountains also increases the rainfall in those areas. Temperatures are very high in summer, up to 43°C, but may drop to as low as 2°C in the higher areas in winter. Frost very seldom occurs.

This Ecozone stretches from the gradually rising Lowveld on the lower eastern Slopes of the Drakensberg, to the higher parts of the Escarpment of the Mountains, which becomes Highveld. Dense forests are found in the Kloofs of the Escarpment, and here fires stop the forest vegetation from expanding. The Plateau (page 34) is a high grassland with some Highveld trees such as Ouhout (page 34), Quilted Buddleja (page 38) and Olive Buddleja (page 39).

The Plains along the foothills are undulating, with different trees in the valleys and on the crests. As the altitude drops, the vegetation on these Plains changes to include more typical Lowveld trees. However this transition from Sour Bushveld to Lowveld is gradual, over tens of kilometres.

On the lower slopes temperatures are much higher and the rainfall is lower. Here trees such as Round-leaved Bloodwood (page 29) are common, as well as Kiaat Bloodwood (page 166) and Mobola-plum (page 170).

Economic uses: Cattle and game farming with subtropical fruit farming, as well as ecotourism and forestry. Conservation status: 9,65% conserved.

*May; Sour Bushveld between the Lowveld in the east and the Drakensberg in the west*

**Sneezewood**
*Ptaeroxylon obliquum  SA Tree no 292*
This tree is easiest to recognise by the once compound leaves that have sickle-shaped leaflets with an off-centre central vein. Leaflets decrease in size from the tip to the base of the leaf. Flowers are sweet-scented, yellow and star-shaped (October to November). The fruit are red-brown papery capsules that split in two to release the winged seeds (December to January).

# MIXED BUSHVELD (M)

Altitude: 700 - 1 100 m; Rainfall 300 - 500 mm per year, mostly in the form of thunderstorms. The summers are hot, reaching temperatures of 35°C and more by day, and dropping to about 16°C by night. In the winter, day temperatures can reach 25°C, but night temperatures can drop to about 6°C, with occasional frost.

This is a very large Ecozone and therefore the vegetation is very varied. Dense thorn thickets of Acacias on clay soils change to more open Plains, with large Burkea (page 236), conspicuous on Sandy soils.

Due to the low rainfall, grasses do not form dense uniform stands as they do in the Highveld, so fires have less effect on tree growth. Frost is not common either, and as a result wide open grassy Plains are uncommon.

Two Mountain ranges, the Magaliesberg and Pilanesberg, have their own unique vegetation patterns, with special trees and Habitats. Pages 36 to 38 cover these areas in detail. A part of this Ecozone also borders on the hot Limpopo Valley, which has unique trees such as Eastern Sesame-bush (page 90) and Fever Croton, discussed below.

Economic uses: Cattle and game farming with some vegetable and crop farming, as well as ecotourism. Conservation status: 2,9% conserved.

*July; Plains sliced by Markwe Dam; foothills of Pilanesberg Mountains; Mixed Bushveld*

**Fever Croton**
*Croton megalobotrys* SA Tree no 329
Common along large Rivers such as the Limpopo, Olifants and Sand, it has a slender, smooth, pale grey trunk, and dense, drooping canopy. Large, simple, alternate leaves are spirally arranged and heart-shaped with a toothed margin. The under-surface of young leaves has silvery-white hairs. Characteristic three-lobed, yellowish-brown fruit capsules look like small apples, and are covered by grey-white, woolly hairs when young (December to March).

# Thorny Bushveld (T)

Altitude: about 1 000 m; Rainfall 450 - 750 mm per year. Temperatures vary from -6°C in winter to 40°C in summer.

The Thorny Bushveld is a large, fairly uniformly flat Plain with no major Mountains. However a few scattered rocky ridges and Rocky Outcrops relieve the landscape, and add tree interest. The Plains have very fertile, black and red clay soils that were formed by the erosion of basalts. The area is fairly uniformly covered with Acacias, that are mostly the same size, and few large trees stand out. However it is an ideal area to enjoy comparing different Acacias, such as Red (described below), Scented-pod (page 254) and Umbrella (page 262). Many of these Acacias and the Sickle-bush (page 258) form dense stands between cultivated areas.

The area is heavily cultivated, with little natural bush on the flat Plains. The red and black soils can be identified by looking at the colour of the soils in the cultivated lands.

Economic uses: Intensively used for crop production and livestock farming. Conservation status: only 0,93% conserved.

*January; Springbok Flats, Thorny Bushveld*

**Red Acacia**
*Acacia gerrardii  SA Tree no 167
Long, droopy, twice compound leaves hug the branches closely, forming sleeves around them. Dark grey bark is fissured lengthways revealing reddish under-bark. Thorns are stout, straight and white. Creamy-white flower-balls grow on long stalks from October to January. Pods are sickle-shaped, flat and velvety and ripen to grey-brown (December to May).*

# Central Mountains (c)

Altitude: 1 200 - 1 500 m; Rainfall 650 - 900 mm per year. The temperatures vary from -6°C in winter to 39°C in summer.

The Waterberg Mountains and surrounding Plains form the main part of this Ecozone. It is a single Mountain range that stretches more or less east-west. On the dry, Rocky Slopes that tend to be North- and West-facing, the white trunks of the Paperbark Albizia (page 178) stand out clearly on the cliffs. Lower down on the cool, moist South- and East-facing Slopes Weeping Faurea (page 350) are more common. Highveld Protea (page 322) and Common Hook-thorn Acacia (page 318) are the most common trees higher up these cool Slopes.

Red Bushwillow form large groups along the dry, gravelly, North-facing Slopes, but where water gathers among loose rocks, Tamboti (page 388), Fever Croton (page 42) and even Red Ivorywood (page 342) can be found. In the overgrazed areas of the Plains, Sickle-bush (page 258) and Umbrella Acacia (page 262) form dense thickets.

Economic uses: Riverine areas under intense agriculture, cattle and game farming, as well as ecotourism are the main form of land use. Conservation status: 8,55% conserved.

*May; Doringdraai Dam Reserve; Central Mountains*

**Thorny-rope Flat-bean**
*Dalbergia armata  SA Tree no 231*
This spiny climber is conspicuous in most dense forests. Huge spines are clumped on dark swellings on the otherwise smooth bark (page 83). The twice compound leaves are Acacia-like and are often only visible high up in the canopy. White, pea-like flowers cover this creeper (October to November).

# Northern Mountains (N)

Altitude: 300 - 2 050 m; Rainfall varies substantially from 350 mm in the north-west near Waterpoort, to 1 700 mm at Hanglip in the east. Temperatures are high in summer, up to 44°C on lower North- or West-facing Slopes. However they can drop to 3°C in winter on higher, South- or East-facing Slopes.

The Soutpansberg and Blouberg Mountains, both run roughly east-west, and together form the main part of this Ecozone. The Soutpansberg Mountains were formed by ancient movements of the Earth causing a dipping in the north, and rising in the south. Cliff faces have therefore formed on the southern Slopes, while the northern Slopes have a gradient of about 45°. The Plains area is relatively small. Because of the huge variation in rainfall, the vegetation also varies greatly. Dense forests are found along the south- or east-facing cliffs, in the Kloofs, and along the River and side-streams of the Sand River, that runs through the Soutpansberg.

Arid-adapted and more drought-resistant trees, such as the succulent-looking Eastern Sesame-bush (page 90), are found on the northern Slopes and Plains. Fever Croton (page 42) are very common on dry, rocky Slopes. Numerous different members of the fascinating Corkwood family thrive on the drier Slopes and are described on page 78.

Economic uses: Cattle and game farming, as well as tourism, are the main forms of land use, although there are some areas under forestry. Conservation status: 12,59% conserved.

*January; Northern Slopes of the Soutpansberg; Northern Mountains*

### Apple-leaf
*Lonchocarpus capassa* SA Tree no 238
This tree has a single, smooth, white-grey, meandering trunk and grows very tall along Rivers. The large, leathery, three-leaflet compound leaves have a very large end leaflet. Large bunches of fragrant, purple, pea-like flowers appear with the new leaves in early spring. Conspicuous bunches of flat, light brown pods can be seen on the tree for most of the year.

45

# Ecozone tree list

This is the list of trees you are most likely to find in each Habitat. The trees you should look for first are shown at the top of the list in the darker colour. The trees in the paler colour are the next "easiest" to look for.

## Ecozone C

| Rivers / Kloofs | | Rocky Areas | | | | Plains | |
|---|---|---|---|---|---|---|---|
| Tree | Page | Tree | Page | Tree | Page | Tree | Page |
| African White-stinkwood | 360 | Eastern Sesame-bush | 90 | Kooboo-berry | 124 | Burkea | 236 |
| Broom-cluster Fig | 364 | Lavender Croton | 280 | Ladies Cabbage-tree | 94 | Camel-thorn Acacia | 240 |
| Flame-pod Acacia | 116 | Naboom Euphorbia | 98 | Large-fruited Bushwillow | 128 | Common Wild Fig | 196 |
| River Bushwillow | 376 | Squat Star-chestnut | 102 | Live-long Lannea | 330 | Leadwood | 226 |
| Robust Acacia | 380 | Stamvrug Milkplum | 296 | Mountain Kirkia | 284 | Silver Cluster-leaf | 244 |
| African Olive | 184 | Bushveld Bead-bean | 112 | Peeling-bark Ochna | 136 | African Weeping-wattle | 214 |
| Black-monkey Acacia | 218 | Hornpod-tree | 268 | Pipe-stem Fingerleaf | 338 | Baobab | 86 |
| Buffalo-thorn Jujube | 188 | Jacket-plum | 272 | Red Bushwillow | 140 | Black-monkey Acacia | 218 |
| Common Wild Fig | 196 | Large Sourplum | 132 | Red Ivorywood | 342 | Black-thorn Acacia | 250 |
| Karree | 368 | Large-leaved Rock Fig | 276 | Robust Acacia | 380 | Hairy-leaved Monkey-orange | 120 |
| Leadwood | 226 | Moepel Red-milkwood | 334 | Rock Karree-rhus | 76 | Naboom Euphorbia | 98 |
| Red Ivorywood | 342 | Paperbark Albizia | 178 | Rock Tree-nettle | 292 | Russet Bushwillow | 144 |
| Sweet-thorn Acacia | 208 | Red-leaved Fig | 288 | Rubber Hedge Euphorbia | 100 | Small-leaved Guarri | 204 |
| Tamboti | 388 | Shepherds-tree | 200 | Sacred Coral-tree | 148 | Umbrella Acacia | 262 |
| Umdoni Waterberry | 392 | Tall Firethorn Corkwood | 300 | Sickle-bush | 258 | White Cats-whiskers | 152 |
| | | | | Silver Cabbage-tree | 96 | | |
| Apple-leaf | 45 | Blue Sourplum | 134 | Silver Raisin | 346 | Blue Acacia | 70 |
| Burkea | 236 | Broad-leaved Coral-tree | 67 | Simple-leaved Cabbage-tree | 96 | Buffalo-thorn Jujube | 188 |
| Bushveld Shepherds-tree | 192 | Bushveld Resin-tree | 314 | Small Knobwood | 384 | Bushveld Resin-tree | 314 |
| Camel-thorn Acacia | 240 | Common Currant-rhus | 76 | Small-leaved Guarri | 204 | Candle-pod Acacia | 62 |
| Common Currant-rhus | 76 | Common Hook-thorn Acacia | 318 | Spine-leaved Monkey-orange | 63 | Common Currant-rhus | 76 |
| Common Hook-thorn Acacia | 318 | Common Spikethorn | xi | Sweet-thorn Acacia | 208 | Common Hook-thorn Acacia | 318 |
| Common Spikethorn | xi | Common Wild Fig | 196 | Velvet Bushwillow | 304 | Common Spikethorn | xi |
| Eastern Rapanea | 32 | Crowberry Currant-rhus | 76 | Velvet Corkwood | 68 | Corky-bark Monkey-orange | 79 |
| False Perdepis | 382 | Deadliest Euphorbia | 100 | Weeping Collina Bushwillow | 75 | Firethorn Corkwood | 78 |
| Fever Croton | 42 | Firethorn Corkwood | 78 | Weeping Faurea | 350 | Glossy-leaved Corkwood | 67 |
| Golden-haired Rock-fig | 77 | Golden-haired Rock-fig | 77 | White Cats-whiskers | 152 | Highveld Silver-oak | 326 |
| Hairy-leaved Monkey-orange | 120 | Hairy-leaved Monkey-orange | 120 | White Kirkia | 308 | Jacket-plum | 272 |
| Highveld Silver-oak | 326 | Highveld Cabbage-tree | 96 | Wild-pear Dombeya | 156 | Ladies Cabbage-tree | 94 |
| Jacket-plum | 272 | Highveld Protea | 322 | | | Large Sourplum | 132 |
| Knob-thorn Acacia | 222 | Highveld Silver-oak | 326 | | | Large-fruited Bushwillow | 128 |
| Kooboo-berry | 124 | | | | | Live-long Lannea | 330 |
| Lover's Cheesewood | 1 | | | | | Marula | 230 |
| Marula | 230 | | | | | Moepel Red-milkwood | 334 |
| Mobola-plum | 170 | | | | | Peeling-bark Ochna | 136 |
| Moepel Red-milkwood | 334 | | | | | Pride-of-De Kaap Bauhinia | 27 |
| Monkey Acacia | 71 | | | | | Red Bushwillow | 140 |
| Pigeonwood | 66 | | | | | Round-leaved Bloodwood | 29 |
| Quilted Buddleja | 38 | | | | | Scented-pod Acacia | 254 |
| Red Acacia | 43 | | | | | Shepherds-tree | 200 |
| Russet Bushwillow | 144 | | | | | Sickle-bush | 258 |
| Scented-pod Acacia | 254 | | | Large-leaved Rock Fig, page 276 | | Silver Raisin | 346 |
| Shepherds-tree | 200 | | | | | Sweet-thorn Acacia | 208 |
| Sickle-bush | 258 | | | | | Tall Firethorn Corkwood | 300 |
| Silver Raisin | 346 | | | | | Tamboti | 388 |
| Sycomore Fig | 77 | | | | | Velvet Corkwood | 68 |
| Thorny-rope Flat-bean | 44 | | | | | Weeping Faurea | 350 |
| Umbrella Acacia | 262 | | | | | Wild-pear Dombeya | 156 |
| Weeping Boer-bean | 31 | | | | | | |
| Weeping Lavender-tree | 354 | | | | | | |
| White Cats-whiskers | 152 | | | | | | |

This list includes Look-alike trees, trees in the Distinctive Striking Features section (pages 58 - 83), and trees described in the introductory pages.

For detailed information on the Central Mountains read page 44.

# CENTRAL MOUNTAINS

| Termite Mounds | | North- or West-facing Slopes | | South- or East-facing Slopes | | Plateaus | |
|---|---|---|---|---|---|---|---|
| Tree | Page | Tree | Page | Tree | Page | Tree | Page |
| African Olive | 184 | Hornpod-tree | 268 | Common Hook-thorn | | Ouhout | 34 |
| Buffalo-thorn Jujube | 188 | Lavender Croton | 280 | Acacia | 318 | African Protea | 324 |
| Bushveld Bead-bean | 112 | Paperbark Albizia | 178 | Highveld Protea | 322 | Common Currant-rhus | 76 |
| Jacket-plum | 272 | Red Bushwillow | 140 | Ladies Cabbage-tree | 94 | Common Spikethorn | xi |
| White Cats-whiskers | 152 | Velvet Bushwillow | 304 | Weeping Faurea | 350 | Highveld Protea | 322 |
| | | | | Weeping Lavender-tree | 354 | Highveld Silver-oak | 326 |
| Burkea | 236 | Bushveld Shepherds-tree | 192 | African Olive | 184 | Ladies Cabbage-tree | 94 |
| Bushveld Resin-tree | 314 | Jacket-plum | 272 | Brittlewood Nuxia | 108 | Silver Protea | 58 |
| Highveld Silver-oak | 326 | Live-long Lannea | 330 | Highveld Silver-oak | 326 | | |
| Karree | 368 | Naboom Euphorbia | 98 | Mountain Kirkia | 284 | | |
| Leadwood | 226 | Red-leaved Fig | 288 | Paperbark Albizia | 178 | | |
| Moepel Red-milkwood | 334 | Rock Tree-nettle | 292 | Peeling-bark Ochna | 136 | | |
| Naboom Euphorbia | 98 | Shepherds-tree | 200 | Pipe-stem Fingerleaf | 338 | | |
| Silver Raisin | 346 | Stamvrug Milkplum | 296 | Red Ivorywood | 342 | | |
| Wild-pear Dombeya | 156 | White Kirkia | 308 | Small Knobwood | 384 | | |
| | | African Olive | 184 | Wild-pear Dombeya | 156 | | |
| Sneezewood | 41 | Baobab | 86 | | | | |
| Weeping Boer-bean | 31 | Hairy-leaved | | African White-stinkwood | 360 | | |
| | | Monkey-orange | 120 | Black-monkey Acacia | 218 | | |
| | | Broad-pod Elephant-root | 61 | Broad-leaved Coral-tree | 67 | | |
| | | Buffalo-thorn Jujube | 188 | Broad-leaved Yellowwood | 33 | | |
| | | Bushveld Resin-tree | 314 | Brown Ivorywood | 344 | | |
| | | Common Spikethorn | xi | Buffalo-thorn Jujube | 188 | | |
| | | Currant Resin-tree | 316 | Flame-pod Acacia | 116 | | |
| | | Glossy-leaved Corkwood | 67 | Forest Bushwillow | 74 | | |
| | | Highveld Silver-oak | 326 | Highveld Cabbage-tree | 96 | | |
| | | Kooboo-berry | 124 | Jacket-plum | 272 | | |
| | | Large-fruited Bushwillow | 128 | Lavender Croton | 280 | | |
| | | Lowveld Silver-oak | 328 | Live-long Lannea | 330 | | |
| | | Moepel Red-milkwood | 334 | Lowveld Silver-oak | 328 | | |
| | | Mountain Kirkia | 284 | Naboom Euphorbia | 98 | | |
| | | Paperbark Corkwood | 79 | Olive Buddleja | 39 | | |
| | | Perdepis | 68 | Perdepis | 68 | | |
| | | Quilted Buddleja | 38 | Pigeonwood | 66 | | |
| | | Red Ivorywood | 342 | Robust Acacia | 380 | | |
| | | Sickle-bush | 258 | Rock Karree-rhus | 76 | | |
| | | Spine-leaved | | Showy Ochna | 60 | | |
| | | Monkey-orange | 63 | Silver Cabbage-tree | 96 | | |
| | | Umbrella Acacia | 262 | Silver Protea | 58 | | |
| | | Velvet Corkwood | 68 | Simple-leaved | | | |
| | | Weeping Faurea | 350 | Cabbage-tree | 96 | | |
| | | Weeping Lavender-tree | 354 | Spine-leaved | | | |
| | | White Cats-whiskers | 152 | Monkey-orange | 63 | | |
| | | Wild-pear Dombeya | 156 | Stamvrug Milkplum | 296 | | |
| | | | | Sweet-thorn Acacia | 208 | | |
| | | | | Umbrella Acacia | 262 | | |
| | | | | Umdoni Waterberry | 392 | | |
| | | | | White Cats-whiskers | 152 | | |

Red-leaved Fig, page 288

47

# Ecozone tree list

This is the list of trees you are most likely to find in each Habitat. The trees you should look for first are shown at the top of the list in the darker colour. The trees in the paler colour are the next "easiest" to look for.

## Ecozone N

| Rivers / Kloofs | Page | Rocky Areas | Page | Rocky Areas (cont.) | Page | Plains | Page |
|---|---|---|---|---|---|---|---|
| **African White-stinkwood** | **360** | **Eastern Sesame-bush** | **90** | Glossy-leaved Corkwood | 67 | **Baobab** | **86** |
| **Broom-cluster Fig** | **364** | **Large-leaved Rock Fig** | **276** | Golden-haired Rock Fig | 35 | **Black-mokey Acacia** | **218** |
| **Flame-pod Acacia** | **116** | **Lavender Croton** | **280** | Hairy-leaved Monkey-orange | 120 | **Common Wild Fig** | **196** |
| **River Bushwillow** | **376** | **Naboom Euphorbia** | **98** | Highveld Silver-oak | 326 | **Knob-thorn Acacia** | **222** |
| **Robust Acacia** | **380** | **Stamvrug Milkplum** | **296** | Jacket-plum | 272 | **Large-fruited Bushwillow** | **128** |
| Big-leaf Fever-tree | 162 | Hornpod-tree | 268 | Lebombo Euphorbia | 100 | African Weeping-wattle | 214 |
| Brittlewood Nuxia | 108 | Ladies Cabbage-tree | 94 | Live-long Lannea | 330 | Buffalo-thorn Jujube | 188 |
| Karree | 368 | Large Sourplum | 132 | Mountain Kirkia | 284 | Burkea | 236 |
| Knob-thorn Acacia | 222 | Moepel Red-milkwood | 334 | Paperbark Albizia | 178 | Kooboo-berry | 124 |
| Leadwood | 226 | Pipe-stem Fingerleaf | 338 | Paperbark Corkwood | 79 | Leadwood | 226 |
| Red Currant-rhus | 372 | Rock Tree-nettle | 292 | Purple-pod Cluster-leaf | 30 | Marula | 230 |
| Russet Bushwillow | 144 | Squat Star-chestnut | 102 | Red Bushwillow | 140 | Russet Bushwillow | 144 |
| Silver Cluster-leaf | 244 | Tall Firethorn Corkwood | 300 | Rubber Hedge Euphorbia | 100 | Sacred Coral-tree | 148 |
| Sweet-thorn Acacia | 208 | Velvet Bushwillow | 304 | Shepherds-tree | 200 | Shepherds-tree | 200 |
| Tamboti | 388 | White Kirkia | 308 | Silver Cluster-leaf | 244 | White Cats-whiskers | 152 |
| African Olive | 184 | Broad-pod Elephant-root | 61 | Silver Raisin | 346 | Black-thorn Acacia | 250 |
| African Schefflera | 67 | Burkea | 236 | Spine-leaved Monkey-orange | 63 | Blue Acacia | 70 |
| Apple-leaf | 45 | Bushveld Shepherds-tree | 192 | Velvet Corkwood | 68 | Blue Sourplum | 134 |
| Black-monkey Acacia | 218 | Bushy Three-hook Acacia | 62 | Velvet-leaved Sweetberry | 26 | Bushveld Bead-bean | 112 |
| Blue Acacia | 70 | Common Hook-thorn Acacia | 318 | Weeping Lavender-tree | 354 | Bushveld Resin-tree | 314 |
| Broad-leaved Yellowwood | 33 | Crowberry Currant-rhus | 76 | Wild-pear Dombeya | 156 | Bushveld Shepherds-tree | 192 |
| Brown Ivorywood | 344 | Deadliest Euphorbia | 100 | Wonderboom Fig | 278 | Camel-thorn Acacia | 240 |
| Buffalo-thorn Jujube | 188 | Giant Raisin | 60 | Zebra-bark Corkwood | 78 | Common Currant-rhus | 76 |
| Camel-thorn Acacia | 240 | | | | | Corky-bark Monkey-orange | 79 |
| Common Hook-thorn Acacia | 318 | | | | | Eastern Sesame-bush | 90 |
| Common Spikethorn | xi | | | | | False-marula Lannea | 82 |
| Eastern Rapanea | 32 | | | | | Giant Raisin | 60 |
| False Perdepis | 382 | | | | | Glossy-leaved Corkwood | 67 |
| False-marula Lannea | 82 | | | | | Large Sourplum | 132 |
| Fever Croton | 42 | | | | | Live-long Lannea | 330 |
| Forest Bushwillow | 74 | | | | | Mopane | 28 |
| Hairy-leaved Monkey-orange | 120 | | | | | Naboom Euphorbia | 98 |
| Lover's Cheesewood | 1 | | | | | Peeling-bark Ochna | 136 |
| Lowveld Silver-oak | 328 | | | | | Purple-pod Cluster-leaf | 30 |
| Monkey Acacia | 71 | | | | | Red Bushwillow | 140 |
| Perdepis | 68 | | | | | Round-leaved Bloodwood | 29 |
| Pigeonwood | 66 | | | | | Scented-pod Acacia | 254 |
| Pride-of-De Kaap Bauhinia | 27 | | | | | Sickle-bush | 258 |
| Quilted Buddleja | 38 | | | | | Silver Cluster-leaf | 244 |
| Red Ivorywood | 342 | | | | | Small-leaved Guarri | 204 |
| Sacred Coral-tree | 148 | | | | | Spine-leaved Monkey-orange | 63 |
| Showy Ochna | 60 | | | | | Spiny Monkey-orange | 79 |
| Simple-leaved Cabbage-tree | 96 | | | | | Squat Star-chestnut | 102 |
| Small-leaved Yellowwood | 33 | | | | | Sweet-thorn Acacia | 208 |
| Spiny Monkey-orange | 79 | | | | | Umbrella Acacia | 262 |
| Sycomore Fig | 77 | | | | | Velvet Corkwood | 68 |
| Thorny-rope Flat-bean | 44 | | | | | Weeping Collina Bushwillow | 75 |
| Umbrella Acacia | 262 | | | | | Wild-pear Dombeya | 156 |
| Umdoni Waterberry | 392 | | | | | Worm-cure Albizia | 61 |
| Weeping Boer-bean | 31 | | | | | | |
| Weeping Lavender-tree | 354 | | | | | | |
| White Cats-whiskers | 152 | | | | | | |

Eastern Sesame-bush, page 90

48

This list includes Look-alike trees, trees in the Distinctive Striking Features section (pages 58 - 83), and trees described in the introductory pages.

For detailed information about Northern Mountains read page 45.

# Northern Mountains

| Termite Mounds | | North- or West-facing Slopes | | South- or East-facing Slopes | | Plateaus | |
|---|---|---|---|---|---|---|---|
| Tree | Page | Tree | Page | Tree | Page | Tree | Page |
| African Olive | 184 | Baobab | 86 | Common Hook-thorn | | Ouhout | 34 |
| Buffalo-thorn Jujube | 188 | Hornpod-tree | 268 | Acacia | 318 | African Protea | 324 |
| Bushveld Bead-bean | 112 | Lavender Croton | 280 | Highveld Protea | 322 | Common Currant-rhus | 76 |
| Jacket-plum | 272 | Live-long Lannea | 330 | Ladies Cabbage-tree | 94 | Common Spikethorn | xi |
| White Cats-whiskers | 152 | Red Bushwillow | 140 | Weeping Faurea | 350 | Highveld Protea | 322 |
| | | | | Weeping Lavender-tree | 354 | Ladies Cabbage-tree | 94 |
| Bushveld Shepherds-tree | 192 | Bushveld Resin-tree | 314 | African Olive | 184 | Rock Karree-rhus | 76 |
| Karree | 368 | Bushveld Shepherds-tree | 192 | Brittlewood Nuxia | 108 | Shepherds-tree | 200 |
| Leadwood | 226 | Eastern Sesame-bush | 90 | Moepel Red-milkwood | 334 | Silver Cabbage-tree | 96 |
| Moepel Red-milkwood | 334 | Jacket-plum | 272 | Peeling-bark Ochna | 136 | Wild-pear Dombeya | 156 |
| Naboom Euphorbia | 98 | Large-leaved Rock Fig | 276 | Pipe-stem Fingerleaf | 338 | | |
| Silver Raisin | 346 | Paperbark Albizia | 178 | Red Currant-rhus | 372 | | |
| Umbrella Acacia | 262 | Squat Star-chestnut | 102 | Red Ivorywood | 342 | | |
| Wild-pear Dombeya | 156 | Stamvrug Milkplum | 296 | Small Knobwood | 384 | | |
| Giant Raisin | 60 | Velvet Bushwillow | 304 | Velvet Bushwillow | 304 | | |
| Tall Firethorn Corkwood | 300 | White Kirkia | 308 | Wild-pear Dombeya | 156 | | |
| Weeping Boer-bean | 31 | Broad-pod Elephant-root | 61 | African Schefflera | 67 | | |
| | | Buffalo-thorn Jujube | 188 | African White-stinkwood | 360 | | |
| | | Burkea | 236 | Baobab | 86 | | |
| | | Bushveld Bead-bean | 112 | Blue Sourplum | 134 | | |
| | | Deadliest Euphorbia | 100 | Broad-leaved | | | |
| | | Giant Raisin | 60 | Yellowwood | 33 | | |
| | | Hairy-leaved | | Broom-cluster Fig | 364 | | |
| | | Monkey-orange | 120 | Brown Ivorywood | 344 | | |
| | | Knob-thorn Acacia | 222 | Buffalo-thorn Jujube | 188 | | |
| | | Large-fruited Bushwillow | 128 | Common Spikethorn | xi | | |
| | | Lebombo Euphorbia | 100 | Crowberry Currant-rhus | 76 | | |
| | | Moepel Red-milkwood | 334 | Flame-pod Acacia | 116 | | |
| | | Paperbark Corkwood | 79 | Forest Silver-oak | 328 | | |
| | | Rock Karree-rhus | 76 | Giant Raisin | 60 | | |
| | | Rock Tree-nettle | 292 | Golden-haired Rock Fig | 35 | | |
| | | Round-leaved Bloodwood | 29 | Kiaat Bloodwood | 166 | | |
| | | Sacred Coral-tree | 148 | Large Sourplum | 132 | | |
| | | Silver Raisin | 346 | Naboom Euphorbia | 98 | | |
| | | Sneezewood | 41 | Olive Buddleja | 39 | | |
| | | Spine-leaved | | Purple-pod Cluster-leaf | 30 | **South- or East-facing** | |
| | | Monkey-orange | 63 | Red-leaved Fig | 288 | **Slopes (continued)** | |
| | | Umbrella Acacia | 262 | Rock Karree-rhus | 76 | Spine-leaved | |
| | | Velvet-leaved Sweetberry | 26 | Scented-pod Acacia | 254 | Monkey-orange | 63 |
| | | Weeping Faurea | 350 | Showy Ochna | 60 | Stamvrug Milkplum | 296 |
| | | Wild-pear Dombeya | 156 | Sickle-bush | 258 | Sweet-thorn Acacia | 208 |
| | | Zebra-bark Corkwood | 78 | Silver Cabbage-tree | 96 | Tamboti | 388 |
| | | | | Silver Cluster-leaf | 244 | Umbrella Acacia | 262 |
| | | | | Silver Protea | 58 | Umdoni Waterberry | 392 |
| | | | | Silver Raisin | 346 | Velvet Corkwood | 68 |
| | | | | Simple-leaved | | Weeping Collina | |
| Squat | | | | Cabbage-tree | 96 | Bushwillow | 75 |
| Star-chestnut, | | | | Small-leaved Yellowwood | 33 | White Cats-whiskers | 152 |
| page 102 | | | | Sneezewood | 41 | White Kirkia | 308 |

49

# Ecozone tree list

This is the list of trees you are most likely to find in each Habitat. The trees you should look for first are shown at the top of the list in the darker colour. The trees in the paler colour are the next "easiest" to look for.

## Ecozone M

| Rivers / Kloofs | Page | Rocky Areas | Page | Plains | Page | | |
|---|---|---|---|---|---|---|---|
| **Flame-pod Acacia** | **116** | **Eastern Sesame-bush** | **90** | **Baobab** | **86** | Silver Raisin | 346 |
| **Karree** | **368** | **Hornpod-tree** | **268** | **Buffalo-thorn Jujube** | **188** | Robust Acacia | 380 |
| **River Bushwillow** | **376** | **Large-leaved Rock Fig** | **276** | **Burkea** | **236** | Sweet-thorn Acacia | 208 |
| **Robust Acacia** | **380** | **Lavender Croton** | **280** | **Camel-thorn Acacia** | **240** | Tamboti | 388 |
| **Tamboti** | **388** | **Stamvrug Milkplum** | **296** | **Leadwood** | **226** | Bushy Three-hook Acacia | 63 |
| | | | | **Marula** | **230** | Wild-pear Dombeya | 156 |
| African White-stinkwood | 360 | Jacket-plum | 272 | African Weeping-wattle | 214 | Worm-cure Albizia | 61 |
| Big-leaf Fever-tree | 162 | Ladies Cabbage-tree | 94 | Black-monkey Acacia | 218 | | |
| Black-monkey Acacia | 218 | Large Sourplum | 132 | Hairy-leaved | | | |
| Bushveld Bead-bean | 112 | Naboom Euphorbia | 98 | Monkey-orange | 120 | | |
| Camel-thorn Acacia | 240 | Red-leaved Fig | 288 | Knob-thorn Acacia | 222 | | |
| Leadwood | 226 | Rock Tree-nettle | 292 | Large-fruited Bushwillow | 128 | | |
| Russet Bushwillow | 144 | Shepherds-tree | 200 | Russet Bushwillow | 144 | | |
| Sweet-thorn Acacia | 208 | Tall Firethorn Corkwood | 300 | Silver Cluster-leaf | 244 | | |
| Umdoni Waterberry | 392 | Velvet Bushwillow | 304 | Small-leaved Guarri | 204 | | |
| White Cats-whiskers | 152 | White Kirkia | 308 | Umbrella Acacia | 262 | | |
| | | | | White Cats-whiskers | 152 | | |
| African Olive | 184 | Blue Sourplum | 134 | | | | |
| Apple-leaf | 45 | Bushveld Bead-bean | 112 | African Olive | 184 | | |
| Black-thorn Acacia | 250 | Bushveld Red Balloon | 37 | Black-thorn Acacia | 250 | | |
| Blue Acacia | 70 | Bushveld Shepherds-tree | 192 | Blue Acacia | 70 | | |
| Brittlewood Nuxia | 108 | Common Hook-thorn | | Broad-pod Elephant-root | 61 | | |
| Broom-cluster Fig | 364 | Acacia | 318 | Bushveld Shepherds-tree | 192 | | |
| Buffalo-thorn Jujube | 188 | Common Spikethorn | xi | Candle-pod Acacia | 62 | | |
| Burkea | 236 | Crowberry Currant-rhus | 76 | Common Currant-rhus | 76 | | |
| Bushy Three-hook Acacia | 62 | Deadliest Euphorbia | 100 | Common Hook-thorn | | | |
| Candle-pod Acacia | 62 | Glossy-leaved Corkwood | 67 | Acacia | 318 | | |
| Common Hook-thorn | | Hairy-leaved | | Common Wild Fig | 196 | | |
| Acacia | 318 | Monkey-orange | 120 | Corky-bark | | | |
| Eastern Rapanea | 32 | Highveld Cabbage-tree | 96 | Monkey-orange | 79 | | |
| Fever Croton | 42 | Highveld Silver-oak | 326 | Eastern Sesame-bush | 90 | | |
| Golden-haired Rock Fig | 35 | Moepel Red-milkwood | 334 | False-marula Lannea | 82 | | |
| Hairy-leaved | | Mountain Kirkia | 284 | Forest Bushwillow | 74 | | |
| Monkey-orange | 120 | Peeling-bark Ochna | 136 | Giant Raisin | 60 | | |
| Large Sourplum | 132 | Purple-pod Cluster-leaf | 30 | Hornpod-tree | 268 | | |
| Monkey Acacia | 71 | Red Bushwillow | 140 | Kiaat Bloodwood | 166 | | |
| Pigeonwood | 66 | Red Ivorywood | 342 | Kooboo-berry | 124 | | |
| Pride-of-De Kaap Bauhinia | 27 | Robust Acacia | 380 | Large Sourplum | 132 | | |
| Quilted Buddleja | 38 | Round-leaved Bloodwood | 29 | Monkey Acacia | 71 | | |
| Red Ivorywood | 342 | Rubber Hedge Euphorbia | 100 | Naboom Euphorbia | 98 | | |
| Rock Karree-rhus | 76 | Russet Bushwillow | 144 | Paperbark Acacia | 174 | | |
| Rock Tree-nettle | 292 | Scented-pod Acacia | 254 | Peeling-bark Ochna | 136 | | |
| Scented-pod Acacia | 254 | Silver Raisin | 346 | Red Acacia | 43 | | |
| Shepherds-tree | 200 | Simple-leaved | | Red Bushwillow | 140 | | |
| Sickle-bush | 258 | Cabbage-tree | 96 | Round-leaved | | | |
| Silver Raisin | 346 | Small Knobwood | 384 | Bloodwood | 29 | | |
| Small-leaved Guarri | 204 | Squat Star-chestnut | 102 | Sand Corkwood | 78 | | |
| Spiny Monkey-orange | 79 | Tamboti | 388 | Scented-pod Acacia | 254 | | |
| Sycomore Fig | 77 | Velvet Corkwood | 68 | Shepherds-tree | 200 | | |
| Thorny-rope Flat-bean | 44 | Velvet-leaved Sweetberry | 26 | Sickle-bush | 258 | | |
| Umbrella Acacia | 262 | Wild-pear Dombeya | 156 | | | | |
| | | Wonderboom Fig | 278 | | | | |

Buffalo-thorn Jujube, page 188

This list includes Look-alike trees, trees in the Distinctive Striking Features section (pages 58 - 83), and trees described in the introductory pages.

For detailed information about the Mixed Bushveld read page 42.

# MIXED BUSHVELD

| Termite Mounds | | North- or West-facing Slopes | | South- or East-facing Slopes | | Plateaus | |
|---|---|---|---|---|---|---|---|
| Tree | Page | Tree | Page | Tree | Page | Tree | Page |
| **African Olive** | **184** | **Bushveld Resin-tree** | **314** | **Common Hook-thorn Acacia** | **318** | **Ouhout** | **34** |
| **Buffalo-thorn Jujube** | **188** | **Hornpod-tree** | **268** | **Highveld Protea** | **322** | African Protea | 324 |
| **Bushveld Bead-bean** | **112** | **Lavender Croton** | **280** | **Ladies Cabbage-tree** | **94** | Highveld Protea | 322 |
| **Leadwood** | **226** | **Red Bushwillow** | **140** | **Moepel Red-milkwood** | **334** | Highveld Silver-oak | 326 |
| **White Cats-whiskers** | **152** | **Velvet Bushwillow** | **304** | **Weeping Faurea** | **350** | Karree | 368 |
| Burkea | 236 | Burkea | 236 | African Olive | 184 | Ladies Cabbage-tree | 94 |
| Bushveld Shepherds-tree | 192 | Eastern Sesame-bush | 90 | Brittlewood Nuxia | 108 | Scented-pod Acacia | 254 |
| Jacket-plum | 272 | Jacket-plum | 272 | Highveld Silver-oak | 326 | Sweet-thorn Acacia | 208 |
| Moepel Red-milkwood | 334 | Large-fruited Bushwillow | 128 | Mountain Kirkia | 284 | Weeping Faurea | 350 |
| Naboom Euphorbia | 98 | Live-long Lannea | 330 | Peeling-bark Ochna | 136 | | |
| Red Ivorywood | 342 | Moepel Red-milkwood | 334 | Pipe-stem Fingerleaf | 338 | | |
| Scented-pod Acacia | 254 | Silver Raisin | 346 | Red Ivorywood | 342 | | |
| Shepherds-tree | 200 | Squat Star-chestnut | 102 | Sacred Coral-tree | 148 | | |
| Silver Raisin | 346 | Stamvrug Milkplum | 296 | Small Knobwood | 384 | | |
| Umbrella Acacia | 262 | Tall Firethorn Corkwood | 300 | Wild-pear Dombeya | 156 | | |
| Large-fruited Bushwillow | 128 | African Weeping-wattle | 214 | Black-thorn Acacia | 250 | | |
| Marula | 230 | Black-monkey Acacia | 218 | Buffalo-thorn Jujube | 188 | | |
| Sickle-bush | 258 | Buffalo-thorn Jujube | 188 | Bushveld Bead-bean | 112 | | |
| Small-leaved Guarri | 204 | Burkea | 236 | Bushveld Resin-tree | 314 | | |
| Squat Star-chestnut | 102 | Common Spikethorn | xi | Common Spikethorn | xi | | |
| Weeping Boer-bean | 31 | Deadliest Euphorbia | 100 | Common Wild Fig | 196 | | |
| Wild-pear Dombeya | 156 | Firethorn Corkwood | 78 | Currant Resin-tree | 316 | | |
| | | Ladies Cabbage-tree | 94 | Golden-haired Rock-fig | 35 | | |
| | | Marula | 230 | Hairy-leaved Monkey-orange | 120 | | |
| | | Peeling-bark Ochna | 136 | Highveld Cabbage-tree | 96 | | |
| | | Robust Acacia | 380 | Hornpod-tree | 268 | | |
| | | Rock Karree-rhus | 76 | Jacket-plum | 272 | | |
| | | Round-leaved Bloodwood | 29 | Karree | 368 | | |
| | | Scented-pod Acacia | 254 | Kiaat Bloodwood | 166 | | |
| | | Sickle-bush | 258 | Large-fruited Bushwillow | 128 | | |
| | | Small-leaved Guarri | 204 | Lover's Cheesewood | 1 | | |
| | | Spine-leaved Monkey-orange | 63 | Lowveld Silver-oak | 328 | | |
| | | Wild-pear Dombeya | 156 | Marula | 230 | | |
| | | | | Monkey Acacia | 71 | | |
| | | | | Olive Buddleja | 39 | | |
| | | | | Perdepis | 68 | | |
| | | | | Pride-of-De Kaap Bauhinia | 27 | | |
| | | | | Robust Acacia | 380 | | |
| | | | | Rock Karree-rhus | 76 | | |
| | | | | Russet Bushwillow | 144 | | |
| | | | | Scented-pod Acacia | 254 | | |
| | | | | Sickle-bush | 258 | | |
| | | | | Silver Cabbage-tree | 96 | | |
| | | | | Silver Protea | 58 | | |
| | | | | Simple-leaved Cabbage-tree | 96 | | |
| | | | | Spine-leaved Monkey-orange | 63 | | |
| | | | | Squat Star-chestnut | 102 | | |
| | | | | Stamvrug Milkplum | 296 | | |
| | | | | Sweet-thorn Acacia | 208 | | |
| | | | | Tamboti | 388 | | |
| | | | | Umbrella Acacia | 262 | | |
| | | | | Velvet Bushwillow | 304 | | |
| | | | | Weeping Lavender-tree | 354 | | |

# Ecozone tree list

This is the list of trees you are most likely to find in each Habitat. The trees you should look for first are shown at the top of the list in the darker colour. The trees in the paler colour are the next "easiest" to look for.

## Ecozone S

| Rivers / Kloofs | | Rocky Areas | | Plains | |
|---|---|---|---|---|---|
| Tree | Page | Tree | Page | Tree | Page |
| **Big-leaf Fever-tree** | **162** | **Large-leaved Rock Fig** | **276** | **Knob-Thorn Acacia** | **222** |
| **Broom-cluster Fig** | **364** | **Naboom Euphorbia** | **98** | **Leadwood** | **226** |
| **Flame-pod Acacia** | **116** | **Red-leaved Fig** | **288** | **Mobola-Plum** | **170** |
| **Robust Acacia** | **380** | **Stamvrug Milkplum** | **296** | **Paperbark Acacia** | **174** |
| **Umdoni Waterberry** | **392** | **Velvet Bushwillow** | **304** | **Silver Cluster-leaf** | **244** |
| African Olive | 184 | Bushveld Shepherds-tree | 192 | African Weeping-wattle | 214 |
| African White-stinkwood | 360 | Eastern Sesame-bush | 90 | Baobab | 86 |
| Black-monkey Acacia | 218 | Hornpod-tree | 268 | Buffalo-thorn Jujube | 188 |
| Knob-thorn Acacia | 222 | Jacket-plum | 272 | Common Wild Fig | 196 |
| Leadwood | 226 | Lavender Croton | 280 | Hairy-leaved Monkey-orange | 120 |
| Red Currant-rhus | 372 | Moepel Red-milkwood | 334 | Kiaat Bloodwood | 166 |
| Red Ivorywood | 342 | Mountain Kirkia | 284 | Kooboo-berry | 124 |
| River Bushwillow | 376 | Rock Tree-nettle | 292 | Large-fruited Bushwillow | 128 |
| Small Knobwood | 384 | Squat Star-chestnut | 102 | Marula | 230 |
| Tamboti | 388 | Tall Firethorn Corkwood | 300 | Sacred Coral-tree | 148 |
| | | | | | |
| Small-leaved Guarri | 204 | Baobab | 86 | African Olive | 184 |
| Small-leaved Yellowwood | 33 | Brittlewood Nuxia | 108 | Apple-leaf | 45 |
| Spiny Monkey-orange | 79 | Broad-pod Elephant-root | 61 | Black-monkey Acacia | 218 |
| Sycomore Fig | 77 | Buffalo-thorn Jujube | 188 | Blue Acacia | 70 |
| Thorny-rope Flat-bean | 44 | Common Hook-thorn Acacia | 318 | Broad-leaved Coral-tree | 67 |
| Umbrella Acacia | 262 | Common Spikethorn | xi | Bushveld Resin-tree | 314 |
| Weeping Boer-bean | 31 | Crowberry Currant-rhus | 76 | Bushy Three-hook Acacia | 62 |
| White Cats-whiskers | 152 | Deadliest Euphorbia | 100 | Common Hook-thorn Acacia | 318 |
| Apple-leaf | 45 | Firethorn Corkwood | 78 | Common Spikethorn | xi |
| Blue Sourplum | 134 | Glossy-leaved Corkwood | 67 | Currant Resin-tree | 316 |
| Broad-leaved Coral-tree | 67 | Ladies Cabbage-tree | 94 | False-marula Lannea | 82 |
| Broad-leaved Yellowwood | 33 | Large Sourplum | 132 | Giant Raisin | 60 |
| Brown Ivorywood | 344 | Lebombo Euphorbia | 100 | Highveld Silver-oak | 326 |
| Buffalo-thorn Jujube | 188 | Purple-pod Cluster-leaf | 30 | Jacket-plum | 272 |
| Bushy Three-hook Acacia | 62 | Red Bushwillow | 140 | Large Sourplum | 132 |
| Common Currant-rhus | 76 | Red Ivorywood | 342 | Monkey Acacia | 71 |
| Common Hook-thorn Acacia | 318 | Rock Karree-rhus | 76 | Mopane | 28 |
| Common Wild Fig | 196 | Rubber Hedge Euphorbia | 100 | Peeling-bark Ochna | 136 |
| Eastern Rapanea | 32 | Shepherds-tree | 200 | Purple-pod Cluster-leaf | 30 |
| False Perdepis | 382 | Silver Raisin | 346 | Red Acacia | 43 |
| False-marula Lannea | 82 | Simple-leaved Cabbage-tree | 96 | Red Bushwillow | 140 |
| Fever Croton | 42 | Small Knobwood | 384 | Round-leaved Bloodwood | 29 |
| Forest Bushwillow | 74 | Velvet Corkwood | 68 | Russet Bushwillow | 144 |
| Forest Lavender-tree | xii | Velvet-leaved Sweetberry | 26 | Scented-pod Acacia | 254 |
| Forest Nuxia | 59 | Weeping Collina Bushwillow | 75 | Sickle-bush | 258 |
| Giant Raisin | 60 | White Kirkia | 308 | Silver Raisin | 346 |
| Golden-haired Rock Fig | 35 | Wild-pear Dombeya | 156 | Small Knobwood | 384 |
| Kooboo-berry | 124 | Wonderboom Fig | 278 | Small-leaved Guarri | 204 |
| Lover's Cheesewood | 1 | | | Spiny Monkey-orange | 79 |
| Lowveld Silver-oak | 328 | | | Sweet-thorn Acacia | 208 |
| Marula | 230 | | | Sycomore Fig | 77 |
| Monkey Acacia | 71 | | | Tall Firethorn Corkwood | 300 |
| Perdepis | 68 | | | Tamboti | 388 |
| Pigeonwood | 66 | | | Umbrella Acacia | 262 |
| Pride-of-de Kaap Bauhinia | 27 | | | White Cats-whiskers | 152 |
| Quilted Buddleja | 38 | | | Wild-pear Dombeya | 156 |
| Rock Tree-nettle | 292 | Tall Firethorn Corkwood, page 300 | | Worm-cure Albizia | 61 |
| Russet Bushwillow | 144 | | | | |
| Scented-pod Acacia | 254 | | | | |
| Silver Cabbage-tree | 96 | | | | |
| Silver Cluster-leaf | 244 | | | | |

This list includes Look-alike trees, trees in the Distinctive Striking Features section (pages 58 - 83), and trees described in the introductory pages.
For detailed information on the Sour Bushveld read page 41.

## SOUR BUSHVELD

| Termite Mounds | | North- or West-facing Slopes | | South- or East-facing Slopes | | Plateaus | |
|---|---|---|---|---|---|---|---|
| Tree | Page | Tree | Page | Tree | Page | Tree | Page |
| **African Olive** | **184** | **Hornpod-tree** | **268** | **Highveld Protea** | **322** | **Ouhout** | **34** |
| **Buffalo-thorn Jujube** | **188** | **Lavender Croton** | **280** | **Mobola-plum** | **170** | African Protea | 324 |
| **Bushveld Bead-bean** | **112** | **Live-long Lannea** | **330** | **Mountain Kirkia** | **284** | Highveld Protea | 322 |
| **Naboom Euphorbia** | **98** | **Red Bushwillow** | **140** | **Weeping Faurea** | **350** | Ladies Cabbage-tree | 94 |
| **Red Ivorywood** | **342** | **Velvet Bushwillow** | **304** | **Weeping Lavender-tree** | **354** | Silver Cabbage-tree | 96 |
| Leadwood | 226 | Hairy-leaved | | African Olive | 184 | | |
| Moepel Red-milkwood | 334 | Monkey-orange | 120 | Broom-cluster Fig | 364 | | |
| White Cats-whiskers | 152 | Jacket-plum | 272 | Common Hook-thorn | | | |
| Wild-pear Dombeya | 156 | Mobola-plum | 170 | Acacia | 318 | | |
| Giant Raisin | 60 | Naboom Euphorbia | 98 | Ladies Cabbage-tree | 94 | | |
| Weeping Boer-bean | 31 | Sacred Coral-tree | 148 | Moepel Red-milkwood | 334 | | |
| | | Squat Star-chestnut | 102 | Red Currant-rhus | 372 | | |
| | | Stamvrug Milkplum | 296 | Red Ivorywood | 342 | | |
| | | Tall Firethorn Corkwood | 300 | Small Knobwood | 384 | | |
| | | White Kirkia | 308 | Umdoni Waterberry | 392 | | |
| | | Wild-pear Dombeya | 156 | Wild-pear Dombeya | 156 | | |
| | | African Olive | 184 | African Schefflera | 67 | | |
| | | Blue Acacia | 70 | African White-stinkwood | 360 | | |
| | | Blue Sourplum | 134 | Big-leaf Fever-tree | 162 | | |
| | | Broad-pod Elephant-root | 61 | Brittlewood Nuxia | 108 | | |
| | | Buffalo-thorn Jujube | 188 | Broad-leaved Yellowwood | 33 | | |
| | | Common Spikethorn | xi | Buffalo-thorn Jujube | 188 | | |
| | | Common Wild Fig | 196 | Common Spikethorn | xi | | |
| | | Currant Resin Tree | 316 | Common Wild Fig | 196 | | |
| | | Firethorn Corkwood | 78 | Eastern Rapanea | 32 | | |
| | | Giant Raisin | 60 | Flame-pod Acacia | 116 | | |
| | | Kooboo-berry | 124 | Forest Lavender-tree | xii | | |
| | | Ladies Cabbage-tree | 94 | Forest Silver Oak | 328 | | |
| | | | | Jacket-plum | 272 | | |
| | | Large-fruited Bushwillow | 128 | Kiaat Bloodwood | 166 | | |
| | | Lowveld Silver-oak | 328 | Large Sourplum | 132 | **South- or East-facing** | |
| | | Marula | 230 | Large-fruited Bushwillow | 128 | **Slopes** (continued) | |
| | | Moepel Red-milkwood | 334 | Live-long Lannea | 330 | Silver Cabbage-tree | 96 |
| | | Peeling-bark Ochna | 136 | Lover's Cheesewood | 1 | Silver Protea | 58 |
| | | Red-leaved Fig | 288 | Lowveld Silver-oak | 328 | Simple-leaved | |
| | | Rock Tree-nettle | 292 | Natal Fig | 198 | Cabbage-tree | 96 |
| | | Round-leaved Bloodwood | 29 | Olive Buddleja | 39 | Small-leaved Yellowwood | 33 |
| | | Sickle-bush | 258 | Paperbark Acacia | 174 | Sneezewood | 41 |
| | | Silver Cluster-leaf | 244 | Peeling-bark Ochna | 136 | Stamvrug Milkplum | 296 |
| | | Silver Raisin | 346 | Perdepis | 68 | Sweet-thorn Acacia | 208 |
| | | Simple-leaved | | Pigeonwood | 66 | Thorny-rope Flat-bean | 44 |
| | | Cabbage-tree | 96 | Pipe-stem Fingerleaf | 338 | Umbrella Acacia | 262 |
| | | Umbrella Acacia | 262 | Pride-of-de Kaap Bauhinia | 27 | Velvet Bushwillow | 304 |
| | | Umdoni Waterberry | 392 | Quilted Buddleja | 38 | Velvet-leaved Sweetberry | 26 |
| | | Velvet Corkwood | 68 | River Guarri | 186 | Weeping Collina | |
| | | Velvet-leaved Sweetberry | 26 | Rock Karree-rhus | 76 | Bushwillow | 75 |
| | | Weeping Faurea | 350 | Sacred Coral-tree | 148 | White Cats-whiskers | 152 |
| | | Weeping Lavender-tree | 354 | Scented-pod Acacia | 254 | | |
| | | White Cats-whiskers | 152 | Showy Ochna | 60 | | |

Tall Firethorn Corkwood, page 300

# Ecozone tree list

This is the list of trees you are most likely to find in each Habitat. The trees you should look for first are shown at the top of the list in the darker colour. The trees in the paler colour are the next "easiest" to look for.

## Ecozone T

### Rivers / Kloofs

| Tree | Page |
|---|---|
| **African White-stinkwood** | **360** |
| **Flame-pod Acacia** | **116** |
| **River Bushwillow** | **376** |
| **Robust Acacia** | **380** |
| **Wild-pear Dombeya** | **156** |
| African Olive | 184 |
| Buffalo-thorn Jujube | 188 |
| Karree | 368 |
| Sacred Coral-tree | 148 |
| Sickle-bush | 258 |
| Silver Cluster-leaf | 244 |
| Sweet-thorn Acacia | 208 |
| Tamboti | 388 |
| Umbrella Acacia | 262 |
| White Cats-whiskers | 152 |
| Common Currant-rhus | 76 |
| Common Hook-thorn Acacia | 318 |
| Common Spikethorn | xi |
| Fever Croton | 42 |
| Hairy-leaved Monkey-orange | 120 |
| Ladies Cabbage-tree | 94 |
| Moepel Red-milkwood | 334 |
| Monkey Acacia | 71 |
| Quilted Buddleja | 38 |

### Rocky Areas

| Tree | Page |
|---|---|
| **Large-leaved Rock Fig** | **276** |
| **Lavender Croton** | **280** |
| **Naboom Euphorbia** | **98** |
| **Red-leaved Fig** | **288** |
| **Stamvrug Milkplum** | **296** |
| Burkea | 236 |
| Common Hook-thorn Acacia | 318 |
| Hornpod-tree | 268 |
| Jacket-plum | 272 |
| Large-leaved Rock Fig | 276 |
| Red Bushwillow | 140 |
| Rock Tree-nettle | 292 |
| Shepherds-tree | 200 |
| Tall Firethorn Corkwood | 300 |
| Broad-pod Elephant-root | 61 |
| Live-long Lannea | 330 |
| Peeling-bark Ochna | 136 |
| Rock Karree-rhus | 76 |
| Rubber Hedge Euphorbia | 100 |
| Small Knobwood | 384 |
| Small-leaved Guarri | 204 |
| Velvet Corkwood | 68 |
| Velvet-leaved Sweetberry | 26 |
| Weeping Collina Bushwillow | 75 |
| Weeping Lavender-tree | 354 |

### Plains

| Tree | Page |
|---|---|
| **Black-thorn Acacia** | **250** |
| **Buffalo-thorn Jujube** | **188** |
| **Scented-pod Acacia** | **254** |
| **Sickle-bush** | **258** |
| **Umbrella Acacia** | **262** |
| African Weeping-wattle | 214 |
| Black-monkey Acacia | 218 |
| Bushveld Shepherds-tree | 192 |
| Common Hook-thorn Acacia | 318 |
| Large-fruited Bushwillow | 128 |
| Marula | 230 |
| Naboom Euphorbia | 98 |
| Russet Bushwillow | 144 |
| Silver Cluster-leaf | 244 |
| Small-leaved Guarri | 204 |
| Blue Acacia | 70 |
| Burkea | 236 |
| Candle-pod Acacia | 62 |
| Common Currant-rhus | 76 |
| Common Spikethorn | xi |
| Highveld Cabbage-tree | 96 |
| Knob-thorn Acacia | 222 |
| Red Acacia | 43 |
| Red Bushwillow | 140 |
| Robust Acacia | 380 |
| Rock Tree-nettle | 292 |
| Rubber Hedge Euphorbia | 100 |
| Shepherds-tree | 200 |
| Sweet-thorn Acacia | 208 |
| White Cats-whiskers | 152 |
| Wild-pear Dombeya | 156 |

Scented-pod Acacia, page 254

This list includes Look-alike trees, trees in the Distinctive Striking Features section (pages 58 - 83), and trees described in the introductory pages.

For detailed information about Thorny Bushveld read page 43.

# THORNY BUSHVELD

| Termite Mounds | | North- or West-facing Slopes | | South- or East-facing Slopes | | Plateaus | |
|---|---|---|---|---|---|---|---|
| Tree | Page | Tree | Page | Tree | Page | Tree | Page |
| **African Olive** | **184** | **Jacket-plum** | **272** | **African Olive** | **184** | | |
| **Buffalo-thorn Jujuba** | **188** | **Lavender Croton** | **280** | **Common Hook-thorn** | | | |
| **Bushveld Bead-bean** | **112** | **Red Bushwillow** | **140** | **Acacia** | **318** | | |
| **Jacket-plum** | **272** | **Velvet Bushwillow** | **304** | **Ladies Cabbage-tree** | **94** | | |
| **White Cats-whiskers** | **152** | **Wild-pear Dombeya** | **156** | **Sweet-thorn Acacia** | **208** | | |
| Bushveld Shepherds-tree | 192 | Buffalo-thorn Jujube | 188 | **Wild-pear Dombeya** | **156** | | |
| Currant Resin-tree | 316 | Live-long Lannea | 330 | African White-stinkwood | 360 | | |
| Karree | 368 | Naboom Euphorbia | 98 | Buffalo-thorn Jujube | 188 | | |
| Ladies Cabbage-tree | 94 | Sickle-bush | 258 | Common Wild Fig | 196 | | |
| Naboom Euphorbia | 98 | Umbrella Acacia | 262 | Large-fruited Bushwillow | 128 | | |
| Sickle-bush | 258 | | | Live-long Lannea | 330 | | |
| Umbrella Acacia | 262 | | | Naboom Euphorbia | 98 | | |
| | | | | Peeling-bark Ochna | 136 | | |
| | | | | Scented-pod Acacia | 254 | | |
| | | | | Shepherds-tree | 200 | | |
| | | | | Highveld Cabbage-tree | 96 | | |
| | | | | Perdepis | 68 | | |
| | | | | Umbrella Acacia | 262 | | |
| | | | | Weeping Collina Bushwillow | 75 | | |

Sickle-bush, page 258

# Trees greet you

**DISTINCTIVE STRIKING FEATURES**

This section of the book summarises the most distinctive of the Striking Features of each tree. When a flower, fruit, pod, leaf or bark jumps out and asks to be recognised, you simply look up the relevant page here. Page numbers of each tree are given to encourage you to look up the other Striking Features of the tree. This will enable you to recognise the tree in other areas, at other times of the year too.

| | |
|---|---|
| Flowers | p. 58 |
| Bean pods | p. 61 |
| Pods and fruit | p. 63 |
| Plums and berries | p. 64 |
| Leaves | p. 65 |
| Families | p. 70 |
| Bark | p. 80 |

The black and red "Mickey Mouse" fruit of the Peeling Ochna (*Ochna pulchra*) give it its other commonly used English name. Here the young fruit is still green, but none the less dramatic to see in the Magaliesberg in November.

# Distinctive Striking Features

The following pages show, flowers, fruit, pods and leaves that are all very striking, or that are so distinctive you can often identify these trees on this information alone. You can use these pages as a quick reference – but it is wise to turn to the full tree description to be sure.

## FLOWERS

Baobab - p. 86
*20% life-size*

Eastern Sesame-bush - p. 90
*20% life-size*

Sacred Coral-tree - p. 148
*40% life-size*

Broad-leaved Coral-tree - p. 150
*10% life-size*

Silver Protea - p. 324
*30% life-size*

Big-leaf Fever-tree - p. 162
*50% life-size*

Ladies Cabbage-tree - p. 94
*50% life-size*

Highveld Protea - p. 322
*40% life-size*

Bushveld Bead-bean - p. 112
*50% life-size*

Pride-of-De Kaap Bauhinia - p. 27
*50% life-size*

Weeping Boer-bean - p. 31
*30% life-size*

Paperbark Albizia - p. 178
Worm-cure Albizia - p. 73
*20% life-size*

# FLOWERS

## SMALL BALLS AND SPIKES

Sweet-thorn
Acacia - p. 208
*life-size*

Common Hook-thorn
Acacia - p. 318
*50% life-size*
(see pages 70 - 73
for Acacias)

Sickle-bush
- p. 258
*60% life-size*

Weeping Faurea
- p. 350
*25% life-size*

**Other flower-ball Acacias**
Camel-thorn - p. 240
Candle-pod - p. 62
Paperbark - p. 174
Red - p. 43
Robust - p. 380
Scented-pod - p. 254
Umbrella - p. 262

**Other flower-spike Acacias**
Black-monkey - p. 218
Bushy Three-hook - p. 70
Flame-pod - p. 116
Knob-thorn - p. 222

## STARS

Wild-pear
Dombeya
- p. 156
*life-size*

Showy Ochna
*life-size*
- p. 63

Peeling-bark Ochna
- p. 136
*life-size*

Pipe-stem
Fingerleaf
- p. 338
*life-size*

Silver Raisin
and Giant Raisin
- p. 346, 348
*50% life-size*

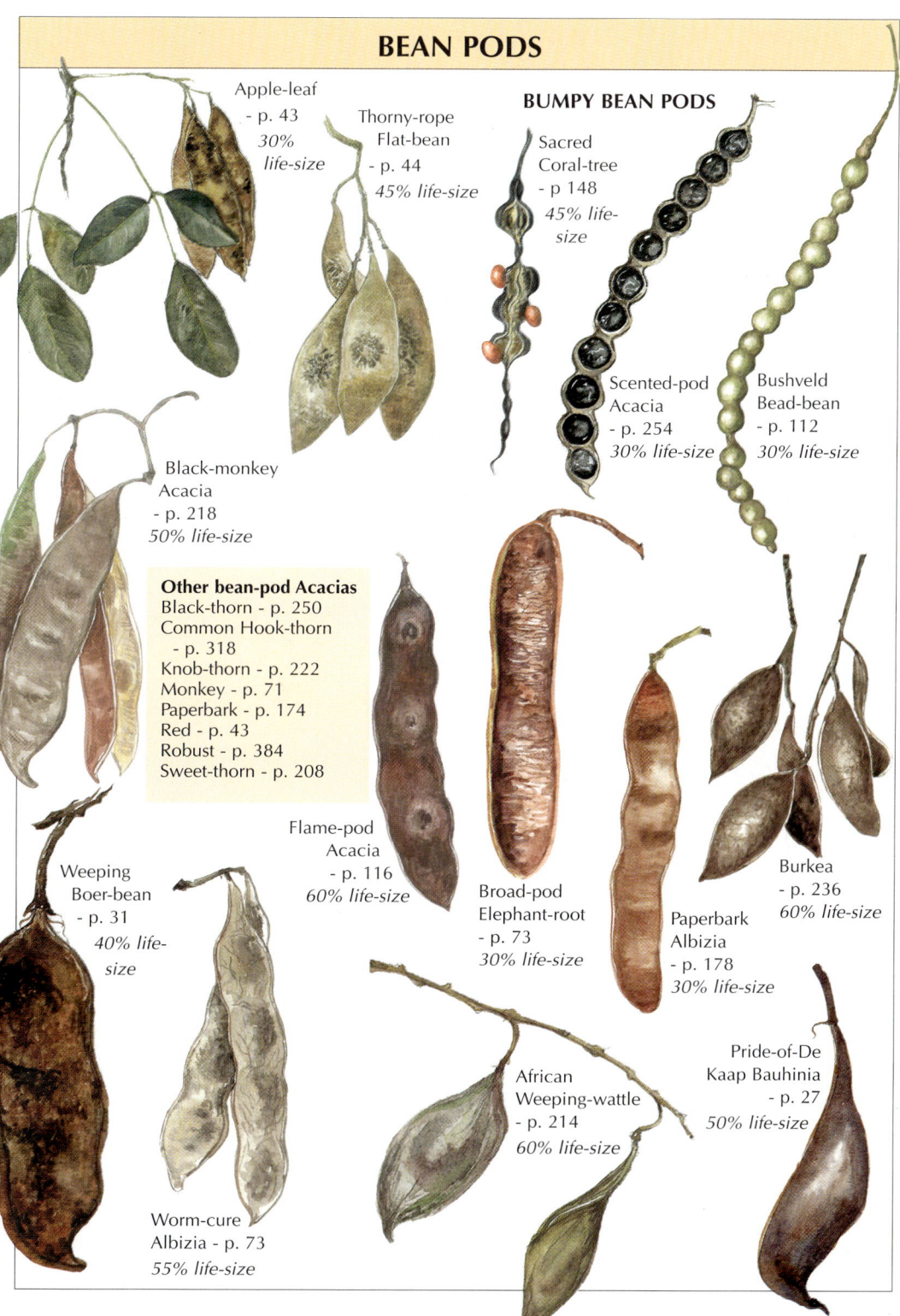

## THREE-VEINED SIMPLE LEAVES

Pigeonwood
- p. 80
*50% life-size*

African White-stinkwood
- p. 360
*50% life-size*

Wild-pear Dombeya
- p. 156 *75% life-size*

Buffalo-thorn Jujube
- p. 188
*70% life-size*

Fever Croton
- p. 42
*40% life-size*

All Monkey-oranges
- p. 79
*80% life-size*

All Raisins - p. 346
*35% life-size*

## HERRINGBONE LEAVES

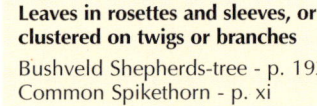

**Leaves in rosettes and sleeves, or clustered on twigs or branches**

Bushveld Shepherds-tree - p. 192
Common Spikethorn - p. xi
Eastern Sesame-bush - p. 90
Golden-haired Rock Fig - p. 35
Hairy-leaved
 Monkey-orange - p. 120
Large Sourplum - p. 132
Peeling-bark Ochna - p. 136
Purple-pod Cluster-leaf - p. 30
Silver Cluster-leaf - p. 244
Umdoni Waterberry - p. 392

Mobola-plum
- p. 170
*50% life-size*

Velvet Bushwillow
- p. 304
*45% life-size*

Velvet-leaved Sweetberry
- p. 26 *45% life-size*

Red Ivorywood
- p. 342 *45% life-size*

Hornpod
- p. 268
*40% life-size*

Bushveld Resin-tree
- p. 314 *30% life-size*

Round-leaved Bloodwood
- p. 29 *20% life-size*

# COMPOUND LEAVES

**BUTTERFLY**

Mopane - p. 28
*45% life-size*

**HAND-SHAPED**

African Schefflera - p. 96
*25% life-size*

Cabbage-trees
*10% life-size*
(see comparisons on p. 96)

Baobab - p. 86
*25% life-size*

Pipe-stem Fingerleaf - p. 338
*40% life-size*

**Simple and compound leaves that have a distinct smell**

*Lemon*
Lavender Croton - p. 280
Small Knobwood - p. 380

*Lavender*
Forest Lavender-tree - p. xii
Lavender Croton - p. 280
Weeping Lavender-tree - p. 354

*Urine*
Perdepis - p. 382

**THREE-LEAFLET**

Karree-rhus species - p. 76
*size varies*

Currant-rhus species - p. 76
*size varies*

Apple-leaf - p. 43
*30% life-size*

Glossy-leaved Corkwood
*life-size*
(some Corkwoods are three-leaflet compound - see p. 78)

Sacred Coral-tree - p. 148
*20% life-size*

Broad-leaved Coral-tree - p. 150
*20% life-size*

STRIKING FEATURES
Distinctive leaves

# ONCE COMPOUND LEAVES

## SPIRALLY ARRANGED AT THE TWIG TIP

Burkea - p. 236
*15% life-size*

White Kirkia - p. 308
*15% life-size*

Marula
- p. 230
*20% life-size*

Live-long Lannea
- p. 330
*20% life-size*

Mountain Kirkia
- p. 284
*20% life-size*

**Compound leaf with a single leaf at the tip**
Burkea - p. 236
False-marula Lannea - p. 232
Kiaat Bloodwood - p. 166
Live-long Lannea - p. 320
Marula - p. 230
Mountain Kirkia - p. 284
Round-leaved Bloodwood
- p. 29
White Kirkia - p. 308

**Compound leaf with a pair of leaves at the tip**
Small Knobwood - p. 384
Sneezewood - p. 41
Weeping Boer-bean - p. 31

eg. Weeping
Boer-bean - p. 31
*10% life-size*

eg. False-marula Lannea
- p. 232
*15% life-size*

**Simple and compound hairy leaves**

*Hairy overall*
Golden-haired Rock Fig - p. 35
Rock Tree-nettle - p. 292
Velvet Bushwillow - p. 304
Velvet Corkwood - p. 78
Velvet-leaved Sweetberry - p. 26
Wild-pear Dombeya - p. 156
Young Silver Protea - p. 58

*Hairy under-surface*
Bushveld Resin-tree - p. 314
Giant Raisin - p. 60
Highveld Silver-oak - p. 326
Live-long Lannea - p. 320
Mobola-plum - p. 170
Ouhout - p. 34
Quilted Buddleja - p. 38
Silver Raisin - p. 346
Squat Star-chestnut - p. 102
Stamvrug Milkplum - p. 296

**STRIKING FEATURES**
Distinctive leaves

# TWICE COMPOUND LEAVES – ACACIAS

## Black-thorn Acacia
*Acacia mellifera* - p. 250
Grows in large uniform groups; low-branching or multi-stemmed with dense, tangled canopy of dark branchlets and twigs; mature trees 3 - 9 m; black, hooked thorns spiral around branches and twigs; bluish-green twice compound leaves (3,5 - 22 x 2 - 16 mm); creamy-white flower-balls cover tree before new leaves appear in spring; flat bean pods are papery, straw-coloured or pale brown (90 x 25 mm) (January - April).

## Black-monkey Acacia
*Acacia burkei* - p. 218
Mature trees up to 12 m; single-trunked, with umbrella-shaped to semi-circular canopy; twice compound leaves are short and stiff (25 - 70 mm; short, dark, sharply-hooked thorns grow in pairs; white flower-spikes grow in small groups (50 - 100 x 10 - 20 mm); (October - January) pods (90 - 160 x 12 - 25 mm).

## Blue Acacia
*Acacia erubescens*
Multi-stemmed shrub or small tree reaching 10 m with somewhat flattened, spreading canopy; often on stream banks; rough, greyish-yellow bark peels in papery layers; paired, hooked thorns are stout, sharp and white or blue; twice compound leaves with leaflets (3 - 7 x 1 - 2 mm); white, sometimes pinkish flower-spikes, up to 45 mm, August - October; flat, brown, leathery, straight pods (130 x 20 mm) (September - January).

## Bushy Three-hook Acacia
*Acacia senegal*
Deciduous, small tree (3 - 8 m), slightly spreading; papery, flaky bark, greyish-yellow to orange-brown; distinctive hooked thorns in 3's, one down, two facing backwards; twice compound leaves are small, with small leaflets (1 - 4 x 0,5 - 1,7 mm); creamy-white flower-spikes are scented (60 - 80 mm); grey-brown or light creamy-brown pods are oblong (40 - 70 x 20 - 30 mm) (February - June).

## Camel-thorn Acacia
*Acacia erioloba* - p. 240
Mature trees 10 m; bark is dark, ropy and deeply fissured lengthways; twice compound leaves in groups of 1 - 7 (30 - 60 mm); straight, white thorns well developed; yellow flower-balls (July - November); hard, wooden pods kidney-shaped, covered by velvety, grey hairs (60 - 130 x 40 - 65 x 13 - 25 mm).

# TWICE COMPOUND LEAVES – ACACIAS

## Candle-pod Acacia
*Acacia hebeclada*
Mature trees 2 m; twice compound leaves, very small, pale, grey-green and feathery (10 - 40 mm); creamy-white flower-balls (July - October); hairy, wooden pods stand upright on twigs and resemble candles (5 - 120 x 15 - 20 mm).

## Common Hook-thorn Acacia
*Acacia caffra* - p. 318
Mature trees 5 m; twice compound leaves droop in a soft canopy (60 - 230 mm); hooked thorns are paired; spikes of cream flowers in early spring; chocolate-brown, flat bean pods, with a pointed tip (70 - 160 x 10 - 13 mm) (ripen December - March).

## Flame-pod Acacia
*Acacia ataxacantha* - p. 116
Multi-stemmed scrambling tree or climber reaching 10 m; twice compound, long, droopy leaves up to 140 mm; dark, hooked thorns, scattered along branchlets and twigs and under-surface of leaf-stem; creamy-yellow flower-spikes appear in spring and summer (70 - 100 mm); pods bumpy, flame-purple (70 - 100 x 12 - 15 mm).

## Knob-thorn Acacia
*Acacia nigrescens* - p. 222
Mature tree 8 - 18 m; knobs on bark, particularly when young; leaves 35 x 86 mm; obvious round leaflet (10 - 30 x 8 - 20 mm); flower-spikes August - September; pods November - April (120 x 70 mm).

## Monkey Acacia
*Acacia galpinii - p. 176, 220*
Large tree (up to 25 m) with a somewhat rounded canopy, grows in open woodland, often near water; yellowish-brown, rough and corky bark; paired, strong, hooked to straightish, whitish thorns in pairs on main trunk and branches; twice compound leaves, with leaflets (4 - 11 x 1 - 3 mm); creamy-yellow to yellow flower-spikes appear before new leaves (September - October); flat pods reddish to purplish-brown (up to 280 x 35 mm) (February - March).

*The art on these pages is not to scale. Please refer to the text for sizes.*

# TWICE COMPOUND LEAVES – ACACIAS

### Paperbark Acacia
*Acacia sieberiana* - p. 174
Single-stemmed, with a moderately thick umbrella canopy; mature trees 7 - 15 m; bark is yellowish-brown and flaking; paired thorns are straight and white; twice compound leaves yellowish-green (60 - 100 mm); conspicuous, sweet-scented flower-balls are creamy-white, October - December; flat, woody, grey-brown pods; (100 - 200 x 20 - 40 mm) (March - June).

### Red Acacia
*Acacia gerrardii* - p. 43
Mature tree 5 - 10 m; leaf attachment like a sleeve covering the branchlets; slender growth-form; reddish bark; leaves 90 mm; leaflet 3 - 7 x 1 - 2 mm; flower-balls October - February; pods November - May (80 - 160 x 6 - 16 mm).

### Robust Acacia
*Acacia robusta* - p. 384
Mature trees 10 m; twice compound leaves form sleeves around branchlets (45 - 90 mm); prickly cushions at base of straight, white thorns; white, ball-like flowers in early spring; sickle-shaped pods in bunches (70 - 160 x 13 - 30 mm) (January - August).

### Scented-Pod Acacia
*Acacia nilotica* - p. 254
Mature tree 6 - 10 m; leaves 40 mm; leaflet 1 x 4 mm; yellow flower-balls October - March; necklace-like pods 15 x 200 mm, ripen during winter.

### Sweet-thorn Acacia
*Acacia karroo* - p. 208
Mature trees 10 m; twice compound leaves (55 - 120 mm) on small knobs in angle of thorns; bark rough and dark; yellow, sweet-smelling, ball-like flowers October to February, after rain; long, paired, white thorns; pods bumpy bean (50 - 130 x 6 - 13 mm).

# TWICE COMPOUND LEAVES – ACACIA AND OTHERS

## Umbrella Acacia
*Acacia tortilis* - p. 262
Mature tree 3 - 6 m; Umbrella form of the tree; leaf 25 mm; leaflet 1 - 2 mm; small, white flower-balls November - December; spiral pods (125 mm) (May - June).

## Paperbark Albizia
*Albizia tanganyicensis* - p. 178
Single-trunked branching high up; usually grow on rocky hillsides; no thorns; thin, pale, orangey-brown bark peels in papery flakes to expose pearly-white, smooth under-bark which stands out from a distance; twice compound leaves; leaflets 12 - 40 x 7 - 12 mm; conspicuous, creamy-white, pincushion flowers appear before new leaves (August - November) 50 mm; broad, flat, reddish-brown pods split on tree (up to 300 mm) (September - January).

## Worm-cure Albizia
*Albizia anthelmintica*
Very striking in early spring when covered by white, typical Albizia, powder-puff flowers; tree is often multi-stemmed and forms many intertwined branchlets; leaves are twice compound with 2 - 4 feather pairs, each with 2 - 4 pairs of leaflets (8 - 25 x 4 - 18 mm); thin bean pods grow in bunches and burst open on the tree (180 x 30 mm).

## African Weeping-wattle
*Peltophorum africanum* - p. 214
Single-stemmed tree branching low down with drooping branches; mature trees 5 - 10 m; no thorns; large, soft, feathery leaves (180 x 90 mm) with rounded leaflets; abundant yellow flowers appear in sprays, November - February; dark brown to black pods (100 x 20 mm) appear in bunches and can be seen throughout the year.

## Broad-pod Elephant-root
*Elephantorrhiza burkei*
Multi-stemmed shrub grows on rocky hillsides; may reach 6 m; no thorns; twice compound, blue-green leaves; leaflets slender and sharply pointed (7 - 15 x 1 - 4 mm); small, creamy-white to yellow flower-spikes up to 100 mm long October - January; woody, reddish-brown, flat pods split in characteristic manner from late summer onwards (up to 300 mm).

## Sickle-bush
*Dichrostachys cinerea* - p. 258
Multi-stemmed tree or shrub (2 - 6 m); heavily intertwined canopy; branches and twigs have long, straight, pale brown spines; long, fine, twice compound leaves (30 - 200 mm) stand out against pale bark; mauve-pink and yellow flower-spikes 40 - 60 mm, October - January; groups of tightly coiled, dark brown pods grow in dense clusters (70 mm diameter) (May - September).

*The art on these pages is not to scale. Please refer to the text for sizes.*

# BUSHWILLOWS

## Forest Bushwillow
*Combretum kraussii* - p. 107
Occurs mainly in forests; mature trees reach 12 m; bark on older trunks dark grey and furrowed with rough flaking; opposite leaves are dark and shiny above and paler below; leaves turn bright red to purple in winter (50 - 120 x 20 - 40 mm), creamy-white flowers in dense heads (25 - 60 mm), August - November; small, 20 x 15 mm, 4-winged seeds which cover tree are light to dark red, and conspicuous brownish-red when dry (16 x 15 mm) (February - June).

## Large-fruited Bushwillow
*Combretum zeyheri* - p. 128
Mature tree 5 - 15 m; leaves 40 - 100 x 30 - 50 mm; flowers September - November; pods February - October; very large fruit (50 - 100 mm).

## Leadwood
*Combretum imberbe* - p. 226
Mature tree 20 m; majestic size and shape; blocky, grey, snake-skin bark; small leaves (35 x 15 mm); flowers November - December; small pods (15 mm) in autumn.

## Red Bushwillow
*Combretum apiculatum* - p. 140
Mature tree 4 - 10 m; most common Combretum occurring on the granites; leaves 65 x 35 mm, twisted at the tip; flowers September - October; pods December - August, (25 x 20 mm).

## River Bushwillow
*Combretum erythrophyllum* - p. 376
Mature tree 5 - 12 m; bark has irregular swellings; occurs only along river beds; leaves 50 - 100 x 20 - 50 mm; flowers August - November; pods January - August, (10 - 15 mm).

# BUSHWILLOWS AND CLUSTER-LEAFS

## Russet Bushwillow
*Combretum hereroense* - p. 144
Mature tree 3 - 5 m; Leaves 30 x 20 mm; flowers August - October; pods January - July; large numbers of russet-coloured seeds, midsummer to autumn (23 x 20 mm).

## Velvet Bushwillow
*Combretum molle* - p. 304
Single-trunked tree (4 - 12 m), dark green canopy; large, oval to rounded, hairy leaves, (60 - 100 x 40 - 60 mm); sweet-scented, conspicuous yellow flower-spikes appear before leaves; abundant four-winged pods turn yellow-green to golden red-brown (September - November) (20 x 16 mm).

## Weeping Collina Bushwillow
*Combretum collinum suluense* - p. 130
Mature tree 4 - 12 m; leaf size varies according to rainfall (7 - 120 x 30 - 45 mm) flowers spikes (50 - 100 mm) August - October; pinkish pods (January - April) (30 - 50 x 45 mm).

## Purple-pod Cluster-leaf
*Terminalia prunioides* - p. 30
Mature tree 3 - 7 m; leaves 35 x 15 mm; strong smelling flower spikes (65 x 20 mm) September - February; purple pods January - September (40 x 30 mm).

## Silver Cluster-leaf
*Terminalia sericea* - p. 244
Mature tree 6 - 20 m; most common on granite seep-lines and sandveld; leaves 100 x 25 mm; flowers (4 mm) October - December; pods January - June (60 x 15 mm).

*The art on these pages is not to scale. Please refer to the text for sizes.*

# RHUS

## Common Currant-rhus
*Rhus pyroides*
Mature trees 3 m; sharp spines on branches; three-leaflet compound leaf, central leaf (18 - 45 x 8 - 25 mm); small, yellow, star-shaped flowers in conspicuous sprays August - March; small, grape-like fruit yellow to reddish-brown (October - May) (3 - 5 mm).

## Crowberry Currant-rhus
*Rhus pentheri*
Small, sturdy, crooked-stemmed tree branches low down and forms a semi-circular canopy (mature trees 2 - 12 m); bark is dark brown and corky, with scattered spines often seen on young branches; leaves shiny, bright green; leaflet margins often toothed on upper third, with hairy leaf-stems (central leaflet: 18 - 45 x 8 - 25 mm); small, yellow, star-shaped flowers grow in bunches (August - March); small, dry, grape-like fruit is shiny yellow to light brown (3 - 5 mm) (September - April).

## Karree
*Rhus lancea* - p. 368
Mature trees 5 m; three-leaflet compound leaves, long and willow-like (central leaflet: 90 - 120 x 6 - 15 mm); leaflets join the leaf-stem at an acute angle; dark brown bark; crushed leaves aromatic smell; grows along rivers and streams; fruit (4 - 5 mm).

## Red Currant-rhus
*Rhus chirindensis* - p. 372
Large tree (3 - 25 m); bark is dark and cracked lengthways; drooping leaves have a long, reddish leaf-stem; elliptic leaflets have a wavy margin (central leaflet: 60 - 130 x 25 - 40mm); small, yellow-green, star-shaped flowers grow in long, delicate sprays 160 - 200 mm, August - January; small, round bunches of red-brown or pink grape-like fruit (4 - 7 mm) (ripen December - March).

## Rock Karree-rhus
*Rhus leptodictya* - p. 370
Mature trees 5 m; three-leaflet compound leaves have toothed margins (central leaflet: 40 - 120 x 10 - 35 mm); leaflets join the leaf-stem almost at right angles; grows on wooded, rocky slopes; fruit (4 - 5 mm).

# FIGS

### ROCK FIGS

Rock Figs are easiest to find in Rocky Areas. The roots grow into small cracks and crevices in search of water and nutrients, and may eventually cause the rock to split further.

### Large-leaved Rock Fig
*Ficus abutilifolia* - p. 276
Small, rock-splitting tree reaching 6 m; has a gnarled, yellow-white trunk and main branches; white roots are visible growing on rocks; papery bark peels off; thick, large leaves shiny, dark green, with prominent yellow veins 60 - 160 x 80 - 250 mm; figs dark red when ripe (10 - 25 mm) (September - March).

### Golden-haired Rock Fig
*Ficus glumosa* - p. 278
Mature trees 13 m; grows on Rocky Outcrops and along dry watercourses; flaky, pale yellow-grey bark; young leaves covered in golden hairs; mature leaves thick, shiny, dark green above, 50 - 150 x 30 - 90 mm; small, hairy fruit, reddish when ripe (8 - 15 mm) (August - March).

### Red-leaved Fig
*Ficus ingens* - p. 288
Mature trees (3 - 12 m); sometimes low, straggly bush in Rocky Areas; spectacular flush of red new leaves; leaves have smooth margins, yellow veins stand out on under-surface, variable in shape, 60 - 150 x 30 - 100 mm; figs are dull red, 10 - 13 mm growing on short stalks (June - March).

### OTHER FIGS

### Broom-cluster Fig
*Ficus sur* - p. 364
Huge (12 - 22 m), grows along Rivers; single-stemmed tree, branches low down to form a wide, dense canopy; buttressed trunk; bark smooth and grey; simple, large, grey-green elliptic leaves have toothed margins, new leaves can be copper-red, 80 - 200 x 25 - 95 mm; plum-sized, red, fleshy figs grow in large bunches (20 - 40 mm) (June - January).

### Sycomore Fig
*Ficus sycomorus*
Mature trees are very large (5 - 25 m), low-branching, spreading, with a buttressed trunk, growing on river banks; yellowish-green to pink bark; pale green, roundish, leathery, rough leaves (50 - 200 x 30 - 150 mm); fleshy figs grow in short, branched masses on trunks and main branches (20 - 50 mm).

### Wonderboom Fig
*Ficus salicifolia* - p. 278
Evergreen tree found in Rocky Outcrops; bark smooth and pale grey in young trees, coarse and brownish-grey in mature trees; leaves broadly elliptic and hard, with net veining visible underneath, (25 - 130 x 15 - 60 mm); leaves narrower at base and slightly smaller than Red-leaved Fig; figs crowded in angles formed by leaves at tips of twigs; red and flecked with white when ripe (5 - 8 mm).

### Common Wild Fig
*Ficus burkei* - p. 196
Medium-sized, single-trunked tree 10 - 20 m; a strangler with aerial roots; small, shiny, dark green leaves 50 - 100 x 10 - 40 mm; long leaf-stems, (up to 45 mm); net veins prominent on both surfaces; small figs (10 mm) have no stalks; red when ripe (August - December).

*The art on these pages is not to scale. Please refer to the text for sizes.*

# CORKWOODS

### THREE SIMILAR CORKWOODS
Most Corkwoods have relatively inconspicuous flowers. The following three Corkwoods have very similar leaves, flowers, fruit and bark, and only one example is illustrated here.

### Firethorn Corkwood
*Commiphora pyracanthoides*
Multi-stemmed shrub or small tree; simple leaves with toothed margin (38 x 25 - 30 mm) clustered on spine-tipped side-branches.

### Sand Corkwood
*Commiphora angolensis* - p. 302
Multi-stemmed, small tree forming dense thickets on deep sands; branchlets are not spine-tipped; compound leaves always have 3 leaflets (60 x 23 mm).

### Tall Firethorn Corkwood
*Commiphora glandulosa* - p. 300
Single-stemmed tree with grey-green, flaky bark; simple leaves (75 x 32 mm), or may be three-leaflet compound, clustered on spine-tipped side-branches; several species look very similar.

### Glossy-leaved Corkwood
*Commiphora schimperi* - p. 302
Compound leaf with 3 leaflets with a much larger central one; grey-green bark that peels in yellow-brown, paper-thin flakes; branches are spine-tipped.

### Velvet Corkwood
*Commiphora mollis* - p. 302
Compound leaves with 4 pairs of fine hairy leaflets and a leaflet at the end (60 x 30 mm); dark grey-brown bark that peels in irregular round patches.

### Zebra-bark Corkwood
*Commiphora viminea* - p. 302
Simple leaves with a toothed edge at the top third (45 x 25 mm); leaves are clustered in rosettes; bark of older trees peels in horizontal bands, with streaks of dark grey, corky bark in between.

# CORKWOODS

## Paperbark Corkwood
*Commiphora marlothii* - p. 302
Compound leaves with up to 4 pairs of hairy leaflets and a leaflet at the tip (30 - 75 x 20 - 40 mm); bark peels off in large creamy-white papery flakes exposing a green under-surface.

# MONKEY ORANGES

## Corky-bark Monkey-orange
*Strychnos cocculoides* - p. 122
Thick, corky bark with very obvious lengthways ridges; distinct, short, curved spines; leaves almost round with tapering tip and base (25 - 50 x 15 - 40 mm), with five veins radiating from the base; upper-surface shiny, dark green, and under-surface paler and dull; fruit 70 mm in diameter, green with white spots, turning yellow when ripe (April - August).

## Hairy-leaved Monkey-orange
*Strychnos madagascariensis* - p. 120
Up to 8 m; often multi-stemmed; bark is light grey and smooth, and does not have spines; simple leaves are broadly elliptic, almost circular, and have 3 - 5 veins from base (20 - 90 x 10 - 60 mm); they are clustered towards the ends of knobbly twigs, hugging the thick branches; striking, hard, orange-like fruit is yellow-orange when ripe (70 - 100 mm).

## Spine-leaved Monkey-orange
*Strychnos pungens* - p. 122
Rough, flaking, bark; leathery leaves are shiny dark green, with 3 distinct veins radiating from the base (30 - 80 x 13 - 50 mm); side veins form a ridge along leaf-edge, and leaves end in a sharp, spine-like tip; bluish-green fruit is large (120 mm) and ripens to yellow (March - August).

## Spiny Monkey-orange
*Strychnos spinosa* - p. 122
Slender, paired, straight or slightly curved, woody spines at base of leaves (15 - 90 x 12 - 75 mm); leaves opposite and not clustered; they are softer and greener than Black Monkey Orange; fruit is large (120 mm), turns yellowish-brown when ripe (March - August).

*The art on these pages is not to scale. Please refer to the text for sizes.*

# BARK

Barks vary greatly from tree to tree, even in the same species. This could be due to differences in climate and locality. However, these pages can be used as a guideline and should help you find new trees, and old friends!

**SMOOTH, WITH SMALL BUMPS OR SPIKES**

Some Corkwoods - p. 78 - 79

**RELATIVELY SMOOTH**

Jacket-plum
- p. 272

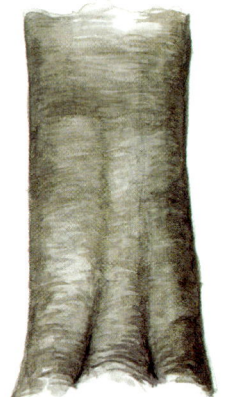

African White-stinkwood
- p. 360

Pigeonwood
- p. 66

Hornpod-tree
- p. 268

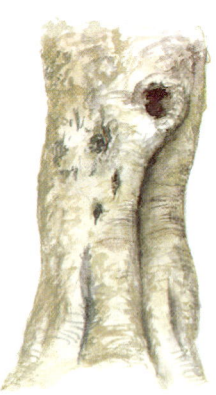

Rock Figs
- p. 77

Shepherds-tree
- p. 200

Eastern Rapanea
- p. 32

Sacred Coral Tree
- p. 148

# BARK

## SMOOTH, PEELING OR FLAKING

Squat Star-chestnut
- p. 102

Eastern Sesame-bush
- p. 90

Blue Acacia
- p. 70

Peeling-bark Ochna
- p. 136

Weeping Lavender-tree
- p. 354

Forest Lavender-tree
- p. xii

Paperbark Albizia
- p. 178

Paperbark Acacia
- p. 174

Some Corkwoods
- p. 78 - 79

**STRIKING FEATURES**
Distinctive bark

81

# BARK

## COARSE AND BLOCKY

Leadwood - p. 226    Tamboti - p. 388

## COARSE AND PEELING

Marula - p. 230    False-marula Lannea

Velvet Bushwillow - p. 304    Kiaat Bloodwood - p. 166

## COARSE AND CORKY

Wild-pear Dombeya - p. 156    Weeping Faurea - p. 350

Red Currant-rhus - p. 372    Mobola-plum - p. 170

Corky-bark Monkey-orange - p. 79    Ladies Cabbage-tree - p. 94

# BARK

## COARSE, ROPEY OR FISSURED

Camel-thorn Acacia
- p. 240

Ouhout
- p. 34

Silver Cluster-leaf
- p. 244

Highveld Silver-oak
- p. 326

## COARSE WITH LARGE BUMPS, KNOBS OR THORNS

River Bushwillow
-p. 376

Small Knobwood
- p. 384

## YELLOWWOODS

Small-leaved Yellowwood
- p. 33

Young Knob-thorn Acacia
- p. 222

Thorny-rope Flat-bean
-p. 44

Broad-leaved Yellowwood
- p. 33

STRIKING FEATURES
Distinctive bark

83

# Trees greet you

### UNIQUE

The trees in this section have such unique forms that you do not need to spend time developing comprehensive Search Images of them. It is helpful to page through this section and look at "Where to find this tree easily", for each tree, to see if it is likely to occur in the area where you are tree spotting. Once you know it is there, you are going to find that it greets you!

| | |
|---|---|
| Baobab | p. 86 |
| Eastern Sesame-bush | p. 90 |
| Ladies Cabbage-tree | p. 94 |
| Naboom Euphorbia | p. 98 |
| Squat Star-chestnut | p. 102 |

This huge, old Ladies Cabbage-tree (*Cussonia spicata*) is on a South-facing Slope in the Eland's Valley, Sour Bushveld (S). It grows near extensive ruins of village walling, and has seen the passage of human history over many, many decades.

# BAOBAB

*Adansonia digitata*

### KAPOK FAMILY
### BOMBACACEAE

SA Tree Number 467

**AFRIKAANS** Kremetart   **N. SOTHO** Seboi   **PEDI** Seboi   **TSONGA** Ximuwu   **TSWANA** Mowana
**VENDA** Muvhuyu

The species name **digitata** refers to the hand-shaped leaves.

## Where you'll find this tree easily
The Baobab grows singly.
- It is easiest to find on the Plains of the Northern Mountains (N).
- It can also be found on the Plains of the Mixed Bushveld (M) and the Central Mountains (C); and in Rocky Areas of the Central Mountains (C); as well as on all Slopes of the Northern Mountains (N).

## Ecozones where this tree occurs

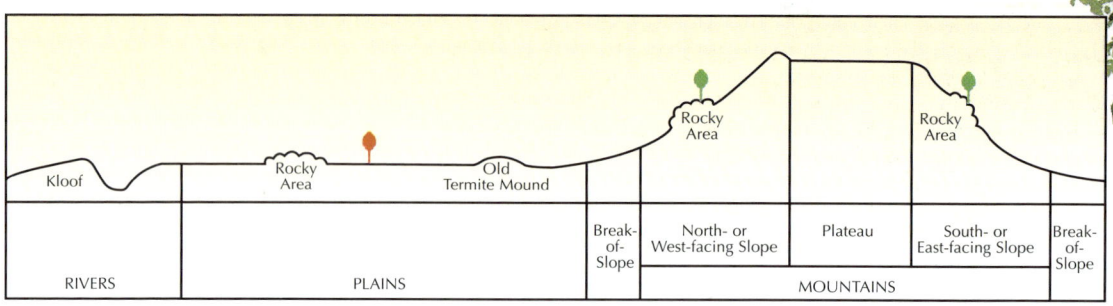

## Striking features
- This gigantic tree with a massive trunk is unmistakable.
- **Massive branches end in very thick stumps that look like roots, giving the tree the appearance of growing upside-down.**
- The bark is shiny, grey-brown and smooth, often dented and grooved.
- Hand-shaped compound leaves grow at the ends of the thick, stubby branchlets and twigs.

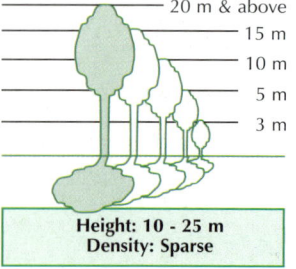

Height: 10 - 25 m
Density: Sparse

UNIQUE
Baobab

# BAOBAB

*Adansonia digitata*

**Links with animals** The Straw-coloured Fruitbat (*Eidolon helvum*) is one of the main pollinators of this tree. The fruit is eaten by baboon, and the bark by elephant. Cattle, elephants and antelope chew on the spongy wood to relieve thirst in times of drought. Böhms Spine-tails build their saucer-like nests in the hollows of these trees.

**Human uses** The trunk is huge, often with hollows deep enough for a human to hide in. Trees with a trunk circumference of 30 metres are estimated to be about 4 000 years old. The trunk decreases in girth during dry seasons, and swells up again after rain. Hollow branches catch rain

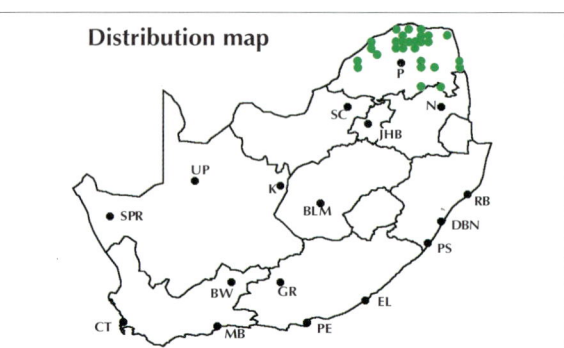

Distribution map

water, and act as a reservoir that can be used by humans and animals. As the spongy wood contains a high proportion of water, humans also chew on the wood to relieve thirst. The trunks that have been hollowed by fire, or sometimes by people, have been used as houses, prisons, storage barns and even water tanks. Fibre, to weave baskets and hats, is made from the bark. Flour is prepared from the roots. Fresh leaves are used as spinach. The fruit is edible, the creamy flesh being sucked from the pips. The pulp is rich in Vitamin C. Cream of tartar was originally made from the mealy substance around the fruit.

A drink prepared from fruit pulp has been used to treat fevers and diarrhoea. Leaves are used against fever, to reduce perspiration and as an astringent. Powdered seeds are given to children as a hiccup remedy. The bark and leaves have been used for treating malaria, dysentery, urinary disorders and mild diarrhoea.

**Wood** The wood is whitish, spongy and light, and contains a high proportion of water.

**Gardening** The Baobab can be very attractive in a large garden. It grows best in warmer areas, on most well-drained soils. It is susceptible to frost, but is fairly drought-resistant. The tree can be grown from seed, and is fairly fast-growing under warm, well-watered conditions.

*The unique growth form of the Boabab makes it easy to identify*

# GROWTH DETAILS

It has a single, straight trunk with branches coming off horizontally to form a round, widely branching, sparse canopy.

**UNIQUE Baobab**

**Leaves**  Mature compound leaves are hand-shaped, with 5 - 7 elliptic leaflets that have smooth margins. They are grouped at the ends of the branches on long leaf-stalks that are about 120 mm long. (Leaflet: 50 - 150 x 30 - 70 mm)

**Fruit**  The characteristic huge, oval to round fruit is covered by yellowish-grey, velvety hairs, and hangs from the tips of branchlets and twigs. The fruit turns brown when ripe, and contains a white, mealy substance surrounding shiny black pips (April to May). (200 - 240 x 100 - 120 mm)

*40% life-size*

**Flowers**  The huge, cup-shaped, white flowers are sweet-scented, and hang downwards. They have crisped-edged petals with long, protruding stamens (October and November). (240 x 120 mm)

**Bark**  The bark is shiny, grey-brown and smooth, often dented and grooved.

## Seasonal changes
Deciduous. Leaves appear late in spring. Because of the massive, unique shape, these trees are easy to identify all year round.

|  | Oct | Nov | Dec | Jan | Feb | Mar | Apr | May | Jun | Jul | Aug | Sep |
|---|---|---|---|---|---|---|---|---|---|---|---|---|
| Leaf |  |  |  |  |  |  |  |  |  |  |  |  |
| Flower |  |  |  |  |  |  |  |  |  |  |  |  |
| Fruit/Pod |  |  |  |  |  |  |  |  |  |  |  |  |

89

# EASTERN SESAME-BUSH

*Sesamothamnus lugardii*                                                Transvaal sesame bush

### SESAME FAMILY
### PEDALIACEAE

SA Tree Number 680

**AFRIKAANS** Transvaalse Sesambos   **TSWANA** Moboana, Siboana   **VENDA** Tshinonzhe

The species name **lugardii** honours Major E J Lugard, a naturalist who collected plants in Namaqualand during the late 1800's.

## Where you'll find this tree easily

This very unusual tree grows singly or in scattered, small groups.

- 🔴 It is easiest to find on the lower North- or West-facing Slopes of the Northern Mountains (N) and Mixed Bushveld (M).
- 🟢 It can also be found in Rocky Areas and on Plains of the Mixed Bushveld (M) and Northern Mountains (N).

## Ecozones where this tree occurs

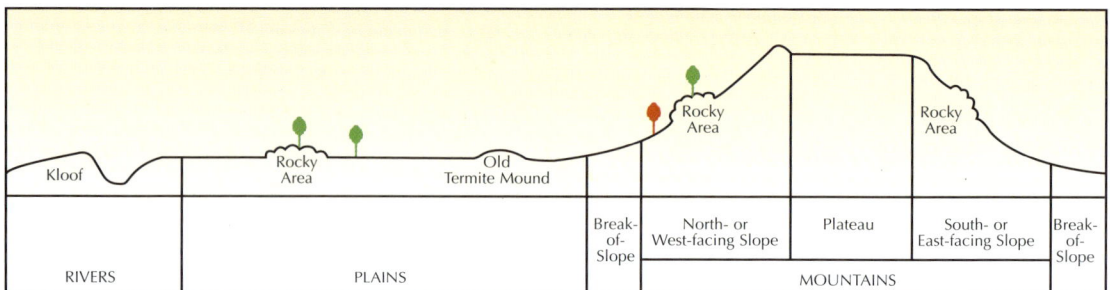

## Striking features

- **This is a stout, succulent-like tree, with a very swollen base and main branches. Branches divide into thick branchlets that taper rapidly towards their tips.**
- The blue-grey-green simple leaves, which are very small for the size of the tree, have very short leaf-stalks and form tight, sparse sleeves around the branchlets and twigs.
- Short, sharp, straight or slightly curved spines grow on twigs and branches.
- The striking, sweet-scented flowers have long, thin, red-brown tubes with white, star-like petals.
- The golden-yellow bark, marked with black, peels off in small flakes, to show shiny green under-bark.

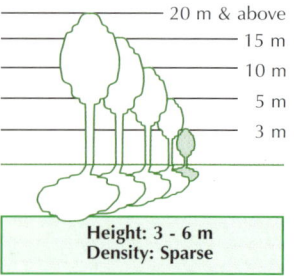

Height: 3 - 6 m
Density: Sparse

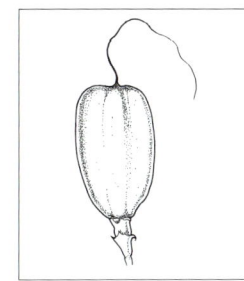

**UNIQUE**
Eastern Sesame-bush

# EASTERN SESAME-BUSH

*Sesamothamnus lugardii*

**Links with animals**  This tree is not used much by animals, but elephants have been known to eat parts of the tree, and sometimes to uproot it.

**Human uses**  There are no recorded human uses for this tree.

**Gardening**  This is an interesting addition to any garden with well-drained soil, especially a rock garden. It is drought- but probably not frost-resistant. These trees are difficult to grow from seed, as planted seeds germinate poorly.

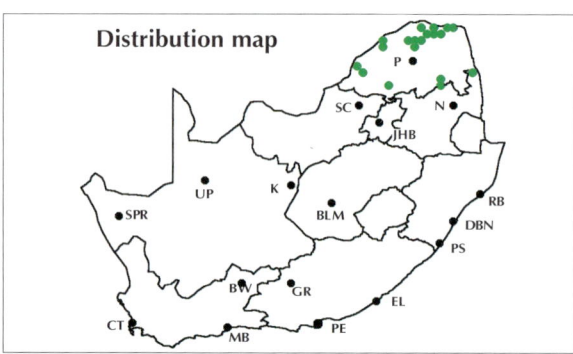

Distribution map

**Wood**  The wood is succulent, very soft, light and fibrous, and has no commercial value.

February; Plains, Northern Mountains

# GROWTH DETAILS

This very unusual succulent-like tree has an exceptionally thick, swollen trunk. It branches very low down into a few thick branches that divide into thin tapering branchlets to form a sparse canopy. The tiny leaves form tight sleeves around the branchlets and twigs.

**Leaves**  The small, simple leaves are found in tufts on knobs, in the angles made by the spines. The leaves have a very short leaf-stalk. They have a smooth margin, rounded-to-notched tip, and a tapering base. Particularly the under-surfaces of the blue-grey-green leaves are covered by many, tiny, star-shaped hairs that give a powdery appearance. The veins, which are without hairs, are prominent on the under-surface. (Leaf: up to 40 x 25 mm)

*30% life-size*

**Flowers**  The striking, large, star-shaped flowers are sweet-scented, and grow singly. The flower consists of a long (up to 100 mm), thin, dark red-brown flower-tube, opening into five, broad, spreading, white petals (November to February). (Flower diameter: 50 - 60 mm)

**Fruit**  The fruit is a pale brown, woody capsule that can be heart-shaped, rectangular or egg-shaped, with a blunt, notched tip sometimes with a long, rigid, hair-like strand. It is thickened in the middle and stands upright. It splits open widely, to release brown seeds with round, papery wings (December to April). (Fruit: 50 x 38 mm)

**Spines**  The branches have dark knobs and short, sharp, straight or slightly curved, stiff spines (10 - 15 mm), which are found just below the leaves.

*30% life-size*

closed fruit    open fruit

**Bark**  The bark is golden-yellow marked with black, and peels slightly in small flakes revealing green under-bark. Branches become darker toward their ends.

## Seasonal changes
Deciduous. It can be identified throughout the year by the unusual succulent trunk and by its growth form.

|  | Oct | Nov | Dec | Jan | Feb | Mar | Apr | May | Jun | Jul | Aug | Sep |
|---|---|---|---|---|---|---|---|---|---|---|---|---|
| Leaf | | █ | █ | █ | █ | █ | █ | | | | | █ |
| Flower | | █ | █ | █ | █ | | | | | | | |
| Fruit/Pod | | | █ | █ | █ | █ | █ | | | | | |

**UNIQUE — Eastern Sesame-bush**

# LADIES CABBAGE-TREE

*Cussonia spicata*

Cabbage tree; Common Cabbage Tree; Kiepersol; Lowveld Cabbage Tree

## CABBAGE TREE FAMILY
## ARALIACEAE

SA Tree Number 564

**AFRIKAANS** Sambreelboom, Laeveldkiepersol  **N. SOTHO** Motšhetše  **SISWATI** umSenge, umSenga  **S. SOTHO** Musenje  **TSONGA** Musenje  **TSWANA** Mosêtsê  **VENDA** Musenzhe  **XHOSA** umSenge  **ZULU** umSenge

The species name **spicata** refers to the flowers that grow in spikes.

## Where you'll find this tree easily

The Ladies Cabbage-tree grows singly among other tree species.

- It is is easiest to find on Rocky Areas and on South- or East-facing Slopes of the Northern Mountains (N), Central Mountains (C) and Sour Bushveld (S).
- It can also be found on North- or West-facing Slopes of the Mixed Bushveld (M), Northern Mountains (N), Sour Bushveld (S) and Central Mountains (C).

## Ecozones where this tree occurs

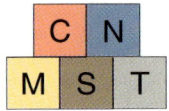

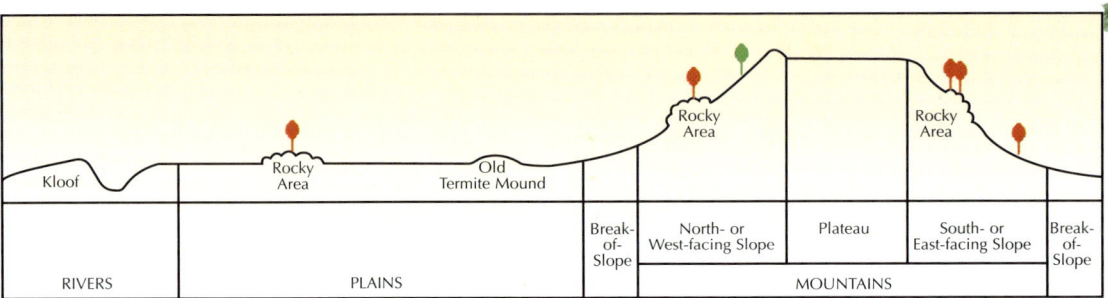

## Striking features

- **This is a single-stemmed tree with a grey, corky bark. It branches fairly high up into many large, crooked branches to form a round, often dense canopy.**
- The compound, hand-shaped leaves are large and blue-grey-green, with very long leaf-stalks.
- The leaves are spirally arranged at the tips of thick branchlets.
- The distinctively shaped leaflets have a toothed margin and are deeply indented, often cutting in very close to the central vein, to form 2 - 3 lobes.
- Up to nine leaflets come from a single point at the tip of the leaf-stalk.

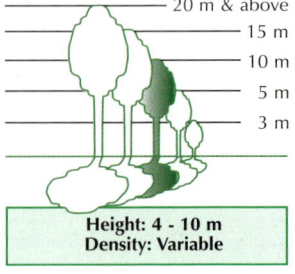

Height: 4 - 10 m
Density: Variable

UNIQUE
Ladies Cabbage-tree

# LADIES CABBAGE-TREE

*Cussonia spicata*

**Links with animals** Black Rhino eat the bark and roots. Baboons and bushpigs also eat bark and roots in times of scarcity. Several species of Charaxes butterflies are attracted to the ripe fruit. Leaves are browsed by domestic stock and game, including elephant and kudu. Barbets eat the fruit. Flowers and fruit are eaten by Sombre and Black-eyed Bulbuls, Knysna Louries, Speckled Mousebirds and Red-winged Starlings.

**Human uses** The roots are eaten when water and food are scarce. The caterpillars that breed on the tree are edible, and are considered a delicacy. Roots, flowers and flower-stalks are used to treat malaria, biliousness and venereal diseases.

**Gardening** This is a fast-growing Cabbage Tree, but is sensitive to frost. It has an invasive root system, and should not be planted close to buildings or paving.

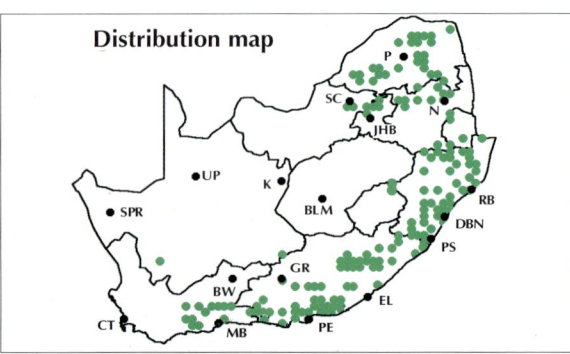

Distribution map

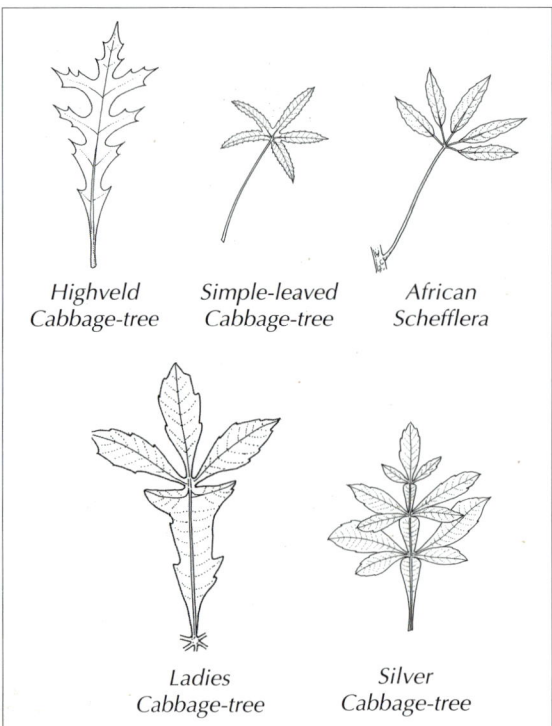

Highveld Cabbage-tree | Simple-leaved Cabbage-tree | African Schefflera

Ladies Cabbage-tree | Silver Cabbage-tree

**Wood** This rare wood is perishable and does not take paint or varnish readily. There is little difference in colour between heartwood and sapwood. It has a straight grain and can be sawn cleanly despite its softness.

**Look-alike trees** The other Cabbage Trees have a very similar growth form, but can be identified by their leaves. The Silver Cabbage-tree (*Cussonia transvaalensis*) has twice compound, blue to grey-green leaves with 7 - 9 subdivided leaflets. The canopy is sparsely branched and small.

The Simple-leaved Cabbage-tree (*Cussonia natalensis*) has simple palmate leaves with 3 - 5 clearly demarcated lobes, with a shiny sheen and a conspicuous central vein in each lobe.

The Highveld Cabbage-tree (*Cussonia paniculata*) has compound leaves and leaflets with a serrated, deeply cut margin but never cutting to the central vein. See **Sappi Tree Spotting Highveld**.

The African Schefflera (*Schefflera umbellifera*), page 67, has smoother bark and is normally more branched; the leaves are compound hand-shaped, with leaflets having a very wavy, sometimes toothed margin.

# GROWTH DETAILS

UNIQUE
Ladies Cabbage-tree

This is a single-stemmed tree that branches into many large branches. The large, hand-shaped leaves are spirally arranged at the tips of large branchlets. The canopy is variable, but often dense, and may be round or irregular.

**Leaves** The compound leaves have 5 - 9 leaflets that are deeply lobed, cutting in close to the central vein. They are shiny and usually blue-grey to grey-green, but may be dark green. The central vein is conspicuous, and the margin is normally toothed. The tips of the leaflets gradually taper to a point, and the base is narrow. The leaf-stalk is sturdy and long. (Leaf: 200 - 1 000 mm; leaf-stalks: 300 - 500 mm)

*10% life-size*

**Flowers** The flowers are small and greenish-yellow. They are densely packed in 8 - 12 candelabra-like spikes, on much-branched stalks, growing at the ends of the branchlets and twigs (April to June). (Spike: 50 - 150 x 15 - 40 mm)

*50% life-size*

**Fruit** The grape-like fruit is densely crowded on the spikes, and purple when ripe (October to December). (Spike: 50 – 150 mm; fruit: 6 mm)

**Bark** The bark is pale brown and corky, becoming darker and fissured with age. The branches show scars from old leaves.

### Seasonal changes
Deciduous, may be evergreen. This tree can be identified by its growth form throughout the year.

|  | Oct | Nov | Dec | Jan | Feb | Mar | Apr | May | Jun | Jul | Aug | Sep |
|---|---|---|---|---|---|---|---|---|---|---|---|---|
| Leaf | ■ | ■ | ■ | ■ | ■ | ■ | ■ | ■ | ■ |  |  | ■ |
| Flower |  |  |  |  |  |  | ■ | ■ | ■ |  |  |  |
| Fruit/Pod | ■ | ■ | ■ |  |  |  |  |  |  |  | ■ | ■ |

97

# NABOOM EUPHORBIA

*Euphorbia ingens*                                     Candelabra Tree; Cactus euphorbia;
                                                       Common Tree Euphorbia

| EUPHORBIA FAMILY  EUPHORBIACEAE | SA Tree Number 351 |

**AFRIKAANS** Gewone Naboom    **N. SOTHO** Mohlohlo-kgomo, Mokgoto    **PEDI** Mokgoro
**SISWATI** iShupa    **TSONGA** Nkondze, Nkonde    **TSWANA** Monkgôpô    **VENDA** Mukonde
**ZULU** umHlonhlo, umPhapha

The species name **ingens** means large.

## Where you'll find this tree easily

The Naboom Euphorbia is fairly wide-spread throughout the Bushveld, but it generally prefers well-drained soils.

- It is easiest to find in Rocky Areas of all Ecozones.
- It can also be found on Old Termite Mounds on the Plains of all Ecozones.

## Ecozones where this tree occurs

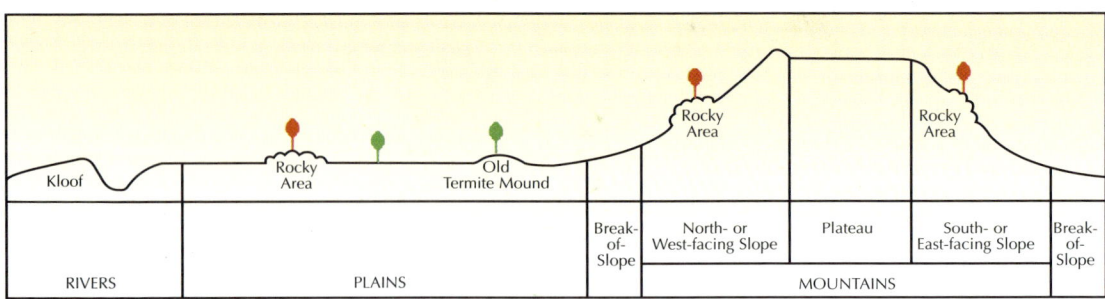

## Striking features

- **This is an evergreen tree that is usually leafless.**
- The trunk is short, with coarse bark.
- **The thick, straight, green branches have constricted, angular segments.**
- The moderate, rounded canopy is formed by branches that leave the trunk and characteristically split again.
- All parts of the tree contain a very irritant, milky latex that may cause blindness if it comes into contact with the eyes.

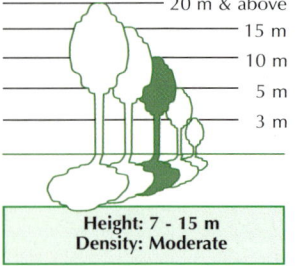

Height: 7 - 15 m
Density: Moderate

UNIQUE
Naboom Euphorbia

# NABOOM EUPHORBIA

*Euphorbia ingens*

**Links with animals** Under drought conditions, Black Rhino eat the branches of young trees. The fruit is eaten by a variety of birds.

**Human uses** The wood is used for planks. The poisonous latex is used to kill maggots in open wounds on cattle, as well as to stupefy fish, which are then easily caught by hand.

**Gardening** This tree can be used effectively in large, rocky, well-drained gardens of the drier areas, although the latex makes it unsuitable for a family garden. It is susceptible to frost but very drought-resistant. It is slow-growing and can be grown from seed or cuttings.

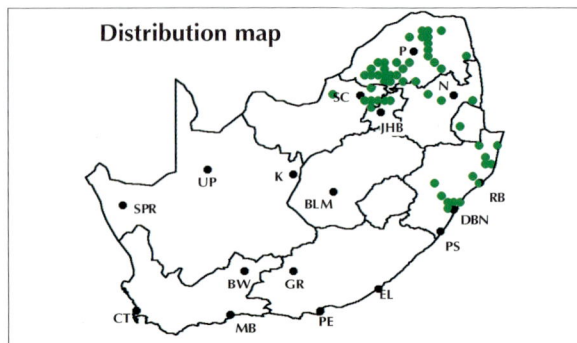

Distribution map

**Wood** The wood is soft, fibrous and white.

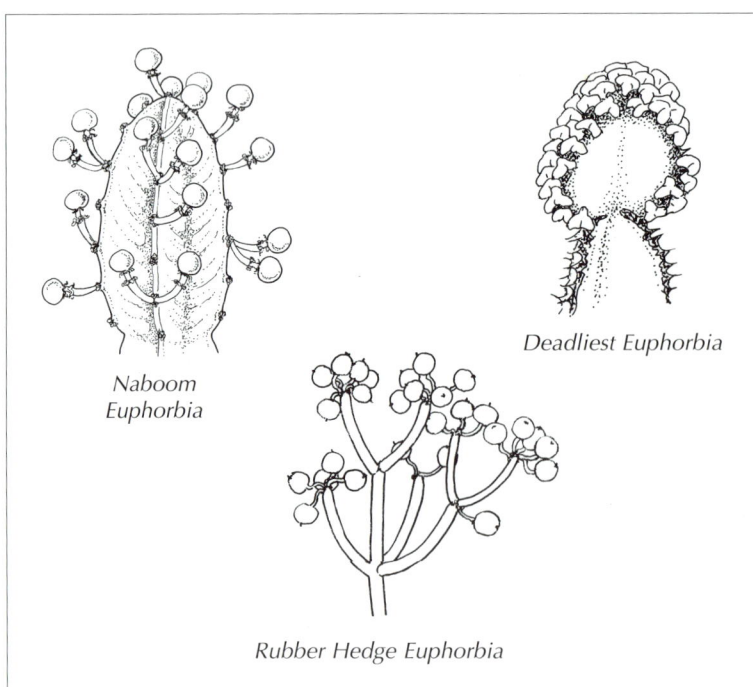

Naboom Euphorbia

Deadliest Euphorbia

Rubber Hedge Euphorbia

**Look-alike trees**
Deadliest Euphorbia (*Euphorbia cooperi*) is very similar, and is also found in Rocky Areas. However the branches do not split and they have thorns on the ridges.

The Rubber Hedge Euphorbia (*Euphorbia tirucalli*) has long, thin, fingerlike branches.

The Lebombo Euphorbia (*Euphorbia confinalis*) has heart-shaped, segmented branches. Individual branches form many side branches that originate at the same level.

# GROWTH DETAILS

It has a single, straight trunk with branches growing upwards to form a cactus-like, rounded, moderate canopy. The thick, straight, green branches characteristically split repeatedly. They have constricted, angular segments with lengthways ridges on which the flowers and fruit grow.

**UNIQUE**
Naboom Euphorbia

**Leaves** The leaves are very small and drop almost immediately. As a result the tree is usually leafless and photosynthesis is the function of the branches.

**Flowers** Inconspicuous, yellow-green flowers appear from autumn to winter growing on the ridges of the branches. (10 mm)

*45% life-size*

**Fruit** Capsule-like, round fruit ripens with a reddish tinge in spring, when it bursts open on the tree. (13 mm)

**Spines** When present these are paired, but are often only 2 mm long, or absent.

**Bark** The bark is coarse.

**Seasonal changes**
Evergreen. This tree does not change seasonally, and can be identified easily in winter.

|  | Oct | Nov | Dec | Jan | Feb | Mar | Apr | May | Jun | Jul | Aug | Sep |
|---|---|---|---|---|---|---|---|---|---|---|---|---|
| Branch | ■ | ■ | ■ | ■ | ■ | ■ | ■ | ■ | ■ | ■ | ■ | ■ |
| Flower |  |  |  |  |  |  |  |  |  |  |  |  |
| Fruit/Pod | ■ |  |  |  |  |  |  |  |  |  | ■ | ■ |

101

# SQUAT STAR-CHESTNUT

*Sterculia rogersii*                                   Common star-chestnut

| STAR-CHESTNUT FAMILY STERCULIACEAE | SA Tree Number 477 |

**AFRIKAANS** Gewone Sterkastaiing  **N. SOTHO** Mokgwakgwatha  **TSONGA** Samani, Nsolodza  **TSWANA** Mokakata  **VENDA** Mukakate  **ZULU** inKhuphenkhuphe

The species name **rogersii** honours Reverend FA Rogers, a keen naturalist and plant collector.

## Where you'll find this tree easily

This uncommon tree grows only in Rocky Areas with sandy soils. It grows singly, and may be the only tree on a rocky outcrop.

- It is easiest to find in Rocky Areas on Plains, and on some North- or West-facing Slopes of the Northern Mountains (N).
- It can also be found on Rocky Areas of the other Ecozones; and in shallow sandy soils on the Plains of Mixed Bushveld (M).

## Ecozones where this tree occurs

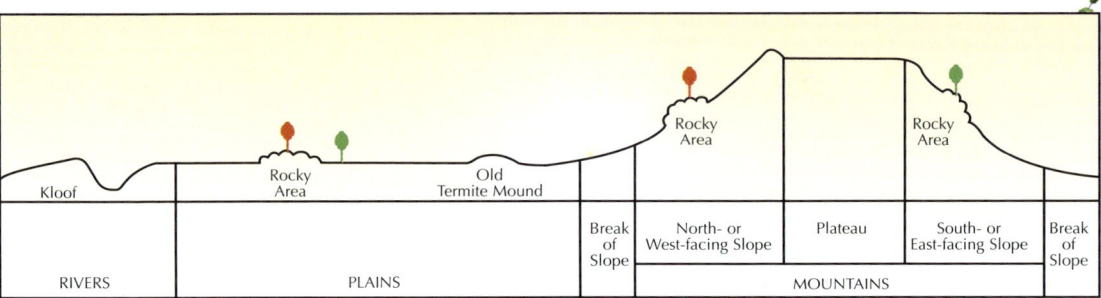

## Striking features

- This stout, low-branching tree has a thick trunk and main branches, which divide abruptly into very thin branchlets and twigs.
- **The dark brown to purplish bark peels patchily in paper-thin flakes, to reveal smooth, creamy, yellow-green under-bark, giving the trunk a distinctive mottled appearance.**
- The simple leaves are small for the size of the tree, which has a sparse, irregular canopy.
- Heart-shaped leaves may have a slightly indented margin.
- The characteristic greyish-pink, chestnut-like fruit consists of 3 - 5 long lobes that end in a long, horn-like point.

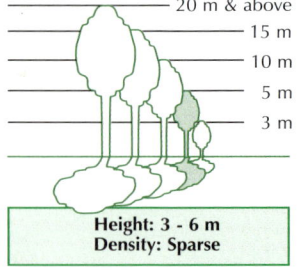

Height: 3 - 6 m
Density: Sparse

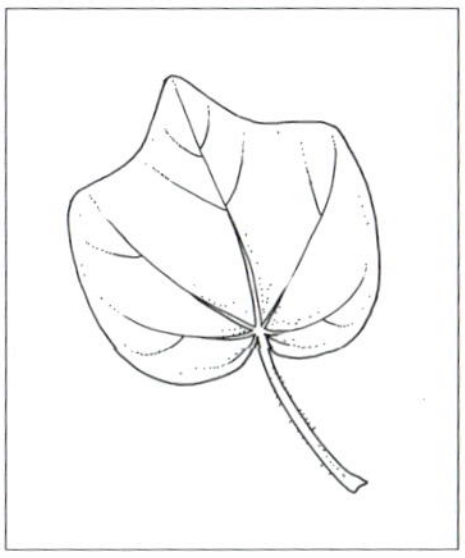

UNIQUE
Squat Star-chestnut

103

# SQUAT STAR-CHESTNUT

*Sterculia rogersii*

**Links with animals**  Elephants are very fond of the young shoots and leaves. The leaves and young stalks are browsed by antelope such as kudu and duiker. The seeds are eaten by birds.

**Human uses**  The heartwood is sometimes eaten when other food is scarce. The bark is used to make rope, string for fishing nets, to tie thatch to the framework of a roof, and to sew sleeping-mats and grain baskets.

**Gardening**  This unusual tree is slow-growing, and the seed takes a long time to germinate. It grows better in drier areas in well-drained soil, and is sensitive to frost.

**Wood**  The wood is greyish-brown to pale brown. It is fibrous, coarse-grained, soft and brittle, and therefore not suitable for use.

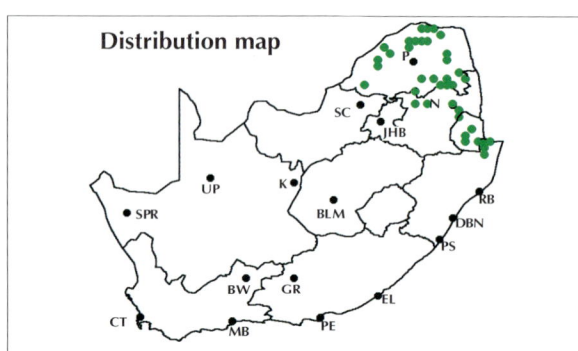

Distribution map

**Look-alike tree**  Because of its stout trunk and thin branchlets, this tree is sometimes mistaken for a young Baobab (*Adansonia digitata*), page 86, which has smooth, grey bark and large, compound hand-shaped leaves.

*Old tree; mottled bark*

# GROWTH DETAILS

This unusual tree is very variable but unmistakable. It is mostly seen as a stout tree, low-branching, with thick trunk and main branches dividing abruptly into very thin branchlets and fine twigs. The canopy is sparse and irregular.

**Leaves** The unusual, simple, small ivy-like leaves are alternate. Young leaves are heart-shaped. Older leaves have a tapering tip and wavy margin, and may be indented to create 3 - 5 'lobes'. Leaf-stalks are long (75 mm). The 5 - 7 veins, which come from the base, are clearly visible. The leaves are shiny green and slightly hairy above, and pale green and hairy below. Leaves turn yellow in autumn. (30 - 60 x 20 - 50 mm)

**Flowers** The star-shaped flowers grow at the ends of branchlets and twigs, and appear before the new leaves. The flowers are red-green on the outside, and yellow-green with vertical, red streaks on the inside (July to January). (10 - 20 mm)

**Fruit** The characteristic greyish-pink, chestnut-like fruit consists of 3 - 5 lobes that are roughly oblong in shape and taper to a long, horn-like point. The ripe fruit is golden-brown, and splits open on the tree to reveal dark grey seeds, which are surrounded by stinging, golden hairs (August to March). (Individual lobe: up to 60 - 80 mm in length)

*life-size*

**Bark** Old trees have rough, dark brown to purplish bark that peels patchily in paper-thin flakes to reveal smooth, shiny, creamy-yellow to yellow-green under-bark, giving the trunk a mottled appearance.

**UNIQUE Squat Star-chestnut**

## Seasonal changes
Deciduous. This tree can be identified throughout the year by its unusual growth form and bark.

|  | Oct | Nov | Dec | Jan | Feb | Mar | Apr | May | Jun | Jul | Aug | Sep |
|---|---|---|---|---|---|---|---|---|---|---|---|---|
| Leaf | 🟩 | 🟩 | 🟩 |  |  |  |  |  |  | 🟩 | 🟩 | 🟩 |
| Flower | 🟧 | 🟧 | 🟧 | 🟧 |  |  |  |  |  | 🟧 | 🟧 | 🟩 |
| Fruit/Pod | 🟧 | 🟧 | 🟧 | 🟧 | 🟧 |  |  |  |  | 🟧 | 🟧 | 🟧 |

105

# You find trees

**SEASONALLY STRIKING**

These trees are particularly easy to find in certain seasons, and, on the whole, are more difficult to spot without their seasonal garb. Read through this section and check the Seasonal Grid for each tree. Also check "Where you'll find this tree easily" to be sure it occurs in the area you are tree spotting. Once you know which trees are seasonally striking in your area, you will have difficulty missing them!

| | |
|---|---|
| Brittlewood Nuxia | p. 108 |
| Bushveld Bead-bean | p. 112 |
| Flame-pod Acacia | p. 116 |
| Hairy-leaved Monkey-orange | p. 120 |
| Kooboo-berry | p. 124 |
| Large-fruited Bushwillow | p. 128 |
| Large Sourplum | p. 132 |
| Peeling-bark Ochna | p. 136 |
| Red Bushwillow | p. 140 |
| Russet Bushwillow | p. 144 |
| Sacred Coral-tree | p. 148 |
| White Cats-whiskers | p. 152 |
| Wild-pear Dombeya | p. 156 |

The Bushwillow (Combretum) family are well-known and well-loved in South Africa, and easily recognised by their characteristic four-winged pods. Arguably the most beautiful of them all is the Forest Bushwillow (*Combretum kraussii*), page 74, with its silvery new leaves and brilliant pink pods. It is probably also the least well-known because of its limited distribution in the eastern forests of South Africa.

# BRITTLEWOOD NUXIA

*Nuxia congesta*                              **Broshout; Brittlewood;
                                               Common Wild Elder**

| **WILD ELDER FAMILY** <br> **LOGANIACEAE** | **SA Tree Number 633** |

**AFRIKAANS**  Witsalie, Gewone Wildevlier    **N. SOTHO**  Motlhabare    **TSWANA**  Mokwêrêkwêrê
**VENDA**  Muteteneka    **XHOSA**  umKhobeza    **ZULU**  umKhobeza

The species name **congesta** refers to the crowded flower-head.

## Where you'll find this tree easily

The Brittlewood Nuxia grows singly among other tree species.

- It is easiest to find in Rocky Areas on South- or East-facing Slopes of the Northern Mountains (N).
- It can also be found in Rocky Areas on South- or East-facing Slopes of the Mixed Bushveld (M), Central Mountains (C) and Sour Bushveld (S); and along Rivers of the Northern Mountain (N).

## Ecozones where this tree occurs

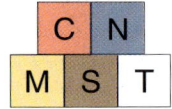

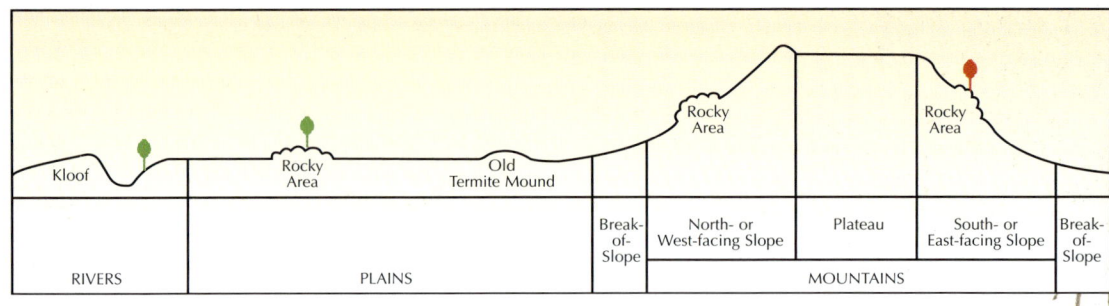

## Striking features

- This is a multi-stemmed tree with crooked stems. Branches grow upwards to form a moderate, round canopy.
- **The shiny leaves are arranged in groups of three around the twigs.**
- **The delicate, white flowers grow in large dense sprays at the tips of twigs and branchlets.**

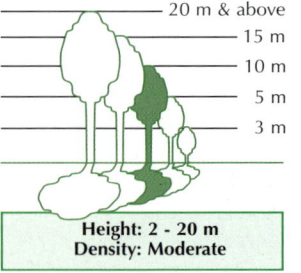

Height: 2 - 20 m
Density: Moderate

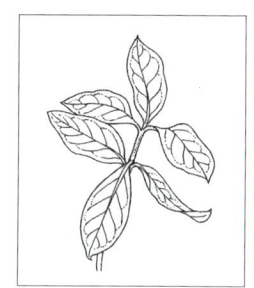

**SEASONALLY STRIKING**
Brittlewood Nuxia

109

# BRITTLEWOOD NUXIA

*Nuxia congesta*

**Links with animals** Bees are attracted to the flowers.

**Human uses** The wood is good for engraving, makes very good fence posts, and has been extensively used for building.

**Gardening** This is an attractive tree but is seldom grown in gardens because it is not frost- or drought-resistant. It is excellent as a bonsai tree.

**Look-alike tree** This tree is very similar to the Forest Nuxia (*Nuxia floribunda*), but the Forest Nuxia has long leaf-stalks and the flowers are arranged in large, loose heads.

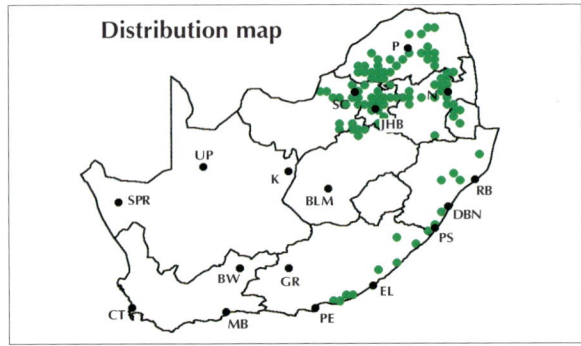

Distribution map

**Wood** The wood is whitish-yellow, hard and heavy.

*Sweet-scented flowers with leaves arranged in groups of three*

# GROWTH DETAILS

This is a multi-stemmed, low-branching tree with crooked stems. Branches grow upwards to form a moderate, rounded canopy. The delicate leaves grow on short, thin branchlets and twigs.

**Leaves** The simple, broadly elliptic leaves are arranged in groups of three towards the ends of the twigs. The margins are usually smooth, but sometimes toothed, and the base and tips taper to a point. Leaves may be shiny and smooth, or hairy, or covered by blue scales that can be rubbed off. The leaf-stalks are short. (Leaf: 10 - 80 x 6 - 40 mm)

**Flowers** Conspicuous white, sweet-scented flowers appear long after the first flower-buds are visible. They are star-shaped and grow in dense, compact heads at the ends of the twigs (March to July). (Spray: 70 - 90 mm; individual: 3 - 5 mm)

**Fruit** The inconspicuous fruit is a small, hairy capsule that develops in the old flower-heads (August to October). (3 mm)

*40% life-size*

**Bark** The light brown to grey bark is rough and finely fissured lengthways, loosely peeling in lengthways strips. Older twigs and branchlets are smooth and grey. Young, velvety twigs are square, and are often red, or light-coloured.

## Seasonal changes
Evergreen. This tree can be identified by its leaves throughout the year.

SEASONALLY STRIKING — Brittlewood Nuxia

|  | Oct | Nov | Dec | Jan | Feb | Mar | Apr | May | Jun | Jul | Aug | Sep |
|---|---|---|---|---|---|---|---|---|---|---|---|---|
| Leaf | ■ | ■ | ■ | ■ | ■ | ■ | ■ | ■ | ■ | ■ | ■ | ■ |
| Flower |  |  |  |  |  | ■ | ■ | ■ | ■ | ■ |  |  |
| Fruit/Pod | ■ |  |  |  |  |  |  |  |  |  | ■ | ■ |

# BUSHVELD BEAD-BEAN

*Maerua angolensis*                                      Bead-bean Tree

| CAPER FAMILY CAPPARACEAE | SA Tree Number 132 |

**AFRIKAANS** Knoppiesboontjieboom  **TSONGA** Palule  **TSWANA** Moomane, Morêketli
**VENDA** Mutamba-na-mme  **ZULU** umEnwayo

The species name **angolensis** refers to Angola, where the first specimen was collected.

## Where you'll find this tree easily

The Bushveld Bead-bean grows singly or among other species of tree, often in the middle of a bush clump where it is protected from fire.

- It is easiest to find in Rocky Areas on the Plains of the Central Mountains (C).
- It can also be found on Old Termite Mounds, on eroded areas and in Rocky Areas in all the Ecozones; and along Rivers and on the South- or East-facing Slopes of the Mixed Bushveld (M).

## Ecozones where this tree occurs

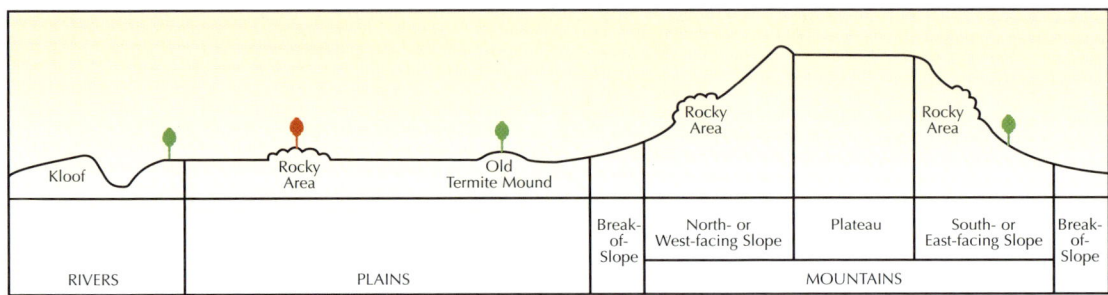

## Striking features

- This tree has a single, pale grey trunk that branches high up to form a moderate, semi-circular canopy.
- Masses of sweet-scented, creamy-white, pincushion flowers with very long stamens cover the tree from July to October.
- Large numbers of characteristic, long, slender, yellow-green, bumpy bean pods resemble a chain of unequal-sized beads, and can be seen on the tree from September to April.
- The simple, broad, elliptic, dark green leaves spiral in clusters, and have a small but distinct, hard, hair-like tip.

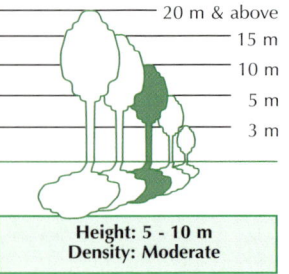

Height: 5 - 10 m
Density: Moderate

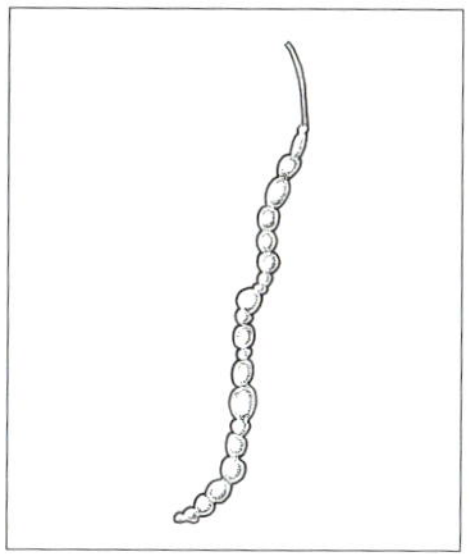

SEASONALLY STRIKING
Bushveld Bead-bean

113

# BUSHVELD BEAD-BEAN

*Maerua angolensis*

**Links with animals** The palatable leaves and bark are eaten by giraffe, kudu, nyala, bushbuck, cattle and goats. The pods are reputed to be poisonous to animals. The caterpillars of various butterfly species eat the leaves.

**Human uses** The wood is used for cabinet-making. An extract of the leaf and bark is used for stomach ache, and as a mild purgative. Steam inhaled from leaves and bark, heated over a fire, helps childhood convulsions and relieves adult headaches. A thick paste made from the leaves is used to treat cancerous areas on the skin. The fruit and the roots are so poisonous to humans that they have been used to poison enemies.

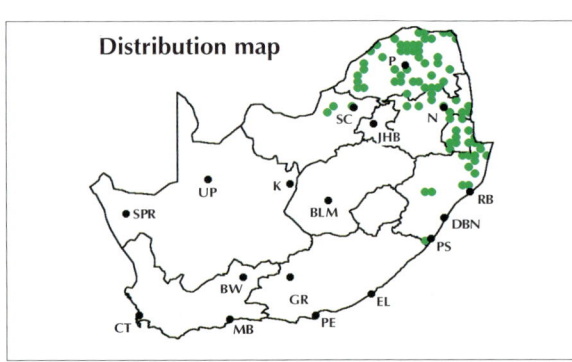

Distribution map

**Wood** The wood is white and medium-heavy, with a fine grain.

**Gardening** This is a very attractive, fast-growing tree. It is frost- and drought-resistant, and grows easily from seed from which the fruit pulp has been removed.

**Look-alike trees** Members of the Albizia genus have flowers that resemble those of this tree, however, all Albizias have twice compound leaves. See page 73 for comparison of Albizias.

*July; near Salt Pan, Soutpansberg; Northern Mountains*

# GROWTH DETAILS

This tree has a single, meandering trunk, which branches high up to form a moderate to dense, semi-circular canopy. The branches divide into fine twigs with spirally arranged leaves crowded towards their tips. The leaves obscure the upper branches.

**Leaves** The simple leaves spiral in clusters. They grow on long leaf-stalks of 18 - 30 mm, with a prominent bend near the leaf-base, and often a swelling just below the leaves. They are broadly elliptic, with a smooth margin, and often a characteristic short, sharp, hair-like tip. The leaves are dark green above and paler below. (Leaf: 25 - 70 x 13 - 55 mm)

**Flowers** The conspicuous sweet-scented, creamy-white, pincushion flowers grow at the ends of branchlets and twigs, in the angle made by the leaves (July to October). (Pincushion thread/stamen): 18 - 40 mm long)

**Pods** The characteristic, long, slender, bumpy bean pods grow towards the tips of branchlets and twigs, and in the angle made by the leaves. They are irregularly constricted between the seeds, resembling a chain of unequal-sized beads. The pods are yellow-green when young, and turn brown when ripe (September to April). (120 - 180 mm)

50% life-size

**Bark** The rough bark is pale grey to dark brown on older branches and stems. Young branches and stems are purple-brown and have white dots (lenticels).

SEASONALLY STRIKING
Bushveld Bead-bean

## Seasonal changes
Sometimes evergreen. This tree can be identified easily from December to July by the conspicuous pods.

|           | Oct | Nov | Dec | Jan | Feb | Mar | Apr | May | Jun | Jul | Aug | Sep |
|-----------|-----|-----|-----|-----|-----|-----|-----|-----|-----|-----|-----|-----|
| Leaf      |     |     |     |     |     |     |     |     |     |     |     |     |
| Flower    |     |     |     |     |     |     |     |     |     |     |     |     |
| Fruit/Pod |     |     |     |     |     |     |     |     |     |     |     |     |

115

# FLAME-POD ACACIA

*Acacia ataxacantha*                                                          Flame Thorn

| THORN-TREE FAMILY MIMOSACEAE | SA Tree Number 160 |

**AFRIKAANS** Rank-wag-'n-bietjie, Vlamdoring  **N. SOTHO** Mologa, Mogaletlwa  **TSONGA** Nuko, Muluwa  **TSWANA** Mogôkatau  **VENDA** Muluwa  **ZULU** umThathawe

The species name **ataxacantha** is compiled from Greek words meaning 'irregular thorns'.

## Where you'll find this tree easily
This often scrambling tree grows in large groups.
- It is easiest to find in Riverine Forests and along Streams of all Ecozones.
- It can also be found on the South- or East-facing Slopes of the Central Mountains (C), Northern Mountains (N) and Sour Bushveld (S).

## Ecozones where this tree occurs

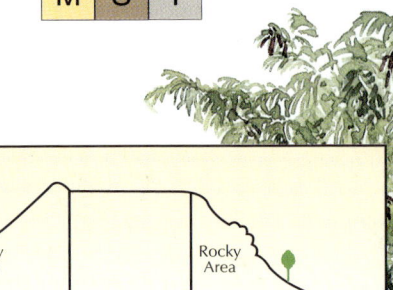

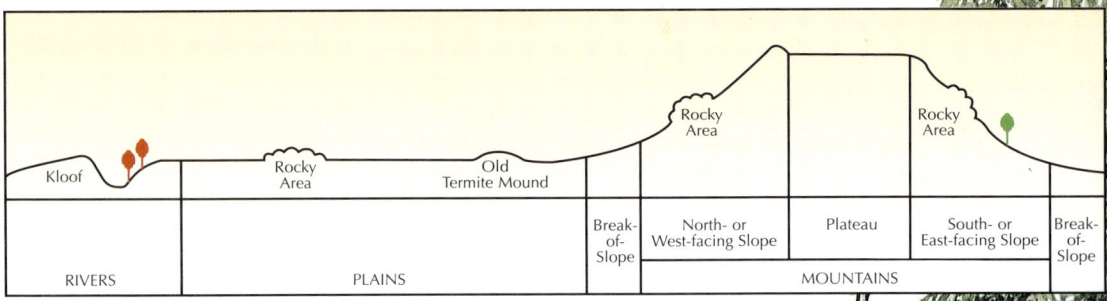

## Striking features
- This is a very thorny, multi-stemmed, scrambling tree or climber with tangled branches that form a moderate, irregular canopy.
- **The hooked thorns are scattered along the branchlets and twigs, and form no specific pattern.**
- The twice compound leaves are long and droopy.
- The creamy-yellow, conspicuous flower-spikes grow at the ends of branchlets and twigs.
- **The seed-pods grow in conspicuous bunches, and turn purple-red when ripe, which gives this tree its English name.**
- It often grows in thick impenetrable groups.

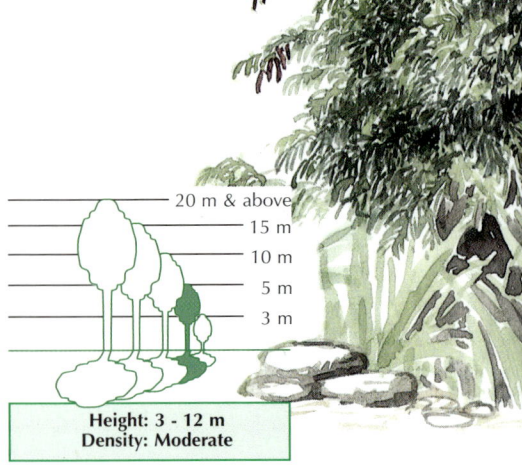

Height: 3 - 12 m
Density: Moderate

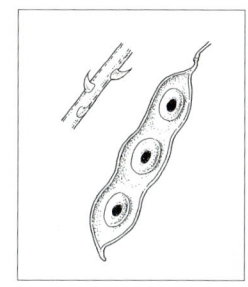

**SEASONALLY STRIKING**
**Flame-pod Acacia**

# FLAME-POD ACACIA

*Acacia ataxacantha*

**Links with animals** The caterpillars of the *Charaxes ethalion ethalion* butterfly eat the leaves. Birds such as the Red-billed Woodhoopoe and Bar-throated Apalis eat insects living on the flowers, leaves and tree trunk.

**Human uses** The wood can be split into paper-like strips without cracking. These strips are used as weaving material for baskets.

**Gardening** The Flame-pod Acacia is not an appealing garden tree as it is untidy, although the bright-coloured pods are attractive in late summer.

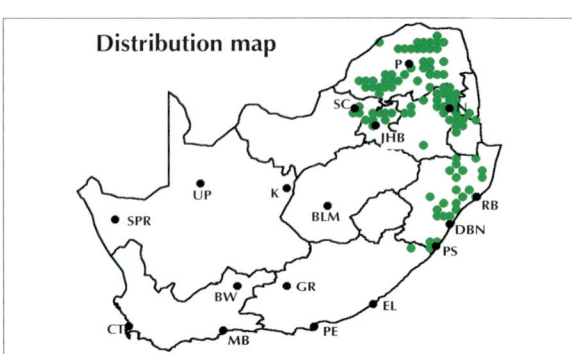

Distribution map

**Wood** The wood can be split, without cracking, to the thickness of paper. These strips are red and white, or white with a dark streak, and are used as weaving material for baskets.

**Look-alike tree** The Common Hook-thorn Acacia (*Acacia caffra*), page 318, also has long, fine, twice compound leaves, but is usually a single-stemmed tree. The hooked thorns are paired, and successive pairs are at right angles to one another. The creamy-white flower-spikes (September to November) are followed by flat bean pods that are chocolate-brown, not purple-red as in the Flame-pod Acacia.

*February; brilliant pods give the tree its name*

# GROWTH DETAILS

This is a very thorny, multi-stemmed, often scrambling tree that branches low down into many smaller, tangled branches. A moderate, leafy canopy is formed with few visible branches.

**Leaves**  The pale green, twice compound leaves have small, hooked thorns on the under-surface of the leaf-stalks. Each leaf has 7 - 17 feather pairs, with 20 - 45 pairs of tiny leaflets. There are often elevations caused by the stalked glands on the leaf-stalk near the base of the leaf. The leaf-buds (stipules) are large and triangular. The leaflets may be slightly hairy. (Leaf: 70 - 140 mm; leaflet: 2 - 5 x 1 mm)

**Flowers**  Conspicuous, creamy-yellow flower-spikes grow in abundance at the ends of the branchlets and twigs, and stand out above the leaves (September to February). (70 - 100 mm)

**Thorns**  Large numbers of small, stout, hooked thorns are purple-brown and are randomly scattered along the branchlets and twigs in no apparent pattern. (5 mm)

*60% life-size*

**Pods**  The bunches of flat bean pods are conspicuous as they ripen to purple-red. The pods become dark brown with age, and split on the tree when ripe. They remain on the tree for long periods (Ripen December to June). (70 - 100 x 12 - 15 mm)

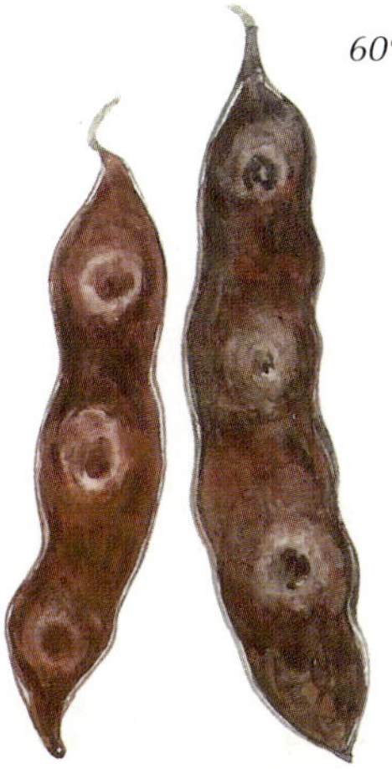

**Bark**  The bark is light brown and smooth in young trees. Older trees have dark brown bark with lengthways fissures that may become flaky.

## Seasonal changes
Deciduous. It can be identified by its growth form and thorn pattern throughout the year.

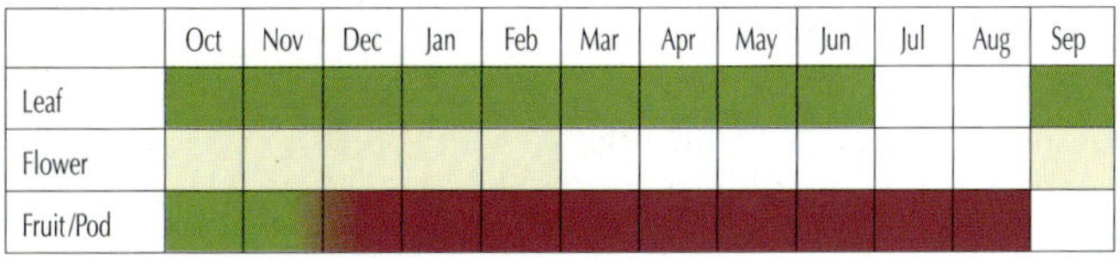

SEASONALLY STRIKING
Flame-pod Acacia

|  | Oct | Nov | Dec | Jan | Feb | Mar | Apr | May | Jun | Jul | Aug | Sep |
|---|---|---|---|---|---|---|---|---|---|---|---|---|
| Leaf |  |  |  |  |  |  |  |  |  |  |  |  |
| Flower |  |  |  |  |  |  |  |  |  |  |  |  |
| Fruit/Pod |  |  |  |  |  |  |  |  |  |  |  |  |

119

# HAIRY-LEAVED MONKEY-ORANGE

*Strychnos madagascariensis*          Black Monkey Orange

### WILD ELDER FAMILY
### LOGANIACEAE

SA Tree Number 626

**AFRIKAANS** Swartklapper, Botterklapper    **N. SOTHO** Morapa    **TSONGA** Nkwakwa
**TSWANA** Mogorwagorwana, Mogwagwa    **VENDA** Mukwakwa    **ZULU** umKwakwa, umGuluguza

The species name **madagascariensis** means 'from Madagascar'.

## Where you'll find this tree easily

The Hairy-leaved Monkey-orange grows singly among other tree species in well-drained soils.

- It is easiest to find in Sandy Areas, on Plains of the Sour Bushveld (S) and the Central Mountains (C).
- It can also be found in Rocky Areas and along Rivers and Streams of the Mixed Bushveld (M), Northern Mountains (N) and Central Mountains (C).

## Ecozones where this tree occurs

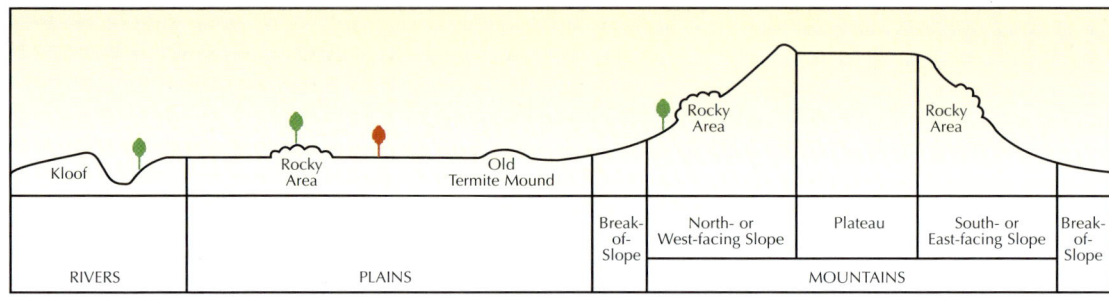

## Striking features

- This variable tree is single- or multi-stemmed with a spreading, irregular, angular canopy.
- The leaves are hairy, dark green and leathery, with 3 - 5 distinct veins radiating from the base.
- **The leaves are clustered in rosettes on very short, thick, knobbly twigs, forming a loose sleeve around the branchlets.**
- The conspicuous, very hard, orange-like fruit is blue-green for most of the year, but turns yellow-orange when ripe.

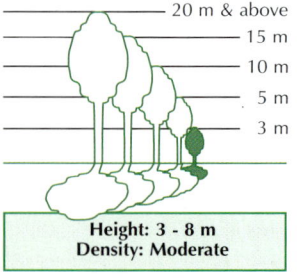

Height: 3 - 8 m
Density: Moderate

SEASONALLY STRIKING
Hairy-leaved Monkey-orange

# HAIRY-LEAVED MONKEY-ORANGE

*Strychnos madagascariensis*

**Links with animals**  The leaves are eaten by duiker, kudu, impala, steenbok, nyala, giraffe and elephant. The fruit is eaten by baboons, monkeys, bushpig, nyala and eland. Dung Beetles help with seed dispersal as the seeds mimic one of the compounds in dung. The Dung Beetle rolls away the seeds in the dung ball, which is then buried.

**Human uses**  The flesh around the seeds is edible and very tasty. The seeds are eaten after being sun-dried and pounded. The dried shells are the traditional sounding boxes of the musical instrument known as the mbila or marimba. They are also made into flutes.

**Gardening**  This is a very interesting addition to the landscape garden. It grows easily from seed, and will grow fairly fast when cultivated. It is sensitive to frost, and prefers well-drained soils.

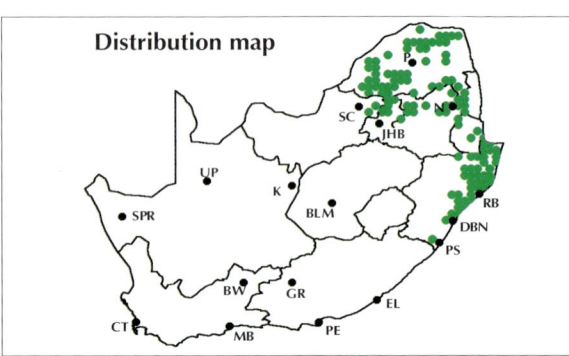
Distribution map

**Wood**  The wood is finely textured, strong, resistant and durable. It is difficult to plane and saw, not suitable for bending, and polishes well.

**Look-alike trees**  The Spine-leaved Monkey-orange (*Strychnos pungens*), the Corky-bark Monkey-orange (*Strychnos cocculoides*) and the Spiny Monkey-orange (*Strychnos spinosa*) are discussed on page 79 under comparison of Corkwoods.

*April; Rocky Area, Sour Bushveld*

# GROWTH DETAILS

This is a very variable tree. It may have a single, grooved and dented trunk, or it may be multi-stemmed, branching low down. The side branches tend to come off at right angles, ending in very short, knobbly twigs. The leaves are clustered on the short, knobbly twigs, forming a sleeve around branches to form a moderate, irregular, angular canopy.

**Leaves** The leaves are simple, and are clustered in rosettes on thick, knobbly twigs. Broadly elliptic leaves are velvety, shiny blue-green above and paler below. The margins are smooth with a round tip and a tapering base. Leaves have 3 - 5 veins radiating from the base, with the outer veins running parallel to the margin.
(Leaf: 20 - 90 x 10 - 60 mm)

**Fruit** The big, round, fleshy, orange-like fruit is characteristic. It has a hard, woody shell. The fruit may take a long time to ripen to yellow-orange, and fruit may still be present into the next flowering season. Large seeds are tightly packed inside the shell, and each seed is covered by yellow pulp (Ripens March to August).
(70 - 120 mm)

*40% life-size*

**Flowers** Small, inconspicuous, greenish-yellow, trumpet-shaped flowers grow in small clusters at the base of the leaves on the old wood. Flowers tend to appear only after good rains (November to December). (8 - 10 mm diameter)

**Bark** The bark of young trees and branches is light grey and smooth, becoming rougher and darker with age. The bark does not have spines, but has knobbly side shoots of 10 - 30 mm.

SEASONALLY STRIKING
Hairy-leaved Monkey-orange

## Seasonal changes
Semi-deciduous. This tree will be easy to find as long as some fruit is present.

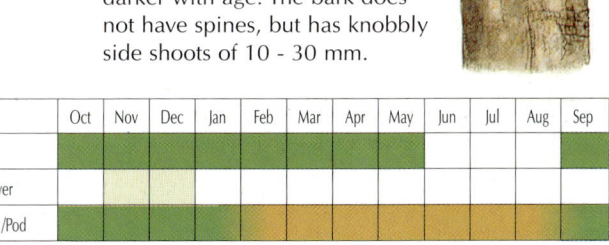

|  | Oct | Nov | Dec | Jan | Feb | Mar | Apr | May | Jun | Jul | Aug | Sep |
|---|---|---|---|---|---|---|---|---|---|---|---|---|
| Leaf | | | | | | | | | | | | |
| Flower | | | | | | | | | | | | |
| Fruit/Pod | | | | | | | | | | | | |

123

# KOOBOO-BERRY

*Mystroxylon aethiopicum (Cassine aethiopica)*   Cape Cherry; Bushveld Cherry

---

**SPIKE-THORN FAMILY**
**CELASTRACEAE**                                           SA Tree Number 410

**AFRIKAANS** Koeboebessie, Lepelhout   **SISWATI** inGulutane   **TSONGA** Nqayi   **VENDA** Mungugunu
**XHOSA** umGxube   **ZULU** umGunguluzane

The species name **aethiopicum** means 'from the country of the black people'.

## Where you'll find this tree easily

The Kooboo-berry grows singly among other trees species.

- It is easiest to find on the Plains of the Mixed Bushveld (M), Northern Mountains (N) and Sour Bushveld (S).
- It can also be found along Rivers and Streams, and on the North- or West-facing Slopes of the Sour Bushveld (S) and Central Mountains (C).

## Ecozones where this tree occurs

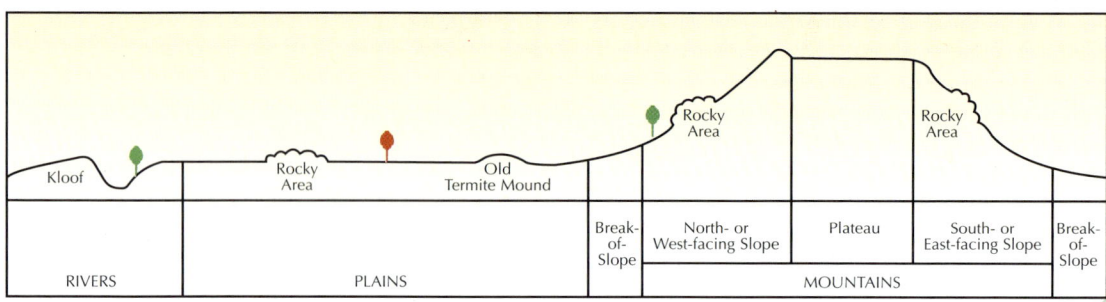

## Striking features

- **This is a single- or multi-stemmed tree that branches low down to form a moderate, irregular, blue-green canopy.**
- Long, smooth, pale grey branches spread outwards, with slender, very pale twigs carrying the leaves in untidy clumps.
- **When ripe, the mass of striking red or yellow, fleshy berries look like tiny, grooved apples (January to June).**
- The simple, elliptic leaves are stiff and leathery, with a finely toothed margin.

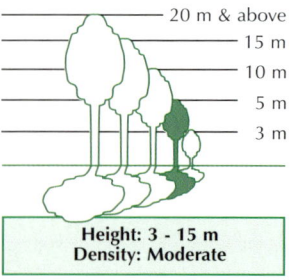

Height: 3 - 15 m
Density: Moderate

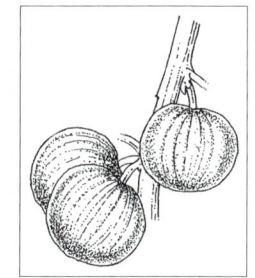

SEASONALLY STRIKING
Kooboo-berry

125

# KOOBOO-BERRY

*Mystroxylon aethiopicum (Cassine aethiopica)*

**Links with animals** The fruit is a favourite with baboons and Samango and Vervet Monkeys, and is eaten on the ground by Grey and Red Duiker, kudu, nyala, bushpigs and warthogs. Birds such as Purple-crested Louries, Green Pigeons, Cape Parrots, Black-eyed Bulbuls and Swainson's Francolin eat the fruit with relish. The leaves are not very palatable, and only duiker and Black Rhino eat them.

**Human uses** The wood is sometimes used for carvings and to make small household articles. The sticks that the Xhosa hold above their heads while dancing are traditionally obtained from this tree.

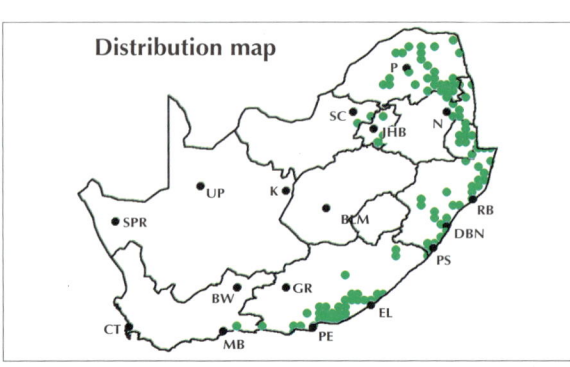

Distribution map

The fruit is sweet and edible. A brown dye comes from the bark, which is used for tanning leather, giving it a characteristic light colour. The bark sap is used as bird lime. Infusions made from the root bark were taken for dysentery and diarrhoea, and the roots were used for heartburn. Bark was used in magical charms by the Vhavenda.

**Wood** The wood has a fine grain, and is tough and hard.

**Gardening** This tree is very attractive, especially when laden with fruit, when it will attract many birds. It tolerates mild frost, is very drought-resistant, and has a moderate growth rate.

*February; young, grooved berries*

# GROWTH DETAILS

This is a single- or multi-stemmed, small tree that branches into many smaller branches to form a moderate, irregular canopy, shaped by the surrounding vegetation.

**Leaves** The simple, spiral, elliptic leaves are leathery. They have a finely toothed, sometimes smooth margin and a short leaf-stalk. The upper-surface is dark blue-green with a paler under-surface that may be slightly hairy. The central and side veins are yellowish. (20 - 90 x 10 - 60 mm)

**Fruit** The striking, berry-like fruit is fleshy, and looks like a little, grooved apple. It changes from lemon-yellow to deep pink, scarlet or purple when ripe, and the skin may be wrinkled, smooth, hairy or shiny (January to June). (8 - 25 mm)

*life-size*

*10 x enlarged*

**Flowers** Inconspicuous, yellow-green, star-shaped, sweet-scented flowers grow in small, dense clusters in the angles of the leaves (October to December). (Cluster: 10 - 13 mm)

**Bark** The bark is dark and rough in older trees, but smooth and pale grey in younger trees and on branches. Young twigs are spirally arranged, and are very pale grey and smooth, but may be hairy.

SEASONALLY STRIKING
Kooboo-berry

|  | Oct | Nov | Dec | Jan | Feb | Mar | Apr | May | Jun | Jul | Aug | Sep |
|---|---|---|---|---|---|---|---|---|---|---|---|---|
| Leaf |  |  |  |  |  |  |  |  |  |  |  |  |
| Flower |  |  |  |  |  |  |  |  |  |  |  |  |
| Fruit/Pod |  |  |  |  |  |  |  |  |  |  |  |  |

**Seasonal changes**
Evergreen. This tree is difficult to identify when it has no fruit.

# LARGE-FRUITED BUSHWILLOW

*Combretum zeyheri*

### BUSHWILLOW FAMILY
### COMBRETACEAE

**SA Tree Number 546**

**AFRIKAANS** Raasblaar  **N. SOTHO** Moduba-tshipi  **PEDI** Moduba  **TSONGA** Mafambaborile
**TSWANA** Modubana, Modube  **VENDA** Mufhatela-thundu, Mufhatela
**ZULU** umBondwe wasembudwini

The species name **zeyheri** honours the German plant collector CLP Zeyher.

## Where you'll find this tree easily

The Large-fruited Bushwillow grows singly among other tree species, but where one is found, there will be others in the vicinity.

- It is easiest to find on the Plains in all Ecozones.
- It can also be found on the North- or West-facing Slopes of the Mixed Bushveld (M), Central Mountains (C), Northern Mountains (N) and Sour Bushveld (S).

## Ecozones where this tree occurs

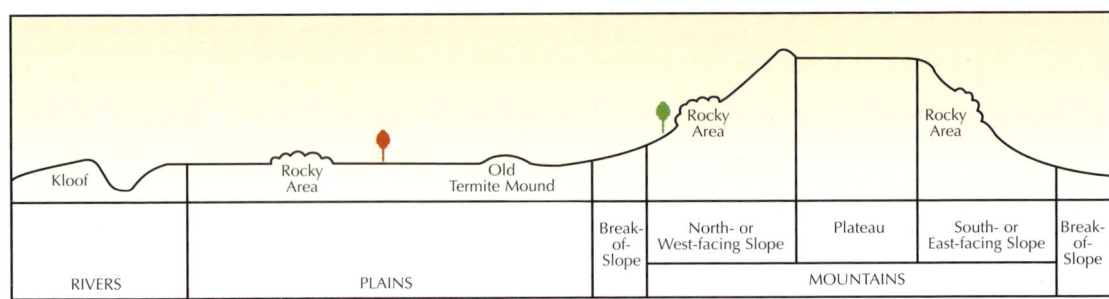

## Striking features

- **This tree has huge, yellowish-brown, four-winged pods for most of the year.**
- It is a single- or multi-stemmed tree with large, drooping leaves.
- The leaves are darkish-green, leathery and dull, and are larger than those of the other similar-looking Bushwillows.
- The branches curve downwards and may hang to the ground.
- As with most Bushwillows many young branches grow as very straight, upward shoots.

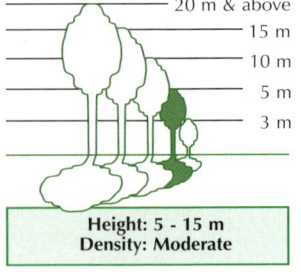

Height: 5 - 15 m
Density: Moderate

**SEASONALLY STRIKING**
Large-fruited Bushwillow

**Largest tree currently registered**

**Diameter:** 0,97 m
**Girth:** 3,04 m
**Height:** 13 m

E.A. Galpin
'Mosdene', Zyferkraal 528
Dist. Potgietersrus

# LARGE-FRUITED BUSHWILLOW

*Combretum zeyheri*

**Links with animals** This tree is not very palatable, but the leaves are eaten by giraffe and elephant. Ripe seeds are eaten by baboons.

**Human uses** The wood makes good timber and is used for yokes. Part of the root is used to make baskets and fishing traps. Leaf extracts are used to treat backache and eye ailments. The bark is used to treat gallstones, and root extracts are taken for bloody diarrhoea. Powdered bark is used to arrest menstrual flow, and as an eye lotion.

**Gardening** This tree is a very decorative addition to the garden. It grows easily but slowly from seed, and is not very resistant to cold.

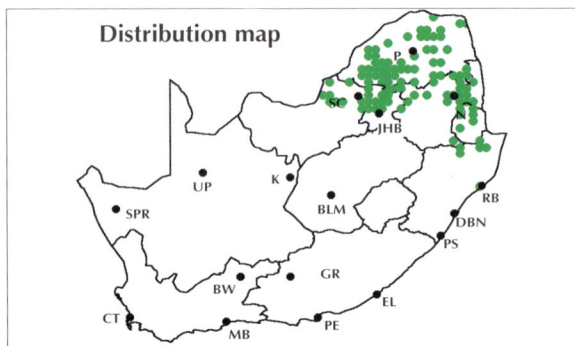

**Wood** The fresh wood is yellow, becoming whitish-yellow as it dries out. The wood is easy to work, but is not durable unless thoroughly seasoned.

**Look-alike tree** The Weeping Collina Bushwillow (*Combretum collinum*), page 75, has large, pinkish-brown, four-winged pods that are slightly smaller than those of the Large-fruited Bushwillow. The young leaves are not hairy. See page 74 - 75 for comparisons of other Bushwillows.

*May; characteristic large four-winged pods*

# GROWTH DETAILS

This is a single-stemmed or multi-stemmed tree that branches low down to form a moderately dense, irregular, roundish canopy, with branches that tend to hang down, and young shoots that grow very straight upwards.

**Leaves** The large leaves are simple and opposite, with a long, hairy leaf-stalk (15 mm). They have wavy margins, and prominent veins especially on the under-surface. They are covered with soft hair when young, but are hairless and leathery when mature. The leaves are elliptic to broadly elliptic with a rounded tip that may be pointed or notched, and a rounded to broadly tapering base. The leaves are yellow-green to dark green above and paler below. The leaves turn brilliant yellow in autumn. (25 - 140 x 30 - 85 mm)

**Pods** The conspicuous pods are the largest of the characteristic four-winged pods of the Bushwillow family. The pods are found in bunches, and are produced in such abundance that they weigh down the branches and branchlets. They are green, turning yellowish-brown when ripe, and may stay on the tree until October (February to October). (Individual pod: 50 - 100 mm diameter)

*35% life-size*

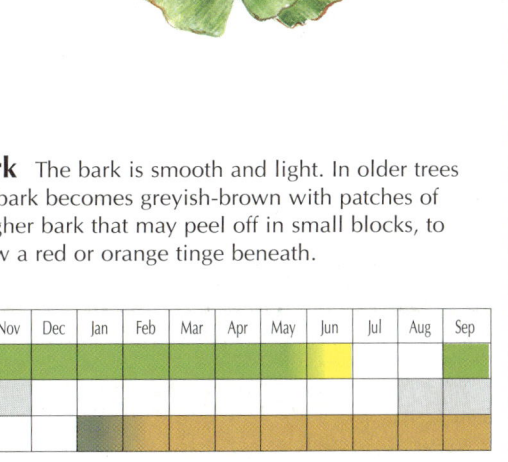

**Flowers** The small, yellow-green to yellow flowers are on dense spikes that grow singly in the angle formed by the leaf. The flowers appear just before, or with, the new leaves, and may be pleasantly or unpleasantly scented (August to November). (Flower-spike: up to 75 x 25 mm)

**Bark** The bark is smooth and light. In older trees the bark becomes greyish-brown with patches of rougher bark that may peel off in small blocks, to show a red or orange tinge beneath.

## Seasonal changes
Deciduous. It can be identified for most of the year while the pods are present.

|  | Oct | Nov | Dec | Jan | Feb | Mar | Apr | May | Jun | Jul | Aug | Sep |
|---|---|---|---|---|---|---|---|---|---|---|---|---|
| Leaf | | | | | | | | | | | | |
| Flower | | | | | | | | | | | | |
| Fruit/Pod | | | | | | | | | | | | |

**SEASONALLY STRIKING**
Large-fruited Bushwillow

# LARGE SOURPLUM

*Ximenia caffra*                                                                                              Sourplum

| SOURPLUM FAMILY OLACACEAE | SA Tree Number 103 |

**AFRIKAANS** Grootsuurpruim  **N. SOTHO** Motšhidi, Hwele  **TSONGA** Ntsengele, Ntsengele-lowu-kulu  **TSWANA** Morêtologane, Morêtologa wa podi  **VENDA** Mutanzwa-dombo, Mutshili  **ZULU** umThunduluka

The species name **caffra** is from the Hebrew 'kafri' meaning 'person living on the land'.

## Where you'll find this tree easily

This tree grows singly among other species of trees, often among rocks.

- It is easiest to find on all Rocky Areas of the Mixed Bushveld (M).
- It can also be found in Rocky Areas and Plains of the Central Mountains (C), the Northern Mountains (N) and the Sour Bushveld (S); and on South- and East-facing Slopes of the Northern Mountains (N) and the Mixed Bushveld (M).

## Ecozones where this tree occurs

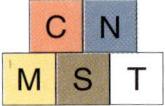

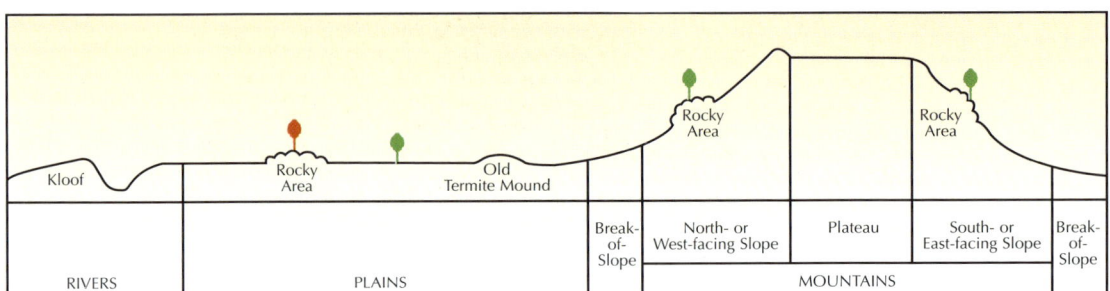

## Striking features

- **This is a small, spiny tree that branches low down into numerous main branches and then grow upwards to form a sparse, untidy, irregular canopy.**
- The dull green, simple leaves grow on short spine-tipped branchlets, and tend to fold inwards.
- The characteristic plum-like fruit turns red when ripe, and has a strong, sourish taste.

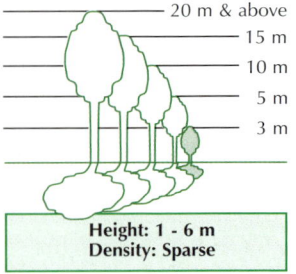

Height: 1 - 6 m
Density: Sparse

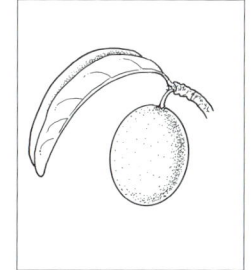

SEASONALLY STRIKING
Large Sourplum

133

# LARGE SOURPLUM

*Ximenia caffra*

**Links with animals** The leaves are browsed by antelope, and the fruit is eaten by birds and animals. Caterpillars of the following butterflies eat the leaves: Natal Bar (*Spindasis natalensis*), Silvery Bar (*Spindasis phanes*), Bowker's Sapphire (*Iolaus bowkeri*), Saffron Sapphire (*Iolaus pallene*), Brown Playboy (*Deudrox antalus*) and Bush Scarlet (*Axiocerses amanga*).

**Human uses** The fruit is tasty, and has a high Vitamin C and potassium content. The oil from the seed is used to rub chapped feet and to anoint the body. An extract from the leaves is used to soothe inflamed eyes, while dried leaves are taken to break fevers. A root extract is used as a remedy for dysentery and diarrhoea, abdominal pains and bilharzia. Powdered roots are used to heal sores.

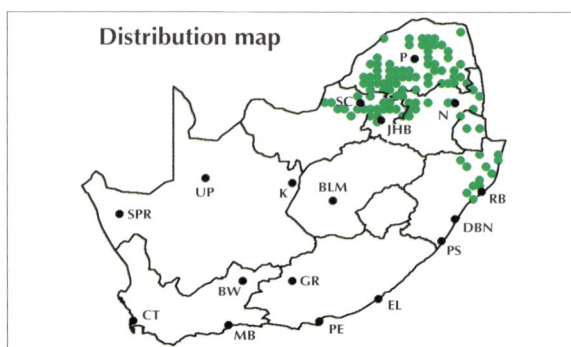
Distribution map

**Wood** The extensive sapwood is yellowish-white, and the irregular heartwood is red-brown. The wood is hard and relatively heavy, has a fine texture, and polishes well.

**Gardening** This tree is an attractive addition to the garden, and makes an ideal container plant. The fruit is beautiful and tasty, and attracts birds. The tree can withstand moderate frost and is drought-resistant when mature. It grows easily from seed, and has a moderate growth rate.

**Look-alike tree** The Blue Sourplum (*Ximenia americana*) is very similar but is a more branched, smaller tree, with blue-green leaves. The fruit of the Blue Sourplum is smaller, and is orange, not red, when ripe.

*December; conspicuous, glossy fruit*

# GROWTH DETAILS

This is a small, spiny, single- or multi-stemmed tree that branches low down and generally grows upwards to form a sparse, untidy, irregular canopy.

**Leaves** The simple leaves tend to fold inwards along the obvious central vein. They have shortish, sometimes hairy leaf-stalks (8 mm), and grow alternately in the angles made by the spines, or in groups on short side branchlets. The leaves are elliptic, and have a rounded-to-notched tip, rounded base and smooth margin. Mature leaves are leathery, dark green and shiny above, and paler green below. Young leaves sometimes have rusty hairs. (30 - 80 x 20 - 40 mm)

**Fruit** The conspicuous plum grows on short stalks. The fruit, speckled with white spots, is initially green and ripens to glossy bright red. Each fruit contains one seed. (Ripens November to January) (40 x 25 mm)

**Thorns** This tree sometimes has scattered hairy spines, or twigs ending in spines, but sometimes entirely lacks spines.

**Flowers** The sweet-scented, creamy-white, star-shaped flowers are found singly or in groups in the angle made by the spine or the leaf. (August to October) (Individual: 12 mm)

*50% life-size*

**Bark** The bark is green to pale brown and covered in dense rusty hairs on younger trees. With age, the bark becomes grey to dark grey and rough, breaking into small, rectangular scales.

## Seasonal changes
Deciduous. The tree will be difficult to identify without leaves.

|  | Oct | Nov | Dec | Jan | Feb | Mar | Apr | May | Jun | Jul | Aug | Sep |
|---|---|---|---|---|---|---|---|---|---|---|---|---|
| Leaf | | | | | | | | | | | | |
| Flower | | | | | | | | | | | | |
| Fruit/Pod | | | | | | | | | | | | |

SEASONALLY STRIKING
Large Sourplum

135

# PEELING-BARK OCHNA

*Ochna pulchra*　　　　　　　　　　　　　　　　Lekkerbreek; Peeling Plane; Wild Pear

## WILD PLANE FAMILY
## OCHNACEAE

SA Tree Number 483

**AFRIKAANS** Lekkerbreek　**N. SOTHO** Monamane　**TSONGA** Nzololo　**TSWANA** Monyêlênyêlê
**VENDA** Tshithothonya, Murambo

The species name **pulchra** means beautiful.

## Where you'll find this tree easily

The Peeling-bark Ochna grows singly among other species of trees, and prefers sandy soils.

- It is easiest to find on the South- or East-facing Slopes of the Mixed Bushveld (M).
- It can also be found on the South- or East-facing Slopes of the other Ecozones; and on the Plains of the Northern Mountains (N) and Central Mountains (C); as well as on the North- or West-facing Slopes of the Sour Bushveld (S) and Mixed Bushveld (M).

## Ecozones where this tree occurs

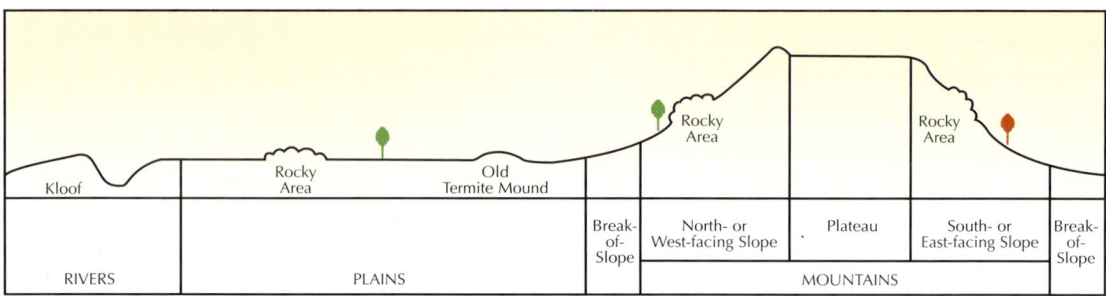

## Striking features

- This is a single-trunked tree that branches fairly low down to form a moderate, spreading canopy.
- **The characteristic pale grey bark peels in large, loose sections to reveal smooth, creamy-yellow patches of under-bark.**
- Pale yellow, star-shaped flowers cover the tree in early spring (August to November).
- The berry-like fruit turns black when ripe, and is surrounded by conspicuous red, flower-like 'petals' (sepals) (October to January).
- The simple, alternate leaves have an obvious central vein. They are coppery-green when young, and become shiny yellow-green when mature.

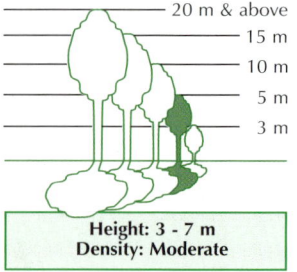

Height: 3 - 7 m
Density: Moderate

**SEASONALLY STRIKING**
Peeling-bark Ochna

**Largest tree currently registered**

**Diameter:** 0,53 m
**Girth:** 1,66 m
**Height:** 12 m

AJ Rodger, Louwskraal,
Dist. Potgietersrus

# PEELING-BARK OCHNA

*Ochna pulchra*

**Links with animals** Mature leaves are eaten by browsers, such as kudu. There are however reports of cattle being poisoned by eating young leaves. Peeling Plane and Wild Seringa are indicators of where the very poisonous Gifblaar (*Dichapetalum cymosum*) occurs.

**Human uses** Tobacco pipes are sometimes made from the wood. The pulp of the fruit is edible, but the seeds are poisonous. Khoisan people roast and eat the green fruit. The oil from the fruit and the seed is used as hair oil, for cooking, and to make candles and soap.

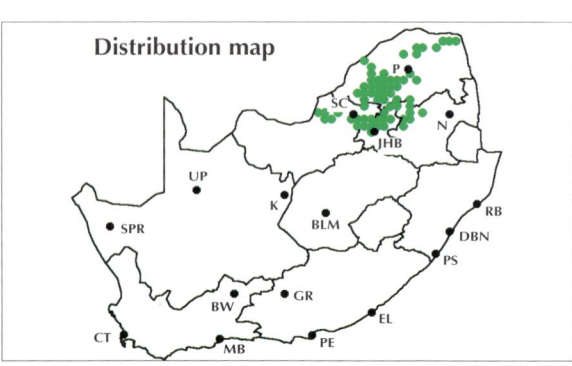

Distribution map

**Wood** The wood is pale red, soft and short-grained. It snaps and cracks easily, and the Afrikaans name 'Lekkerbreek' is derived from this. The grain is fine, and cross-cuts can be smoothly worked and well polished.

**Gardening** This attractive little tree has lovely flowers and fruit. It grows well, but slowly, in warm areas with well-drained soil. It is difficult to grow from seed, apparently needing to be processed by the acids of a bird's digestive system first. It is fairly frost-resistant, but can withstand dry periods.

**Look-alike tree** The Showy Ochna (*Ochna natalitia*), page 60, has very similar flowers and fruit, but the margins of the leaves are toothed. It is a smaller multi-stemmed tree, with rough, grey bark that does not peel. The Showy Ochna is more common than the Peeling-bark Ochna in the Sour Bushveld.

*Striking peeling bark helps with identification*

# GROWTH DETAILS

This is an often single-trunked, fairly low-branching, small to medium-sized tree with a moderate, spreading canopy. The tree usually has a fairly straight trunk, and the leaves are crowded towards the ends of branchlets and twigs.

**Leaves** The simple, alternate leaves have a short leaf-stalk (3 - 5 mm), and are crowded towards the ends of thickish twigs, forming rosettes. They are broadly elliptic with a smooth margin that may be slightly toothed towards the rounded tip. The central vein is obvious on both surfaces. New leaves are pale coppery-green, maturing to fresh pale green or yellowish-green. (35 - 185 x 13 - 57 mm)

**Fruit** The flower-like fruit consists of 1 - 3 kidney-shaped berries that are initially pale green, but turn black when ripe. Attached to the base of the fruit are showy pink to coral red, flower-like 'petals' (sepals) (Ripens October to January). (14 mm long)

*80% life-size*

**Flowers** The small, sweet-scented, pale yellow flowers are star-shaped, and are found in sprays at the ends of twigs. They appear with, or just before, the new leaves (August to November). (Spray: up to 130 mm long; individual: 20 mm diameter)

**Bark** The diagnostic bark is pale grey and peels loosely to reveal a creamy-yellow under-surface, which can be seen from a distance. The branchlets and twigs also have pale bark.

SEASONALLY STRIKING
Peeling-bark Ochna

## Seasonal changes
Deciduous. Can be identified by its bark throughout the year.

|  | Oct | Nov | Dec | Jan | Feb | Mar | Apr | May | Jun | Jul | Aug | Sep |
|---|---|---|---|---|---|---|---|---|---|---|---|---|
| Leaf |  |  |  |  |  |  |  |  |  |  |  |  |
| Flower |  |  |  |  |  |  |  |  |  |  |  |  |
| Fruit/Pod |  |  |  |  |  |  |  |  |  |  |  |  |

139

# RED BUSHWILLOW

*Combretum apiculatum*

## BUSHWILLOW FAMILY
## COMBRETACEAE

S A Tree Number 532

**AFRIKAANS** Rooiboswilg  **N. SOTHO** Mohwelere  **SISWATI** umBondomyana, inKukutu
**TSONGA** Xikukutsi  **TSWANA** Mofudiri, Mogodiri  **VENDA** Musingidzi  **ZULU** umBondwe omnyama

The species name **apiculatum** refers to the sharp tip of the leaf.

## Where you'll find this tree easily

This tree normally grows in loose, scattered groups.
- It is easiest to find on North- or West-facing Slopes of all Ecozones.
- It can also be found on the Plains and in Rocky Areas of all Ecozones.

## Ecozones where this tree occurs

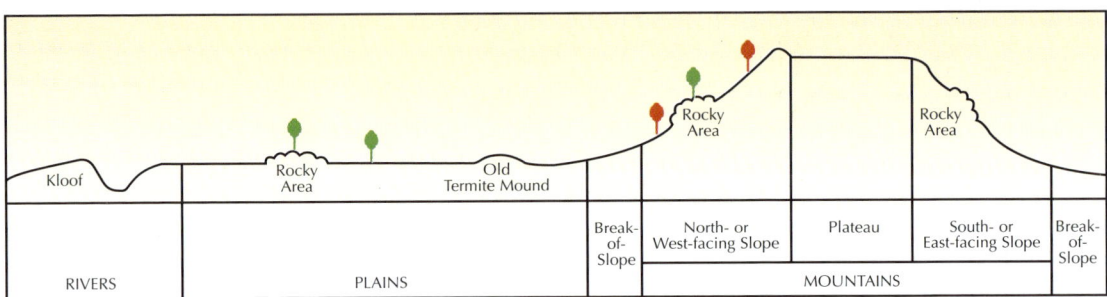

## Striking features

- This is a single- or multi-stemmed tree with a short, often curved stem, and a spreading, irregular canopy.
- The long, slender branches hang low down, giving some trees a drooping, willow-like appearance.
- **The medium-sized, rich yellow-brown, four-winged pods are visible most of the year.**
- **The simple leaves have a sharp, twisted tip.**
- Groups of trees with their red, yellow and brown leaves are conspicuous in autumn, even from quite a distance away.

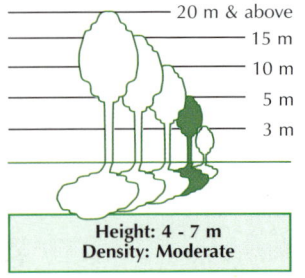

Height: 4 - 7 m
Density: Moderate

SEASONALLY STRIKING
Red Bushwillow

141

# RED BUSHWILLOW

*Combretum apiculatum*

**Links with animals** Young or fallen leaves are eaten by kudu, bushbuck, eland, giraffe and elephant. The seeds are eaten by Brown-headed Parrots.

**Human uses** The wood is used for fence posts and to make furniture. Extracts of the leaves were used for stomach complaints.

**Gardening** This is an attractive garden tree, and established trees are frost- and drought-resistant. The tree grows slowly.

**Look-alike trees** All Bushwillows have simple opposite leaves and winged pods. For a detailed comparison of other Bushwillows found in the Bushveld, see pages 74 - 75.

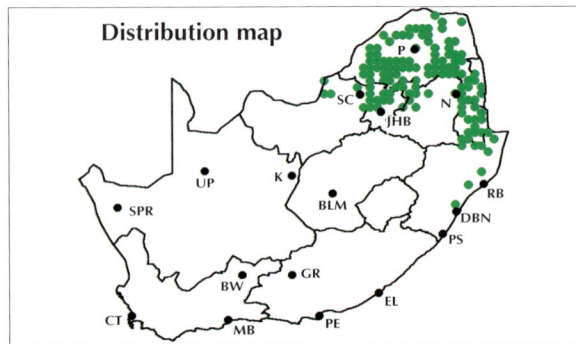

**Wood** The wood is exceptionally hard and durable, with black heartwood and yellow sapwood. It is suitable for turning.

*Striking autumn colours; West-facing Slope, Mixed Bushveld*

# GROWTH DETAILS

This is a single- or multi-stemmed tree with an irregular, moderate canopy. The end branches and twigs are thin, and tend to droop down.

**Leaves**  Leaves are simple, opposite and broadly elliptic, with a slightly wavy margin. They are shiny yellow-green, and yellow leaves are seen among the green ones for most of the year. The tip of the leaf is sharp and twisted, and the veins are obvious on both the upper- and under-surfaces.
(30 - 100 x 20 - 60 mm)

**Pods**  The characteristic four-winged pods, with a single seed in the centre, hang in large bunches that ripen to a rich yellow-brown (Ripen January to May). Pods often stay on the tree until the next flowers appear in August.
(20 - 30 mm)

*50% life-size*

**Flowers**  The creamy-yellow, sweet-smelling flower-spikes grow in groups of 1 - 4 in the angles of the leaves. They are not very conspicuous, but give the tree a lemon-yellow tinge in spring and early summer when they appear with the new leaves (September to October). (Spike: 70 x 20 mm)

**Bark**  The bark is grey to blackish, and cracks into irregular blocks that flake off in flat pieces. The bark on the smaller branches and twigs is green to light brown, and smooth.

## Seasonal changes
Deciduous. This tree is very difficult to find in winter if there are no pods to help identification.

|  | Oct | Nov | Dec | Jan | Feb | Mar | Apr | May | Jun | Jul | Aug | Sep |
|---|---|---|---|---|---|---|---|---|---|---|---|---|
| Leaf | | | | | | | | | | | | |
| Flower | | | | | | | | | | | | |
| Fruit/Pod | | | | | | | | | | | | |

SEASONALLY STRIKING
Red Bushwillow

# RUSSET BUSHWILLOW

*Combretum hereroense*

---

## BUSHWILLOW FAMILY
## COMBRETACEAE

SA Tree Number 538

**AFRIKAANS** Kierieklapper  **N. SOTHO** Mokabi  **PEDI** Mokata  **SISWATI** isiHlahlavane
**TSONGA** Mpotsa  **TSWANA** Mokabi  **VENDA** Mugavhi  **ZULU** umHlalavane

The species name **hereroense** refers to the Herero people of Namibia.

## Where you'll find this tree easily
The Russet Bushwillow grows in scattered groups.
- It is easiest to find on the Plains of the Mixed Bushveld (M).
- It can also be found on the Plains of the Thorny Bushveld (T), Northern and Central Mountains (C, N), and Sour Bushveld (S); and along Rivers and Streams of the Mixed Bushveld (M).

## Ecozones where this tree occurs

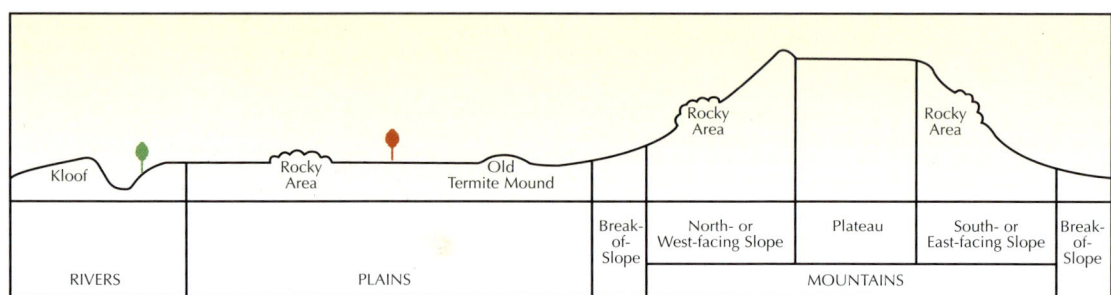

## Striking features
- This is a small, often multi-stemmed tree, with one or more thick, crooked, often curved stems.
- **From January to July it often has an overall coppery appearance because of large numbers of conspicuous russet pods.**
- The pods are the characteristic four-winged Combretum shape, but are smaller than those of other similar-sized Bushwillow trees.
- It is densely branched, and, as with most Bushwillows, new young branches form very straight, upward shoots.

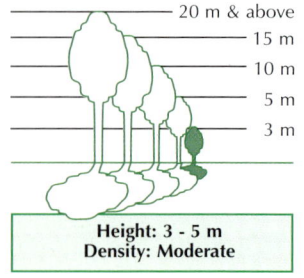

Height: 3 - 5 m
Density: Moderate

SEASONALLY STRIKING
Russet Bushwillow

145

# RUSSET BUSHWILLOW

*Combretum hereroense*

**Links with animals** The leaves are eaten by kudu, impala, steenbok, elephant and giraffe.

**Human uses** The wood is used as supports in mines, and to make pick and hoe handles. Straight branches are used to make kieries (walking sticks), hence the Afrikaans name 'Kierieklapper'. Root extracts are used for stomach complaints, as enemas, to treat venereal diseases, and for pains in the body. Bark is used for heart disease and heartburn. Dried young shoots are used for tonsilitis and coughs.

**Gardening** This is not a very attractive garden plant, except in autumn when it is covered in coppery fruit. However it should grow well in most gardens as it is drought-resistant and can withstand fairly sharp frost. It can be grown from seed, and will grow quite fast when well-watered. The seeds are thought to be poisonous.

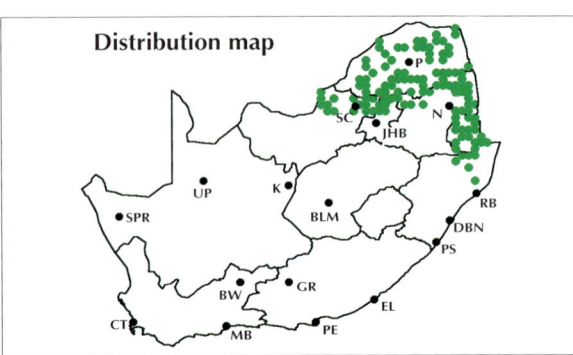

**Wood** The wood is very hard and heavy. The sapwood is brown, and the heartwood reddish-brown with dark markings. It is termite- and borer-proof.

**Look-alike trees** All Bushwillows have simple opposite leaves and winged pods. For a detailed comparison of other Bushwillows found in the Bushveld, see pages 74 - 75.

*Tree with pods in autumn; Plains, Central Mountains*

# GROWTH DETAILS

It is small and multi-stemmed, with branchlets growing vertically upwards from bigger, horizontal branches. It often has an overall coppery appearance due to masses of pods.

**Leaves** Simple, opposite, elliptic to heart-shaped leaves have a smooth margin. They are bicoloured, with dark green above and light green-brown below. (30 x 20 mm)

**Pods** The four-winged pods grow abundantly in prominent bunches, and, although smaller, are characteristic of the Bushwillow family. They are brilliant russet-red in summer, changing to a light, coppery-brown later in the season. Pods appear in mid to late summer, and remain on the tree for long periods, often until July. (Pods: approximately 23 x 20 mm)

**Flowers** The sweet-smelling flowers vary from white or cream-coloured, to yellow, and are found in dense spikes that grow in the angle formed by leaves, or on the tips of twigs. The flowers appear before, or with, the new leaves (August to November). (Flower-spike: up to 60 x 15 mm)

*75% life-size*

**Bark** The bark is grey with longitudinal grooves that may peel off.

**Seasonal changes**
Deciduous. Leaves and fruit fall in late autumn, after which identification is difficult.

|  | Oct | Nov | Dec | Jan | Feb | Mar | Apr | May | Jun | Jul | Aug | Sep |
|---|---|---|---|---|---|---|---|---|---|---|---|---|
| Leaf |  |  |  |  |  |  |  |  |  |  |  |  |
| Flower |  |  |  |  |  |  |  |  |  |  |  |  |
| Fruit/Pod |  |  |  |  |  |  |  |  |  |  |  |  |

# SACRED CORAL-TREE

*Erythrina lysistemon*  **Common Coral Tree; Lucky Bean Tree**

## PEA FAMILY
## FABACEAE

**SA Tree Number 245**

**AFRIKAANS** Gewone Koraalboom  **N. SOTHO** Mokhupye, Mmalê  **SISWATI** umSisi
**TSONGA** Nsisimbana, Muvale  **TSWANA** Mophêthê  **VENDA** Muvhale  **XHOSA** umSintsi
**ZULU** umSinsi

The species name **lysistemon** refers to the stamen that stands separate in the tube-like flower.

## Where you'll find this tree easily

The Sacred Coral-tree grows singly among other tree species.

- It is easiest to find on the Plains of the Northern Mountains (N) and Sour Bushveld (S).
- It can also be found along Rivers and Streams of the Thorny Bushveld (T); and on South- or East-facing Slopes of the Mixed Bushveld (M) and Sour Bushveld (S); as well as on North- or West-facing Slopes of the Sour Bushveld (S).

## Ecozones where this tree occurs

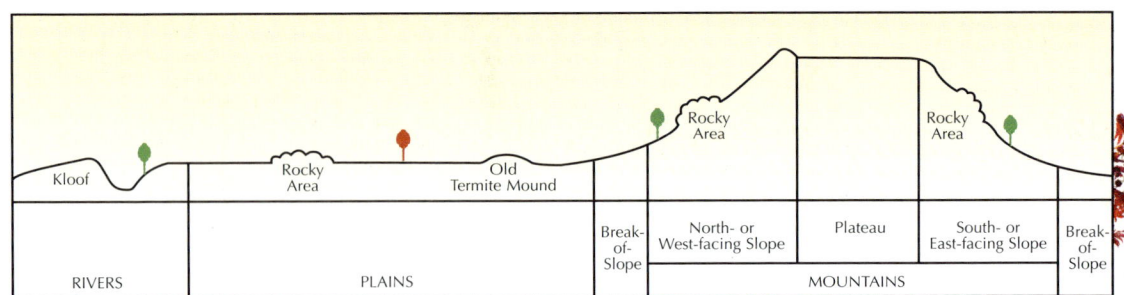

## Striking features

- This is a single-trunked tree that forms a moderate, rounded canopy, with large, angular branches visible among the leaves.
- The bark is light grey-brown. On the trunk and branches it is smooth between shallow lengthways grooves, and dark, slightly hooked thorns.
- **The compound leaves have three heart-shaped leaflets, the terminal one distinctly larger, with a longer leaflet-stalk.**
- **The red flowers are aloe-like and conspicuous in winter and early spring on the leafless tree.**
- The bumpy bean pods burst open on the tree to reveal characteristic black-and-red seeds (September to February).

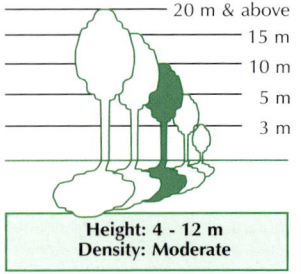

Height: 4 - 12 m
Density: Moderate

SEASONALLY STRIKING
Sacred Coral-tree

# SACRED CORAL-TREE

*Erythrina lysistemon*

**Links with animals**  The leaves and bark are eaten by Black Rhino, elephant, baboons, kudu, nyala and klipspringer. Unripe seeds are a favourite of the Brown-headed Parrot, and many sunbirds and insects are attracted to the nectar. Vervet Monkeys regard flower-buds as a delicacy.

**Human uses**  Canoes and troughs are made from hollowed trunks, and wood is used as floats for fishing nets. It has many medicinal uses: a poultice of the bark for swellings, sores, wounds, abscesses and arthritis; an infusion of bark for toothache, and an infusion of leaves for ear-drops to relieve earache; crushed leaves clear the maggots from infested wounds, and counteract inflammation. A branch from this tree growing near a man's hut was planted on his grave, and the seeds are often still used as lucky charms.

**Gardening**  This is a very attractive, fast-growing garden tree. It grows easily from seed, and may flower within a year. It is fairly drought-resistant, and will tolerate several degrees of frost.

**Look-alike tree**  The Broad-leaved Coral-tree (*Erythrina latissima*), page 67, has similar flowers, but the leaflets are large (200 - 600 mm), rounded and very hairy, and the bark is coarse and rough.

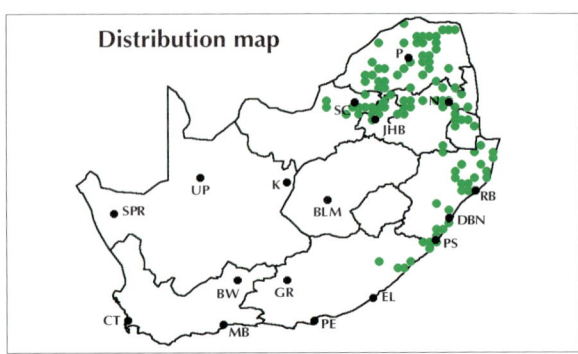

Distribution map

**Wood**  The wood has a straight grain with white heartwood and sapwood. It has poor nail-holding properties, saws cleanly and is not suitable for turning.

*July; flowers on bare twigs*

# GROWTH DETAILS

This is a single-trunked tree that forms a moderate, rounded canopy, with large, angular branches visible among the leaves.

**Leaves**  The three-leaflet compound leaves are alternate, and are crowded towards the ends of the branchlets and twigs. The heart-shaped, dark green leaflets have smooth margins, and the central vein is prominent on both surfaces. New leaves are a bright, light green. The end leaflet is larger, with a longer leaflet-stalk than the side leaflets. The leaf-stalks are long (160 mm) and may have scattered thorns. (Leaf: 60 - 220 mm; end leaflet: 110 - 125 mm; side leaflets: 80 - 110 mm)

*55% life-size*

**Flowers**  Conspicuous, erect, red flower-spikes usually appear before the leaves in winter and early spring. The tightly packed flowers each consist of a large, tube-like petal. This encloses the stamens and smaller petals so that they are not visible (June to October). (Spray: 90 mm; individual: 40 - 60 mm)

**Thorns**  Slightly hooked thorns are dark brown, with a broad base and a very sharp point, resembling those of a rose. Thorns are sparsely scattered on the main trunk and branches, but are much closer together on the smaller branchlets and twigs. (3 - 7 mm)

**Pods**  Tightly constricted, bumpy bean pods hang in clusters. When ripe, they burst open to expose shiny, black-and-red, bead-like seeds that resemble lucky beans. Pods stay on the tree for long periods (September to February). (90 - 200 x 11 - 15 mm)

**Bark**  The bark is pale grey-brown, fairly smooth and often grooved lengthways, with scattered brown, hooked thorns.

SEASONALLY STRIKING
Sacred Coral-tree

## Seasonal changes
Deciduous. Leaves turn yellow in autumn. The tree can often still be identified by its bark, thorns and pods even when no leaves are present.

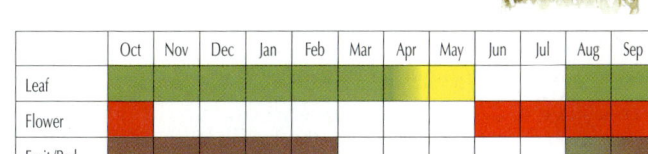

|  | Oct | Nov | Dec | Jan | Feb | Mar | Apr | May | Jun | Jul | Aug | Sep |
|---|---|---|---|---|---|---|---|---|---|---|---|---|
| Leaf | | | | | | | | | | | | |
| Flower | | | | | | | | | | | | |
| Fruit/Pod | | | | | | | | | | | | |

# WHITE CATS-WHISKERS

*Clerodendrum glabrum*

White cat's whiskers; Tinderwood; Stinkleaf Tree; Resin-leaf

**VERBENA FAMILY**
**VERBENACEAE**

SA Tree Number 667

**AFRIKAANS** Tontelhout, Stinkboom  **N. SOTHO** Mohlokohloko  **TSONGA** Xinhun'welambeva
**VENDA** Munukha-tshilongwe  **XHOSA** umQwaqu, umQangazani  **ZULU** umQaqongo

The species name **glabrum** refers to the leaves, which are mostly without hairs.

## Where you'll find this tree easily

The White Cats-whiskers normally grows singly or in scattered groups, and is very striking when flowering.

- It is easiest to find on the Plains of the Mixed Bushveld (M) and Sour Bushveld (S).
- It can also be found on the plains of the Thorny Bushveld (T), along Rivers and Streams and on South- or East-facing Slopes of the Sour Bushveld (S), Central Mountains (C) and Northern Mountains (N); and on the North- or West-facing Slopes of the Central Mountains (C) and the Sour Bushveld (S).

## Ecozones where this tree occurs

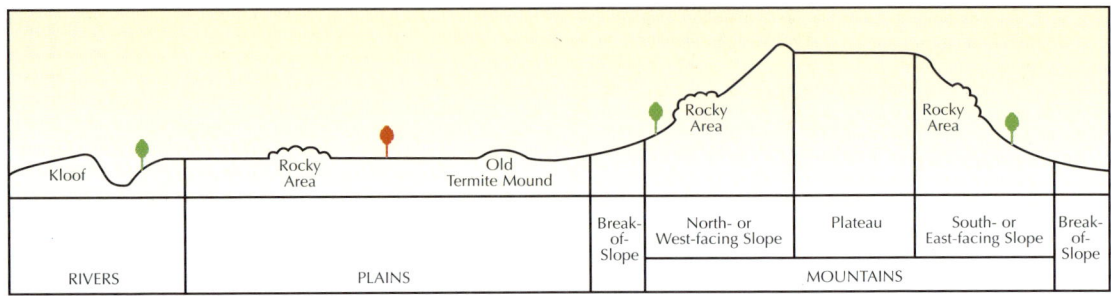

## Striking features

- This is a multi-stemmed or low-branching, single-stemmed tree, with main branches forming a dense, V-shaped canopy.
- The leaves grow in whorls of three, and each leaf arches downwards towards the branchlet or twig.
- Leaves are clustered towards the ends of the twigs and branchlets.
- The compact clusters of white flowers grow at the ends of the twigs and branches, above the leaves, making the tree very striking from November to April.
- The straw-coloured, fleshy, berry-like fruit is clustered at the ends of the branchlets and twigs from February to July.

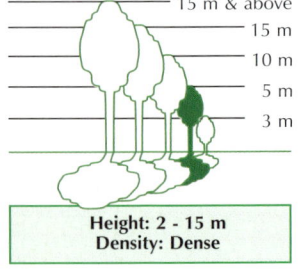

Height: 2 - 15 m
Density: Dense

SEASONALLY STRIKING
White Cats-whiskers

153

# WHITE CATS-WHISKERS

*Clerodendrum glabrum*

**Links with animals** The flowers attract many insects, especially butterflies, and the tree is the breeding place for the caterpillars of two butterflies. This is one of the 'rain trees' of South Africa – small insects known as Frog-hoppers suck the moisture from the branches; it is then excreted as drops of water that fall to the ground below. The caterpillars of the Natal Red Bar butterfly live in tubes in the stems, formed by ants eating out the pith, and from these they emerge at night to eat the leaves. The fruit is eaten by White-eyes and Bulbuls.

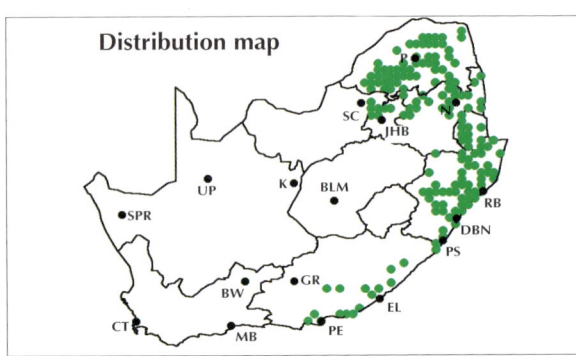

Distribution map

**Human uses** The wood was used as firesticks to start fires. Parts of the plant are repellent to beetles, and the leaves are rubbed over the hands and face before collecting honey, to keep bees from attacking. A solution of the leaves was used to treat coughs and colds, to aid sleep and to prevent bad dreams.

**Wood** The wood is hard and closely grained. It is suitable for turning, and varnishes well.

**Human uses (continued)** Leaf extracts were used to expel roundworm and threadworm, as a disinfectant, and to prevent maggot infection in wounds. The root is a widely known snakebite remedy, used in particular for mamba bites. Leaves were used to drive away evil spirits.

**Gardening** This is a fast-growing, attractive tree. It may be grown from seed or cuttings. It will flower about one year after planting.

*January: conspicuous flower-heads on the ends of branchlets*

# GROWTH DETAILS

This is a single- or multi-stemmed, often low-branching tree. The branches grow upwards to form a dense, V-shaped canopy. The leaves are clustered towards the tips of the branches, and hang down like drooping feathers, creating a soft, rounded effect.

**Leaves**  The simple, broadly elliptic leaves arch downwards and grow in whorls of three or four, and are crowded towards the ends of the branchlets and twigs. The leaves have a slightly wavy margin and a tapering tip and base. There is a prominent central vein, and the side veins curl at the margin of the leaf. The upper-surface is shiny dark or grey-green, and the under-surface is paler and may be covered by short hairs. The leaves have an unpleasant smell when crushed. The leaf size is very variable. (Leaf: 20 - 250 x 10 - 70 mm)

**Flowers**  Small, white to pinkish, trumpet-shaped flowers have long filaments and are crowded in conspicuous, large, compact heads. These grow at the ends of branchlets and twigs in the centre of the leaf-rosettes. They are strong-smelling, and the smell may be offensive or sweet (November to April). (Head: 50 mm; individual: 10 mm)

*60% life-size*

**Fruit**  The fleshy, berry-like fruit is crowded together in a compact head that stands out above the leaf-rosette. Each 'berry' (drupe) is held in a brown, cup-like structure (calyx). The fruit is light yellow when ripe (February to July). (Head: 50 - 80 mm; individual: 10 mm)

**Bark**  The light brown-grey bark becomes cracked and flaky with age to reveal pale brown under-bark. The branchlets are light grey and are characteristically covered by distinct white marks (lenticels). Twigs may be hairy when young.

## Seasonal changes
Deciduous. This tree is easiest to identify when in flower or fruit.

|  | Oct | Nov | Dec | Jan | Feb | Mar | Apr | May | Jun | Jul | Aug | Sep |
|---|---|---|---|---|---|---|---|---|---|---|---|---|
| Leaf | | | | | | | | | | | | |
| Flower | | | | | | | | | | | | |
| Fruit/Pod | | | | | | | | | | | | |

SEASONALLY STRIKING
White Cats-whiskers

# WILD-PEAR DOMBEYA

*Dombeya rotundifolia*

Wild pear; Common Wild Pear; Blossom tree

### STAR-CHESTNUT FAMILY
### STERCULIACEAE

SA Tree Number 471

**AFRIKAANS** Drolpeer, Gewone Drolpeer  **N. SOTHO** Mokgoba  **SISWATI** umBikanyaka, umWane  **TSONGA** Xiluvarhi, Nsihaphukuma  **TSWANA** Mokgofa, Motubane  **VENDA** Tshiluvhari  **ZULU** uNhliziyonkulu

The species name **rotundifolia** refers to the round form of the leaf.

## Where you'll find this tree easily

The Wild-pear Dombeya grows singly among other tree species.

- It is easiest to find on South- or East-facing Slopes of all Ecozones.
- It can also be found in Rocky Areas, on Old Termite Mounds on the Plains, and on North- or West-facing Slopes of Mixed Bushveld (M), Northern Mountains (N) and Sour Bushveld (S); and along Rivers.

## Ecozones where this tree occurs

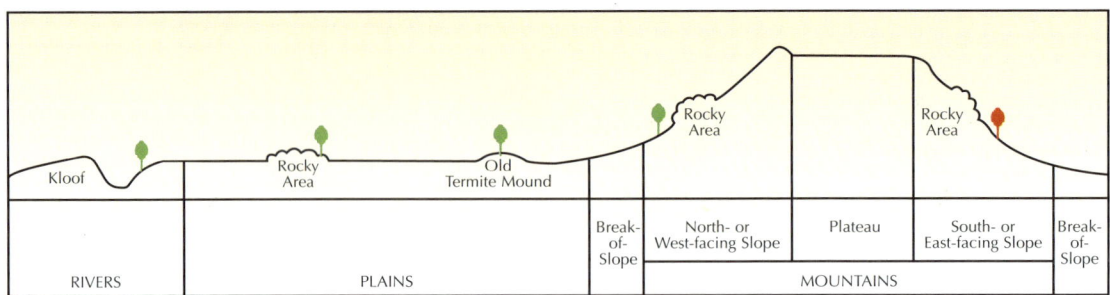

## Striking features

- This is a single-stemmed tree with a moderate, irregular canopy.
- The star-like, papery flowers are cream-coloured to pink, and cover the whole tree in late winter and early spring before the leaves appear.
- The simple, rigid leaves are hairy, rough and parchment-like, and are conspicuously round.
- The bark is rough and dark brown to black.

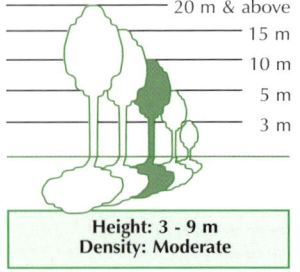

Height: 3 - 9 m
Density: Moderate

SEASONALLY STRIKING
Wild-pear Dombeya

# WILD-PEAR DOMBEYA

*Dombeya rotundifolia*

**Links with animals** Many butterflies are attracted to the flowers, and the caterpillars of three species of butterfly eat the leaves.

**Human uses** The wood is used for yokes and mine props. The bark fibre is used to make rope. The tree is widely used for medicinal purposes: the inner bark to treat heart weakness, and nausea in pregnant women; infusions of the bark or wood as enemas and for intestinal ulceration; the flowers for a love potion.

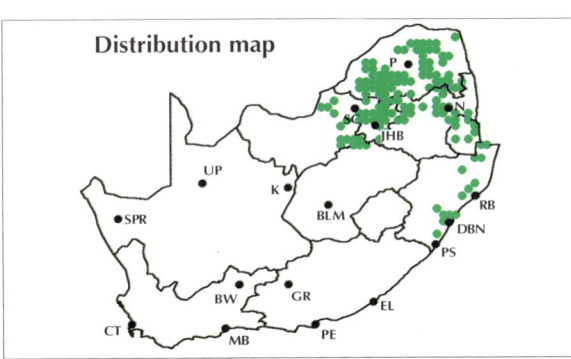

Distribution map

**Wood** The wood has a pale pinky-brown heartwood with creamy-brown sapwood. It holds nails well and varnishes to a good finish.

**Gardening** This tree is very attractive in spring. It grows fast and well from seed in well-prepared soil with adequate moisture. It is resistant to light frost and drought. It is suitable as a bonsai tree.

*Profusion of spring flowers before the leaves*

# GROWTH DETAILS

This is a single-stemmed tree with a straight trunk and a densely branched, moderate, irregular canopy. Large branches are normally visible in the canopy.

*life-size*

**Leaves** Simple, round leaves are alternate on older twigs and spiral on young twigs. The margins of the round leaves are irregularly and roundly toothed. The leaves are rigid and covered by coarse hairs, giving the leaf a sandpapery feel. The upper-surface is dark green with a paler under-surface. Three to five thick veins originate at the base, and protrude from the leaf-surface. (Leaf: 30 x 150 mm)

**Flowers** In late winter and early spring, before the leaves appear, conspicuous, white to light pink, star-shaped flowers grow in abundance in sprays at the ends of twigs. Flowers turn brownish when old. This is one of the first trees to flower in spring, and is very striking from July to October. (Individual: 15 - 20 mm; spray: 70 x 60 mm)

*70% life-size*

**Fruit** The seeds grow in small capsules surrounded by the brownish, dry flower-petals. Seeds are covered by silky hairs, and are dark when mature (October to December). (6 mm)

**Bark** The bark is smooth in young branches and trees, but in older trunks is very rough and dark, and deeply fissured into long, irregular blocks.

## Seasonal changes
Semi-deciduous. This tree is easiest to identify in early spring when it is conspicuously covered with white flowers. It is difficult to identify when no leaves or flowers are present.

|  | Oct | Nov | Dec | Jan | Feb | Mar | Apr | May | Jun | Jul | Aug | Sep |
|---|---|---|---|---|---|---|---|---|---|---|---|---|
| Leaf | ■ | ■ | ■ | ■ | ■ | ■ | ■ |  |  |  |  | ■ |
| Flower | ■ |  |  |  |  |  |  |  |  | ■ | ■ | ■ |
| Fruit/Pod | ■ | ■ | ■ |  |  |  |  |  |  |  |  | ■ |

**SEASONALLY STRIKING** — Wild-pear Dombeya

159

# You find trees

**ECOZONE SPECIALISTS**

Most trees included in this book are common in many areas of the Bushveld. However these few have been chosen because of their unique charm – despite being relatively selective and growing in only one or two Ecozones.

| | |
|---|---|
| Big-leaf Fever-tree | p. 162 |
| Kiaat Bloodwood | p. 166 |
| Mobola-plum | p. 170 |
| Paperbark Acacia | p. 174 |
| Paperbark Albizia | p. 178 |

The dramatic bark of the Paperbark Albizia (*Albizia tanganyicensis*) is one of the many rewarding surprises that greet tree spotters in the Central and Northern Mountains (C, N).

# BIG-LEAF FEVER-TREE

*Anthocleista grandiflora*

Forest Fever Tree; Big-leaf Tree; Wild Tobacco Tree

## WILD ELDER FAMILY
## LOGANIACEAE

SA Tree Number 632

**AFRIKAANS** Boskoorsboom, Wildetabakboom  **N. SOTHO** Mophala  **TSONGA** Galudzu  **VENDA** Mueneene

The species name **grandiflora** refers to the large flowers.

## Where you'll find this tree easily

The Big-leaf Fever-tree grows singly.

- It is easiest to find in low-lying areas along Rivers and Streams of the Sour Bushveld (S).
- It can also be found along Rivers of the Northern Mountains (N); and in medium-to-low altitude forests on the South- or East-facing Slopes of the Sour Bushveld (S).

## Ecozones where this tree occurs

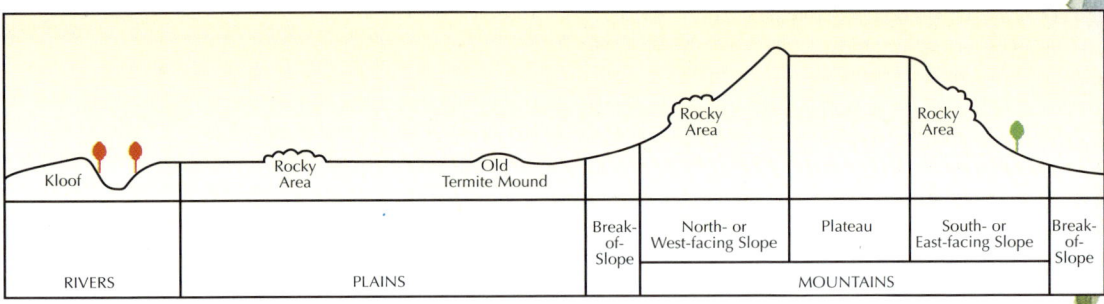

## Striking features

- This is a very striking, slender, tall, single-trunked tree, which branches high up into a few large, upward-growing branches with almost no twigs.
- **The trunk, branches and branchlets are bare, with leaves clustered at their ends.**
- **The leaves are huge, dark green and distinctly paddle-shaped, with a slightly wavy appearance.**

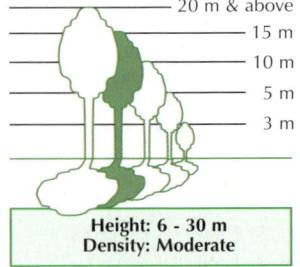

Height: 6 - 30 m
Density: Moderate

ECOZONE SPECIALISTS
Big-leaf Fever-tree

Unlike most other trees in this book, the Forest Fever Tree can be identified even when very young, as illustrated here.

**Largest tree currently registered**

**Diameter:** 1,27 m
**Girth:** 3,99 m
**Height:** 30 m

Lekgalameetse Nature Reserve
Cyprus

# BIG-LEAF FEVER-TREE

*Anthocleista grandiflora*

**Links with animals** Elephants eat the leaves and branches. Monkeys and birds eat the ripe fruit, and bushpigs eat the dropped fruit from the forest floor. Many species of insects are attracted to flowering trees, and in turn attract many insect-eating birds.

**Human uses** An extraction of the bark and leaves is taken to treat malaria, diarrhoea, diabetes, high blood pressure and venereal diseases, and to get rid of roundworm infestations.

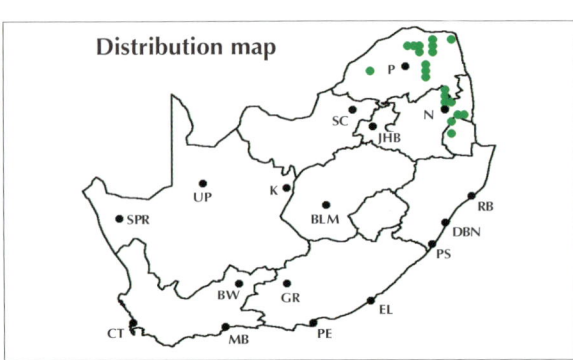

Distribution map

**Wood** The wood is whitish-yellow, soft and light, and is not put to use.

**Gardening** This is one of the most decorative trees for a garden or park. It grows very fast, and can be grown from seed after the fruit pulp has been removed. The Big-leaf Fever-tree thrives on a lot of water in the summer, but frost and cold winds usually kill it. It is suitable to grow as a bonsai.

*Fluted trunk of Riverine tree; Soutpansberg; Northern Mountains*

# GROWTH DETAILS

This single-trunked tree branches high up into a few large branches that grow upwards. The large leaves grow at the tips of the branches and branchlets to form dense, cabbage-like clusters. In large, older trees along Rivers the trunk can be fluted or buttressed.

**Leaves** The huge, simple leaves are arranged in opposite pairs at right angles to one another. They have a short leaf-stalk, a rounded tip and a tapering base, and are paddle-shaped, with a slightly wavy appearance. They are dark, glossy green above and pale green below. The yellow central vein is obvious on the lower surface. (Leaf: 1 000 x 450 mm in younger trees; 500 x 200 mm in older trees)

**Flowers** The conspicuous, sweet-scented, white flowers consist of a tube of up to 30 mm in length, and petals curving backwards. The flowers grow in clusters at the ends of branches and branchlets (September to January).

*25% life-size*

**Fruit** The glossy, dark green, plum-like fruit turns brown when mature (January to June). (30 x 20 mm)

**Bark** The bark is smooth and pale grey or brown.

**Seasonal changes**
Evergreen. This unique tree can be identified easily throughout the year.

|  | Oct | Nov | Dec | Jan | Feb | Mar | Apr | May | Jun | Jul | Aug | Sep |
|---|---|---|---|---|---|---|---|---|---|---|---|---|
| Leaf | | | | | | | | | | | | |
| Flower | | | | | | | | | | | | |
| Fruit/Pod | | | | | | | | | | | | |

ECOZONE SPECIALISTS
Big-leaf Fever-tree

165

# KIAAT BLOODWOOD

*Pterocarpus angolensis*

Kiaat; Wild Teak;
Bloodwood; Transvaal teak

## PEA FAMILY
## FABACEAE

SA Tree Number 236

**AFRIKAANS** Kiaat, Bloedhout  **N. SOTHO** Morôtô  **PEDI** Mmilo, Morôtô
**SWAZI** umVangatsi, umWangati  **TSONGA** Mvhangazi  **TSWANA** Mokwa  **VENDA** Mutondo
**ZULU** umVangazi, umBilo

The species name **angolensis** refers to Angola.

## Where you'll find this tree easily

The Kiaat Bloodwood grows singly. It prefers areas with more than 500 mm annual rainfall, and well-drained soils.

- It is easiest to find on the Plains of the Sour Bushveld (S).
- It can also be found on South- or East-facing Slopes of the Northern Mountains (N) and Sour Bushveld (S).

## Ecozones where this tree occurs

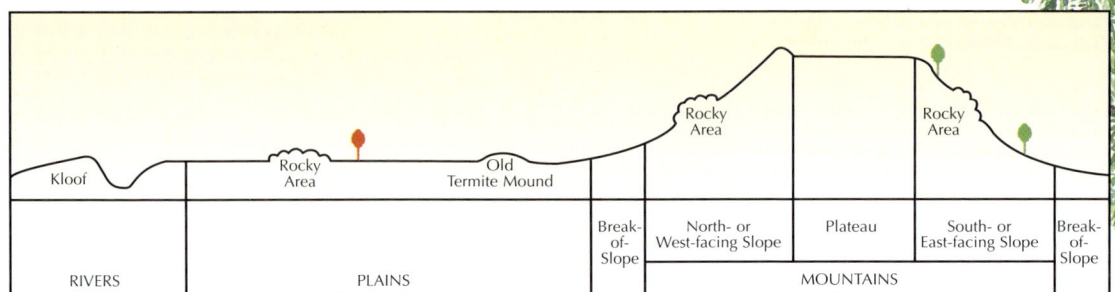

## Striking features

- This is a large, striking, single-trunked tree with a few large branches growing upwards and outwards.
- Feathery, drooping leaves grow only very high up, to form an umbrella-like canopy.
- **Winged pods have a characteristic round centre that is covered with stiff bristles. They are conspicuous, especially when the leaves have dropped.**
- The bark of the trunk and large branches are dark brown to black. When sections flake off there are lighter under-bark patches.

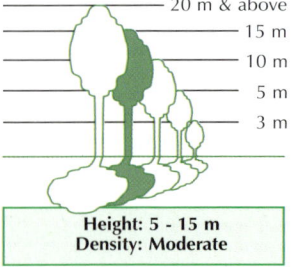

Height: 5 - 15 m
Density: Moderate

ECOZONE SPECIALISTS
Kiaat Bloodwood

# KIAAT BLOODWOOD

*Pterocarpus angolensis*

**Links with animals**  The leaves are eaten by elephant and kudu. Baboon eat the young pods. The seeds are eaten by Tree Squirrels, baboons and monkeys. Elephants often push the trees over, or ringbark them.

**Human uses**  The wood is an excellent timber for making furniture and curios. It is also used for canoes and building. The red gum and sap are used as a dye. The sap is used to cure cuts and sores, diarrhoea and intestinal worm infestations.

**Gardening**  It is extremely difficult to grow from seed, but it can be grown from cuttings (trucheons) taken in spring. It grows slowly on most soil types, and is not frost-resistant.

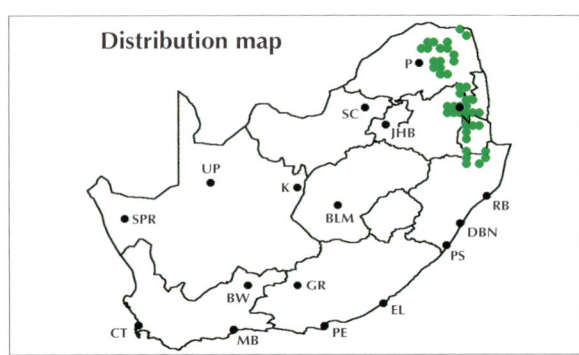

**Wood**  The wood is medium-hard. It varies greatly in weight and colour, but in general the sapwood is off-white to yellow, and the heartwood is light brown to dark reddish-brown.

*Near Hazyview in June; Plains, Sour Bushveld*

# GROWTH DETAILS

This is a single-trunked, high-branching tree with a few large branches growing upwards and outwards, with the leaves growing very high up to form a moderately dense, flat-to-umbrella-shaped canopy with drooping leaves.

**Leaves** The leaves are compound with a single leaflet at the tip, and the leaflets are alternate. There are 11 - 25 pairs of leaflets. They are elliptic, with a prominent twisted tip and a smooth margin. The leaflets are shiny dark green above and have fine hairs below. Leaves are droopy, and hang down, and turn yellow to yellow-brown before dropping in late autumn and early winter. Young leaflets are soft and covered in brown hairs. (Leaf: 230 - 250 mm; leaflets: 20 - 70 x 25 - 45 mm)

*30% life-size*

**Pods** Distinctive pods have a central, round seed-case covered with long, stiff bristles. This is surrounded by a round, flat, papery plate. The pods grow singly or in groups on long twigs. They ripen in late summer and remain on the tree long after the leaves have fallen (February to August). (80 - 150 mm diameter)

**Flowers** The striking orange-yellow, sweet-scented, pea-shaped flowers are found in abundance in branched sprays, usually on older, darker branches. The flowers appear before or with the new leaves, from August to October, and the main flowering period lasts 2 - 4 weeks. (Spray: 100 - 200 mm long; individual flower: 10 - 20 mm long)

**Bark** The bark is dark grey to dark brown, and in very old trees may be black. It is rough and fissured, or cracked into lengthways sections. Red gum oozes out when the bark is damaged, and young twigs are smooth and grey, and covered with hairs.

## Seasonal changes
Deciduous. The tree can be identified easily in all seasons by its characteristic form and the presence of the pods for most of the year.

|  | Oct | Nov | Dec | Jan | Feb | Mar | Apr | May | Jun | Jul | Aug | Sep |
|---|---|---|---|---|---|---|---|---|---|---|---|---|
| Leaf | | | | | | | | | | | | |
| Flower | | | | | | | | | | | | |
| Fruit/Pod | | | | | | | | | | | | |

ECOZONE SPECIALISTS
Kiaat Bloodwood

169

# MOBOLA-PLUM

*Parinari curatellifolia*                                   Mobola Plum; Cork Tree; Hissing tree

## COCO PLUM FAMILY
## CHRYSOBALANCEAE
SA Tree Number 146

**AFRIKAANS** Grysappel, Bosappel   **N. SOTHO** Mmola   **TSONGA** Mbulwa   **TSWANA** Mobola
**VENDA** Muvhula   **ZULU** amaBulwa

The species name **curatellifolia** refers to the South American genus Curatella, with leaves similar to the Mobola Plum.

### Where you'll find this tree easily
The Mobola-plum grows singly, but where one is found, there are likely to be others in the vicinity.

- It is easiest to find on the lower South- or East-facing Slopes of the Sour Bushveld (S).
- It can also be found on the North- or West-facing Slopes of the Sour Bushveld (S), where specimens grow further apart.

### Ecozones where this tree occurs

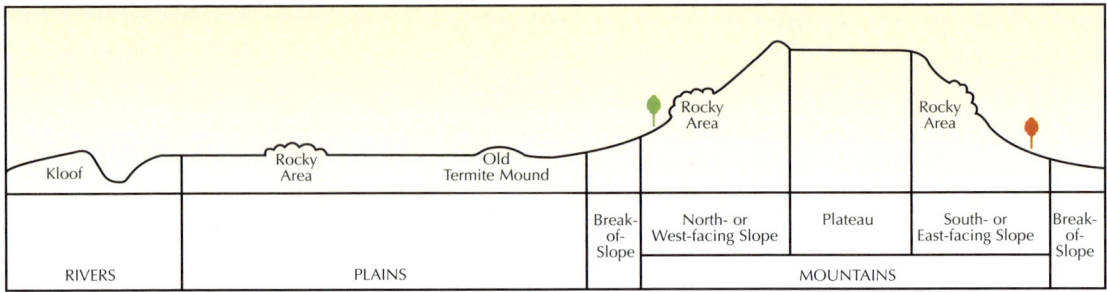

### Striking features

- This is a single-trunked tree with a meandering trunk and large branches, with dark corky bark.
- **The semi-circular, blue-grey-green canopy stands out amongst other vegetation.**
- The simple leaves are bicoloured, dark grey-green above, and silvery-white below.
- **The fine herringbone veins are obvious on both surfaces.**
- The plum-like fruit is orange-yellow when ripe, and is often speckled with grey.

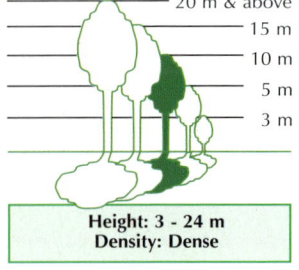

Height: 3 - 24 m
Density: Dense

**ECOZONE SPECIALISTS**
Mobola-plum

**Largest tree currently registered**

**Diameter:** 0,94 m
**Girth:** 2,95 m
**Height:** 20 m

A S Knoetze
'Tuinplaas', Beaufort
Dist. Soutpansberg

# MOBOLA-PLUM

*Parinari curatellifolia*

**Links with animals** Leaves and fruit are eaten by elephant and game. The caterpillars of the Striped Policeman butterfly (*Coeliades forestan*) eat the leaves.

**Human uses** The wood is sometimes used for poles, and to make boats. The edible fruit is boiled to make a nutrituous syrup and beer. Meal made from the fruit is eaten raw, or mixed with wild spinach or cooked as a vegetable. Extracts of the bark are used for tanning and to treat pneumonia. The roots are used to treat earache and cataracts.

**Gardening** This attractive garden tree grows fast from seed, but is sensitive to frost and cold winds.

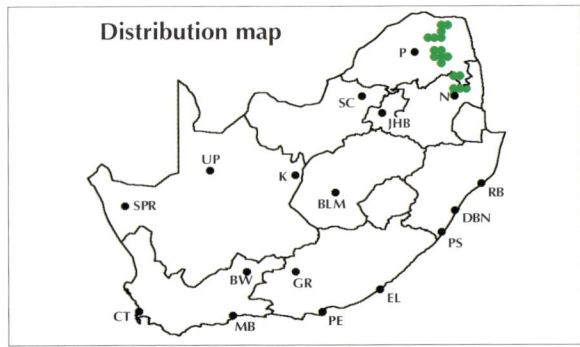

Distribution map

**Wood** The wood is hard and pale-coloured with red heartwood. It is difficult to work with.

*Near Graskop; lower East-facing Slope, Sour Bushveld*

# GROWTH DETAILS

This is a single-trunked tree that branches high up into a few large meandering branches to form a moderate to dense, semi-circular to irregular-shaped canopy of dark grey-green leaves.

**Leaves** The simple, alternate leaves tend to be folded inwards, and have a short and hairy leaf-stalk. Leaves are elliptic with a rounded tip and base, and a herringbone vein pattern that can be seen on both surfaces. They are stiff and leathery, dark grey-green above, and covered in dense white-to-yellowish hairs below, giving them a silvery-white appearance. When young, the entire leaf is covered by velvety hairs. (30 - 100 x 20 - 50 mm)

**Fruit** The characteristic plums grow in profusion at the ends of short twigs, and can take up to a year to ripen. The ripe fruit is orangey-yellow and lightly speckled with grey, and usually ripens on the ground (October to January). (30 - 50 x 15 - 35 mm diameter)

**Flowers** The sweet-scented, white-to-yellow, bell-shaped flowers grow in branched sprays in the angles formed by the leaves, as well as at the tips of twigs. The flower-stalks and new flowers are covered in dense, rusty, woolly hairs (July to November). (5 mm)

*20% life-size*

*60% life-size*

**Bark** The dark grey bark is rough and corky. On young branchlets and twigs the bark is covered with yellowish, woolly hairs.

## Seasonal changes
Evergreen. This tree can be identified throughout the year by its leaves.

|  | Oct | Nov | Dec | Jan | Feb | Mar | Apr | May | Jun | Jul | Aug | Sep |
|---|---|---|---|---|---|---|---|---|---|---|---|---|
| Leaf | | | | | | | | | | | | |
| Flower | | | | | | | | | | | | |
| Fruit/Pod | | | | | | | | | | | | |

**ECOZONE SPECIALISTS** — Mobola-plum

173

# PAPERBARK ACACIA

*Acacia sieberiana*                                                    Paperbark Thorn

| THORN-TREE FAMILY MIMOSACEAE | SA Tree Number 187 |

**AFRIKAANS** Papierbasdoring, Verveldoring  **N. SOTHO** Mphoka, Mošibihla  **SISWATI** umNganduzi
**TSONGA** Nkowankowa  **TSWANA** Mokha  **VENDA** Musaunga, Muunga-luselo  **ZULU** umKhamba

The species name **sieberiana** honours Franz Wilhelm Sieber, a Bohemian botanist, plant collector and traveller of the early 18th Century.

## Where you'll find this tree easily

The Paperbark Acacia normally grows in loose, widespread groups.

- It is easiest to find on the Plains of the Sour Bushveld (S).
- It can also be found on the Plains of the Mixed Bushveld (M); and on the lower foothills of the South- or East-facing Slopes.

## Ecozones where this tree occurs

## Striking features

- **This is a single-stemmed Thorn-tree with a moderately thick umbrella canopy.**
- **The straw-coloured bark forms irregular flakes, revealing deeper yellow under-bark.**
- The twice compound leaves are yellowish-green, and the elliptic leaflets are very narrow.
- Thick, flat, hard pods hang in bunches and do not open on the tree.
- The thorns may not be conspicuous, but when present are straight and joined at the base.

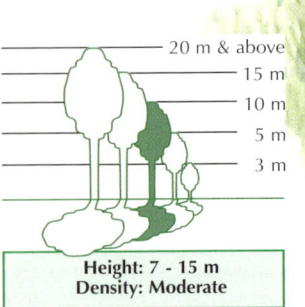

Height: 7 - 15 m
Density: Moderate

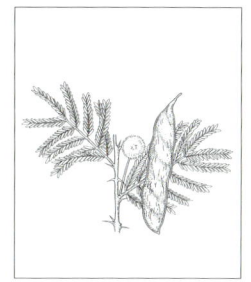

**ECOZONE SPECIALISTS**
Paperbark Acacia

**Largest tree currently registered**

**Diameter:** 1,74 m
**Girth:** 5,46 m
**Height:** 13 m

R Vise, Wallace Dale,
Dist. Soutpansberg

175

# PAPERBARK ACACIA

*Acacia sieberiana*

**Links with animals** The fallen pods and leaves are eaten by cattle and game. Young green pods and the foliage, especially when wilted, contain a large amount of poisonous prussic acid, and can be dangerous to stock. The tree attracts birds, especially the Bar-throated Apalis, which eats insects off flowers, leaves and tree-trunks. Sunbirds such as the Malachite, Greater Double-collared, Scarlet-chested, Black, and Collared, are also attracted to the tree.

**Human uses** The gum is edible, and has good adhesive properties. Bark and root extracts were used to treat arthritis and tapeworm infestations; root infusions were used as antiseptics, used orally and as a wash for children with fevers or stomach ache.

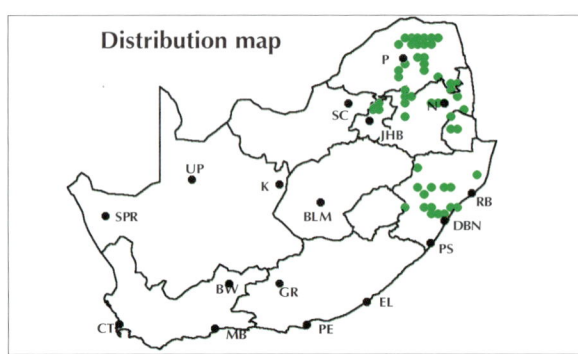

Distribution map

**Wood** The wood is soft, and easily destroyed by termites and borer beetles. It has white heartwood and sapwood, and a coarse texture. It varnishes well but is not suitable for turning.

**Gardening** This is a fast-growing, attractive tree for the landscape garden. Although it is not very frost-resistant, it is probably more resistant than most other Acacias.

**Look-alike trees** Monkey Acacia (*Acacia galpinii*), page 71, has yellow-brown, corky bark that is fissured lengthways; short, slightly curved hook thorns; fine, feathery leaves with 7 - 14 pairs of feathers, and 12 - 40 pairs of leaflets; flowers in spikes; and smooth, brittle pods that turn purplish-brown when ripe.

Black-monkey Acacia (*Acacia burkei*), page 218, has a thicker and less spreading canopy, and the bark forms deep fissures and does not flake; the leaves are smaller with only a few leaflets, and the flowers are in spikes.

This tree can be confused with other Acacias. See pages 70 - 73 for comparisons.

*Leaves twigs and bark; summer silouette*

# GROWTH DETAILS

This is a single-stemmed tree with a straight trunk that branches low down into several large branches. These spread out horizontally to form a wide, moderately thick umbrella canopy. Large branches are visible well into the canopy, and only form smaller branchlets and twigs high up. The branchlets are covered in golden hairs.

*55% life-size*

**Leaves** The twice compound leaves are yellowish-green and have 3 - 20 feather pairs, with 12 - 40 pairs of leaflets. The elliptic leaflets are very narrow. There is a small, knob-like gland at the base of each leaf. Young leaves are covered by thick, yellow hairs. (Leaf: 60 - 100 mm; leaflet: 2 - 6 x 0,6 - 1,6 mm)

**Flowers** The conspicuous, creamy-white flower-balls are sweet-scented, and grow in groups of 1 - 4 on long stalks between the leaves. This tree is one of the last of the Acacias to flower in spring, and continues to flower sporadically throughout the summer (October to December). (10 - 15 mm)

**Pods** The stout, hard, woody, flat bean pods are hairy when young. The pods turn grey-brown when ripe, and do not split open on the tree (March to June). (100 - 150 x 20 - 30 x 13 mm)

*55% life-size*

**Thorns** The paired thorns are short, straight and white. However, they are variable and are not always well developed. It may be difficult to see that this is a Thorn-tree. (25 - 100 mm)

**Bark** The bark is straw-coloured and corky, and forms flakes that may be large and obvious in some trees, but much smaller and almost inconspicuous in others.

**ECOZONE SPECIALISTS** — Paperbark Acacia

### Seasonal changes
Deciduous. This tree can be identified by its bark throughout the year.

|  | Oct | Nov | Dec | Jan | Feb | Mar | Apr | May | Jun | Jul | Aug | Sep |
|---|---|---|---|---|---|---|---|---|---|---|---|---|
| Leaf | ■ | ■ | ■ | ■ | ■ | ■ | ■ | ■ | ■ | ■ |  | ■ |
| Flower | ■ | ■ | ■ |  |  |  |  |  |  |  |  |  |
| Fruit/Pod |  |  |  | ■ | ■ | ■ | ■ | ■ | ■ |  |  |  |

177

# PAPERBARK ALBIZIA

*Albizia tanganyicensis*                              Paperbark False-thorn

## THORN-TREE FAMILY
## MIMOSACEAE
## SA Tree Number 157

**AFRIKAANS** Papierbasvalsdoring, Koorsboom  **TSONGA** Dzuvudzuvu  **VENDA** Mulelu, Munungufhefhe

The species name **tanganyicensis** refers to Tanganyika, now part of Tanzania.

## Where you'll find this tree easily

The Paperbark Albizia grows singly, often on the sandy soils of Rocky Areas. It is often found on quartzite and granite hills.

- It is easiest to find on the North- or West-facing Slopes of the Central Mountains (C).
- It can also be found in Rocky Areas and on North- or West-facing Slopes of the Northern Mountains (N).

## Ecozones where this tree occurs

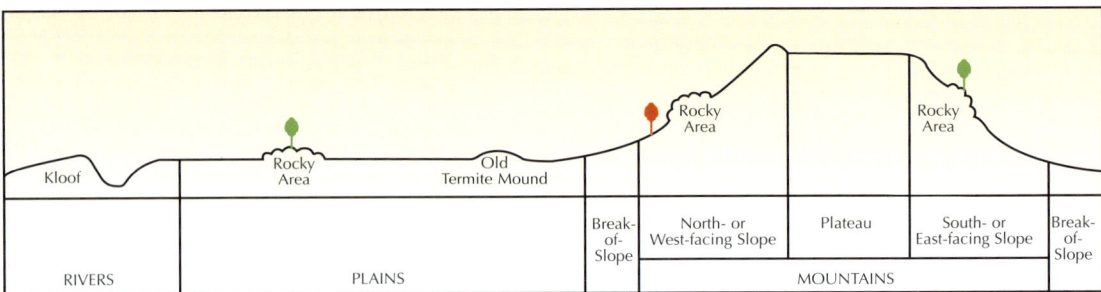

## Striking features

- This is a thornless, single-trunked tree that resembles a Thorn-tree, and branches high up into a few large branches, to form a sparse, deep green canopy that can be umbrella-like.
- From a distance the pale trunk stands out on rocky hillsides, contrasting with the deep green canopy.
- The thin, orangey-brown outer bark is broken into irregular blocks, and peels leaving paler orangey-brown, papery flakes, which flap in the wind. The large areas of exposed under-bark are pearly-white to yellowish and smooth.
- Leaves are twice compound, and leaflets are relatively large for an Albizia.
- Creamy-white pincushion flowers can be seen from August to November, and broad, flat pods from September to May.

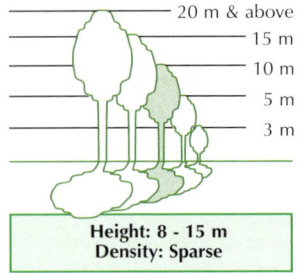

Height: 8 - 15 m
Density: Sparse

ECOZONE SPECIALISTS
Paperbark Albizia

179

# PAPERBARK ALBIZIA

*Albizia tanganyicensis*

**Links with animals** Elephants eat the leaves and young branches, and kudu and impala eat the flowers. The pods are poisonous, and cause nervous disorders in animals. Caterpillars of the Satyr Charaxes butterfly (*Charaxes ethalion*) eat the leaves. Brown-headed Parrots eat the green seeds.

**Human uses** The wood contains an ingredient that can irritate the nose and throat when it is worked. An extraction made from the bark is taken for coughs.

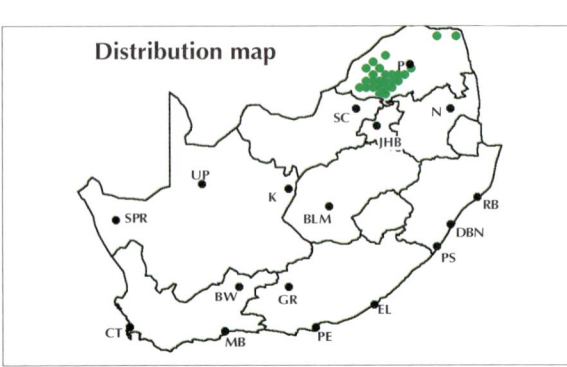

Distribution map

**Wood** The wood is white, soft, coarse-grained and light.

**Gardening** This tree is eye-catching and very attractive in a rock garden, but has a rather aggressive root system. However, it also makes a very unusual container plant. The Paperbark Albizia can withstand cold but not frost, and is extremely drought-resistant. It grows fast from fresh seed soaked overnight in hot water before planting.

*June; North-facing Slope, Northern Mountains*

# GROWTH DETAILS

This is a single-trunked tree that branches high up into a few large branches. The trunk is often crooked.

**Leaves** The large, twice compound leaves have a prominent gland near the base of the leaf-stalk. Leaves have 2 - 6 pairs of opposite feathers, with 5 - 13 pairs of opposite leaflets. (Leaf: 250 - 300 mm; leaflet: 12 - 40 mm x 7 - 12 mm)

**Pods** The broad-bean pods are thin, and reddish-brown when ripe, and they split open on the tree (September to December). (up to 300 mm)

*40% life-size*

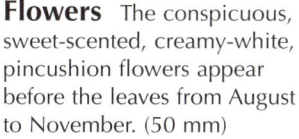

**Flowers** The conspicuous, sweet-scented, creamy-white, pincushion flowers appear before the leaves from August to November. (50 mm)

**Bark** Thin orange-brown outer bark breaks into irregular blocks. It peels in orange-brown, papery flakes that can be huge and seen from afar, moving in the wind. The under-surface is smooth and pearly-white to yellowish in older trees, and greenish-cream on young branches.

## Seasonal changes
Deciduous. This tree is easy to recognise throughout the year by its bark.

|  | Oct | Nov | Dec | Jan | Feb | Mar | Apr | May | Jun | Jul | Aug | Sep |
|---|---|---|---|---|---|---|---|---|---|---|---|---|
| Leaf | ■ | ■ | ■ | ■ | ■ | ■ | ■ | ■ |  |  |  | ■ |
| Flower | ■ | ■ |  |  |  |  |  |  |  |  | ■ | ■ |
| Fruit/Pod | ■ | ■ | ■ |  |  |  |  |  |  |  | ■ | ■ |

**ECOZONE SPECIALISTS** — Paperbark Albizia

181

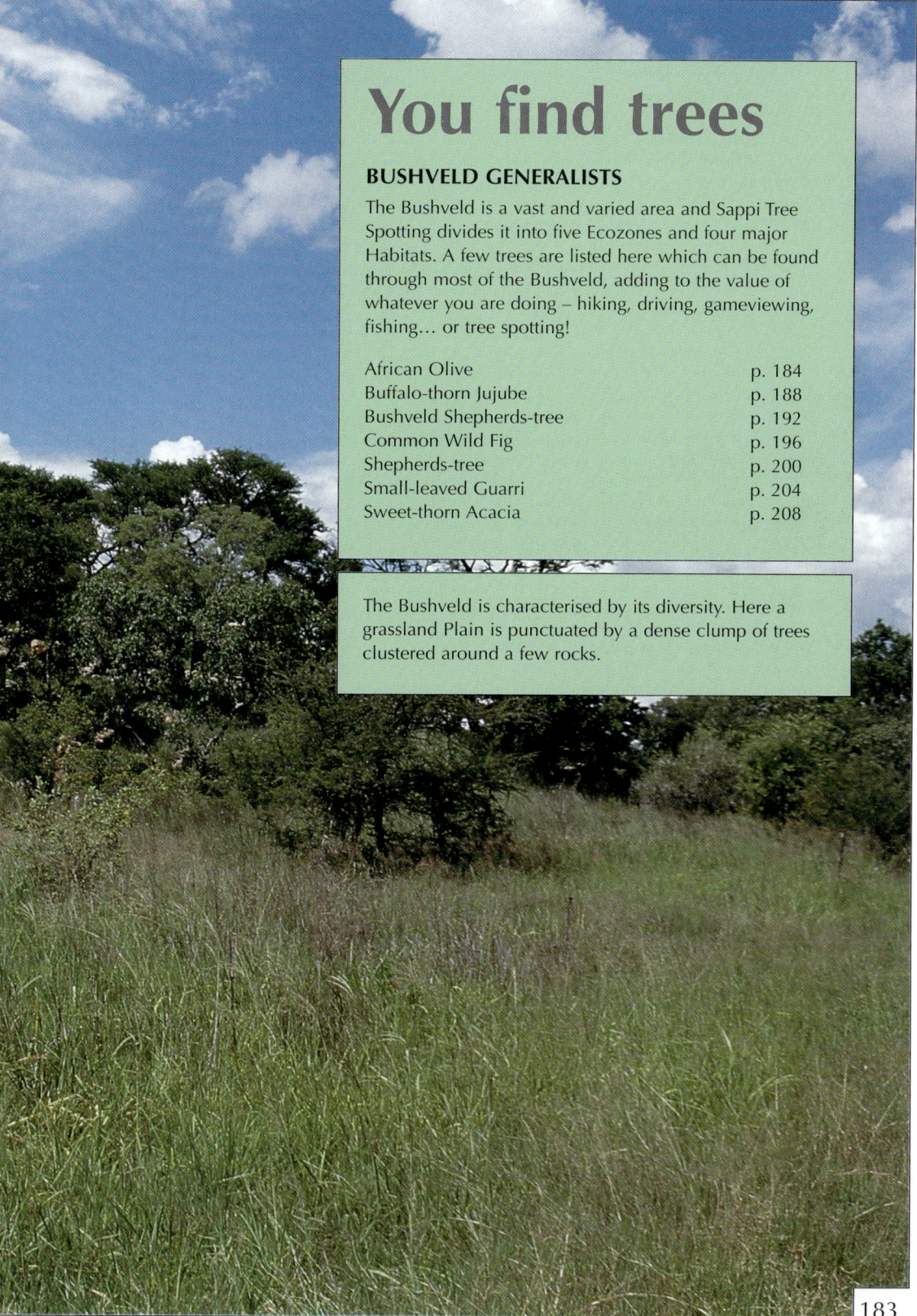

# You find trees

## BUSHVELD GENERALISTS

The Bushveld is a vast and varied area and Sappi Tree Spotting divides it into five Ecozones and four major Habitats. A few trees are listed here which can be found through most of the Bushveld, adding to the value of whatever you are doing – hiking, driving, gameviewing, fishing… or tree spotting!

| | |
|---|---|
| African Olive | p. 184 |
| Buffalo-thorn Jujube | p. 188 |
| Bushveld Shepherds-tree | p. 192 |
| Common Wild Fig | p. 196 |
| Shepherds-tree | p. 200 |
| Small-leaved Guarri | p. 204 |
| Sweet-thorn Acacia | p. 208 |

The Bushveld is characterised by its diversity. Here a grassland Plain is punctuated by a dense clump of trees clustered around a few rocks.

# AFRICAN OLIVE

*Olea europaea*                                                                 Wild Olive

| OLIVE FAMILY OLEACEAE | SA Tree Number 617 |

**AFRIKAANS** Olienhout, Swartolienhout  **N. SOTHO** Mohlware  **SISWATI** umNquma
**S. SOTHO** Mohloaare, Mohloare  **TSONGA** Mutlhwari  **TSWANA** Motlhware
**VENDA** Mutwari  **XHOSA** umNquma  **ZULU** umNqumo

The species name **europaea** refers to its close relationship with the European Olive.

## Where you'll find this tree easily

The African Olive normally grows singly, and occurs in a wide variety of Habitats ranging from Kloofs and River banks to grasslands and Rocky Areas on Plains.

- It is easiest to find on the South- or East-facing Slopes of all Ecozones.
- It can also be found along Rivers and Streams and Old Termite Mounds of all Ecozones; and on some of the Plains of the Mixed Bushveld (M) and Sour Bushveld (S); as well as on some North- or West-facing Slopes of the Sour Bushveld (S).

## Ecozones where this tree occurs

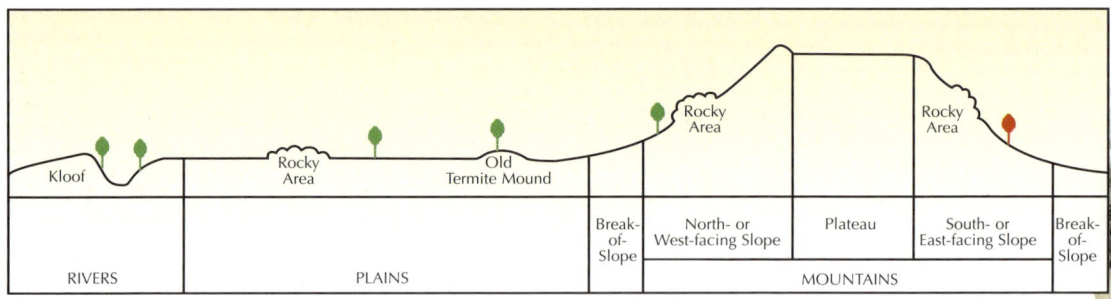

## Striking features

- This is a single-trunked tree with a dense, bicoloured canopy, and a regular, round canopy.
- The trunk is often fluted and usually gnarled.
- The simple, narrowly elliptic, leathery, rigid leaves are shiny dark green above, and paler below.
- The side veins and the leaves are opaque when the leaf is held against the light.

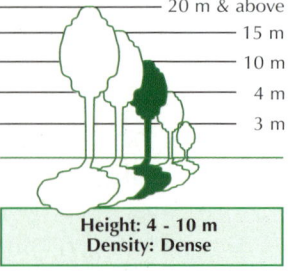

Height: 4 - 10 m
Density: Dense

**BUSHVELD GENERALISTS**
*African Olive*

**Largest tree currently registered**

**Diameter:** 1,59 m
**Girth:** 4,99 m
**Height:** 14 m

Ds AMJD Alberts, Schaaphok, Dist. Potgietersrus

# AFRICAN OLIVE

*Olea europaea*

**Links with animals**  The foliage is tough and unpalatable in the mature tree. However, it is favoured by browsers when young, and may be useful as a fodder plant during drought. The fruit is eaten and dispersed by birds such as Red-winged and Pied Starlings, and Rameron Pigeons.

**Human uses**  The juice of the fruit can be made into ink, and the leaves into palatable tea. The wood makes beautiful furniture and is good for fencing posts. The tree is still used in traditional medicine today: an infusion of the bark to relieve colic; infusion of the leaves as an eye lotion and gargle; the leaf and bark for intermittent fever.

**Gardening**  This is an attractive tree, and is easy to cultivate. It is drought- and frost-resistant, but it grows slowly. The commercial Olive Tree can be successfully grafted onto this tree as they are very closely related. It is excellent as a bonsai tree.

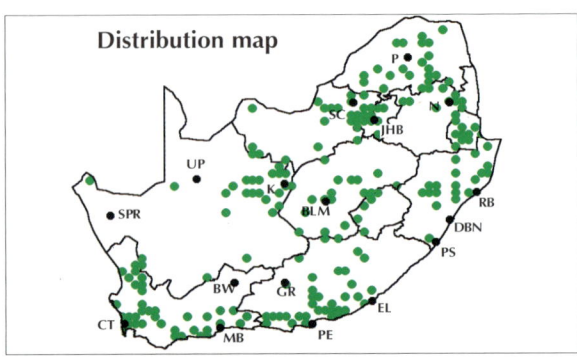

Distribution map

**Wood**  The wood has a wavy grain with attractive yellow-brown heartwood and yellow sapwood. It is very durable, is too hard to nail, but turns and polishes well.

East-facing Slope, Sour Bushveld

**Look-alike trees**  This tree can easily be confused with the River Guarri (*Euclea schimperi*), which has a less regular outline, formed by clumped, upright leaves. The leaf margin is wavy, and the side veins are transparent when held against the light. Fruit and flowers grow among the leaves. See **Sappi Tree Spotting KwaZulu-Natal** for descriptions of this tree.

The Olive Buddleja (*Buddleja saligna*), page 39, has pale, peeling, lengthways-fissured bark. The canopy is irregular and tangled, with leaves only on the outside of the canopy. The leaf-bearing twigs are square, and the flower-heads are large, white and conspicuous. See **Sappi Tree Spotting Highveld** for full description of this tree.

# GROWTH DETAILS

This is a single-trunked tree with a crooked, often fluted, gnarled trunk that branches low down to form a dense, round, bicoloured canopy with a smooth outline. More exposed trees are smaller, while those in very windy areas may be weather-beaten and more irregular. Young stems are square with four ridges.

**Leaves** Simple, narrowly elliptic leaves are opposite. They are leathery, rigid, shiny and dark green above, becoming greyer with maturity. The leaves are distinctly bicoloured, the under-surface much paler and covered with silvery or brownish scales. The tips end in a sharp point that may turn slightly downwards. The base is tapering, and the margin is thickened. The side veins and the leaf are opaque when the leaf is held against the light. (Leaf: 20 - 100 x 7 - 16 mm)

**Fruit** The berry-like, fleshy fruit turns purplish-black when ripe from March to July. (8 x 10 mm)

**Flowers** Inconspicuous, small, cream-green flowers are faintly scented, and grow in short, branched sprays in the angles of the leaves (October to February). (6 - 10 mm)

*life-size*

**Bark** The bark is smooth and grey-brown in younger branchlets and twigs. It turns darker and rougher with age, flaking in irregular strips and blocks. Twigs are covered with small, raised dots, from old leaf-stalks.

**BUSHVELD GENERALISTS**
African Olive

## Seasonal changes
Evergreen. This tree can be found throughout the year.

|            | Oct | Nov | Dec | Jan | Feb | Mar | Apr | May | Jun | Jul | Aug | Sep |
|------------|-----|-----|-----|-----|-----|-----|-----|-----|-----|-----|-----|-----|
| Leaf       |     |     |     |     |     |     |     |     |     |     |     |     |
| Flower     |     |     |     |     |     |     |     |     |     |     |     |     |
| Fruit/Pod  |     |     |     |     |     |     |     |     |     |     |     |     |

187

# BUFFALO-THORN JUJUBE

*Ziziphus mucronata*                                                    Buffalo-thorn

## DOGWOOD FAMILY/BLINKBLAAR FAMILY
## RHAMNACEAE                                          SA Tree Number 447

**AFRIKAANS** Blinkblaar-wag-'n-bietjie, Haak-en-steek-wag-'n-bietjie  **N. SOTHO** Mokgalwa, Mokgalô
**SISWATI** umLahlabantu  **TSONGA** Mphasamhala  **TSWANA** Mokgalo, Mokalabata
**VENDA** Mutshetshete, Mukhalu  **XHOSA** umPhafa  **ZULU** umPhafa, isiLahlankosi, isiLahla, umHlahlankosi

The species name **mucronata** refers to the pointed leaves.

## Where you'll find this tree easily

The Buffalo-thorn Jujube occurs in a wide variety of Habitats.
It normally grows singly among other tree species.
- It is easiest to find as a large tree on the Plains of the Mixed Bushveld (M).
- It can also be found along Rivers and Streams and on the Slopes of all Ecozones.

## Ecozones where this tree occurs

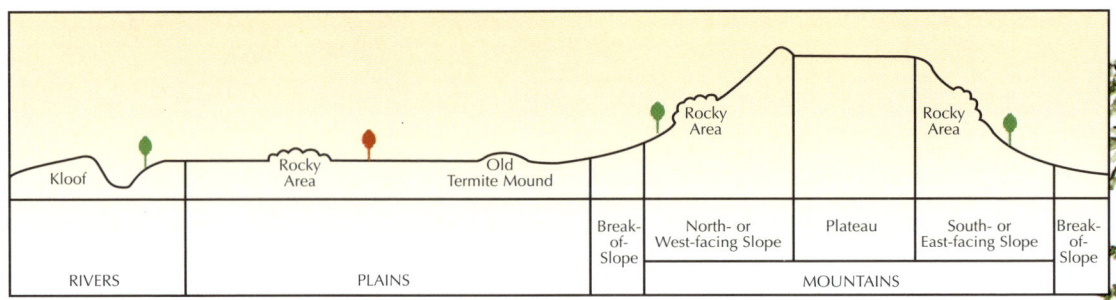

## Striking features
- This is a single-trunked tree with a moderate, spreading canopy.
- Branchlets divide into fine twigs that are slightly zig-zagged.
- Leaves tend to grow on the same flat plane, facing the light.
- **The leaves are distinctly shiny, and have three veins radiating from the base.**
- Pairs of reddish-brown thorns, one hooked and one straight, grow at the base of the leaves, in the angles of the twigs.
- The large, round, red-brown berries are conspicuous, and stay on the tree for long periods.

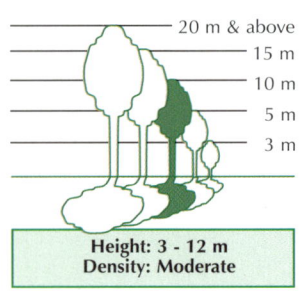

Height: 3 - 12 m
Density: Moderate

**BUSHVELD GENERALISTS**
Buffalo-thorn Jujube

**Largest tree currently registered**

**Diameter:** 1,37 m
**Girth:** 4,30 m
**Height:** 12 m

CG & MM Cunningham
Meseg Cemetery, Enzelsberg,
Dist. Marico

# BUFFALO-THORN JUJUBE

*Ziziphus mucronata*

**Links with animals**  The leaves are eaten by giraffe, antelope, cattle and goats, and the fruit by many animals such as small antelope, baboons, monkeys and warthog, as well as Green Pigeons. The caterpillars of many butterflies feed on the tree.

**Human uses**  The fruit is edible, and is used to make porridge and meal. The seeds can be roasted as a coffee substitute. This was an important medicinal tree, and is still used in traditional medicine today: for stomach ailments, skin ulcers and chest problems; and a paste of the leaves to treat boils and glandular swellings. It was the burial tree of the Zulu and the Sotho. Trees were planted to surround the body, and branches were used to attract the ancestral spirits from one dwelling place to the next.

**Gardening**  This is a very pretty tree but it tends to drop thorny branches. The tree grows fast from seed and is fairly drought- and frost-resistant. It is suitable as a bonsai tree.

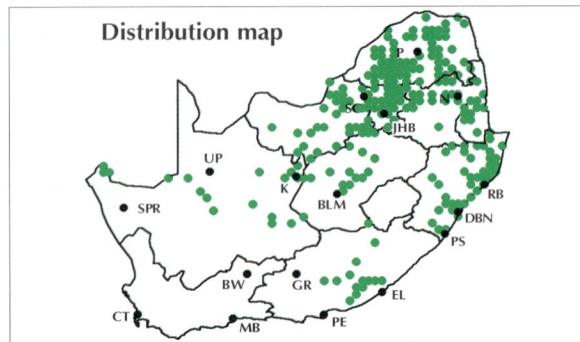

Distribution map

**Wood**  It has yellow-brown heartwood, sometimes with reddish-brown, dark streaks, and the sapwood is yellow. It is hard and is suitable for turning, but warps easily.

*Winter shows zig-zag twigs clearly*

# GROWTH DETAILS

This is a single-trunked tree with a short, often crooked trunk that branches fairly low down to form a shiny, moderate, spreading canopy. It can grow very tall in forests. Long, slender branchlets and twigs are red-brown. Twigs and leaves create a flat plane with leaves facing the light. Twigs are slightly zig-zag.

**Leaves** Simple, alternate, elliptic leaves are slightly folded, and grow on the angles of the twigs. They are distinctly shiny with slightly toothed edges, and have three veins radiating from the base. Young leaves may be hairy and are bright spring-green. In protected areas the leaf-stalk is long and prominent. (30 - 120 x 20 - 70 mm)

**Fruit** The hard, round, berry-like fruit is shiny and red-brown when ripe. The fruit is often still visible on the leafless trees in winter (Ripens February to June). (15 - 25 mm)

**Thorns** Pairs of reddish-brown thorns, one straight and one hooked, grow at the base of the leaves, in the angles of the twigs. Mature trees may have virtually no thorns. In drier areas the younger trees and younger branchlets and twigs tend to be more thorny. (Straight: 10 - 20 mm; curved: 5 - 7 mm)

*60% life-size*

**Flowers** Inconspicuous, small, star-like, yellow-green flowers grow in clusters at the base of the leaves. They produce copious nectar (October to January). (6 mm)

**Bark** The bark is light grey-brown and smooth when young, becoming grooved with age. In forests the bark is distinctive, flaking in rectangular blocks that run lengthways down the trunk.

**BUSHVELD GENERALISTS** — Buffalo-thorn Jujube

### Seasonal changes
Semi-deciduous. The presence of fruit and the characteristic thorns makes it possible to identify this tree in winter.

|  | Oct | Nov | Dec | Jan | Feb | Mar | Apr | May | Jun | Jul | Aug | Sep |
|---|---|---|---|---|---|---|---|---|---|---|---|---|
| Leaf | | | | | | | | | | | | |
| Flower | | | | | | | | | | | | |
| Fruit/Pod | | | | | | | | | | | | |

191

# BUSHVELD SHEPHERDS-TREE

*Boscia foetida*                                    Smelly shepherd's tree; Stink-bush

| CAPER FAMILY CAPPARACEAE | SA Tree Number 125 |
|---|---|

**AFRIKAANS** Stinkwitgat, Fynblaarwitgat  **TSWANA** Mopipi  **ZULU** umVithi

The species name **foetida** refers to the unpleasant smell of the flowers.

## Where you'll find this tree easily

The Bushveld Shepherds-tree grows singly among other species of trees, and where one is found there are usually more in the vicinity.

- It is easiest to find on the North- or West-facing Slopes of the Central Mountains (C).
- It can also be found on Old Termite Mounds; and on the Plains of the Northern Mountains (N), the Thorny Bushveld (T) and the Mixed Bushveld (M).

## Ecozones where this tree occurs

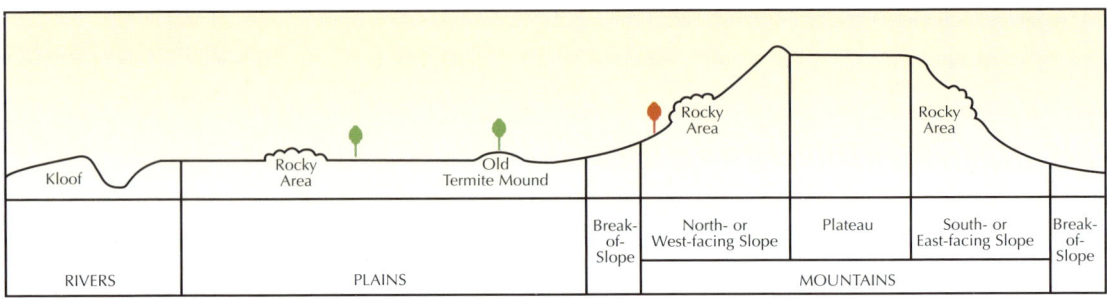

## Striking features

- This is a very striking tree with a dense, untidy, semi-circular to V-shaped canopy. Myriads of branchlets and twigs interweave and tangle, and project rigidly outwards from the canopy.
- **Tiny, hard leaves grow in tight clusters and form dense sleeves around thin branchlets and twigs, obscuring them when seen from a distance.**
- It has smooth, whitish-grey bark that is sometimes folded and pleated with scars and depressions, giving the bark an ancient appearance.
- Small, greenish-yellow flowers have an offensive carrion-like smell, hence the name of the tree.

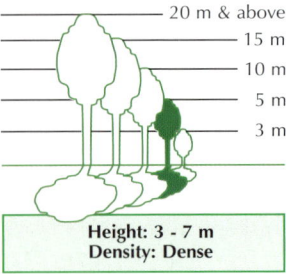

Height: 3 - 7 m
Density: Dense

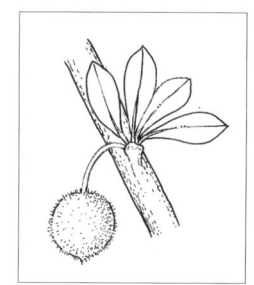

**BUSHVELD GENERALISTS**
Bushveld Shepherds-tree

# BUSHVELD SHEPHERDS-TREE

*Boscia foetida*

**Links with animals** This is a good fodder tree. The flowers attract many insects, and the fruit is eaten by birds.

**Human uses** Freshly sawn wood has an unpleasant smell. The fruit is edible. The root is occasionally used as a chicory substitute in coffee. An extract of the leaves is used to treat earache and for back pain. The leaves and flowers have caused poisoning in sheep.

**Gardening** It is usually not suitable for a small garden because of the offensive smell of the flowers.

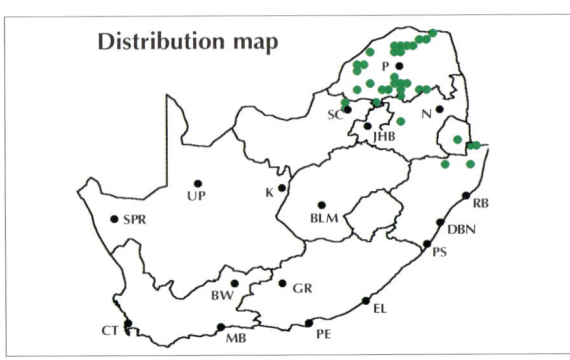

**Wood** The wood is white, hard, close-grained and often twisted.

**Look-alike tree** The Shepherds-tree (*Boscia albitrunca*), page 200, can have a similar growth form and bark, but it usually has a single trunk, and the leaves are larger and do not form sleeves.

*May; Plains, Northern Mountains*

# GROWTH DETAILS

This is a small, single- or multi-stemmed, low-branching tree. It forms a dense canopy that varies in form. The canopy consists of myriads of branchlets and twigs that interweave and sometimes tangle, and project rigidly outwards from the canopy. These twigs are often noticeably angular.

**Leaves** The minute, hard leaves have very short leaf-stalks and cluster tightly around the branchlets and twigs to form dense sleeves. Leaves are more-or-less oval-shaped, and have a broadly tapering to rounded, sometimes notched tip, and a tapering base. The leaves are leathery and dark blue-green to greyish-green, and may be with or without hairs. (Leaf: 8 - 25 mm long)

**Fruit** The small, round, velvety fruits are found in bunches, and are yellowish to yellowish-brown when ripe (Ripens November to April). (Individual fruit: 10 mm diameter)

*90% life-size*

**Flowers** The inconspicuous, small greenish-yellow flowers have an offensive carrion-like smell, and grow in small, closely packed bunches (August to October). (4 mm)

**Bark** The grey to whitish-grey bark is smooth, but can be folded and pleated with scars and depressions, giving the bark an ancient appearance. The twigs and branches are sometimes spine-tipped.

**Seasonal changes**
Evergreen. The tree can be identified throughout the year by its characteristic growth form.

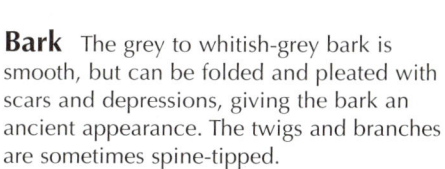

|          | Oct | Nov | Dec | Jan | Feb | Mar | Apr | May | Jun | Jul | Aug | Sep |
|----------|-----|-----|-----|-----|-----|-----|-----|-----|-----|-----|-----|-----|
| Leaf     |     |     |     |     |     |     |     |     |     |     |     |     |
| Flower   |     |     |     |     |     |     |     |     |     |     |     |     |
| Fruit/Pod|     |     |     |     |     |     |     |     |     |     |     |     |

BUSHVELD GENERALISTS
Bushveld Shepherds-tree

# COMMON WILD FIG

*Ficus burkei (Ficus thonningii)*

| | |
|---|---|
| **MULBERRY FAMILY** **MORACEAE** | **SA Tree Number 48** |

**AFRIKAANS** Gewone Wildevy, Wurgvy  **N. SOTHO** Moumo  **TSONGA** Xirhomberhombe
**TSWANA** Moumo  **VENDA** Muumo  **XHOSA** umThombe, uluZi  **ZULU** umThombe, umBombe

The species name **burkei** is named after Joseph Burke, a plant collector in the Magaliesberg area.

## Where you'll find this tree easily

The Common Wild Fig grows singly.

- It is easiest to find as a large tree on the Plains of the Sour Bushveld (S).
- It can also be found on the Plains of the Mixed Bushveld (M), the Northern Mountains (N) and the Central Mountains (C); and along Rivers and on all Slopes of the Sour Bushveld (S).

## Ecozones where this tree occurs

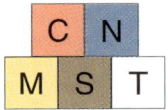

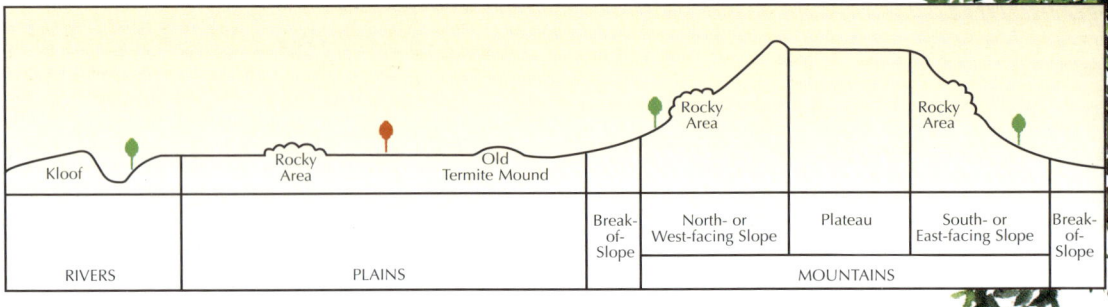

## Striking features

- This is a large, single-trunked tree that branches low down to form a wide-spreading, semi-circular canopy.
- **The bark is smooth and pale grey, and aerial roots may often be seen hanging from the main trunk and branches. Strangler roots are often visible, as are either the trunk or branches of the original support tree.**
- **The simple, shiny, dark green leaves are spirally arranged. They have long leaf-stalks and the yellowish central vein is clearly visible on the upper-surface.**
- The leaf is translucent, and the fine network of side veins can be seen when the leaf is held against the light.
- The small, short-stalked or stalkless, berry-like figs are green with white spots, and turn red when ripe.

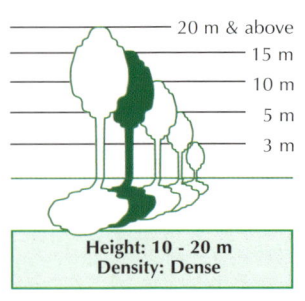

Height: 10 - 20 m
Density: Dense

BUSHVELD GENERALISTS
Common Wild Fig

# COMMON WILD FIG

*Ficus burkei (Ficus thonningii)*

**Links with animals** The fruit is eaten by Vervet and Samango Monkeys, baboons and a wide variety of fruit-eating birds and bats. Leaves, twigs and fallen fruit are eaten by elephant, giraffe, kudu, nyala, bushbuck and impala. Caterpillars of the Fig-tree Blue butterfly (*Myrina silenus ficedula*) eat the young leaves of the tree.

**Human uses** The fruit is edible and is used to make beer. Bark fibre is used for making mats, and twined bark to make a strong rope. An extraction of the bark is used for colds and throat infections, to prevent constipation, to stop nose-bleeding and to stimulate lactation. It is believed that miscarriage can be prevented by drinking a tea made from the root. The milky latex, dropped into the affected eye, is used to treat cataracts.

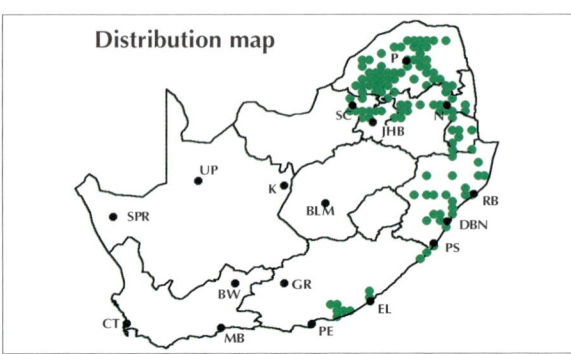
Distribution map

**Wood** The wood is not used commercially, but is often cut into straight planks and used as farm timber.

**Gardening** This is an attractive, fairly fast-growing tree that will attract birds to the garden. It can be grown from cuttings and from seed. It has an aggressive root system, but makes a good container plant, and is ideal as a bonsai. The tree is fairly drought- and frost-resistant, but is sensitive to cold winds, and young trees should be protected for the first 2 - 3 years.

**Look-alike trees** There are other Figs in this book, some of which are similar. See the Fig comparisons on page 77.

*Characteristic grey bark, long leaf-stalks and very short fig-stalks*

# GROWTH DETAILS

This is a medium-to-large tree with a broad, often twisting, buttressed trunk. It branches low down to form a wide-spreading, moderate-to-dense, semi-circular canopy. This is a strangler fig, and often masses of aerial roots can be seen hanging from the branches and main trunk. Often the trunk or branches of the original host tree are discernible from the difference in bark or leaves. All parts contain milky latex.

**Leaves** The simple, spirally arranged leaves have long leaf-stalks of 7 - 45 mm. They are broadly elliptic with a broad base and a broad tip. The leaves have a smooth margin, and are shiny dark green above and paler green below. The yellowish central vein is clearly visible on the upper-surface, and the fine network of side veins can be seen when the leaf is held up against the light. The veins and the leaf are translucent. (50 - 100 mm x 10 - 40 mm)

**Fruit** The small, berry-like, usually hairy figs have short stalks or no stalks. They are initially green with white spots, and ripen to red. The figs grow singly or in pairs in the angles formed by the leaves (August to December). (10 mm diameter)

*65% life-size*

**Flowers** As in all figs, the flowers are inside the fruit and are not visible.

**Bark** The bark is smooth and pale grey.

### Seasonal changes
Semi-deciduous tree. This tree can be identified by its aerial roots and growth form throughout the year.

|  | Oct | Nov | Dec | Jan | Feb | Mar | Apr | May | Jun | Jul | Aug | Sep |
|---|---|---|---|---|---|---|---|---|---|---|---|---|
| Leaf | █ | █ | █ | █ | █ | █ | █ | █ | █ |  | █ | █ |
| Flower |  |  |  |  |  |  |  |  |  |  |  |  |
| Fruit/Pod | █ | █ | █ |  |  |  |  |  | █ | █ | █ | █ |

199

# SHEPHERDS-TREE

*Boscia albitrunca*  
Shepard's tree; White-stem Tree; Coffeee-tree

| CAPER FAMILY CAPPARACEAE | SA Tree Number 122 |
|---|---|

**AFRIKAANS** Witgat, Witstamboom   **N. SOTHO** Mohlôpi   **PEDI** Mohlôpi   **TSONGA** Xukutsi
**TSWANA** Motlhôpi   **VENDA** Muṯhobi   **ZULU** umVithi

The species name **albitrunca** refers to the pale-coloured bark.

## Where you'll find this tree easily

The Shepherds-tree is associated with hot dry areas.
It prefers well-drained soils such as sandy or rocky soils.
- It is easiest to find in Rocky Areas on the Plains of the Mixed Bushveld (M).
- It can also be found in the other Ecozones on Rocky Areas on the Plains and the North- and West-facing Slopes, and along Rivers and Streams.

## Ecozones where this tree occurs

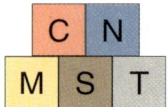

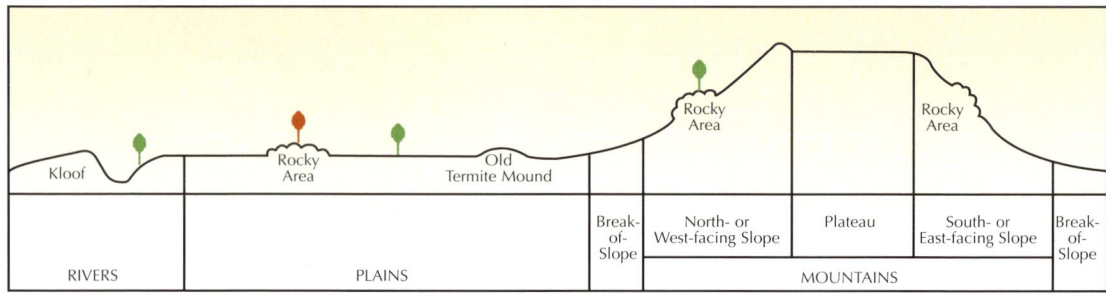

## Striking features

- This is a single-trunked tree that branches into a few large, but short, branches.
- Branches divide profusely to form a patchy, dense, V-shaped to semi-circular canopy.
- **The bark is noticeably pale grey with white patches, particularly on the branches which are clearly visible between the dense leaves.**
- **The young, dull green twigs stand out from the canopy and are covered with tight, spirally arranged, simple, leathery leaves.**

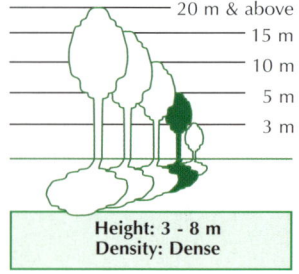

Height: 3 - 8 m
Density: Dense

**BUSHVELD GENERALISTS**
Shepherds-tree

# SHEPHERDS-TREE

*Boscia albitrunca*

**Links with animals** The leaves and flowers are valuable fodder for both domestic and wild animals, especially during drought periods. They are eaten by all antelope, and favoured by giraffe. The leaves are very nutritious as they are high in protein and Vitamin A.

**Human uses** Wood is used to make household utensils such as spoons and bowls. Coffee and porridge are made from the powdered roots, and the fruit is eaten in drier areas. The green fruit is used in the treatment of epilepsy. Infusions of the leaves are used to treat eye diseases in cattle.

**Gardening** This can be an attractive shade tree in gardens in dry areas. It can be grown easily from seed, as well as from root or shoot cuttings. It grows slowly and is drought-resistant but not very frost-resistant.

**Look alike tree** The Bushveld Shepherds-tree (*Boscia foetida*), page 192, is very similar in growth form, but tends to be multi-stemmed.

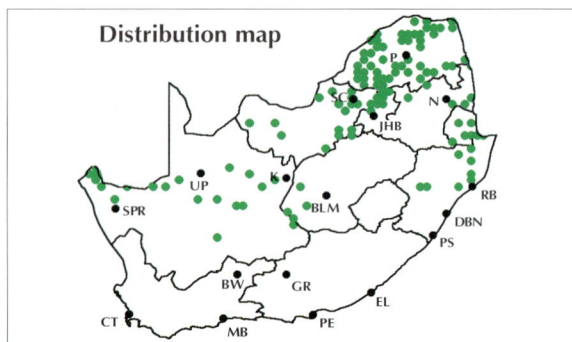

Distribution map

**Wood** The wood is dull white to pale yellowish-brown, moderately heavy, close-grained and tough. It has prominent annual rings and pores.

*January; characteristic white trunk and dense canopy; Plains, Mixed Bushveld*

# GROWTH DETAILS

It can have a very variable growth form, but is most often seen as a single-trunked, high-branching tree with a heavily branched, V-shaped to semi-circular canopy. The trunk is usually crooked or twisted.

**Leaves** The leaves are clustered in bunches of 4 - 5 on both older branches and short, spiky side-branchlets, and are usually alternate on new growth. They are narrowly elliptic, with a rounded tip and smooth margin, and have a short leaf-stalk. The leaves are grey-green to green, tough and leathery, and may be slightly hairy. (Leaf variable, usually 20 - 60 x 4 - 20 mm)

**Fruit** The smooth, round, berry-like fruit is light brown to yellowish when ripe, and about 10 mm in diameter (Ripens October to March).

**Flowers** The small, sweet-scented, greenish-yellow flowers grow singly or in small, dense bunches on short side-branchlets or in the angles formed by the leaves, usually on older growth. Flowering trees have a striking yellow-green tinge. Flowers appear from July to November, but mostly from August to November, depending on rain. (Individual flower: 4 mm diameter)

*90% life-size*

**Bark** Conspicuous whitish bark makes the tree look as if it has been whitewashed. It is often pitted and folded, and may have holes. In some areas the bark may become yellowish or blackish and can be flaky.

**Seasonal changes**
Evergreen. The presence of leaves all year round, with the white bark, makes it possible to identify the tree easily throughout the year.

|  | Oct | Nov | Dec | Jan | Feb | Mar | Apr | May | Jun | Jul | Aug | Sep |
|---|---|---|---|---|---|---|---|---|---|---|---|---|
| Leaf | | | | | | | | | | | | |
| Flower | | | | | | | | | | | | |
| Fruit/Pod | | | | | | | | | | | | |

BUSHVELD GENERALISTS
Shepherds-tree

# SMALL-LEAVED GUARRI

*Euclea undulata*                                    Common Guarri

---

### EBONY FAMILY
### EBENACEAE
**SA Tree Number 601.1**

**AFRIKAANS** Gewone Ghwarrie, Raasbessie  **N. SOTHO** Mohlakola  **TSONGA** Nhlangula
**TSWANA** Motlhakola  **VENDA** Tshitangule  **XHOSA** umGwali, umTshekisane  **ZULU** umShekisane

The species name **undulata** refers to the wavy leaf-margin.

## Where you'll find this tree easily

The Small-leaved Guarri grows singly, often under or among other trees.

- It is easiest to find on the Plains of the Mixed Bushveld (M).
- It can also be found on the Plains of the Thorny Bushveld (T), the Northern Mountains (N) and the Central Mountains (C); and along Rivers and Streams and on Old Termite Mounds of the Mixed Bushveld (M).

## Ecozones where this tree occurs

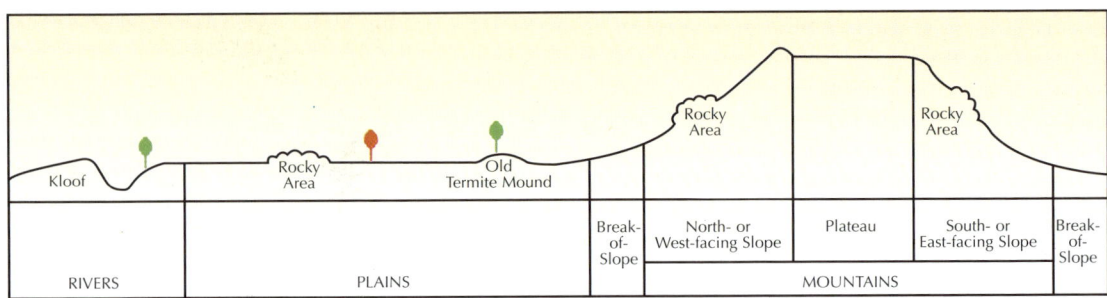

## Striking features

- This is a multi-stemmed shrub or small tree that branches low down to form a dense, neat, rounded canopy.
- Leaves are tightly packed in whorls at the ends of branchlets and twigs, one pair of leaves at right angles to the next.
- **The margin of the small, simple, blue-green leaf is usually conspicuously wavy.**
- **The grey bark is fissured lengthways, and in young trees and branches is smooth and pale.**

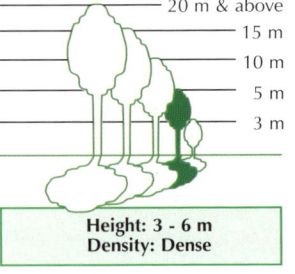

Height: 3 - 6 m
Density: Dense

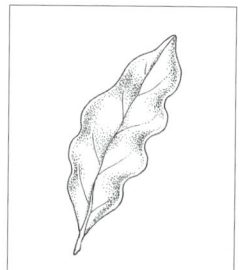

**BUSHVELD GENERALISTS**
Small-leaved Guarri

# SMALL-LEAVED GUARRI

*Euclea undulata*

**Links with animals** The leaves are browsed by domestic stock and game. The fruit is eaten by monkeys and birds.

**Human uses** The trunks are often used for fence posts. The berries are edible. Infusions of the roots have traditionally been used to treat heart disease. Because of the anaesthetic and anti-inflammatory properties, the roots have also been used to treat headache and toothache. An infusion of the root bark is used as a purgative.

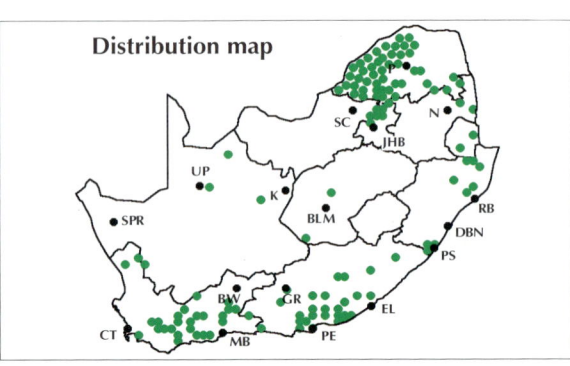
Distribution map

**Wood** The wood is brown, hard, close-grained, tough and durable, and is used in joinery.

**Gardening** This is a very attractive tree in a small garden, and will grow on soils that do not have a lot of nutrients. It is difficult to grow from seed as many seeds are parasitised. It is extremely frost- and drought-resistant.

*February; growing in loose groups; Mixed Bushveld, near Warmbaths*

# GROWTH DETAILS

This is a single- or multi-stemmed small tree that branches low down to form a dense, neat, rounded canopy. The leaves are tightly packed in whorls towards the ends of branchlets and twigs.

**Leaves** The simple, leathery leaves are elliptic to almost round. The margins are distinctively wavy, but may sometimes be smooth. Each pair of opposite leaves is at right angles to the next pair. The leaves are dark green or blue-green above, and paler, dotted with rust-brown glands below. (20 - 40 mm x 5 - 15 mm)

**Fruit** The reddish-brown berries become black when ripe, and are found in small bunches among the leaves (April to October). (4 - 6 mm diameter)

*life-size*

**Flowers** The inconspicuous, sweet-scented, white, bell-shaped flowers are found in branched sprays in the angles formed by the leaves. Similar male and female flowers grow on separate trees (December to April). (Flowering spray: up to 20 mm long)

**Bark** The grey bark is fissured lengthways. Young branchlets and twigs are smooth and pale, and covered in rusty scales.

**Seasonal changes**
Evergreen. The tree can be identified throughout the year.

|  | Oct | Nov | Dec | Jan | Feb | Mar | Apr | May | Jun | Jul | Aug | Sep |
|---|---|---|---|---|---|---|---|---|---|---|---|---|
| Leaf | ■ | ■ | ■ | ■ | ■ | ■ | ■ | ■ | ■ | ■ | ■ | ■ |
| Flower |  |  |  |  |  |  |  |  |  |  |  |  |
| Fruit/Pod | ■ |  |  |  |  | ■ | ■ | ■ | ■ | ■ | ■ | ■ |

BUSHVELD GENERALISTS
Small-leaved Guarri

# SWEET-THORN ACACIA

*Acacia karroo*

Sweet Thorn; Karoo thorn;
Cape Thorn Tree; Mimosa Thorn

## THORN-TREE FAMILY
## MIMOSACEAE

SA Tree Number 172

**AFRIKAANS** Soetdoring, Karoodoring  **N. SOTHO** Mooka  **SISWATI** isiNga  **S. SOTHO** Leoka
**TSONGA** Munga  **TSWANA** Mooka, Mookana  **VENDA** Muunga, Muunga-ludzi
**XHOSA** umNga  **ZULU** umuNga

The species name **karroo** refers to the fact that this is the most conspicuous tree of the arid areas of South Africa.

## Where you'll find this tree easily

The Sweet-thorn Acacia is one of the most widespread and common trees in South Africa. It often occurs in large groups on grassland, and single trees are found along drainage lines.

- It is easiest to find along Rivers and Streams in all Ecozones.
- It can also be found on the Plains; and Rocky Outcrops on the South- or East-facing Slopes in all Ecozones.

## Ecozones where this tree occurs

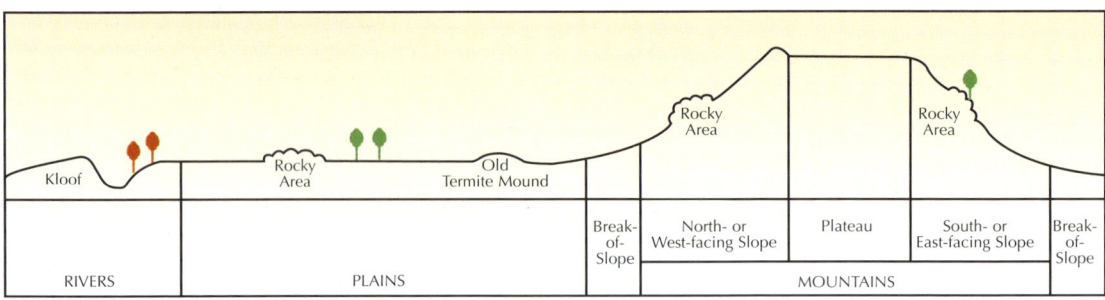

## Striking features

- This is a single- or multi-trunked Thorn-tree that branches low down into several large branches to form a wide canopy.
- The bright green, twice compound leaves and straight, long, paired, white thorns contrast strongly with the dark, rough bark.
- Many sturdy twigs in the outer canopy give this tree a spiky outline.
- The yellow, sweet-smelling flower-balls appear after rain, mostly from October to February, but often until April.

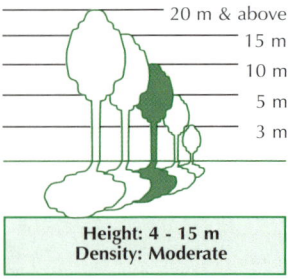

Height: 4 - 15 m
Density: Moderate

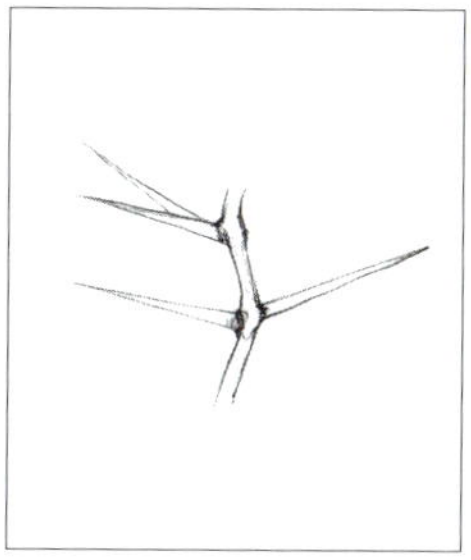

**BUSHVELD GENERALISTS**
*Sweet-thorn Acacia*

**Largest tree currently registered**

**Diameter:** 0,78 m
**Girth:** 2,45 m
**Height:** 27 m

O Q Smith, Oudehoutspruit, Dist. Standerton

209

# SWEET-THORN ACACIA

*Acacia karroo*

**Links with animals** This is a very good fodder tree, all parts being eaten by cattle and goats. Monkeys, parrots and many other birds and insects are attracted to the flowers, and baboons eat the pods. Nitrogen-fixing bacteria are found on the roots of Acacias. This increases the fertility of the soil in the vicinity, and ultimately adds to the nutritional value of the grasses that grow there. Many grazers are attracted to these areas.

**Human uses** The wood is used for building. It was also used for spokes, wheels and yokes, as well as tool handles. The bark can be used to tan leather red. It is used in certain areas as a Christmas tree.

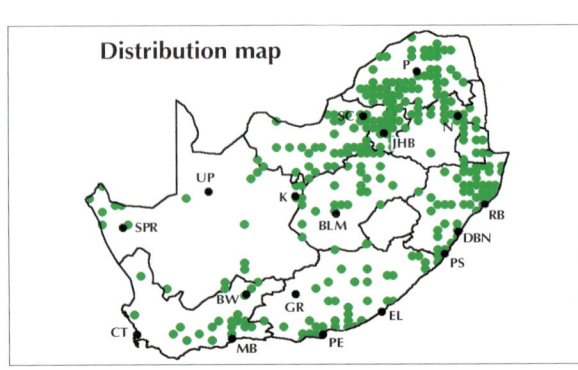
Distribution map

**Wood** The wood is durable, hard and tough, with yellow heartwood.

**Gardening** This is an attractive tree that is frost- and drought-resistant, and grows quickly. It grows easily from seed, but the seeds should be soaked in hot water before planting. It is suitable as a bonsai tree.

**Look alike trees** Acacias all have twice compound leaves, and many have yellow flower-balls. See Acacia comparisons pages 70 - 73.

*Conspicuous flower-balls; sprays at ends of twigs*

# GROWTH DETAILS

This single- or multi-trunked tree often has a crooked trunk that branches low down. Multiple small, sturdy, dark branchlets and twigs in the outer canopy give the tree a spiky outline. The moderate canopy is spreading but less dense in areas of lower rainfall. The young twigs grow in a zig-zag pattern, with the thorns on the angles.

**Leaves**  Twice compound leaves grow on small cushions in the angles of the thorns. There are 2 - 12 feather pairs, with 8 - 20 pairs of leaflets. (Leaf: 55 - 120 mm; leaflet: 3 - 10 x 1,5 - 5 mm)

**Flowers**  The conspicuous, yellow flower-balls are sweet-scented, and grow in sprays at the ends of the twigs. This tree is one of the last of the Thorn-trees (Acacias) to flower in late spring or early summer, often only after rain. It flowers intermittently throughout the summer. The trees may be covered in a mass of yellow flower-balls after good rains (October to April). (10 - 13 mm)

**Thorns**  The characteristic thorns are long, white and paired. The trees in the drier areas tend to be more thorny. (30 - 150 mm)

*40% life-size*

**Pods**  The bumpy bean pods curl into a sickle-shape. They split open on the tree when ripe, from January to May. Pods may stay on the tree well into winter. (50 - 130 x 6 - 13 mm)

**Bark**  The bark is dark red to black, rough, and fissured lengthways, peeling loosely to reveal red under-bark. New branches, branchlets and twigs are smooth and red-brown.

## Seasonal changes
Deciduous, but may be evergreen under favourable conditions. During drier periods and in drier areas, the leaves change into autumn colours before they drop. It is difficult to find without leaves and/or pods.

|  | Oct | Nov | Dec | Jan | Feb | Mar | Apr | May | Jun | Jul | Aug | Sep |
|---|---|---|---|---|---|---|---|---|---|---|---|---|
| Leaf | | | | | | | | | | | | |
| Flower | | | | | | | | | | | | |
| Fruit/Pod | | | | | | | | | | | | |

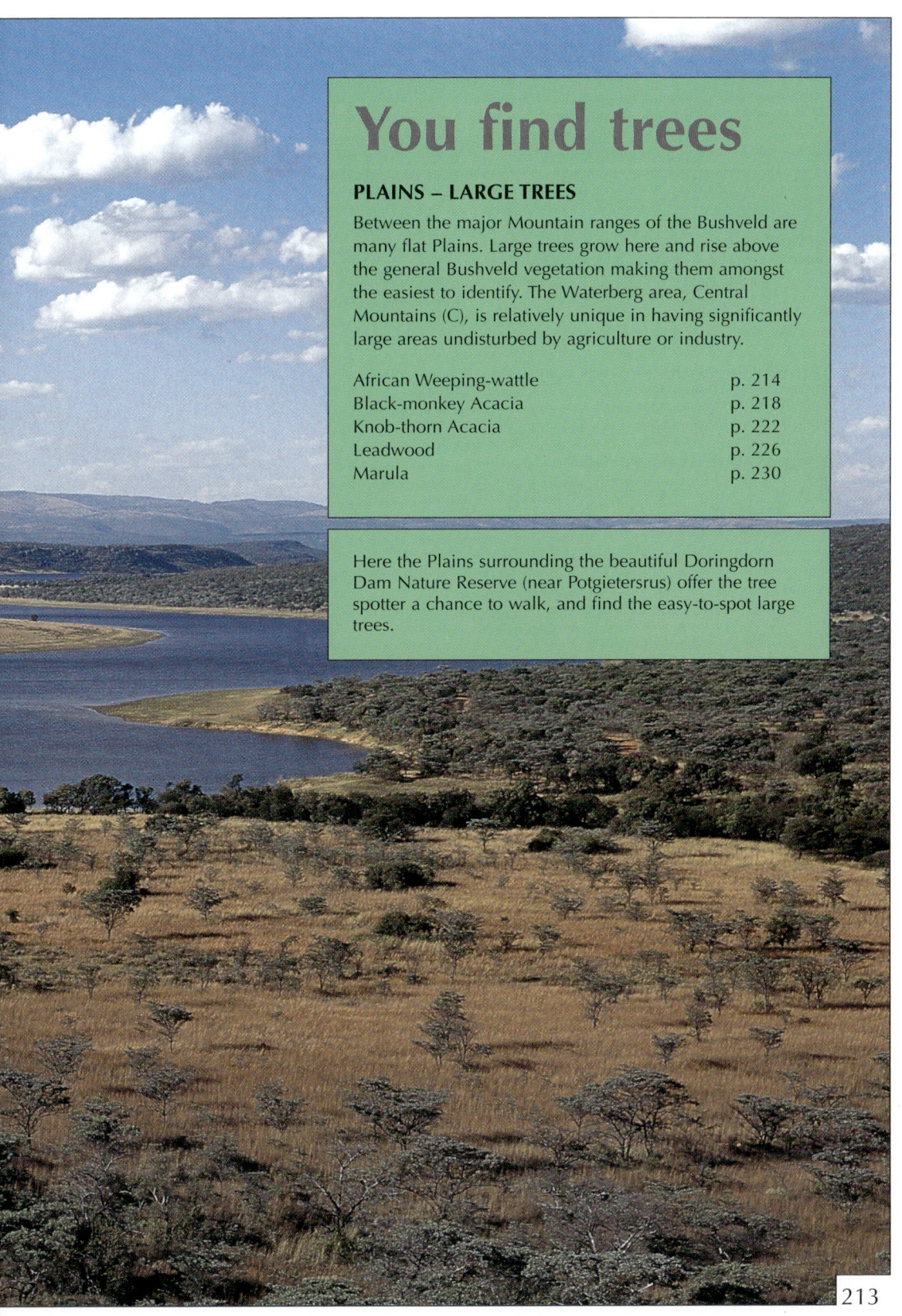

# You find trees

## PLAINS – LARGE TREES

Between the major Mountain ranges of the Bushveld are many flat Plains. Large trees grow here and rise above the general Bushveld vegetation making them amongst the easiest to identify. The Waterberg area, Central Mountains (C), is relatively unique in having significantly large areas undisturbed by agriculture or industry.

| | |
|---|---|
| African Weeping-wattle | p. 214 |
| Black-monkey Acacia | p. 218 |
| Knob-thorn Acacia | p. 222 |
| Leadwood | p. 226 |
| Marula | p. 230 |

Here the Plains surrounding the beautiful Doringdorn Dam Nature Reserve (near Potgietersrus) offer the tree spotter a chance to walk, and find the easy-to-spot large trees.

# AFRICAN WEEPING-WATTLE

*Peltophorum africanum*  **Weeping wattle; African Wattle; Rhodesian Wattle**

## FLAMBOYANT FAMILY
## CAESALPINIACEAE

**SA Tree Number 215**

**AFRIKAANS** Huilboom, Rooikiaat    **N. SOTHO** Mosehla, Mosese    **PEDI** Mosehla
**SISWATI** isiKhabakhombe    **TSONGA** Ndzedze    **TSWANA** Mosêtlha    **VENDA** Musese
**ZULU** umSehle

The species name **africanum** refers to Africa.

## Where you'll find this tree easily

The African Weeping-wattle grows singly among other tree species, but where one is found, others are usually nearby.

- It is easiest to find on the Plains of all Ecozones.
- It can also be found on the North- and West-facing Slopes; and on the foothills of the South- and East-facing Slopes.

## Ecozones where this tree occurs

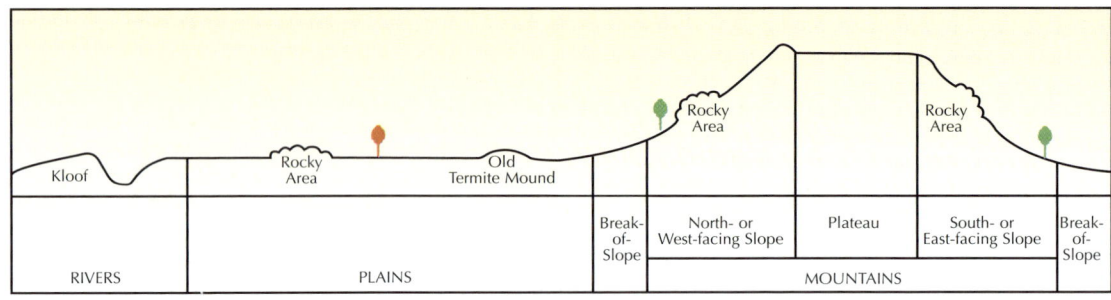

## Striking features

- **This tree has dull green, large, soft, feathery, Acacia-like leaves.**
- It does not have thorns.
- It branches low down from a stem that is often crooked, to form a spreading, irregular and untidy canopy.
- The mature leaves, at the tips of the branches, are often yellowish.
- **Abundant, yellow flowers among the large, feathery leaves are striking in summer.**

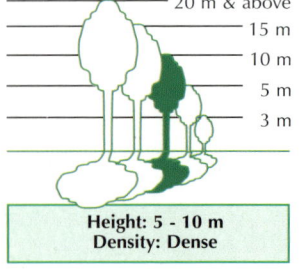

Height: 5 - 10 m
Density: Dense

PLAINS – LARGE TREES
African Weeping-wattle

# AFRICAN WEEPING-WATTLE

*Peltophorum africanum*

**Links with animals** In summer the tree is often infested with the Spittle Bug, *Ptyelus grossus*. The bugs' secretions drip down, causing it to 'rain' under the tree. The tree is not browsed regularly, but young shoots may be eaten by Black Rhino, elephant, giraffe and kudu.

**Human uses** The wood is used to make furniture, axe handles, buckets and ornaments. It is also used as fuel. Root extracts are used as enemas, and to treat sterility and backache. Bark extracts are used for coughs, sore throats, fevers, stomach complaints, wounds, intestinal parasites, eye complaints and venereal diseases.

**Gardening** This decorative tree will grow in most gardens. It is sensitive to severe frost, but drought-resistant once established. It grows easily from seed, and is fast-growing when planted in fertile soils and watered well.

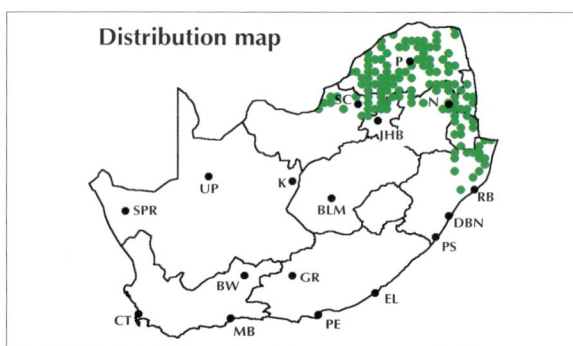

Distribution map

**Wood** The heartwood is reddish, close-grained, fairly hard and tough. It polishes well, and is easy to work.

*Large tree; often obscured trunk; Plains, Mixed Bushveld*

# GROWTH DETAILS

There is a single, crooked stem. It branches low down with several downward curving branches to form an irregular, dense canopy. The trunk is often obscured by drooping branchlets and leaves.

**Flowers** The conspicuous, sweet-scented, bright yellow flowers grow in sprays at the ends of twigs or in the angles formed by the leaves. The flowers have crinkled petals up to 20 mm in diameter. The flower-stalk and the back of the petals are covered in reddish-brown hairs (September to February). (Spray: up to 150 x 80 mm; individual flower: up to 20 mm wide)

**Leaves** The alternate, feathery, Acacia-like leaves are twice compound, with 4 - 9 pairs of feathers, and 10 - 23 pairs of leaflets. The small, soft leaflets are silvery and dull green above, and paler below. The leaflets are oblong to almost square. The feather-stalks and central vein, as well as the leaf-stalk, are covered in reddish-brown hairs. (Leaf: up to 120 - 180 mm; leaflet: 5 - 9 x 1,5 - 3 mm)

**Pods** The greyish-brown to dark brown pods grow in conspicuous hanging bunches. The pods are thinly woody, and contain one or two seeds, which can be seen as bulges. At least a few pods can be seen on the tree for most of the year, but pods are found in much greater numbers from February to May. (Pod: 40 - 100 x 12 - 20 mm)

*70% life-size*

**Bark** The bark of older trees is dark grey-brown with shallow grooves.

### Seasonal changes
Deciduous. The leaves are lost late in the winter. The tree can be identified for most of the year, as either the leaves or pods are normally present.

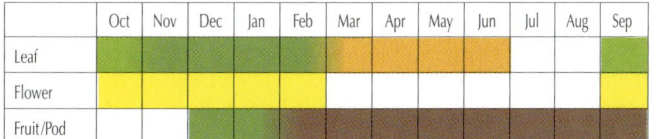

|  | Oct | Nov | Dec | Jan | Feb | Mar | Apr | May | Jun | Jul | Aug | Sep |
|---|---|---|---|---|---|---|---|---|---|---|---|---|
| Leaf | green | green | green | green | green | orange | orange | orange | orange |  |  | green |
| Flower | yellow | yellow | yellow | yellow | yellow |  |  |  |  |  |  | yellow |
| Fruit/Pod |  |  | green | green | brown | brown | brown | brown | brown | brown | brown | brown |

# BLACK-MONKEY ACACIA

*Acacia burkei*                                    Black Monkey Thorn

---

### THORN-TREE FAMILY
### MIMOSACEAE
### SA Tree Number 161

**AFRIKAANS** Swartapiesdoring, Apiesdoring  **TSONGA** Nkasinga  **TSWANA** Mokgwa
**ZULU** umKhaya wehlalahlathi

The species name **burkei** refers to the naturalist / botanist Joseph Burke who catalogued the tree in the 1840s.

## Where you'll find this tree easily

The Black-monkey Acacia grows singly but where one is found others will be found in the vicinity.

- It is easiest to find as a tall tree on the Plains of the Mixed Bushveld (M).
- It can also be found on the Plains and along Rivers and Streams of the Central (C) and Northern Mountains (N) and Thorny Bushveld (T); and along Rivers of the Mixed Bushveld (M) and Sour Bushveld (S).

## Ecozones where this tree occurs

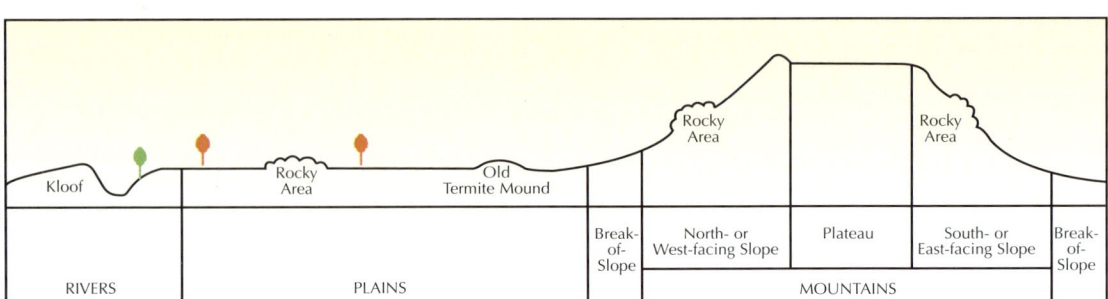

## Striking features

- **This is a tall, single-trunked tree, often high-branching, with a dense, dark green, semi-circular to deep-umbrella canopy.**
- The twice compound leaves are short and stiff, stand upright, and hardly move in the wind.
- The bark is dark and rough, and forms deep, lengthways fissures exposing yellowish under-bark.
- The white flower-spikes bloom from October to January after the leaves have appeared.
- **The flat bean pods have a pointed tip, and are dark brown when ripe.**

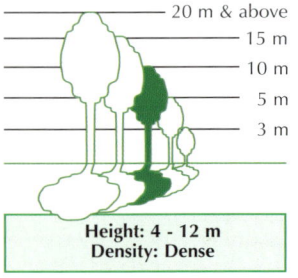

Height: 4 - 12 m
Density: Dense

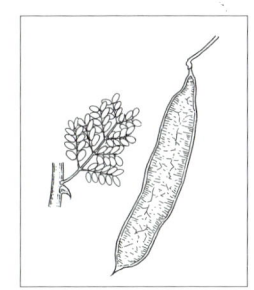

**Largest tree currently registered**

**Diameter:** 0,90 m
**Girth:** 2,83 m
**Height:** 14 m

EA Galpin, 'Mosdene',
Zyferkraal,
Dist. Potgietersrus

PLAINS – LARGE TREES
Black-monkey Acacia

# BLACK-MONKEY ACACIA

*Acacia burkei*

**Links with animals** The dry pods have a high nutritional value, and are eagerly eaten by cattle, game and bushbabies. The green leaves are eaten by Black Rhino, elephant, giraffe, kudu, nyala and impala, and fallen leaves are eaten by Grey Duiker and steenbok. Monkeys eat the gum. These trees are favoured by nesting birds.

**Human uses** The wood is used to make furniture and tool handles. It makes good fence posts as it is termite-resistant, although it must be protected against wood-borers. The tree was believed to attract lightning.

**Gardening** This tree can provide valuable shade in warm Sandveld areas, but the root systems are invasive. It can be grown from seed easily, but it is a slow grower and prefers well-drained soil. The tree can withstand low temperatures but not cold wind. It is excellent as a bonsai tree.

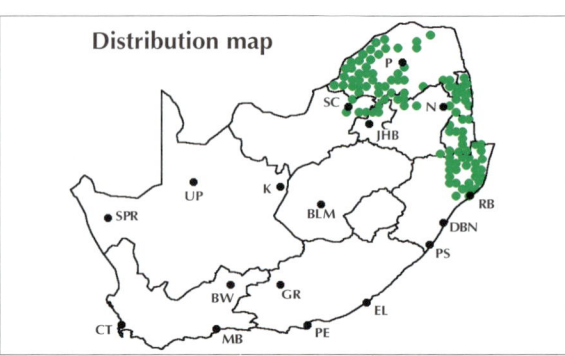
Distribution map

**Wood** The yellow-brown to dark brown wood is fine grained, strong, hardy and heavy.

**Look-alike trees** Knob-thorn Acacia (*Acacia nigrescens*), page 222, has a lengthways-fissured bark with pale yellow under-bark; conspicuous knobs with hooked thorns on young branches and trunks; large paired leaflets that may resemble butterfly leaves; and flower-spikes that appear before the leaves.

Monkey Acacia (*Acacia galpinii*), page 71, has yellowish, corky bark with flaky, lengthways fissures; the 8 - 10 mm-long thorns are slightly curved; leaves are long, with 7 - 14 pairs of feathers, and 12 - 40 pairs of fine leaflets; flowers are in spikes; flat, purplish-brown bean pods split on the tree.

This tree can be confused with other Acacias. See pages 70 - 73 for comparisons.

*Early winter; Plains, Mixed Bushveld*

# GROWTH DETAILS

This is a single-trunked tree that branches to form a semi-circular to deep-umbrella canopy. In Riverine forests it often branches high up and has a more rounded canopy.

**Leaves**  Twice compound leaves are alternate, and the leaf-stalk is often covered in fine, white hairs. The leaf may have 3 - 10 opposite or sub-opposite feather pairs, with fewer pairs in drier areas and more in wetter areas. There are 2 - 16 pairs of dark green leaflets that vary in shape and size, tending to be larger and rounder in the drier areas. The leaves are short and stiff, stand upright, and hardly move in the wind. (Leaf: 25 - 70 mm; leaflet: 4 - 20 x 2 - 12 mm)

**Pods**  The flat bean pods have a pointed tip, and turn red-brown to dark brown as they ripen. They are conspicuously veined, particularly when young. Ripe pods turn black, and split open on the tree. They may remain on the tree until late autumn (December to May). (90 - 160 x 12 - 25 mm)

*80% life-size*

**Thorns**  Short, dark, sharply hooked thorns grow in pairs, far apart, below the leaf-buds. (3 - 9 mm)

**Flowers**  White flower-spikes in small groups appear long after the leaves in late spring or summer (October to January). (50 - 100 x 10 - 20 mm)

**Bark**  The dark brown bark is rough, and forms deep, lengthways fissures, exposing yellowish under-bark. The branches often have dark, hooked thorns on knobs. Young branchlets are covered with fine, brown hairs that turn grey with age.

**Seasonal changes**
Evergreen. This unique tree can be identified easily throughout the year.

|  | Oct | Nov | Dec | Jan | Feb | Mar | Apr | May | Jun | Jul | Aug | Sep |
|---|---|---|---|---|---|---|---|---|---|---|---|---|
| Leaf | ■ | ■ | ■ | ■ | ■ | ■ | ■ | ■ | ■ |  |  | ■ |
| Flower | ■ | ■ | ■ |  |  |  |  |  |  |  |  |  |
| Fruit/Pod |  | ■ | ■ | ■ | ■ | ■ | ■ | ■ |  |  |  |  |

PLAINS — LARGE TREES
Black-monkey Acacia

# KNOB-THORN ACACIA

*Acacia nigrescens*          Knob Thorn

## THORN-TREE FAMILY
## MIMOSACEAE

SA Tree Number 178

**AFRIKAANS** Knoppiesdoring, Perdepram    **N. SOTHO** Moritidi    **SISWATI** umKhaya    **TSONGA** Nkaya    **TSWANA** Mokoba, Mokala    **VENDA** Munanga    **ZULU** umKhaya

The species name **nigrescens** means 'black', and probably refers to the pods.

## Where you'll find this tree easily

The Knob-thorn Acacia is most common on clay soils. It is a large tree that stands out among other trees and normally grows singly, but where one is found others are usually in the vicinity.

- It is easiest to find on the Plains of the Mixed Bushveld (M).
- It can also be found on the Plains of the other Ecozones; and on the North- or West-facing Slopes of the Northern Mountains (N); as well as along Rivers and Streams of the Sour Bushveld (S) and the Northern Mountains (N).

## Ecozones where this tree occurs

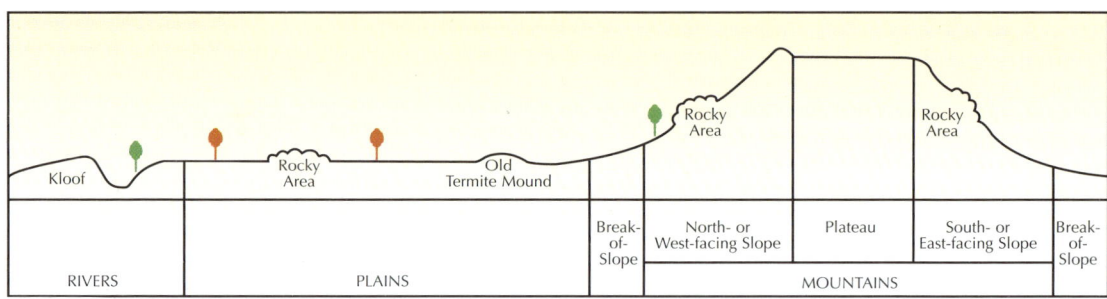

## Striking features

- This is an upright thorn tree, with a straight, single trunk that branches high up to form a moderate, irregular canopy.
- There are woody knobs on the young trunks and large branches of many specimens.
- The leaflets are large for an Acacia, and paired. Each pair resembles a butterfly leaf.
- In late winter and early spring, before the new leaves appear, the tree is covered with conspicuous, creamy-white flower-spikes.

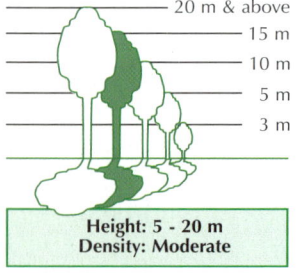

Height: 5 - 20 m
Density: Moderate

**Largest tree currently registered**

**Diameter:** 0,97 m
**Girth:** 3,05 m
**Height:** 13 m

Nwanedi Resort, Northern Province

PLAINS – LARGE TREES
Knob-thorn Acacia

# KNOB-THORN ACACIA

*Acacia nigrescens*

**Links with animals** This tree is vulnerable to insects. When the bark has been removed, the tree is often attacked, and may even be killed, by wood-borers. The flowers are eaten by baboons, monkeys and giraffe. However, in the process many of the flowers are pollinated by giraffe! Leaves and shoots form an important food source for elephant, kudu, giraffe, cattle and goats. The pods are an important source of protein for giraffe in winter. Holes in the trunk and branches provide nesting sites for birds.

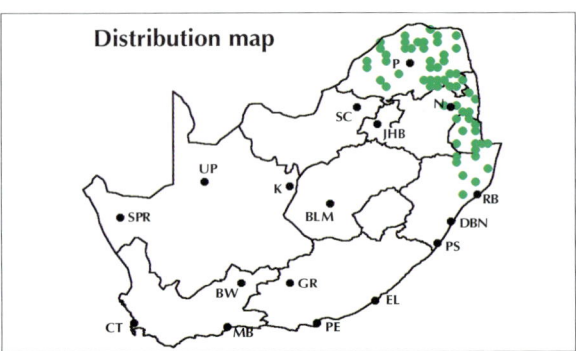

**Human uses** The wood is used for fence posts. Young branches make ideal knobkieries (fighting sticks) but, despite the name, the knobs play no part in this. Poles were planted in the ground to prevent lightning from striking a village. The bark was used for tanning leather.

**Wood** The heartwood is yellow-brown and the sapwood is yellow. The wood has an irregular grain, is difficult to saw, and planes well to a smooth finish. It turns readily and varnishes satisfactorily, but does not hold nails well.

**Gardening** The tree grows well in most gardens. It likes warm conditions and is susceptible to frost, but is fairly drought-resistant. The tree is a disadvantage in home gardens as it tends to drop thorny twigs. It grows very easily but very slowly from seed. It is excellent as a bonsai tree.

**Look-alike trees** Despite the knobs on some trees, this tree can be confused with other Acacias. See pages 70 - 73 for comparisons.

*Young trees; protruding knobs*

# GROWTH DETAILS

The tree has a single, straight trunk that branches to form a moderate, irregular canopy.

*50% life-size*

**Leaves** The twice compound, alternate leaves have pale green leaflets that are almost round and have a smooth margin. There are 1 - 3 feather pairs, each feather consisting of 1 - 2 pairs of leaflets, each pair resembling a butterfly leaf. (Leaf: 35 x 80 mm; leaflet: 10 - 30 x 8 - 25 mm)

**Thorns** Downward-curving, hooked thorns grow on characteristic protruding knobs on the thicker branches and young trunks. Smaller hooked thorns grow in pairs on branchlets and twigs. (5 - 10 mm)

**Pods** The flat bean pods hang down in clusters. They change from pale green to brown as they ripen. Pods never open on the trees, but break up on the ground (December to June). (110 - 140 x 70 mm)

**Flowers** From late June to early July the tree has a plum-coloured sheen from the developing flower-buds. They open to form a spectacular creamy-white display, covering the leafless trees in spring (July to September). The sweet-scented flower-spikes grow in clusters of 2 - 3 at the leaf-buds. Flowers are most abundant after good, late summer rains during the previous season. (80 - 100 mm)

**Bark** The bark is dark brown, rough and deeply fissured lengthways, revealing a yellowish under-bark. Younger branches and trees have paler bark, and have the characteristic knobs with hooked thorns.

**Seasonal changes** Deciduous. Leaves turn yellow before they fall in autumn. The knobs are still visible in winter, making the tree easy to find.

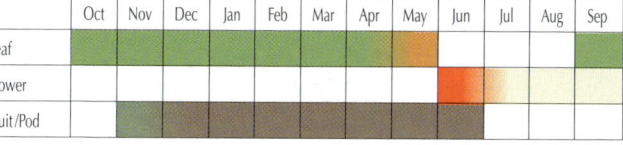

PLAINS – LARGE TREES
Knob-thorn Acacia

225

# LEADWOOD

*Combretum imberbe*

---

### BUSHWILLOW FAMILY
### COMBRETACEAE

**SA Tree Number 539**

**AFRIKAANS** Hardekool, Loodhout  **N. SOTHO** Mohwelere-tšhipi, Mmotô
**PEDI** Motswiri  **SISWATI** umMono, imPondozendhlovu  **TSONGA** Mondzo  **TSWANA** Motswiri
**VENDA** Mudzwiri, Muhiri  **ZULU** imPondondlovu

The species name **imberbe** refers to the hairless leaves.

## Where you'll find this tree easily

The Leadwood grows singly.
- It is easiest to find on the Plains of the Mixed Bushveld (M).
- It can also be found on the Plains on Old Termite Mounds and along Rivers and Streams of the Northern Mountains (N), Central Mountains (C) and Sour Bushveld (S).

## Ecozones where this tree occurs

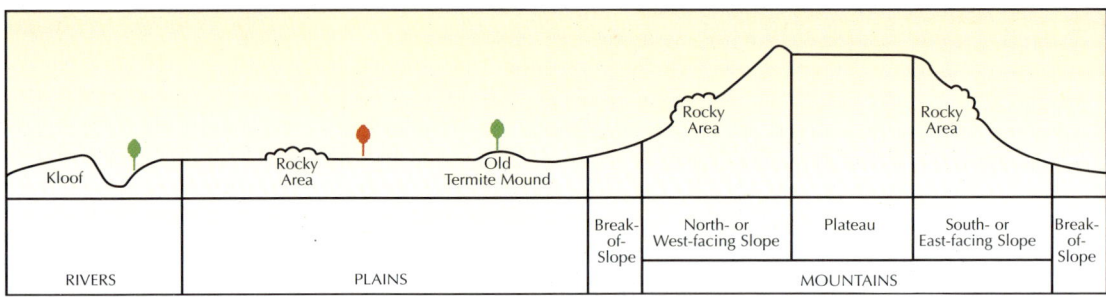

## Striking features

- This is a very tall, high-branching, majestic tree.
- The sparse foliage has a yellow tinge throughout the year.
- **The light grey bark, which breaks up into small, regular blocks (like snake-skin), is striking and characteristic.**
- Mature trees often have dead, bare branches and twigs.
- **The tree has small, four-winged pods.**

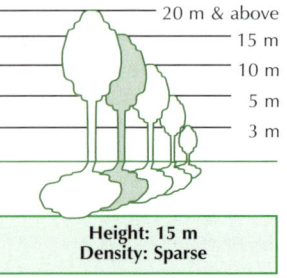

Height: 15 m
Density: Sparse

**Largest tree currently registered**

**Diameter:** 1,40 m
**Girth:** 4,40 m
**Height:** 20 m

B G Bronn, 24 Kruis Road,
('Korthoek') Dist. Ellisras

PLAINS – LARGE TREES
Leadwood

# LEADWOOD

*Combretum imberbe*

**Links with animals** The leaves are eaten by giraffe, elephant, kudu and impala. Trees damaged by elephants or other animals usually recover well.

**Human uses** As the wood burns slowly and forms good coals, it is highly sought-after as cooking fuel. However, to protect our trees, wood fires are discouraged. The calcium-rich ash is used as a whitewash on houses. The flowers are used in a cough mixture, and smoke from the burning leaf is inhaled to relieve coughs and colds. The leaves and fruit are believed to have mystical powers.

**Gardening** The Leadwood will grow in most well-drained gardens. It is fairly drought-resistant, but could be damaged by frost. It grows easily, but extremely slowly, from seed. The seeds are thought to be poisonous.

**Wood** The heartwood is dark brown, hard and very heavy, while the sapwood is thin and yellowish. Although it is difficult to work, rapidly blunting and breaking tools, it is used to make ornaments. The wood is termite- and borer-proof.

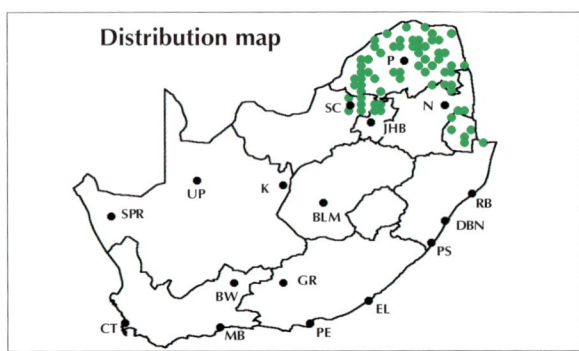

Distribution map

*August; late evening; dead Leadwood in Malatse Dam, Pilanesberg*

# GROWTH DETAILS

It has a single, straight trunk that branches high up, with branches tending to grow horizontally and upwards. The canopy is wide-spreading and sparse. New branches, and the branches of young trees, are thick and end in spines. Older trees often display dead, bare branches and twigs. Leaves and pods are relatively small for the size of the tree.

50% life-size

**Leaves** The simple, opposite leaves are broadly elliptic to oval, with a wavy margin. The tip and the base of the leaves are rounded to broadly tapering. The leaves are characteristically grey-green to grey-yellow-green, because they are covered with minute silvery scales. They are rather leathery and without hairs. (25 - 80 x 10 - 30 mm)

**Pods** The pod is four-winged, and is characteristic of the Bushwillow family. It is small for the size of the tree, and is yellowish-green, also covered with minute silvery scales, and drying to light brown. The pods do not remain on the tree for long periods, as with most other Bushwillows, but often drop just after ripening in autumn (February to June). (Pod: 15 - 19 mm diameter)

**Flowers** The creamy to creamy-yellow flowers are sweet-smelling. The long, slender spikes grow in the angles formed by the leaves or at the ends of branches (November to March). (Flower spikes: 40 - 80 x up to 15 mm)

**Bark** The light grey bark, which breaks up into small, regular blocks (like snake-skin), is striking and characteristic.

## Seasonal changes
Deciduous. Leaves turn yellow-brown before falling in winter. The majestic growth form and characteristic light grey, snake-skin bark make identification possible throughout the year.

|          | Oct | Nov | Dec | Jan | Feb | Mar | Apr | May | Jun | Jul | Aug | Sep |
|----------|-----|-----|-----|-----|-----|-----|-----|-----|-----|-----|-----|-----|
| Leaf     |     |     |     |     |     |     |     |     |     |     |     |     |
| Flower   |     |     |     |     |     |     |     |     |     |     |     |     |
| Fruit/Pod |    |     |     |     |     |     |     |     |     |     |     |     |

PLAINS – LARGE TREES
Leadwood

# MARULA

*Sclerocarya birrea*

| MANGO FAMILY ANACARDIACEAE | SA Tree Number 360 |
|---|---|

**AFRIKAANS** Maroela  **N. SOTHO** Morula  **SISWATI** UmGana  **TSONGA** Nkanyi  **TSWANA** Morula  **VENDA** Mufula  **ZULU** umGanu

The species name **birrea** is based on the common name of the tree ('birr') in Senegal and Gambia.

## Where you'll find this tree easily

Marula trees very seldom grow in groups, but once one is found, other trees are usually visible in the vicinity. It grows on most soil types at medium-to-low altitudes.

- It is easiest to find on the Plains of the Mixed Bushveld (M).
- It can also be found on the Plains of the Northern Mountains (N), the Central Mountains (C) and the Sour Bushveld (S); and on the North- or West-facing Slopes of the Mixed Bushveld (M) and the Sour Bushveld (S).

## Ecozones where this tree occurs

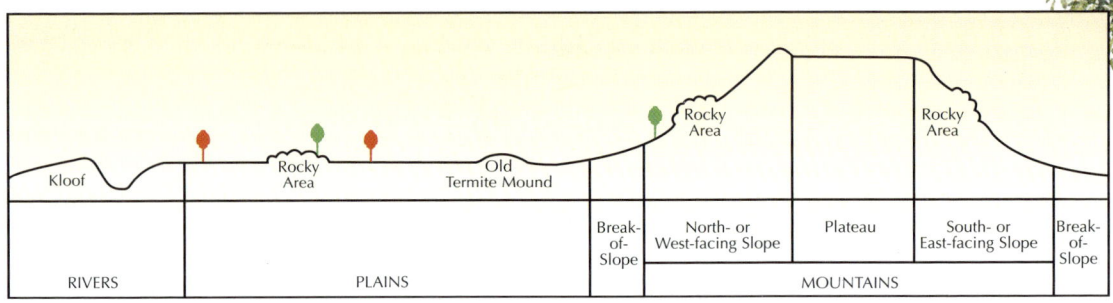

## Striking features

- It is a single-trunked tree, dividing high up into a few bare branches and a semi-circular canopy.
- **The bark often peels in conspicuous, characteristic rounded depressions, revealing smooth, pink-brown under-bark.**
- In summer blue-green, compound leaves hang, crowded towards the end of thickened twigs; in winter the bare twigs stand out like stubby fingers.
- Unripe green and ripe yellow fruit are often seen on the ground under the female trees (January to March).

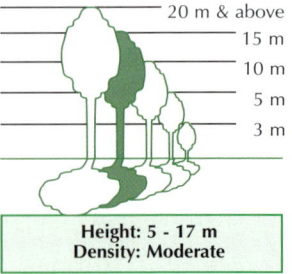

Height: 5 - 17 m
Density: Moderate

**Largest tree currently registered**

**Diameter:** 1,33 m
**Girth:** 4,18 m
**Height:** 19 m

N G Kerk Kranspoort Mission Station, Dist. Soutpansberg

PLAINS – LARGE TREES
Marula

# MARULA

*Sclerocarya birrea*

**Links with animals** Mosquitoes often breed in the hollows between branches. The caterpillars of eight species of butterfly eat the foliage. The bark is often infected by insects that cause huge, dark swellings (galls) to form on the main trunk. The fleshy fruit is a favourite of many mammals such as elephant, monkeys, baboons, kudu, duiker, impala and zebra. The leaves and bark are often eaten by elephant.

**Human uses** The wood is used for furniture, carvings and household articles. The fruit is tasty and rich in Vitamin C. Jelly, jam, beer and Amarula liqueur are made from it. The kernel of the seed is edible, and oil pressed from it can be used as a preservative. An extract of the bark is used to treat dysentery and diarrhoea, and to prevent malaria, while the inner bark is effective in soothing insect bites and the burns of hairy caterpillars. Newly-born baby girls and their mothers were traditionally washed in water heated on a fire made from the twigs.

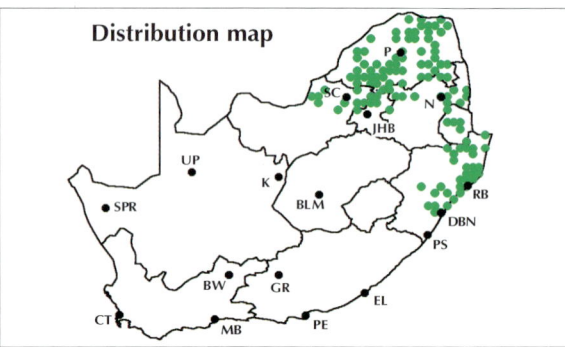
Distribution map

**Wood** The wood is soft, perishable and permeable. The heartwood is pinky-red, sometimes with blue patches. It turns well and sharp tools are required when planing.

**Gardening** This is a very attractive shade tree. It grows fast and easily form seed. It is drought-resistant, but young trees are frost-sensitive.

**Look-alike trees** False-marula Lannea (*Lannea schweinfurthii*), page 82, has similar growth form, but with thinner twigs, and the bark peels in large, irregular scales. There are 1 - 3 pairs of leaflets, plus a terminal that is more pointed. They tend to lose their leaves later than Marulas. The fruit is grape-like and hangs in bunches.

Two other trees with compound leaves that grow at the tips of thick, stubby twigs, are Burkea (*Burkea africana*), page 236, which has yellowish leaflet- and leaf-stalks, and Live-long Lannea (*Lannea discolor*), page 330, which is usually a smaller tree, and has green leaf- and leaflet-stalks. See comparisons on page 69.

*Winter; stubby finger twigs; Plains, Sour Bushveld*

# GROWTH DETAILS

This tree has a single, straight trunk that branches high up into a few bare main branches. These grow slightly upwards and outwards, to form a moderate-to-dense, semi-circular canopy.

**Leaves** Compound, alternate leaves have 3 - 7 pairs of opposite, elliptic leaflets with a single leaflet at the tip. New leaves are coppery, turning shiny bright green before they mature to blue-green above and paler below. They hang crowded towards the ends of the branchlets and twigs. Leaflets have a tapering tip and smooth margin. Leaf- and leaflet-stalks are pinkish. (Leaf: 150 - 300 mm; leaflet: 30 - 100 x 15 - 40 mm)

**Flowers** Flower-buds are plum-red. They appear with, or before, the new leaves in spring. Male and female flowers grow on separate trees. Inconspicuous pink-and-white male flowers grow in sprays at the ends of branches and twigs. Female flowers are reddish-green and grow singly from the twig ends (September to November). (Spray: 50 - 80 mm)

*30% life-size*

**Fruit** The oval, plum-sized, fleshy fruit develops on female trees only, and drops while it is still green. It ripens to pale yellow on the ground, giving off a strong fruity smell (January to March). Often the central woody stones, with two or three seed-holes, can be found nearby. (Fruit: 40 x 40 mm)

**Bark** The bark often peels in conspicuous, characteristic rounded depressions, exposing smooth, pink-brown under-bark. In forests the bark tends to form more regular blocks, and has a pinkish-grey tinge.

## Seasonal changes
Deciduous. The leaves turn yellow-green before they drop, and the tree has long periods without leaves. The bark and stubby branchlets are very characteristic, making identification possible throughout the year.

|  | Oct | Nov | Dec | Jan | Feb | Mar | Apr | May | Jun | Jul | Aug | Sep |
|---|---|---|---|---|---|---|---|---|---|---|---|---|
| Leaf | | | | | | | | | | | | |
| Flower | | | | | | | | | | | | |
| Fruit/Pod | | | | | | | | | | | | |

PLAINS – LARGE TREES
Marula

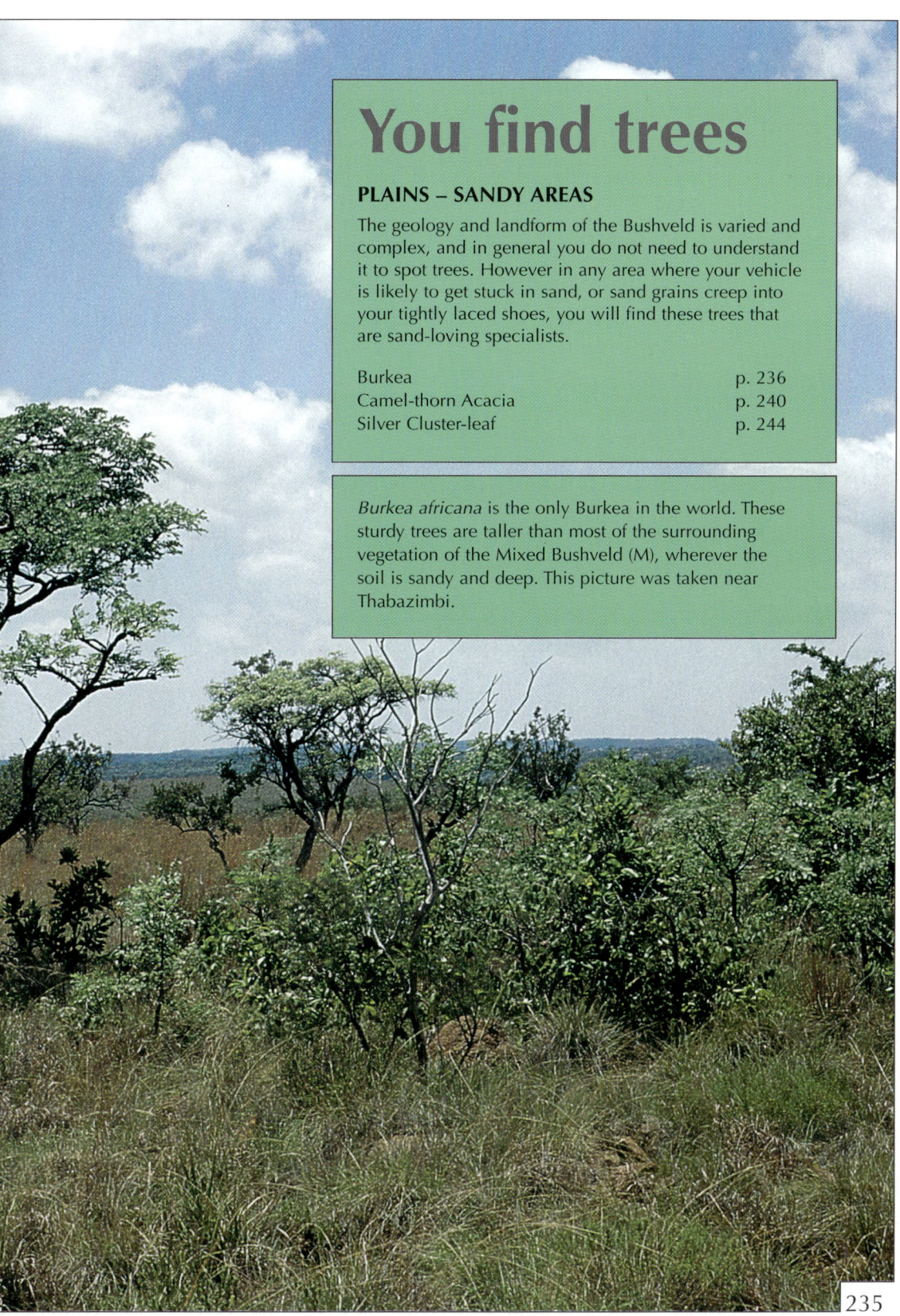

# You find trees

### PLAINS – SANDY AREAS

The geology and landform of the Bushveld is varied and complex, and in general you do not need to understand it to spot trees. However in any area where your vehicle is likely to get stuck in sand, or sand grains creep into your tightly laced shoes, you will find these trees that are sand-loving specialists.

| | |
|---|---|
| Burkea | p. 236 |
| Camel-thorn Acacia | p. 240 |
| Silver Cluster-leaf | p. 244 |

*Burkea africana* is the only Burkea in the world. These sturdy trees are taller than most of the surrounding vegetation of the Mixed Bushveld (M), wherever the soil is sandy and deep. This picture was taken near Thabazimbi.

# BURKEA

*Burkea africana*  Red syringa; Wild Seringa

| FLAMBOYANT FAMILY CAESALPINIACEAE | SA Tree Number 197 |

**AFRIKAANS** Sandsering, Wildesering  **N. SOTHO** Monatô  **TSONGA** Mpulu
**TSWANA** Monatô  **VENDA** Mufhulu

The species name **africana** refers to Africa.

## Where you'll find this tree easily

The Burkea grows singly, but where one is found there are bound to be others in the vicinity, occasionally forming uniform groups.

- It is easiest to find on the Plains and, especially in sandy soils, of the Mixed Bushveld (M).
- It can also be found on the Plains of the Central Mountains (C) and the lower North- or West-facing Slopes of the Northern Mountains (N); and on Old Termite Mounds; as well as along Rivers of the Mixed Bushveld.

## Ecozones where this tree occurs

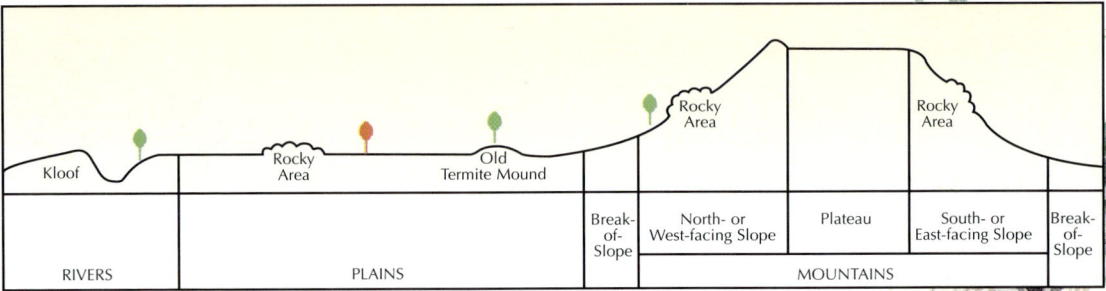

## Striking features

- This is a single-trunked, V-shaped, often high-branching tree, which branches into a few large branches.
- The leaves form moderate, flat-topped layers, with lacy edges, towards the ends of thick branchlets.
- The bark is dark grey and rough, forming distinct blocks, and contrasts with the dark green canopy.
- The large, dark green, twice compound leaves crowd at the tips of thick branchlets and twigs, and have yellowish leaflet- and leaf-stalks.
- Young shoots and tips of young branches are densely covered by velvety, rusty-red to maroon hairs.
- The pale brown, flat, pointed bean pods hang in conspicuous clusters at the ends of thick branchlets.

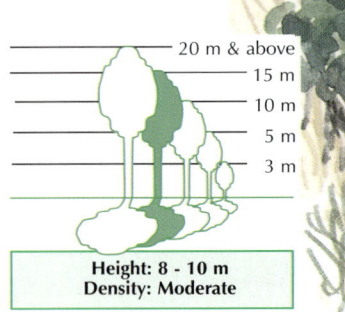

Height: 8 - 10 m
Density: Moderate

236

PLAINS – SANDY AREAS
Burkea

# BURKEA

*Burkea africana*

**Links with animals** Elephants eat the branches and leaves, and monkeys eat the flowers and pods. The widespread Common Blue butterfly (*Syntarucus telicanus*) lays its eggs on the flower-buds.

**Human uses** The wood is used for fence posts, parquet flooring, furniture, mine props, railway sleepers and wagons. The gum is edible. The pods and bark are used for tanning. The pods are also used to treat dysentery, and the bark to treat septic sores. Headaches and stomach aches are relieved by an extract of the leaves. The caterpillars of one of the Emporor Moths (*Cirina forda*) eat the leaves, and they themselves can be eaten after they are boiled, lightly roasted or dried.

**Gardening** This is a very attractive garden tree, especially on sandy soils as it grows slowly in clay soils. It is not easy to grow from seed. It is drought- but not very frost-resistant.

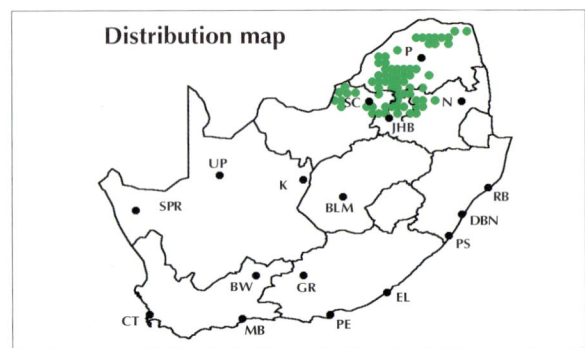

Distribution map

**Wood** The wood is hard, tough and heavy, and varies in colour from whitish-yellow to red-brown, sometimes with black-and-gold marking. Both sapwood and heartwood have a lovely lustre. It can be difficult to plane because of the cross-grains.

**Look-alike trees** Trees with leaves that grow at the tips of thick, stubby twigs are Marula (*Sclerocarya birrea*), page 230, which has red leaf- and leaflet-stalks; and Live-long Lannea (*Lannea discolor*), page 330, which has green leaf- and leaflet-stalks. Other similar trees are compared on page 69.

*Burkea in winter; Plains, Mixed Bushveld*

# GROWTH DETAILS

This is a single-trunked tree that usually branches high up in a V-shape to form an irregular, layered, canopy with flat-topped clusters of leaves. The leaves crowd at the tips of thick, stubby twigs and branchlets.

**Leaves** The opposite, twice compound leaves are dark green on the upper-surface and paler below. They have 2 - 3 feather pairs, with 4 - 8 pairs of alternate leaflets and a leaflet at the tip. The leaf- and feather-stalks are thickened at their bases. The leaflet and leaves have yellow stalks, and the pale yellow central vein is clearly visible on both surfaces. Tips of twigs and emerging leaves are covered in rusty hairs, and in autumn leaves turn red and coppery before dropping. (Leaf: 250 - 600 mm; leaflet: 50 x 25 mm)

*25%life-size*

**Flowers** The conspicuous, creamy-white, strong-smelling flower-spikes are crowded towards the ends of the thick twigs (September to November). (Individual flower: 5 mm; spray: 240 - 250 mm x 8 mm)

**Pods** The pale brown, short, flat bean pods each contain a single papery seed, and hang in conspicuous clusters at the ends of thick branchlets (February to July). (70 x 20 mm)

**Bark** The dark grey bark is rough and flaking, and broken into irregular blocks; the under-bark is deep red. Young shoots and tips of young branches are covered by dense, velvety, rusty-red to maroon hairs.

## Seasonal changes
Deciduous. This tree could be difficult to identify for the first time without its leaves, although the growth form is striking.

|  | Oct | Nov | Dec | Jan | Feb | Mar | Apr | May | Jun | Jul | Aug | Sep |
|---|---|---|---|---|---|---|---|---|---|---|---|---|
| Leaf | green | green | green | green | green | green | green | yellow |  |  |  | green |
| Flower | yellow | yellow |  |  |  |  |  |  |  |  |  | yellow |
| Fruit/Pod |  |  |  |  | orange | orange | orange | orange | orange | orange |  |  |

PLAINS – SANDY AREAS
Burkea

# CAMEL-THORN ACACIA

*Acacia erioloba*

**Camel thorn; Giraffe Tree; Black-barked Camel Thorn**

### THORN-TREE FAMILY
### MIMOSACEAE

**SA Tree Number 168**

**AFRIKAANS** Kameeldoring, Grootdoring  **NORTH SOTHO** Mogohlo, Mošu
**TSWANA** Mogôtlhô, Motlhabakgosi  **VENDA** Musivhitha

The species name **erioloba** refers to the velvety, hairy fruit.

## Where you'll find this tree easily

The Camel-thorn Acacia prefers deep, sandy, well-drained soils. It grows singly, but where one is found, others are usually nearby.

- It is easiest to find on the Plains of the Mixed Bushveld (M).
- It can also be found on the Plains of the Northern Mountains (N) and Central Mountains (C); and along Rivers and Streams of the Mixed Bushveld (M) and Central Mountains (C).

### Ecozones where this tree occurs

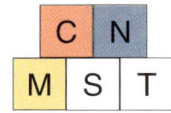

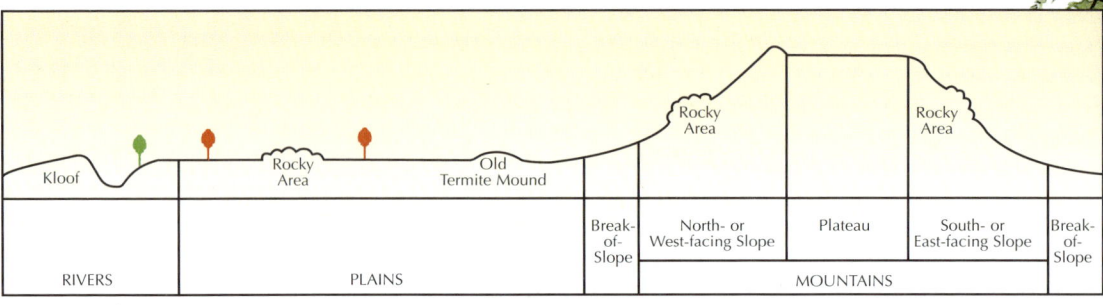

## Striking features

- This is a single-trunked tree with a large, spreading canopy.
- **The bark is dark, ropey and deeply fissured lengthways.**
- The straight, white thorns are well developed, and often have a swollen base.
- The young twigs grow in a zig-zag pattern between each pair of thorns.
- **The hard wooden pods are characteristically kidney-shaped and covered by velvety grey hairs.**
- The yellow flower-balls, which appear before the leaves, are conspicuous from late July to November.

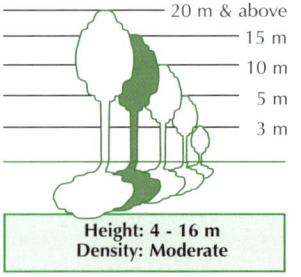

Height: 4 - 16 m
Density: Moderate

PLAINS – SANDY AREAS
Camel-thorn Acacia

# CAMEL-THORN ACACIA

*Acacia erioloba*

**Links with animals** The flowers and leaves are eaten eagerly by giraffe, from which the Afrikaans name Kameeldoring is derived. The pods are known among farmers to be very nutritious, and cattle and game will eat them whenever they are available. Wilted green pods, however, are high in prussic acid, a very poisonous substance that kills livestock. The gum is one of the favourite foods of the Kori Bustard.

**Human uses** Spoons and knife handles are carved from the wood. In the old mining days the heartwood was used to make strong, long-lasting bearings. The bark was used to treat headaches, and tea made from the leaves was a treatment for coughs and lung infections.

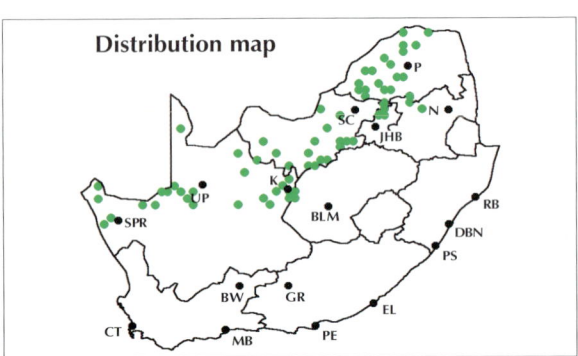
Distribution map

**Wood** The wood is very hard and heavy, and is dark reddish.

**Gardening** This is an attractive tree for gardens w well-drained soils. It is frost- and drought-resistant, but grows very slowly. It is difficult to grow from seed b once established is suitable a bonsai tree.

**Look-alike trees** This tree can be confused with other Acacias. See pages 70 - 73 for comparisons.

*January; White-browed Sparrow Weavers' nests in Camel-thorn Acacia*

# GROWTH DETAILS

PLAINS – SANDY AREAS
Camel-thorn Acacia

This is a single-trunked tree, often with a crooked trunk. Thick, spreading, angular branches form a moderate, wide, almost umbrella-like canopy. The dark branches are very obvious in the canopy, where the leaves grow on fine, reddish twigs. The young twigs grow in a zig-zag pattern, with paired thorns on the angles.

**Leaves** Twice compound leaves grow in groups of 1 - 7 on small knobs in the angles of the thorns. There are 1 - 4 feather pairs with 6 - 12 pairs of leaflets. Elliptic leaflets have a smooth margin. (Leaf: 30 - 60 mm; leaflet: 4 - 13 x 1 - 4 mm)

**Flowers** Conspicuous yellow flower-balls are sweet-scented, and appear in groups of 1 - 4 just before or with the new leaves. They grow towards the ends of the twigs and branchlets (July to November). (8 - 12 mm)

*60% life-size*

**Pods** The distinctive kidney-shaped pods are hard when mature, and are covered by a dense layer of thick, grey, velvety hairs. The pods are white and spongy inside, and contain hard, brown seeds. Pods ripen from December to March but may be present on the tree for most of the year. Pods do not burst open on the tree. (60 - 130 mm long x 40 - 65 mm wide, and 13 - 25 mm thick)

**Thorns** The straight, paired thorns grow in the angles of the twigs. The base of a pair of thorns is fused and is often enlarged. Young thorns are white, whereas older thorns tend to be browner. (30 - 60 mm)

**Bark** The bark is grey to black-brown, rough, and deeply fissured lengthways. It is loose, stringy and rope-like in older trees. On young branches and twigs the bark is reddish.

## Seasonal changes
Deciduous, but may be evergreen under very favourable conditions. The tree can be identified by the pods and bark throughout the year.

|  | Oct | Nov | Dec | Jan | Feb | Mar | Apr | May | Jun | Jul | Aug | Sep |
|---|---|---|---|---|---|---|---|---|---|---|---|---|
| Leaf | | | | | | | | | | | | |
| Flower | | | | | | | | | | | | |
| Fruit/Pod | | | | | | | | | | | | |

243

# SILVER CLUSTER-LEAF

*Terminalia sericea*      Silver terminalia; Transvaal Silver-leaf

## BUSHWILLOW FAMILY — COMBRETACEAE     SA Tree Number 551

**AFRIKAANS** Vaalboom, Sandvaalbos   **N. SOTHO** Mogônônô, Moletša-ňakana
**PEDI** Mogô-nônô   **SISWATI** umHonono   **TSONGA** Nkonono, Nkonola
**TSWANA** Mogonono, Mokubu   **VENDA** Mususu   **ZULU** amaNgwe amhlophe

The species name **sericea** refers to the soft, hairy leaves.

## Where you'll find this tree easily

The Silver Cluster-leaf grows in scattered groups, and is most common on sandy soils.

- It is easiest to find on the Plains of the Mixed Bushveld (M).
- It can also be found on the Plains of the Thorny Bushveld (T), Northern Mountains (N), Central Mountains (C) and Sour Bushveld (S); and along Rivers and Streams of the Northern Mountains (N).

## Ecozones where this tree occurs

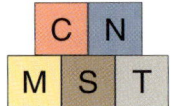

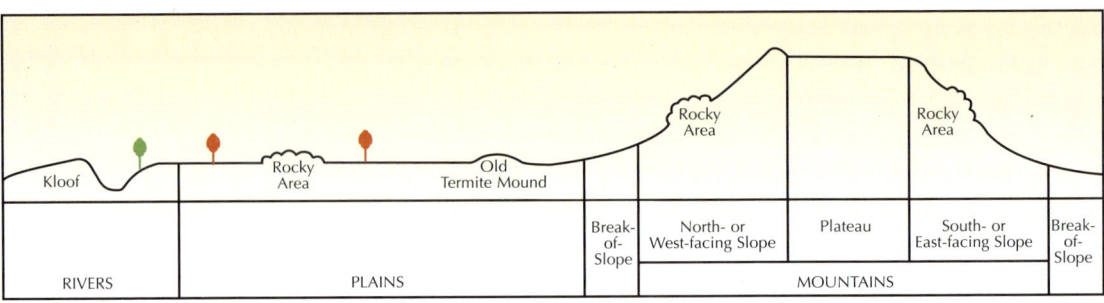

## Striking features

- This is a silvery-blue-green, upright, single-trunked tree.
- **The branches leave the trunk at different levels to form distinct horizontal layers.**
- The simple leaves are clustered towards the tips of slender branchlets and twigs.
- **The young leaves have silver hairs, giving the tree a characteristic silver shine.**
- The rough, dark bark is deeply fissured lengthways.
- **The two-winged pods are pinky-red to brown, and remain on the tree for long periods.**

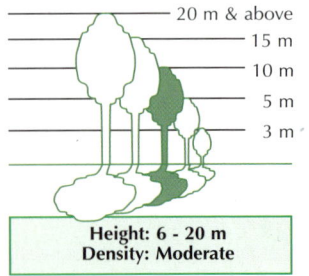

Height: 6 - 20 m
Density: Moderate

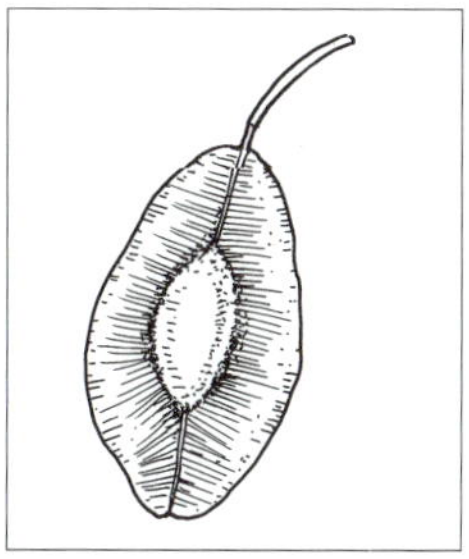

PLAINS – SANDY AREAS
Silver Cluster-leaf

245

# SILVER CLUSTER-LEAF

*Terminalia sericea*

**Links with animals** Although the nutritional value is low, leaves and young shoots are eaten by elephant, giraffe, kudu, impala and goats. Dry leaves on the ground are eaten by wildebeest. The branches are eaten by elephant and giraffe.

**Human uses** The wood is used for fence poles, household goods, firewood and axe handles. The gum is edible. Extracts of the bark are used as an antidote to poisons, and for tanning. Root extracts are used as a remedy for stomach disorders and diarrhoea; extracts and infusions are used as eye lotions and to treat pneumonia. Bark is used to treat diabetes and wounds.

**Gardening** This tree grows well in deep, sandy soils, and may be an attractive addition to gardens. It is frost- and drought-resistant, but is difficult to grow from the few undamaged seeds that may be found.

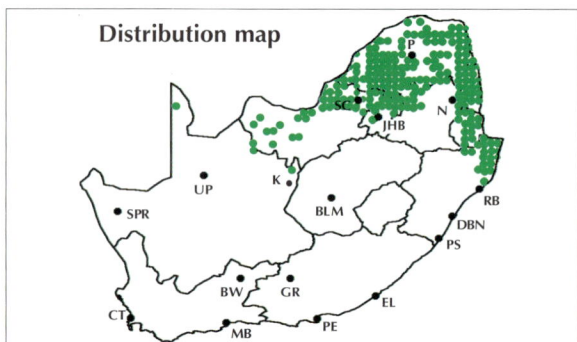

Distribution map

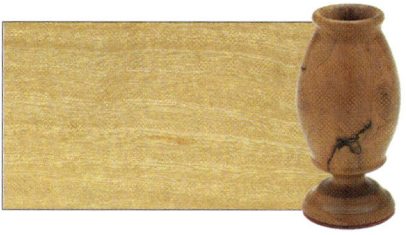

**Wood** The wood is yellow, hard and close-grained. It is strong and elastic, and termite- and wood-borer proof when properly seasoned. The wood is quite difficult to work.

*A mini-forest of Silver Cluster-leafs; sandy soil at base of Rocky Area; Soutpansberg, Northern Mountains*

# GROWTH DETAILS

The single trunk is relatively short, straight and upright. The branches are low down, leaving the trunk horizontally, to form a moderately dense, spreading canopy.

**Leaves** The simple, spirally arranged leaves are clustered towards the tips of slender branchlets. They are elliptic with a broadly tapering tip that tends to be pointed, and a narrowly tapering base. The pale green to grey-silvery-green leaves are leathery, and have a smooth margin. The young leaves are covered in silky, silvery hairs. (55 - 120 x 13 - 45 mm)

**Pods** The two-winged pods grow in bunches at the ends of branchlets and twigs. They are pink to red when mature, later drying to brown. The pods may remain on the tree until the next flowering season (January to June). (Individual: 25 - 60 x 15 - 25 mm)

*45% life-size*

**Flowers** The inconspicuous, unpleasantly-scented, cream-to-yellow flowers grow on spikes that are found in the angles made by the leaves (October to January). (Spike: up to 70 mm long; individual flower: 4 mm diameter)

**Bark** The bark is rough and dark grey or brown, and is deeply fissured lengthways on older branches and trunks. The branchlets are dark brown or purplish, and flake in rings and strips, to reveal light brown under-bark. Young twigs are covered in fine, silvery hairs.

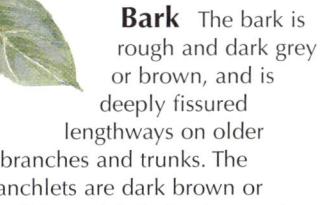

## Seasonal changes
Deciduous. Although this tree is without leaves for most of the winter, the horizontal, branching growth form is characteristic and makes identification easy. In summer the new leaves with their silvery hairs assist identification.

PLAINS – SANDY AREAS
Silver Cluster-leaf

|  | Oct | Nov | Dec | Jan | Feb | Mar | Apr | May | Jun | Jul | Aug | Sep |
|---|---|---|---|---|---|---|---|---|---|---|---|---|
| Leaf |  |  |  |  |  |  |  |  |  |  |  |  |
| Flower |  |  |  |  |  |  |  |  |  |  |  |  |
| Fruit/Pod |  |  |  |  |  |  |  |  |  |  |  |  |

247

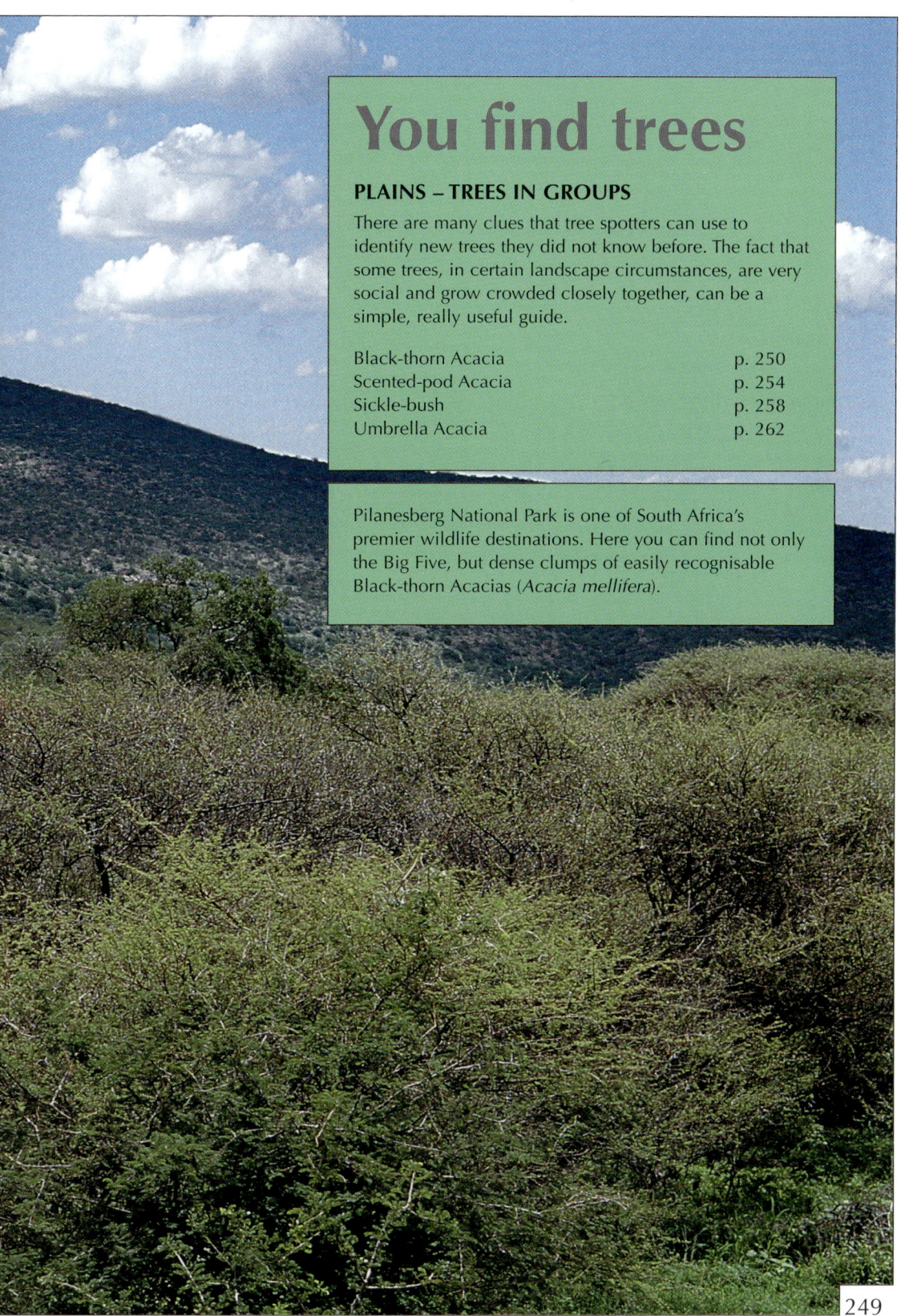

# You find trees

## PLAINS – TREES IN GROUPS

There are many clues that tree spotters can use to identify new trees they did not know before. The fact that some trees, in certain landscape circumstances, are very social and grow crowded closely together, can be a simple, really useful guide.

| | |
|---|---|
| Black-thorn Acacia | p. 250 |
| Scented-pod Acacia | p. 254 |
| Sickle-bush | p. 258 |
| Umbrella Acacia | p. 262 |

Pilanesberg National Park is one of South Africa's premier wildlife destinations. Here you can find not only the Big Five, but dense clumps of easily recognisable Black-thorn Acacias (*Acacia mellifera*).

# BLACK-THORN ACACIA

*Acacia mellifera*                                                Black Thorn

| THORN-TREE FAMILY MIMOSACEAE | SA Tree Number 176 |
|---|---|

**AFRIKAANS** Swarthaak, Bruinhaakdoring   **N. SOTHO** Mongangatau   **TSWANA** Mongana
**VENDA** Munembedzi

The species name **mellifera** means 'honey-bearing', and refers to the flowers.

## Where you'll find this tree easily

The Black-thorn Acacia grows in large uniform groups, especially in disturbed and overgrazed areas.

- It is easiest to find on the Plains of the Thorny Bushveld (T).
- It can also be found on the Plains of the Mixed Bushveld (M), the Northern Mountains (N) and the Central Mountains (C), where it may grow singly or in groups.

## Ecozones where this tree occurs

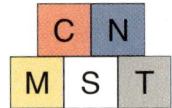

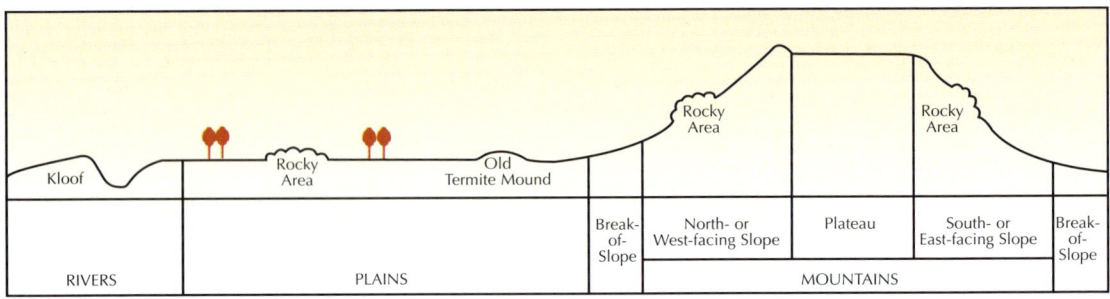

## Striking features

- This is a small, low-branching tree with a dense, tangled canopy of dark, rigid branchlets and twigs.
- The hooked thorns are black on older branches, grow in pairs, and spiral around the branchlets and twigs.
- The leaves grow on short leaf-stalks close to the dark, rigid branchlets and twigs.
- The bluish-green leaves are twice compound, and are small despite the leaflets being particularly large for a Thorn-tree.
- Creamy-white flower-balls cover the tree in spring before the leaves appear.

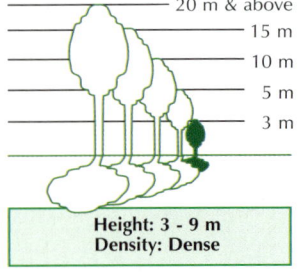

Height: 3 - 9 m
Density: Dense

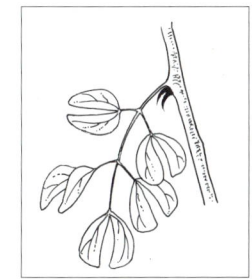

PLAINS – TREES IN GROUPS
Black-thorn Acacia

251

# BLACK-THORN ACACIA

*Acacia mellifera*

**Links with animals** This is a valuable fodder tree on cattle and game farms. The leaves, young branchlets and pods are very nutritious, containing a high percentage of protein. Leaves are browsed by Black Rhino, giraffe, eland, kudu and many other antelope. The flowers are eaten by kudu and by stock, particularly sheep and goats.

**Human uses** The wood is used for axe and pick handles. Heartwood is termite- and borer-proof, and larger stems make excellent fencing posts. The sap of the Black-thorn Acacia was mixed with a powdered grub for use on Khoisan poison arrows. The gum is edible, and is sometimes mixed with clay to make floors. Extractions made from the roots are used for the relief of stomach pains and to treat gonorrhoea. Extracts of the roots and leaves are used to treat colds, eye inflammation, diarrhoea and bleeding.

**Look-alike trees** See pages 70 - 73 for Acacia look-alikes.

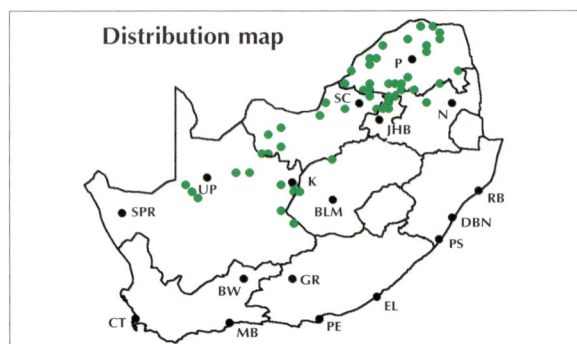

Distribution map

**Wood** Dark brown to greenish-black heartwood turns almost black when oiled. The whitish sapwood is thick, and the wood takes a high polish. It is very tough and elastic and does not split.

**Gardening** This can be an attractive addition to a waterwise indigenous garden. It grows moderately fast from seed, but seeds must be soaked overnight before planting. The tree can tolerate a little frost, and is drought-resistant. Black-thorn Acacia is suitable as a bonsai tree.

*July; Plains, Mixed Bushveld*

# GROWTH DETAILS

This is usually a small, multi- or single-trunked tree that branches low down to form a tangled, much-branched, moderate-to-dense canopy of variable shape when mature.

**Leaves** The leaves are twice compound and bluish-green. The leaflets are large compared to other members of the Thorn-tree family. The leaves have 2 - 3 pairs of feathers with 1 - 2 pairs of opposite leaflets. (Leaflet: 4 - 15 mm x 3 - 10 mm; leaf: about 30 mm)

**Thorns** The hooked thorns are found in pairs just below each leaf-bud, and spiral around the branchlets and twigs. The thorns are usually black on older and green on younger branchlets and twigs. (5 mm)

**Pods** The flat bean pods are papery, and straw-coloured or pale brown when ripe, and split open on the tree (January to April). (90 x 25 mm)

*life-size*

**Flowers**
The conspicuous, creamy-white, sweet-scented flower-balls are closely packed along the rigid, dark brown branchlets. They appear before the leaves from August to November, when the whole tree is covered in creamy-white blossoms. (Flower: 10 mm)

**Bark** The bark is rough and dark brown to black on the main stem and older branches, with lengthways fissures showing the yellowish under-bark. The bark is grey to yellowish-brown on young branches.

**PLAINS – TREES IN GROUPS**
**Black-thorn Acacia**

## Seasonal changes
Deciduous. The tree can be identified by its much-branched canopy and hooked thorns throughout the year.

|  | Oct | Nov | Dec | Jan | Feb | Mar | Apr | May | Jun | Jul | Aug | Sep |
|---|---|---|---|---|---|---|---|---|---|---|---|---|
| Leaf |  |  |  |  |  |  |  |  |  |  |  |  |
| Flower |  |  |  |  |  |  |  |  |  |  |  |  |
| Fruit/Pod |  |  |  |  |  |  |  |  |  |  |  |  |

# SCENTED-POD ACACIA

*Acacia nilotica*

Scented Thorn; Black Thorn;
Red-heart Thorn Tree

## THORN-TREE FAMILY
## MIMOSACEAE

SA Tree Number 179

**AFRIKAANS** Lekkerruikpeul, Swartsaadpeul  **N. SOTHO** Mogohlo, Mooka
**SISWATI** isiThwethwe, umNcawe  **TSONGA** Nxangwa  **TSWANA** Motsha  **ZULU** umNqawe

The species name **nilotica** refers to the distribution of the tree along the Nile River.

## Where you'll find this tree easily

The Scented-pod Acacia grows in uniform groups or scattered among other trees.

- It is easiest to find on the Plains of the Thorny Bushveld (T).
- It can also be found on the Plains of the other Ecozones; and in many Habitats in the Mixed Bushveld (M); as well as on the South- or East-facing Slopes of the Northern Mountains (N) and Sour Bushveld (S).

## Ecozones where this tree occurs

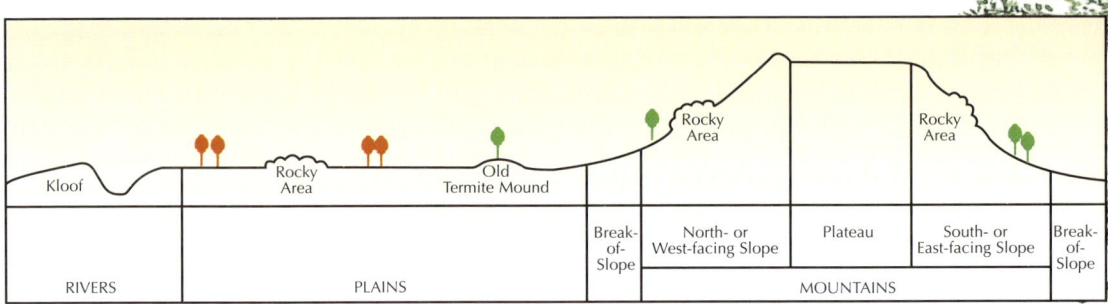

## Striking features

- This is a single-stemmed tree that branches high up to form a semi-circular canopy.
- **The characteristic pods look similar to a beaded necklace.**
- The bottle-green leaves are stiff and sturdy, and do not move easily in the wind, despite small leaflets.
- **The flower-balls are yellow.**
- The thorns are paired and white, and curve slightly backwards.
- The bark is dark brown and has deep lengthways fissures.

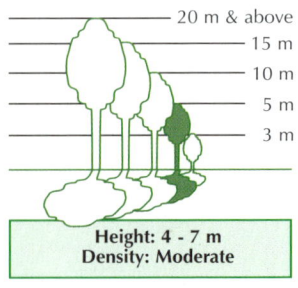

Height: 4 - 7 m
Density: Moderate

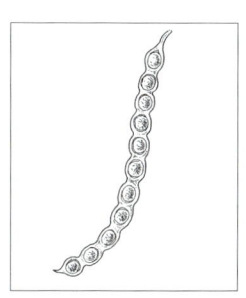

**PLAINS – TREES IN GROUPS**
Scented-pod Acacia

# SCENTED-POD ACACIA

*Acacia nilotica*

**Links with animals** The leaves are eaten by most browsers. The mature pods are eaten by Black Rhino, baboons, giraffe, impala, nyala and cattle, and seeds are dispersed in this way.

**Human uses** The wood can be used as fence posts and to make furniture, especially riempie benches. Extracts of the unripe pods and bark were used for tanning. The gum is edible and can be used as glue. An extract of the bark was used to loosen phlegm, for treating eye diseases, as a tranquiliser and as an aphrodisiac. A root extract was used to treat tuberculosis, impotence, diarrhoea, haemorrhage, toothache, dysentery and gonorrhoea. Leaf extracts treated menstrual problems, eye infections, diarrhoea, sores caused by leprosy, stomach ulcers, indigestion and haemorrhage.

**Gardening** This small tree will grow in most gardens. It is fairly frost- and drought-resistant, and is easily grown from treated seeds, but grows slowly. The Scented-pod Acacia attracts garden birds as it is always alive with insects and small reptiles. The tree starts to flower after five years.

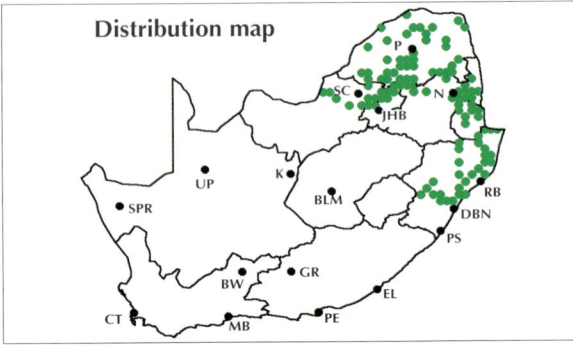
Distribution map

**Wood** The wood is reddish, has a very fine texture and is hard, durable and termite- and wood-borer resistant.

**Look-alike trees** Without its distinctive pods, this tree is difficult to distinguish from other Acacias. See the table on pages 70 - 73 for twice compound leaf comparisons.

April; Plains, Thorny Bushveld

# GROWTH DETAILS

This small to medium-sized, single-stemmed tree has branches that spread out to form a moderate, semi-circular canopy. The trunk is often crooked. The new leaves and twigs are green to reddish, and are covered by short, grey hairs.

*55% life-size*

**PLAINS – TREES IN GROUPS** — Scented-pod Acacia

**Leaves** The twice compound leaves are stiff, with 3 - 4 leaves clumped at the base of the thorns. They consist of 3 - 9 feather pairs and 8 - 20 pairs of leaflets. The leaflets are small and elliptic, and are bottle-green to bright green. The leaf-stalks are hairy. (Leaf: 40 - 50 mm; leaflet: 4 x 1 mm)

**Flowers** The yellow, scented flower-balls with hairy stalks grow in groups of up to four on the new branchlets. The tree may flower for most of the summer, although it is never covered in flowers (September to May). (12 mm)

**Pods** The long, narrow pods are characteristic. They are constricted between seeds, which gives the appearance of a string of beads. Young green pods are covered with fine, reddish hairs, and the pods turn black as they mature. They do not split open on the tree, but break up on the ground. Mature pods have a strong, sweet, 'apple' scent irresistible to browsers (Ripen March to September). (120 - 200 x 31 - 15 mm)

**Thorns** The paired, white thorns are curved slightly backwards, and have a few hairs when young. The thorns grow from a single base and vary in size, with some being overdeveloped and others underdeveloped. (50 - 90 x 4 mm)

**Bark** The bark is reddish-brown and smooth in young trees. In older trees, the bark is dark grey to black, and rough with lengthways fissures.

## Seasonal changes
Semi-deciduous. Although these trees are difficult to identify without the pods, there are usually some pods on the tree or on the ground all year round.

|  | Oct | Nov | Dec | Jan | Feb | Mar | Apr | May | Jun | Jul | Aug | Sep |
|---|---|---|---|---|---|---|---|---|---|---|---|---|
| Leaf | 🟢 | 🟢 | 🟢 | 🟢 | 🟢 | 🟢 | 🟢 | 🟢 |  |  |  | 🟢 |
| Flower | 🟡 | 🟡 | 🟡 | 🟡 | 🟡 | 🟡 | 🟡 | 🟡 |  |  |  | 🟡 |
| Fruit/Pod |  |  | 🟤 | 🟤 | 🟤 | 🟤 | 🟤 | 🟤 | 🟤 | 🟤 | 🟤 | 🟤 |

# SICKLE-BUSH

*Dichrostachys cinerea*                    Sickle Bush; Large-leaved Sickle Bush

---

**THORN-TREE FAMILY**
**MIMOSACEAE**                                        **SA Tree Number 190**

**AFRIKAANS** Sekelbos, Soetpeul   **N. SOTHO** Morêtsê   **SISWATI** umSilazembe   **TSONGA** Ndzenga
**TSWANA** Mosêlêsêlê   **VENDA** Murenzhe   **ZULU** uGagane, umThezane

The species name **cinerea** refers to the ashy colour of the bark.

## Where you'll find this tree easily

The Sickle-bush prefers loamy soils, and is often found close to Rivers and on Plains. In these Habitats and in badly over-grazed areas it grows in dense, uniform groups.

- It is easiest to find on the Plains of the Thorny Bushveld (T).
- It can also be found on the Plains of all other Ecozones (C, N, M, S); and along Rivers and Streams and on Old Termite Mounds of the Thorny Bushveld (T) and Mixed Bushveld (M); as well as on South- or East-facing Slopes of the Northern Mountains (N) and Mixed Bushveld (M).

## Ecozones where this tree occurs

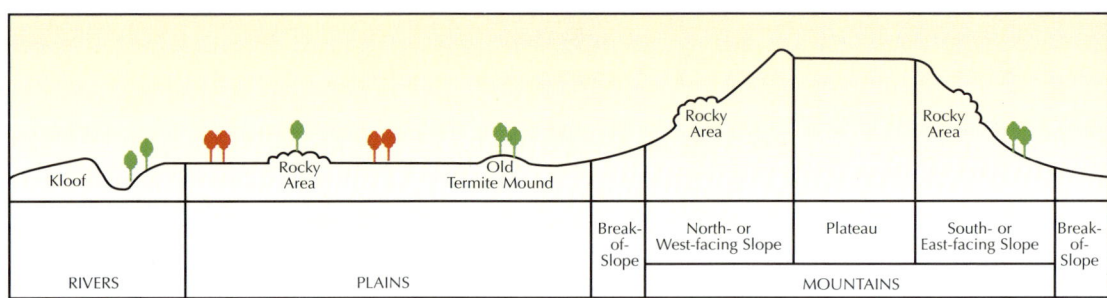

## Striking features

- **This multi-stemmed, small tree is low-branching and has a heavily intertwined or matted canopy, with long, fine, feathery leaves.**
- The branches and twigs have long, straight, pale brown spines.
- **The mauve-pink and yellow flower-spikes resemble Chinese lanterns.**
- **Groups of tightly coiled pods growing in dense clusters are distinctive.**
- The delicate, twice compound olive-green leaves add contrast to the pale ashy bark.

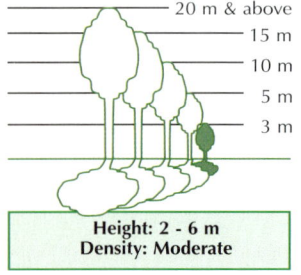

Height: 2 - 6 m
Density: Moderate

**PLAINS – TREES IN GROUPS**
Sickle-bush

**Largest tree currently registered**

Diameter: 0,67 m
Girth: 2,10 m
Height: 6 m

JJH Engelbrecht
Maroelasfontein,
Dist. Waterberg

# SICKLE-BUSH

*Dichrostachys cinerea*

**Links with animals**  Pods are very nutritious, and eaten by a wide variety of animals such as Black Rhino, monkey, giraffe, bushpig, impala, nyala, kudu and even buffalo. Caterpillars of the Satyr Charaxes butterfly (*Charaxes ethalion ethalion*) feed on the Sickle Bush.

**Human uses**  The tree is used widely for medicinal purposes: pods to treat sores and scabies, and leaves as a local anaesthetic; chewed leaves placed on scorpion stings and snake bites draw the poison; leaf extracts for earache, sore throat, and headache; leaf and root extracts relieve toothache, sore eyes and stomach troubles; powdered bark placed locally draws skin abscesses.

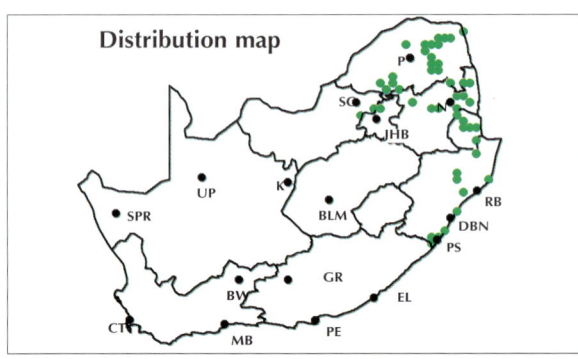

**Wood**  The wood is hard, dark, durable and borer- and termite-proof. It is suitable for turning and produces a good quality charcoal.

**Gardening**  Although it grows slowly unless well watered, the Sickle-bush can be an attractive tree or hedge, and is used by insects and thus attracts birds. It can be grown easily from seed or root cuttings. It is not frost-resistant, but is drought-resistant. It is very good as a bonsai tree.

**Look-alike trees**
See pages 70 - 73 for a comparison of trees with twice compound leaves.

*October; Chinese lantern flower-spikes and leaves*

# GROWTH DETAILS

This is a small, multi-stemmed, low-branching tree. The stems and branches divide profusely to form a densely intertwined, matted canopy of branchlets and twigs, with fine, feathery foliage.

**Leaves** The long, twice compound, olive-green leaves are alternate. The very small, delicate leaflets are elliptic with a smooth margin. There are 8 - 12 pairs of feathers and 15 - 30 pairs of leaflets. (Leaf: 20 - 200 mm; leaflet: 3 x 0,5 mm)

**Spines** The long, straight, light grey spines are modified side branchlets, and are so tough that they can puncture tractor tyres. Sometimes they have leaves growing on them. (20 - 40 mm)

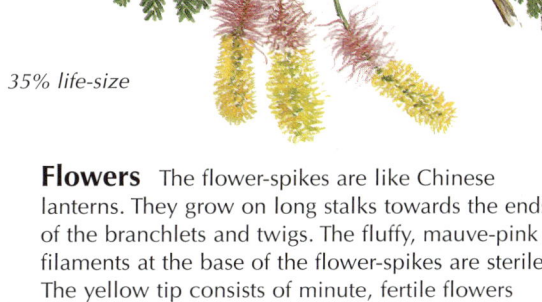

*35% life-size*

**Flowers** The flower-spikes are like Chinese lanterns. They grow on long stalks towards the ends of the branchlets and twigs. The fluffy, mauve-pink filaments at the base of the flower-spikes are sterile. The yellow tip consists of minute, fertile flowers closely packed together (October to January). (40 - 60 mm)

**Pods** The closely packed, fertilised flowers mature to form many tightly coiled pods, growing bunched together from each flower-spike. The clusters of pods ripen to dark brown and do not split open on the tree. Pods may remain on the tree even after the leaves have dropped (May to September). (Cluster: 70 - 100 mm diameter)

**Bark** The bark is light brown to ash-grey as the scientific name indicates, with shallow lengthways grooves.

### Seasonal changes
Deciduous. The tree can be identified in winter by its growth form, spines and pods.

|            | Oct | Nov | Dec | Jan | Feb | Mar | Apr | May | Jun | Jul | Aug | Sep |
|------------|-----|-----|-----|-----|-----|-----|-----|-----|-----|-----|-----|-----|
| Leaf       | ■   | ■   | ■   | ■   | ■   | ■   | ■   | ■   |     |     |     | ■   |
| Flower     | ■   | ■   | ■   |     |     |     |     |     |     |     |     |     |
| Fruit/Pod  |     |     |     |     | ■   | ■   | ■   | ■   | ■   | ■   | ■   | ■   |

PLAINS – TREES IN GROUPS
Sickle-bush

261

# UMBRELLA ACACIA

*Acacia tortilis*  
Umbrella Thorn

## THORN-TREE FAMILY
## MIMOSACEAE
### SA Tree Number 188

**AFRIKAANS** Haak-en-steek, Withaakdoring   **N. SOTHO** Mošu, Mošwana   **SISWATI** IsiThwethwe  
**TSONGA** Nsasani   **TSWANA** Mosu   **VENDA** Muunga-khanga, Muswu   **ZULU** umSasane, isiThwethwe

The species name **tortilis** refers to the twisted pods.

## Where you'll find this tree easily

The Umbrella Acacia may grow singly or in groups.
- It is easiest to find as an umbrella-shaped tree on the Plains of the Thorny Bushveld (T).
- It is also common growing in a group of mixed Thorn-trees on the Plains and along Rivers and Streams, on Old Termite Mounds and on all Slopes of all Ecozones.

### Ecozones where this tree occurs

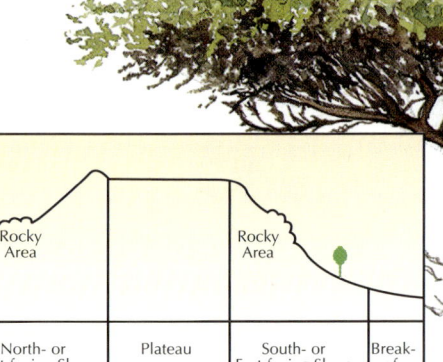

## Striking features

- **This is the most striking of the umbrella trees of the Thorny Bushveld, with a particularly flat umbrella canopy of grey-green leaves.**
- The leaflets are very tiny, giving the umbrella canopy a fine feathery appearance.
- There are some straight and some hooked thorns, singly or in pairs, in different arrangements on different branches.
- Each pod is tightly coiled.
- In early summer the tree becomes covered in numerous small, white flower-balls.

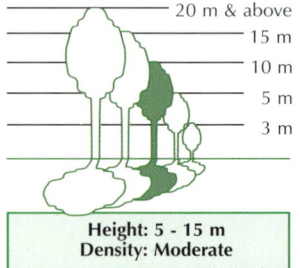

Height: 5 - 15 m  
Density: Moderate

**PLAINS – TREES IN GROUPS**
Umbrella Acacia

**Largest tree currently registered**
**Diameter:** 0,90 m
**Girth:** 2,83 m
**Height:** 17 m

Letaba Camp,
Kruger National Park

# UMBRELLA ACACIA

*Acacia tortilis*

**Links with animals**  The foliage is browsed by antelope and giraffe. The pods are eaten by virtually every grazing and browsing mammal, often in preference to any other pod. The coiled pod shape makes it easy for grazers to pick up the pod without a mouthful of grit. The bark is also eaten by domestic and wild animals. Meyer's and Brown-headed Parrots relish the green seeds. Live trees are attacked by wood-borers, and are often damaged by elephants.

**Human uses**  The wood makes good wagon beams, yokes and some furniture, if treated carefully. The gum is edible. The inner bark can be used to make rope. Bark is used in traditional medicine.

**Gardening**  It grows easily from seed and is extremely hardy, and drought- and frost-resistant, but is rather slow growing. It is suitable as a bonsai tree.

**Look-alike trees**  See pages 70 - 73 for a comparison of trees with twice compound leaves.

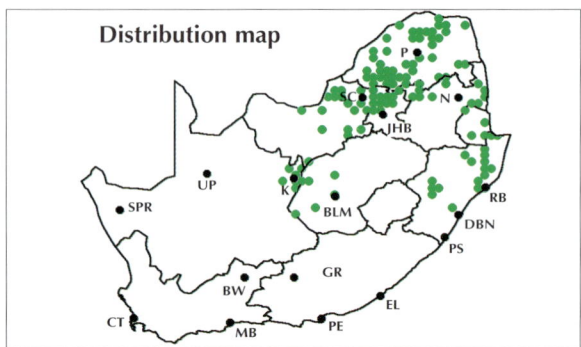

**Wood**  The outer wood is whitish and soft with conspicuous growth rings, while the heartwood is red.

*November; Plains, Mixed Bushveld; near Thabazimbi; umbrella shape variation*

# GROWTH DETAILS

This is often a single-stemmed tree with a straight trunk, but its growth form is very variable (see photo on the opposite page). Branches come off horizontally to form a flat umbrella canopy. Young trees, and mature trees growing on shallow soil, tend to form a rounder canopy, with the thin branchlets and twigs intertwining.

**Leaves** The twice compound leaves are grouped at the leaf-bud. The leaves are very small and delicate with 4 - 10 pairs of feathers and 5 - 15 pairs of leaflets. (Leaf: 20 - 30 mm; leaflet: 1 - 2 x 1,4 mm)

**Thorns** The sharp, white thorns are not always obvious. There are some straight and some hooked thorns, singly or in pairs, in different arrangements on different branches. (Straight thorn: 50 - 90 mm; hooked: 3 - 15 mm)

*life-size*

**Flowers** Large numbers of small, sweet-scented, white flower-balls grow on older twigs, often shortly after rain (October to February). (5 - 10 mm)

**Pods** The pale brown, coiled pods hang in bunches. The pods do not split open on the tree (December to June). (Pods: up to 125 mm long when stretched out, 8 mm wide)

**Bark** In mature trees the bark is dark grey and rough, with deep, lengthways fissures. Younger trees have smoother, lighter bark.

**Seasonal changes**
Semi-deciduous. Many mature trees are easy to find because of their umbrella-shaped canopy.

|  | Oct | Nov | Dec | Jan | Feb | Mar | Apr | May | Jun | Jul | Aug | Sep |
|---|---|---|---|---|---|---|---|---|---|---|---|---|
| Leaf | ■ | ■ | ■ | ■ | ■ | ■ | ■ | ■ | ■ | ■ |  |  |
| Flower | ■ | ■ | ■ |  |  |  |  |  |  |  |  |  |
| Fruit/Pod |  | ■ | ■ | ■ | ■ | ■ | ■ | ■ | ■ |  |  |  |

PLAINS – TREES IN GROUPS
Umbrella Acacia

265

# You find trees

## ROCKY AREAS

Some trees need the added protection, nutrients and moisture provided by Rocky Areas to really thrive. Rock-lovers can often be found on Plains or Mountain Slopes, but always with their roots in amongst boulders or on large stones.

| | |
|---|---|
| Hornpod-tree | p. 268 |
| Jacket-plum | p. 272 |
| Large-leaved Rock Fig | p. 276 |
| Lavender Croton | p. 280 |
| Mountain Kirkia | p. 284 |
| Red-leaved Fig | p. 288 |
| Rock Tree-nettle | p. 292 |
| Stamvrug Milkplum | p. 296 |
| Tall Firethorn Corkwood | p. 300 |
| Velvet Bushwillow | p. 304 |
| White Kirkia | p. 308 |

The magnificent autumn foliage of the White Kirkia (*Kirkia acuminata*) is a breathtaking discovery in amongst rocks, near Thabazimbi in Mixed Bushveld (M).

# HORNPOD-TREE

*Diplorhynchus condylocarpon*      Horn-pod tree; Transvaal Rubber Tree

| OLEANDER FAMILY APOCYNACEAE | SA Tree Number 643 |

**AFRIKAANS** Horingpeultjieboom, Melkbos   **TSONGA** Ntsowa   **TSWANA** Moleye   **VENDA** Muthowa

The species name **condylocarpon** refers to the knuckle-shaped fruit.

## Where you'll find this tree easily

The Hornpod-tree grows in scattered, large groups.

- It is easiest to find on North- or West-facing Slopes of the Mixed Bushveld (M).
- It is also common on the North- or West-facing Slopes and can also be found on the South- or East-facing Slopes and Rocky Areas of the Northern Mountains (N), the Sour Bushveld (S) and the Central Mountains (C).

## Ecozones where this tree occurs

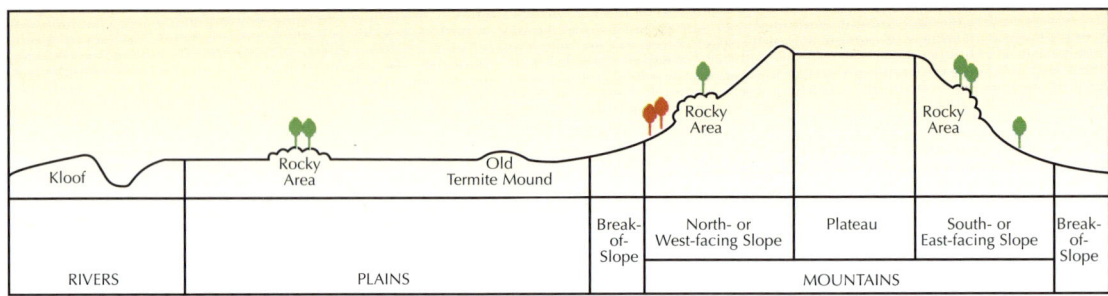

## Striking features

- This is a small, multi-stemmed tree with a moderate, spreading canopy and long branchlets that may arch and hang downwards.
- **The distinctive pair of sharp, pointed, kidney-shaped pods are horn-like (March to August).**
- The simple, opposite leaves are yellowish-green with a shiny upper-surface.
- The central vein and leaf-stalk are yellow, and the very thin, soft twigs are russet.
- **All parts contain milky latex.**

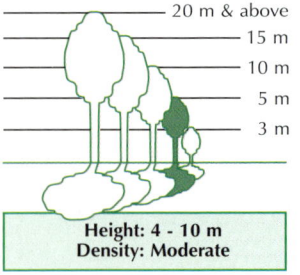

Height: 4 - 10 m
Density: Moderate

**ROCKY AREAS**
**Hornpod-tree**

269

# HORNPOD-TREE

*Diplorhynchus condylocarpon*

**Links with animals** The leaves are eaten by elephant, and the fruit by duiker.

**Human uses** The timber is used to make assegai and arrow shafts, gun-butts and porridge spoons. The outer bark is used as a tobacco substitute in Zambia. The leaves are chewed as a remedy for headache, upset stomach, indigestion, bloody urine and syphilis. A strong extract of the root was used by early settlers to treat blackwater fever. It is also used as a treatment for snakebite and other bite wounds, and as an emetic. The latex is used to fix punctures and as birdlime to catch birds. The vapour from the fruit and root, boiling in water, is inhaled to treat chronic cough and pulmonary tuberculosis.

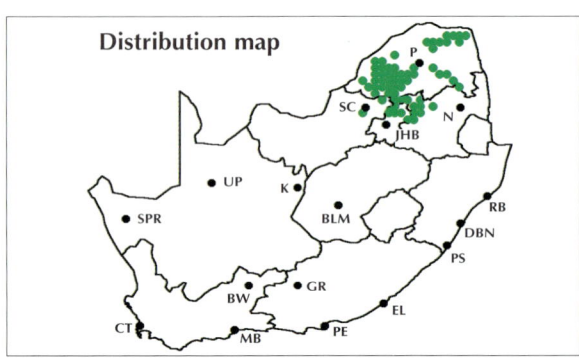

Distribution map

**Wood** The wood is pale and is attractive when polished. It is relatively hard, medium-heavy and tough. It has a fine grain and polishes smoothly.

**Gardening** This can be an attractive garden tree if grown with care in sandy soil, under the right climatic conditions. It grows easily from seed, and will grow fairly quickly. The tree grows medium-fast, and is not frost-resistant.

*Multi-stemmed; Rocky Area, Mixed Bushveld*

# GROWTH DETAILS

This is a small, multi- or single-stemmed, low-branching tree. The short stems are often crooked. The tree has a moderate, irregular, spreading canopy. Long, thin branchlets and soft, thin, russet twigs hang downwards, and move easily in the wind. All parts contain milky latex.

**Leaves** The simple, opposite leaves, with leaf-stalks of up to 25 mm, have a smooth-to-wavy margin, are elliptic, and taper broadly to a sharp point. They are yellowish-green, with a shiny upper surface. The central vein and leaf-stalk are yellow, and the side veins form a faint herringbone pattern. Young leaves may be softly hairy. (Leaf 30 - 70 mm x 20 - 45 mm)

**Pods** The distinctive pairs of sharp, pointed, kidney-shaped pods are horn-like. They are green and covered in white spots when young, and dark brown-red when ripe. The pods split open along one side, to release 2 - 4 flat, winged seeds while still on the tree. Some pods may remain on the tree for long periods (March to August). (Individual pod: 35 - 50 mm x 15 - 20 mm)

*life-size*

**Flowers** The sweet-scented, star-shaped flowers are white to cream, and are found in loose flower-sprays near the ends of twigs (September to December). (Individual flower: 10 mm diameter)

**Bark** The young bark is haphazardly streaked lengthways, with grey and cream. Older bark is uniformly creamy grey, and may either peel off in square, grey-brown flakes, or have small knobs resembling the skin of a toad.

**ROCKY AREAS**
Hornpod-tree

## Seasonal changes
Deciduous. The tree can be identified most of the year either by its leaves or the distinctive pods that remain on the tree for many months.

|  | Oct | Nov | Dec | Jan | Feb | Mar | Apr | May | Jun | Jul | Aug | Sep |
|---|---|---|---|---|---|---|---|---|---|---|---|---|
| Leaf | | | | | | | | | | | | |
| Flower | | | | | | | | | | | | |
| Fruit/Pod | | | | | | | | | | | | |

271

# JACKET-PLUM

*Pappea capensis*

## LITCHI FAMILY
## SAPINDACEAE

SA Tree Number 433

**AFRIKAANS** Doppruim, Wildepruim  **N. SOTHO** Mopsinyugane  **SISWATI** umLahlabantu
**TSONGA** Xikwakwaxu, Gulaswimbi  **TSWANA** Mopennwêeng, Motlhatlha
**VENDA** Tshikavhavhe, Tshikwakwashi  **XHOSA** iliTye, umGqalutye  **ZULU** umGqogqo

The species name **capensis** means 'from the Cape'.

## Where you'll find this tree easily

The Jacket-plum grows singly among other tree species and has a wide distribution.

- It is easiest to find in Rocky Areas on North- or West-facing Slopes of all Ecozones.
- It can also be found in Rocky Areas and Old Termite Mounds on the Plains, and less often on South- or East-facing Slopes of all Ecozones.

## Ecozones where this tree occurs

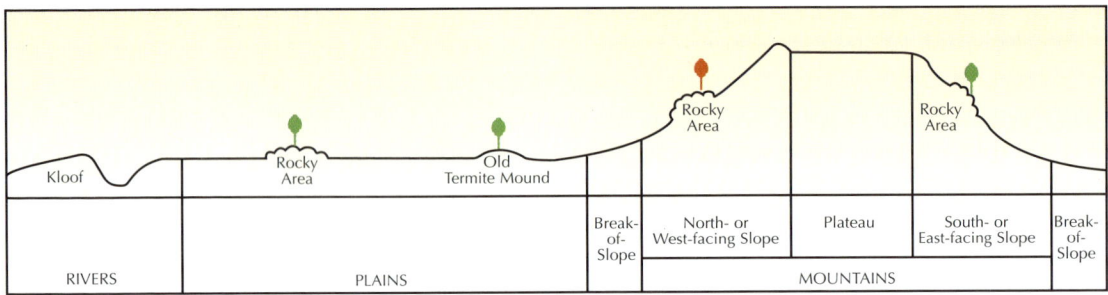

## Striking features

- The rounded canopy is formed by an intense tangle of short, grey branchlets and twigs.
- The tree has a overall dull green appearance, and the pale grey branches are very obvious.
- **The leaves are alternate but form rosettes at the ends of the branchlets.**
- **Mature leaves are hard and leathery, and have a prominent, sunken, yellow central vein.**
- Young leaves are lime-green and soft, and have toothed edges.
- **The characteristic, velvety-green fruit is plum-like, and bursts open to expose bright red, glistening flesh (December to July).**

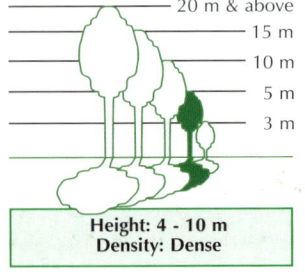

Height: 4 - 10 m
Density: Dense

*Immature leaf*

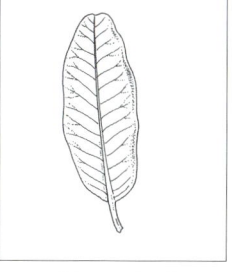
*Mature leaf*

**ROCKY AREAS
Jacket-plum**

# JACKET-PLUM

*Pappea capensis*

**Links with animals** The fruit is eaten by a wide variety of animals and birds, particularly by Green Pigeons. The leaves are not palatable and are seldom eaten.

**Human uses** The wood may be used to make poles, yokes, furniture and spoons. The fruit is edible and tasty. Vinegar and jelly are made from the fruit. The seeds contain oil that is used for various purposes. This tree is still important in traditional medicine today.

**Gardening** This is an attractive tree that will grow well in most gardens. It grows very well from seed, but extremely slowly. It is fairly drought-resistant, and is suitable as a bonsai tree.

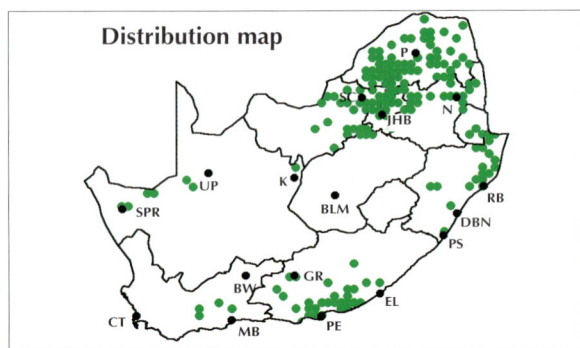

Distribution map

**Wood** The wood is a uniform light brown with a red tint. It is tough and heavy, but easy to work.

*Plains, Old Termite Mound; Jacket-plum, Red Bushwillow and Umbrella Thorn Acacia*

# GROWTH DETAILS

The short trunk may be straight or crooked. It branches low-down to form an intricately branched, dense, roundish canopy, but the growth form varies depending on rainfall. Under well-watered conditions it is a tall tree while in drier areas it is small and stout.

**Leaves** The leaves are elliptic with a rounded tip but vary in size, depending on the rainfall. They are simple and alternate on older branches, and crowded to form rosettes towards the ends of young twigs. The margins are smooth when mature, but sharply toothed in young leaves. The leaves are leathery, rough, dark olive-green above and pale underneath, with a conspicuous yellow central vein that is visible from both sides. (25 x 100 - 80 x 160 mm)

**Fruit** The velvety-green, plum-like fruit grows in bunches. When ripe it bursts open to expose shiny, bright red, glistening flesh that covers the black seeds (December to July). The dark shells of the fruit may be seen long after the fruit has dropped. (20 mm)

*50% life-size*

**Flowers** Small, pale green, scented flowers grow in spikes between the leaves. Male and female flowers are on separate trees (October to March). (Spike: 25 - 160 mm)

**Bark** The bark of young branches is smooth and pale grey and may be broken into small blocks. The bark of older trees and branches is darker and rough, with irregular patches of light and dark bark. The bark is often covered in lichen. The branchlets are pale grey.

**Seasonal changes**
Deciduous in drier areas to evergreen in the higher rainfall areas and along rivers. As this tree has leaves for most of the year it is normally easy to recognise.

|  | Oct | Nov | Dec | Jan | Feb | Mar | Apr | May | Jun | Jul | Aug | Sep |
|---|---|---|---|---|---|---|---|---|---|---|---|---|
| Leaf | █ | █ | █ | █ | █ | █ | █ | █ | █ | █ | █ | |
| Flower | ░ | ░ | ░ | ░ | ░ | ░ | | | | | | |
| Fruit/Pod | | ▓ | ▓ | ▓ | ▓ | ▓ | ▓ | ▓ | ▓ | ▓ | | |

**ROCKY AREAS** — Jacket-plum

275

# LARGE-LEAVED ROCK FIG

*Ficus abutilifolia*

| | |
|---|---|
| **MULBERRY FAMILY**<br>**MORACEAE** | **SA Tree Number 63** |

**AFRIKAANS** Grootblaarrotsvy, Klipvy  **N. SOTHO** Monokane  **TSONGA** Nkuwamaribye  **TSWANA** Momelantsweng  **VENDA** Tshikululu  **ZULU** imPayi

The species name **abutilifolia** refers to the fact that the leaves resemble those of the genus *Abutilon*.

## Where you'll find this tree easily

The Large-leaved Rock Fig grows singly on rock faces where there is good drainage. The roots of the tree split rocks when they grow into the crevices.

- It is easiest to find in Rocky Areas with large boulders in all Ecozones.

## Ecozones where this tree occurs

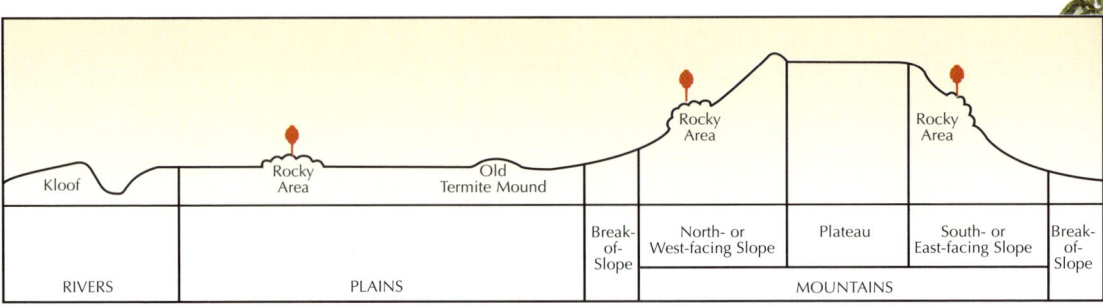

## Striking features

- **It has a gnarled, yellow-white, smooth trunk with papery bark that peels off.**
- Conspicuous white roots are visible, spreading over the rock face.
- **The large leaves are smooth and heart-shaped, with prominent veins that are reddish when the leaves are young.**
- All parts of the tree contain copious amounts of white latex.

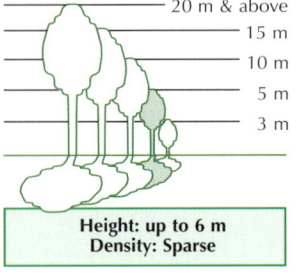

Height: up to 6 m
Density: Sparse

ROCKY AREAS
Large-leaved Rock Fig

# LARGE-LEAVED ROCK FIG

*Ficus abutilifolia*

**Links with animals**  Baboon, monkey, bushbuck, duiker, nyala and bushpig eat the fruit.

**Human uses**  The tasty fruit is a valued food. Bark extracts are taken as strengthening tonics by men.

**Gardening**  This tree can be used very effectively in a rocky garden. It is not frost-resistant but can withstand drought. It can be grown from cuttings and, although slow-growing, it responds well to watering in well-drained soils.

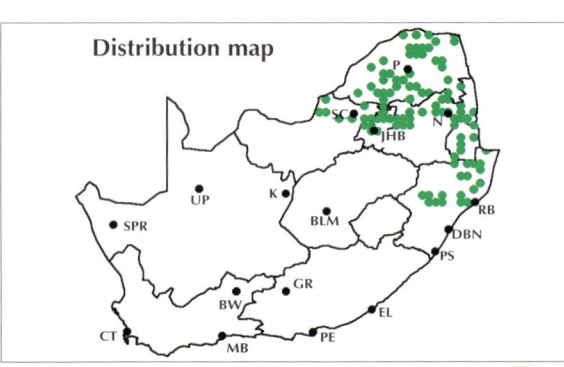

Distribution map

**Wood**  The wood is light and tough, and pale brown with a yellowish tint.

**Look-alike trees**  Other Figs that tend to grow on rocks are Red-leaved Fig (*Ficus ingens*), page 288, Golden-haired Rock Fig (*Ficus glumosa*) page 77 and Wonderboom Fig (*Ficus salicifolia*). See page 77 for comparison with other figs.

*Young Rock Fig roots starting to grow; Central Mountains*

# GROWTH DETAILS

The single, crooked trunk branches low down at irregular angles to form an irregular, sparse canopy. The white roots grow prominently over rock faces. All parts of the tree contain copious amounts of white latex.

**Leaves**  The large, simple leaves are spirally arranged or alternate, and they have a smooth margin that may be wavy. The leaves are heart-shaped to round, with a rounded tip that often ends in a point. The base is distinctly deeply lobed. Leaves are dark green above and paler below. The veins are clearly visible on both surfaces, and are pale red-brown to yellow, but reddish in young leaves. The central vein stands out underneath. The leaf-stalks are long, varying from 25 to 170 mm. (Leaf: 60 - 160 x 80 - 250 mm)

**Fruit**  The round fig grows singly, or in small groups, on a short stalk, or directly on the branches in the angle formed by the leaf. The figs are pale green with white spots, and ripen to red (August to March). (Individual fig: 15 - 25 mm diameter)

*25% life-size*

**Flowers**  As in all figs, the flowers are not visible as they grow inside the fruit.

**Bark**  The bark is white to pale grey and smooth, and on older branches and trunks often flakes or peels in layers. The trunk is often twisted.

ROCKY AREAS
Large-leaved Rock Fig

## Seasonal changes
Semi-deciduous. It can be identified throughout the year by the characteristic growth form and bark colour.

|  | Oct | Nov | Dec | Jan | Feb | Mar | Apr | May | Jun | Jul | Aug | Sep |
|---|---|---|---|---|---|---|---|---|---|---|---|---|
| Leaf | ■ | ■ | ■ | ■ | ■ | ■ | ■ | ■ |  |  |  | ■ |
| Flower |  |  |  |  |  |  |  |  |  |  |  |  |
| Fruit/Pod | ■ | ■ | ■ | ■ | ■ | ■ |  |  |  | ■ | ■ | ■ |

279

# LAVENDER CROTON

*Croton gratissimus*  **Lavender Fever-berry**

## EUPHORBIA FAMILY
## EUPHORBIACEAE

**SA Tree Number 328**

**AFRIKAANS** Laventelkoorsbessie, Bergboegoe  **N. SOTHO** Mologa  **TSWANA** Moologa
**VENDA** Mufhorola, Nyasimbitane  **ZULU** uMahlabekufeni

The species name **gratissimus** means 'very pleasant', and probably refers to the smell of the leaves and the image of the tree.

### Where you'll find this tree easily

The Lavender Croton is conspicuous where it grows in large scattered groups.

- It is easiest to find on the Rocky Areas on the North- or West-facing Slopes in the Mixed Bushveld (M).
- It can also be found on the Rocky Areas of both the Plains and the North- or West-facing Slopes of the Northern Mountains (N) and the Sour Bushveld (S); and on Rocky Areas of all Slopes of the Central Mountains (C).

### Ecozones where this tree occurs

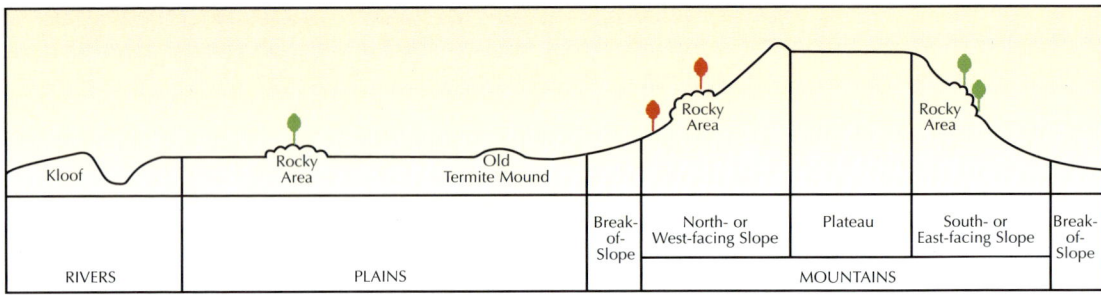

## Striking features

- This is usually a small to medium-sized tree that branches low down to form an irregular canopy.
- **The simple, bicoloured leaves have a striking silvery under-surface that is evident from a distance as it contrasts with the green upper-surface, forming an overall yellow-green canopy.**
- **The silvery-gold under-surface is covered in dense, orange-brown scales, giving a characteristic speckled appearance.**
- Orange leaves are usually visible in the canopy from February until the leaves drop.
- Tiny new leaves at the tips of twigs are conspicuously covered in dense russet hairs.
- From October to May the pink to rusty-brown flower-buds dominate the colour of the canopy.

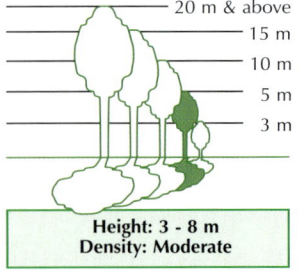

Height: 3 - 8 m
Density: Moderate

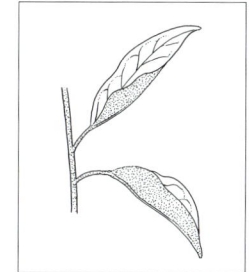

**ROCKY AREAS**
**Lavender Croton**

281

# LAVENDER CROTON

*Croton gratissimus*

**Links with animals** The fruit is eaten by birds, and the leaves are occasionally browsed by game and stock. Elephant and kudu are some of the few wild mammals that feed on this tree. The fruit is eaten by many species of fruit-eating birds such as Crested Guineafowl, Green-spotted Doves, Tambourine Doves, Terrestrial Bulbuls and francolins.

**Human uses** The wood is used for fencing, roofs and hut posts. Children make catapults out of the twigs. San women use the leaves for perfume. As suggested by the name, the leaves are commonly used to treat fevers. Leaf extracts are also used for coughs. The bark is used to treat bleeding gums, rheumatism, chest complaints, indigestion and oedema. Zulus inhale the fumes from ground leaves mixed into a paste with goat fat and placed on hot coals, as a cure for insomnia and restlessness.

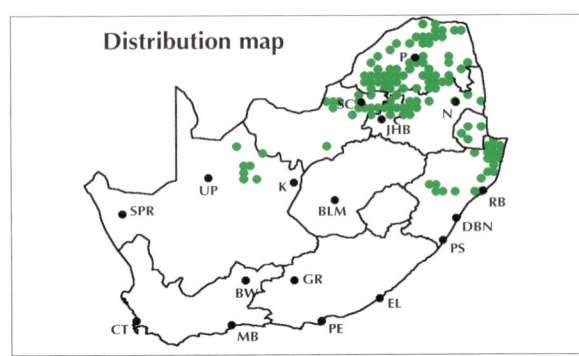

Distribution map

**Wood** The wood is relatively hard and heavy, and has a fairly fine texture. The sapwood is pale brown, and the prominent heartwood is dark brown. The wood can be worked, and polishes fairly well.

**Gardening** This is an attractive tree in any garden but is unfortunately a medium-to-slow grower. The tree has some resistance to frost and is drought-resistant.

*North-facing Slope, Mixed Bushveld*

# GROWTH DETAILS

This is a small to medium-sized tree that is single or multi-stemmed and branches low down to form a moderate, irregular, often V-shaped canopy. The stems are straight, and grow upwards. The thin branchlets in the canopy branch into straight twigs.

**Leaves** The simple, alternate leaves are spirally arranged, They generally have a smooth margin that can sometimes be wavy. They are elliptic, with a long, russet leaf-stalk of up to 30 mm. The leaves are dark, shiny green above, and have a striking, silvery-gold under-surface. The under-surface is covered in dense, orange-brown scales that give the surface a characteristic speckled appearance. The central vein stands out underneath. Tiny new leaves and the tips of twigs are conspicuously covered in dense, russet hairs. The leaves tend to droop when wilted. Crushed leaves have a lavender smell.
(Leaf 70 - 80 mm x 20 - 40 mm)

**Fruit** The silver, three-lobed, berry-like capsules grow in spikes, and become yellow and split open when ripe (December into winter).
(7 - 12 mm)

**Flowers** The creamy-yellow flower-spikes are found at the ends of twigs. The pink to rusty-brown flower-buds are on the tree for months before the flowers open, and give the tree an immediately recognisable, overall pinky-brown appearance (October to May).
(Individual flower: 6 mm; spikes: up to 100 mm long)

*45% life-size*

**Bark** The bark is rough and brown. The young stems are shiny silver-yellow with brown dots.

ROCKY AREAS
Lavender Croton

## Seasonal changes
Deciduous. The tree is difficult to recognise without leaves.

|  | Oct | Nov | Dec | Jan | Feb | Mar | Apr | May | Jun | Jul | Aug | Sep |
|---|---|---|---|---|---|---|---|---|---|---|---|---|
| Leaf | ■ | ■ | ■ | ■ | ■ | ■ | ■ | | | | | ■ |
| Flower | ■ | ■ | ■ | ■ | ■ | ■ | ■ | ■ | | | | |
| Fruit/Pod | | | ■ | ■ | ■ | ■ | ■ | ■ | ■ | | | |

# MOUNTAIN KIRKIA

*Kirkia wilmsii*   Mountain syringa; Mountain Seringa; Wild Pepper Tree; Bastard Pepper Tree

| TREE-OF-HEAVEN FAMILY SIMAROUBACEAE | Tree no 269 |
|---|---|

**AFRIKAANS** Bergsering, Wildepeperboom  **N. SOTHO** Modumela

The species name **wilmsii** refers to the plant collector F. Wilms, who first found this species near Lydenburg.

## Where you'll find this tree easily

This tree grows singly among other species of trees, but where one is found, others will be found in the vicinity.

- It is easiest to find on Rocky Areas on the South- or East-facing Slopes of the Sour Bushveld (S).
- It can also be found on Rocky Areas on the South- or East-facing Slopes of the Mixed Bushveld (M); and on the Rocky Areas of both the Plains and sometimes the North- or West-facing Slopes of the Northern Mountains (N), Central Mountains (C), Mixed Bushveld (M) and Sour Bushveld (S).

## Ecozones where this tree occurs

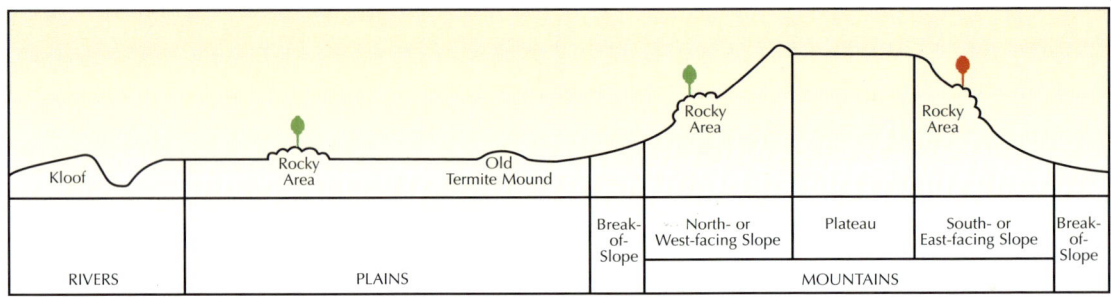

## Striking features

- **The brilliant autumn colours make this tree easy to identify in Rocky Areas during April and May.**
- It is a multi-stemmed tree with an irregular, spreading canopy, with foliage separated into small dense clusters.
- Branchlets and twigs tend to grow upwards, and twigs end bluntly.
- **The slender, compound leaves are clustered at the tips of the blunt, thick twigs forming whorls.**
- The long leaves are feathery. They consist of 30 pairs of small leaflets with no leaflet-stalks.
- The bark is grey and smooth.

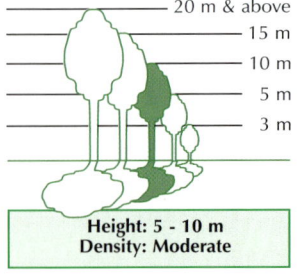

Height: 5 - 10 m
Density: Moderate

ROCKY AREAS
Mountain Kirkia

285

# MOUNTAIN KIRKIA

*Kirkia wilmsii*

**Links with animals**  Browsing animals seldom use this tree, but it is favoured by elephant.

**Human uses**  The bark, young shoots and roots provide a good, strong fibre suitable for plaiting. The roots are swollen with water that can be used for drinking during dry periods.

**Gardening**  This can be a very attractive shade tree for the garden. It needs well-drained soil, and will grow best in warm, sheltered gardens. It will grow easily from seed sown in spring or from hard-wood cuttings in summer. It will withstand frost once it is well established.

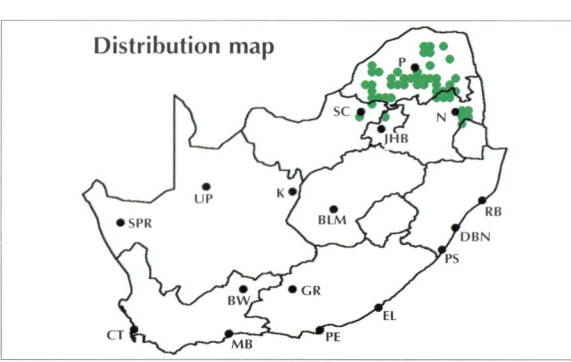

**Wood**  The light, coarse-grained wood is greyish.

**Look-alike trees**  This tree can be confused with four others that have compound leaves clustered at the ends of twigs. These are compared on page 69. It is most similar to White Kirkia (*Kirkia acuminata*), page 308, but White Kirkia is very rarely multi-stemmed.

*Tibani Resort, Potgietersrus; Rocky Areas, Central Mountains*

# GROWTH DETAILS

The tree is multi-stemmed, and divides into a few large, spreading branches to form a rounded canopy with a fine, feathery foliage. Branchlets are usually marked with old leaf-scars, and have stubby tips.

**Leaves** The compound leaves are clustered at the ends of branchlets and twigs on long leaf-stalks (40 mm) forming whorls. The leaves consist of 10 - 40 pairs of opposite to sub-opposite leaflets, and a leaflet at the tip. The leaflets are small and narrowly elliptic, and have a tapering or pointed tip and a rounded base, with a coarsely toothed margin. The leaves produce brilliant yellow, orange, red and purple autumn colours. (Leaf: 100 - 200 x up to 50 mm; leaflet: up to 25 x 5 mm)

**Fruit** The fruit capsule is woody, and brown when mature. The capsule consists of four sections, each containing one seed. The sections split apart but remain joined at the tip to a central axis, resembling a small, half-open umbrella. The split fruit often remains on the tree for long periods (January to July). (Fruit: up to 12 x 5 mm)

*70% life-size*

**Flowers** The small flowers are greenish-white to yellow-green. They grow in branched sprays on long flower-stalks in the angles formed by the leaves, near the ends of the twigs. The flower-stalks are reddish-brown (September to December). (Spray: 40 - 220 mm long)

**Bark** The bark is smooth and grey. On older trunks patches of dead bark form irregular blocks. The branches are usually marked with conspicuous leaf-scars.

**ROCKY AREAS** — Mountain Kirkia

## Seasonal changes
Deciduous. Even though the growth form and preference for Rocky Areas will help with identification throughout the year, it is only easy to identify while the tree has leaves.

| | Oct | Nov | Dec | Jan | Feb | Mar | Apr | May | Jun | Jul | Aug | Sep |
|---|---|---|---|---|---|---|---|---|---|---|---|---|
| Leaf | | | | | | | | | | | | |
| Flower | | | | | | | | | | | | |
| Fruit/Pod | | | | | | | | | | | | |

287

# RED-LEAVED FIG

*Ficus ingens*  
Red-leaved Rock Fig

## MULBERRY FAMILY
## MORACEAE

SA Tree Number 55

**AFRIKAANS** Rooiblaarrotsvy, Rooiblaarvy  **N. SOTHO** Monokane  **TSONGA** Nkuwamaribye  
**TSWANA** Motlhatsa  **VENDA** Tshikululu  **XHOSA** umThombe  **ZULU** umGonswane, umDenda obomvu

The species name **ingens** means 'large', referring to the leaves.

## Where you'll find this tree easily

The Red-leaved Fig grows singly.

- It is easy to find in Rocky Areas or growing over large boulders in all Ecozones.
- It can also be found in Rocky Areas on the edges of Rivers and Streams and in thick woodland of the Northern Mountains (N), Central Mountains (C) and the Sour Bushveld (S).

## Ecozones where this tree occurs

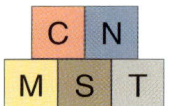

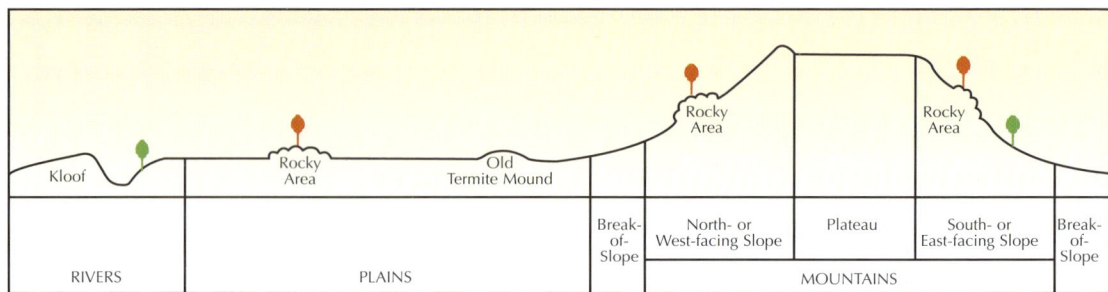

## Striking features

- This tree branches low down and spreads widely, to form a semi-circular canopy.
- The large, simple leaves are long and narrowly elliptic, with distinct, yellowish, indented central and side veins.
- The trees stand out clearly among the other vegetation in spring, when there is a spectacular flush of wine-red to coppery leaves.
- All parts of the tree contain some milky latex.
- The small, berry-like figs are smooth or slightly hairy, and are dull-red to coppery when ripe (June to December).

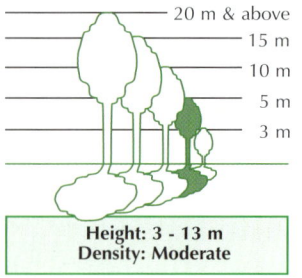

Height: 3 - 13 m  
Density: Moderate

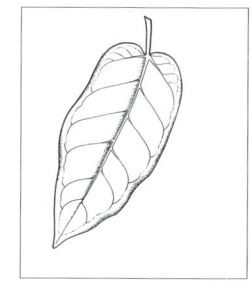

**ROCKY AREAS**
Red-leaved Fig

**Largest tree currently registered**

**Diameter:** 1,93 m
**Girth:** 6,60 m
**Height:** 10 m

Padreserwe,
Nylstroom / Vaalwater
Plaas Waterval, Dist. Waterberg

# RED-LEAVED FIG

*Ficus ingens*

**Links with animals** Mature leaves are seldom eaten, but young leaves turning green are favoured by Grey Duiker, kudu and nyala. Ripe fruit is eaten by monkeys, baboons, squirrels, dassies, bushbabies, and a wide variety of fruit-eating birds, while the fruit that falls is eaten by Grey Duiker, suni, nyala, warthog and bushpig.

**Human uses** The fruit is edible. An extraction of the bark is used to treat anaemia, and the milky latex is used as a disinfectant and astringent. Cows with a low milk-yield are also treated with an extraction of the bark to improve production.

**Gardening** This is an attractive, fast-growing tree that grows well in warm, sunny areas. It can be grown from the fruit, if harvested before it drops. The fine seed should be mixed with river sand. It is fairly frost-resistant and very drought-resistant. It has an aggressive root system, but makes a good container plant and is popular as a bonsai.

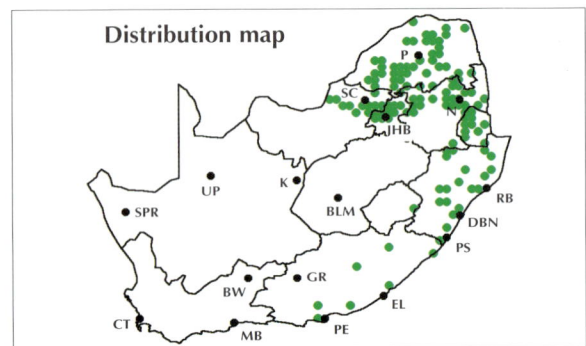

Distribution map

**Wood** The wood is pale with darker annual rings and fine jagged stripes in between. It is light but tough, and can be cut and worked easily, but does not give a smooth finish.

**Look-alike tree** Wonderboom Fig (*Ficus salicifolia*) also grows on rocks, and has very similar fruit. The leaves of Wonderboom Fig are thickly leathery, and the base is roughly triangular to almost heart-shaped. Red-leaved Fig's leaves are narrowly elliptic, thin and brittle.

*Characteristic white roots; Rocky Area, Plains, Sour Bushveld*

# GROWTH DETAILS

The growth form varies from being a small tree with obvious white roots to a single-trunked tree with a fluted trunk. It grows much taller along rivers and in areas with deeper soil, and branches low down to form a dense, semi-circular canopy, with leaves obscuring the branches. All parts contain milky latex.

**Leaves** The simple leaves are spirally arranged on long leaf-stalks. The leaves are long, narrowly elliptic, thin and brittle, with a squarish base and a tapering tip. They are dark green above and paler green below. The yellowish, indented, central and side veins are obvious on both surfaces. New leaves are wine-red to coppery, and form a conspicuous spring flush. (60 - 150 mm x 30 - 100 mm)

*50% life-size*

**Fruit** The small, berry-like figs are smooth or slightly hairy, and have a very short stalk. The figs grow in the angles formed by the leaves, and are dull-red to coppery when ripe (June to December). (10 - 13 mm diameter)

**Flowers** As in all figs, the flowers are not visible as they grow inside the fruit.

**Bark** The smooth bark is yellowish-grey.

**ROCKY AREAS — Red-leaved Fig**

**Seasonal changes** Deciduous. The tree can be identified throughout the year by its growth form.

|  | Oct | Nov | Dec | Jan | Feb | Mar | Apr | May | Jun | Jul | Aug | Sep |
|---|---|---|---|---|---|---|---|---|---|---|---|---|
| Leaf | ■ | ■ | ■ | ■ | ■ | ■ | ■ | ■ |  |  | ■ | ■ |
| Flower |  |  |  |  |  |  |  |  |  |  |  |  |
| Fruit/Pod | ■ | ■ | ■ |  |  |  | ■ | ■ | ■ | ■ | ■ | ■ |

291

# ROCK TREE-NETTLE

*Obetia tenax (Urera tenax)*

Mountain Nettle

### NETTLE FAMILY
### URTICACEAE

SA Tree Number 70

**AFRIKAANS** Bergbrandnetel  **TSONGA** Ntadzwa  **TSWANA** Moralejwe, Mmabi
**VENDA** Muthanzwa, Murovha-dembe  **XHOSA** umBabazane  **ZULU** imBati

The species name **tenax** refers to the dense, stinging hairs.

## Where you'll find this tree easily

The Rock Tree-nettle grows singly, often amongst other species of trees, and is often found near water.

- It is easiest to find in Rocky Areas of the Plains and North- or West-facing Slopes in all Ecozones.
- It can also be found on North- or West-facing Slopes and along Rivers and Streams of the Mixed Bushveld (M), the Sour Bushveld (S), the Northern Mountains (N) and Central Mountains (C).

## Ecozones where this tree occurs

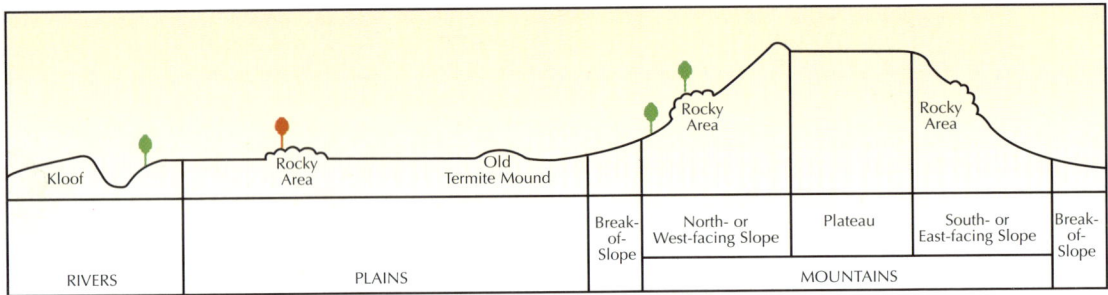

## Striking features

- This small tree branches low down into a few upward-growing branches to form an irregular, sparse canopy.
- **The distinctive pale, lime-green, round to heart-shaped leaves have long leaf-stalks, and are covered by long, rigid stinging hairs.**
- Rigid, stinging hairs are obvious on the twigs, branchlets and even the main stem, and cause an immediate uncomfortable reaction on the skin.
- The leaves are crumpled and wrinkled with sunken veins creating ridges, which resemble caterpillar bodies.

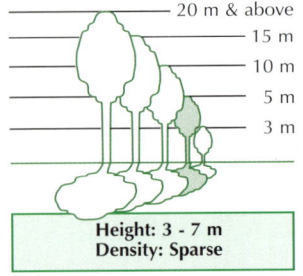

Height: 3 - 7 m
Density: Sparse

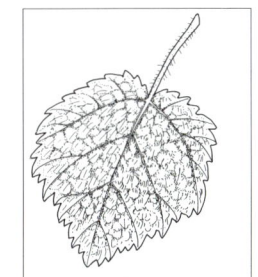

**ROCKY AREAS**
Rock Tree-nettle

293

# ROCK TREE-NETTLE

*Obetia tenax (Urera tenax)*

**Links with animals** Black Rhinos browse the stems and leaves. The caterpillars of the Pale Yellow Acraea butterfly (*Acraea obeira burni*) also eat the leaves.

**Human uses** A strong fibre can be made from the bark, which the Voortrekkers used to make rope and local tribes used to make cord.

**Gardening** This tree grows from seeds and cuttings, but should not be used as a garden tree, because contact with its hairs causes intense itching.

**Wood** The wood is white, very light, soft and brittle, and has a particularly rough grain.

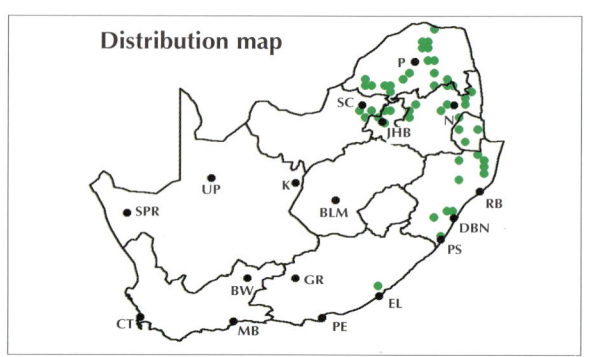

Distribution map

*March; Rocky River edge, Pilanesberg*

# GROWTH DETAILS

This is a multi- or single-stemmed shrub or small tree that branches low down into a few upward-growing branches and branchlets, that do not divide into twigs. It forms an irregular, sparse canopy.

**Leaves**  The large, simple, alternate leaves have long, yellowish leaf-stalks of up to 140 mm. The leaves are pale lime-green, and round to heart-shaped, and are deeply toothed. They are soft, crumpled and wrinkled, and although the entire leaf is covered by stinging hairs, there are more on the under-surface. (70 - 150 x 70 - 120 mm)

**Flowers**  The inconspicuous, greenish-yellow to whitish flowers appear before the leaves. They are found in much-branched sprays in the angles formed by the leaves. Separate male and female flowers grow on the same tree (August to September). (3 mm)

*50% life-size*

ROCKY AREAS
Rock Tree-nettle

**Fruit**  The very small, berry-like fruit is found in branched spikes. The fruit is purplish-brown, and is also covered in stinging hairs (October to November). (Individual fruit: 2 - 3 mm)

**Bark**  The smooth bark is pinkish-bronze to grey, with fine vertical streaking and little dark knobs. Even the main stem has rigid stinging hairs.

## Seasonal changes
Deciduous. The tree can be identified throughout the year by the stinging hairs on its stem.

|  | Oct | Nov | Dec | Jan | Feb | Mar | Apr | May | Jun | Jul | Aug | Sep |
|---|---|---|---|---|---|---|---|---|---|---|---|---|
| Leaf | | | | | | | | | | | | |
| Flower | | | | | | | | | | | | |
| Fruit/Pod | | | | | | | | | | | | |

295

# STAMVRUG MILKPLUM

*Englerophytum magalismontanum*

Stamvrug; Transvaal Milkplum; Wild Plum; Stem-fruit Tree

## MILKWOOD FAMILY
## SAPOTACEAE

SA Tree Number 581

**AFRIKAANS** Stamvrug  **N. SOTHO** Mohlatswa  **SISWATI** umNumbela  **TSONGA** Nombhela
**TSWANA** Motlhatswa, Motlhakwa  **VENDA** Munombelo  **ZULU** umNumbela

The species name **magalismontanum** means 'from the Magaliesberg'.

## Where you'll find this tree easily
The Stamvrug Milkplum grows singly or in small groups.
- It is easiest to find in Rocky Areas of all Ecozones.

## Ecozones where this tree occurs

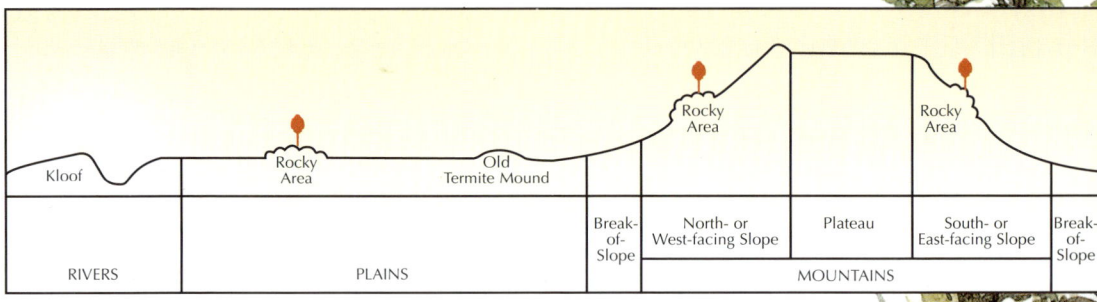

## Striking features
- This is a low-branching, multi-stemmed tree or shrub that grows among rocks.
- **The leaves form blue-green rosettes with conspicuous, young, golden-brown leaves at the tips of the rosettes.**
- The leaves are covered by a transparent, whitish, waxy bloom that can be rubbed off.
- **The plum-like fruit is red when ripe, and grows directly on the large branches and branchlets.**

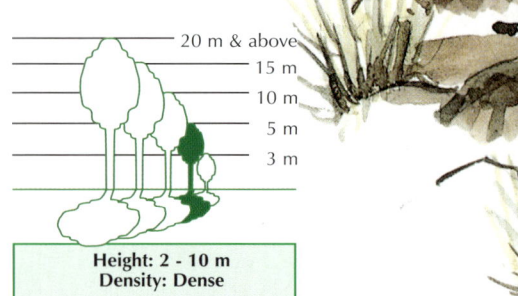

Height: 2 - 10 m
Density: Dense

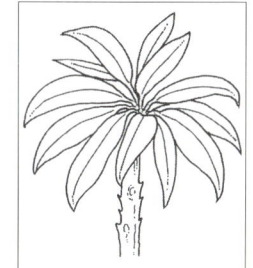

**ROCKY AREAS**
Stamvrug Milkplum

# STAMVRUG MILKPLUM

*Englerophytum magalismontanum*

**Links with animals** The fruit is readily eaten by baboons and monkeys, and bushpigs eat the roots.

**Human uses** The fruit, high in Vitamin C, is eaten fresh and is also used to make wine, jelly, brandy and syrup. Finely mashed fruit and roots were used to treat headaches and epilepsy. The powdered root, rubbed into incisions over the affected part, is used to relieve rheumatism.

**Gardening** This attractive tree is frost- and drought-resistant. It is fast growing and easy to grow from seed and cuttings.

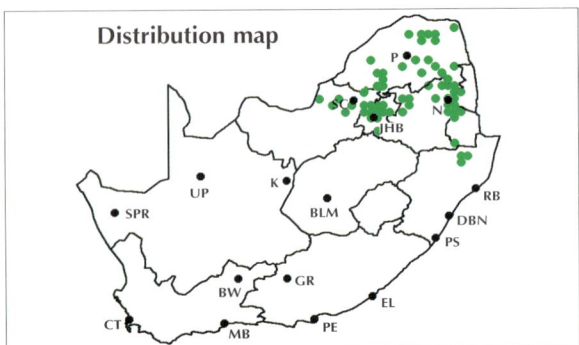

**Wood** This coarse-grained wood is white to reddish, and hard and tough. It has been extensively used in building.

*Multi-stemmed, dense canopy; Sour Bushveld*

# GROWTH DETAILS

This is a compact, multi-stemmed tree, with a short, thick stem that branches to form a round, dense, bluish-green canopy. It is very low-branching, and branches often hang to the ground. It contains milky latex.

**Leaves** Simple, alternate leaves are crowded towards the ends of the stubby branchlets, forming rosettes. Leaves are thick, rigid, dark green and shiny, and are covered by a whitish, waxy bloom that can be rubbed off easily. The central vein is sunken in on the upper-surface. It is prominent on the under-surface, which is dull olive-green and covered by golden-brown hairs. The margin of the elliptic leaf is smooth and slightly folded in underneath. Young leaves, which are covered by golden-brown hairs, look like flowers. (Leaf: 70 - 140 x 20 - 30 mm)

**Fruit** The plum-shaped fruit has a sharp tip and contains sticky, milky juice. Fruit is densely crowded on the stalks, branches and older branchlets, and is bright red when ripe (December to February). (15 - 25 x 10 - 18 mm)

**Flowers** Strong-smelling, creamy-white to pink, star-shaped flowers grow directly from the knobs on stalks, branches and older branchlets. Unopened flowers and their stalks are thickly covered by red-brown hairs (June to December). (10 mm)

*60% life-size*

**Bark** The bark is light brown to grey, rough and scaly, and cracks with age. Scars from previous fruit attachments form knobbly growths on the stems and branches.

**ROCKY AREAS — Stamvrug Milkplum**

## Seasonal changes
Evergreen. This tree is easy to identify throughout the year.

|  | Oct | Nov | Dec | Jan | Feb | Mar | Apr | May | Jun | Jul | Aug | Sep |
|---|---|---|---|---|---|---|---|---|---|---|---|---|
| Leaf | | | | | | | | | | | | |
| Flower | | | | | | | | | | | | |
| Fruit/Pod | | | | | | | | | | | | |

299

# TALL FIRETHORN CORKWOOD

*Commiphora pyracanthoides*                    **Tall Common Corkwood**

### MYRRH FAMILY
### BURSERACEAE

**SA Tree Number 285.1**

**AFRIKAANS** Groot Gewone Kanniedood  **TSONGA** Xifati  **TSWANA** Morôka  **VENDA** Mutalu  **ZULU** iMinyela

The species name **glandulosa** refers to the glandular hairs on the flower-stalks and calyces.

## Where you'll find this tree easily

The Tall Firethorn Corkwood grows singly, but where one is found, others are usually nearby. It normally grows in hot, dry places, and generally prefers well-drained soils, such as deep sandy soils and Rocky Areas.

- It is easiest to find on North- or West-facing Slopes of the Mixed Bushveld (M).
- It can also be found in Rocky Areas on the Plains in all Ecozones.

## Ecozones where this tree occurs

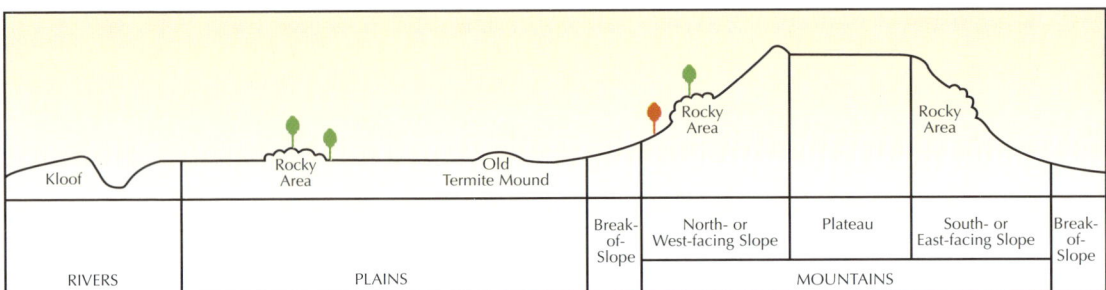

## Striking features

- This tree has a robust, fleshy, single, grey-green trunk, and a sparse, semi-circular canopy.
- The bark peels in small, straw-coloured, papery strips to expose the shiny green under-bark.
- It has a few short branches and branchlets, which divide profusely into fine, spine-tipped twigs.
- The branchlets and twigs come off at right angles from the trunk and branches, giving the tree a spiky appearance.
- The simple leaves are characteristically clustered on twigs.

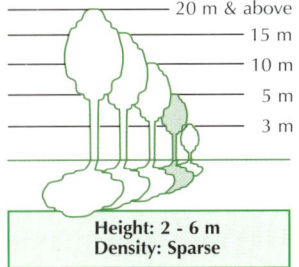

Height: 2 - 6 m
Density: Sparse

**ROCKY AREAS**
**Tall Firethorn Corkwood**

301

# TALL FIRETHORN CORKWOOD

*Commiphora pyracanthoides*

**Links with animals** The fruit is eaten by Yellow-billed Hornbills. Young shoots and leaves are eaten by duiker and elephant.

**Human uses** The wood is used to make cups and buckets.

**Gardening** This tree can be planted to form a hedge. It grows fast from seed and easily from cuttings. It is fairly frost-resistant and very drought-resistant.

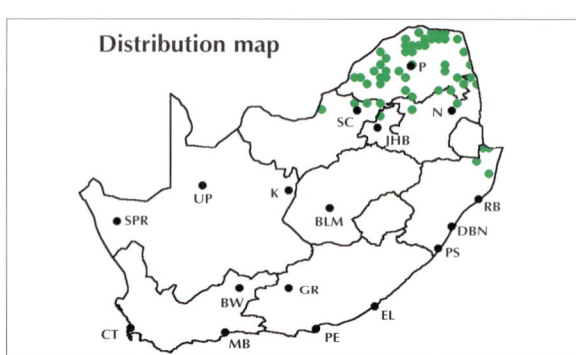
Distribution map

**Wood** The grey-white wood is very soft, and coarsely textured.

**Look-alike trees** Other fairly common corkwoods are Poison-grub Corkwood (*Commiphora africana*), Paperbark Corkwood (*Commiphora marlothii*), Zebra-bark Corkwood (*Commiphora viminea*), Velvet Corkwood (*Commiphora mollis*), Glossy-leaved Corkwood (*Commiphora schimperi*) and Sand Corkwood (*Commiphora angolensis*). See page 78 for details of Corkwood comparisons.

*June; West-facing Slope, Mixed Bushveld*

# GROWTH DETAILS

This is a single-stemmed tree that branches profusely low-down to form a semi-circular canopy. The branches are stiff but often arch downwards. The branchlets come off at right angles from the main stem and branches, and end in spines, giving the tree a spiky appearance. The very young twigs are often red.

**Leaves** The simple leaves are clustered in rosette-like groups on short, spiny twigs. However young leaves are often three-leaflet compound, with a big terminal and two smaller leaflets. They are elliptic to broadly elliptic in shape, with a broadly tapering tip that may be pointed, and a tapering base. The upper two-thirds of the leaf margin is toothed. Leaves are bright green to grey-green above and paler-green below, and turn yellow in autumn. The central and side-veins are yellow, and are clearly visible on the upper-surface. (30 - 75 x 20 - 35 mm)

**Spines** Twigs often end in hard spines, and there are sometimes single spines that grow on the main stem or branches.

*50% life-size*

**Fruit** The berry-like fruit is egg-shaped and red-green to brown. When ripe the fruit splits open to expose black and red seeds. It has a pleasant, fresh, medicinal smell (February to April). (13 x 10 mm)

**Flowers** Inconspicuous, small, narrow, pink or reddish trumpet-like flowers are grouped on short, knob-like, side branches. Female and bisexual flowers usually grow on separate trees. Flowers appear before the leaves (September to October).

**Bark** The bark is typical of most Corkwoods. It peels in small, papery flakes, exposing grey-green, shiny, oily under-bark.

## Seasonal changes
Deciduous. The characteristic bark and growth form of this tree makes identification easy throughout the year.

|  | Oct | Nov | Dec | Jan | Feb | Mar | Apr | May | Jun | Jul | Aug | Sep |
|---|---|---|---|---|---|---|---|---|---|---|---|---|
| Leaf | █ | █ | █ | █ | █ | █ | █ | █ |  |  |  | █ |
| Flower |  |  |  |  |  |  |  |  |  |  |  | █ |
| Fruit/Pod |  |  |  | █ | █ | █ | █ |  |  |  |  |  |

ROCKY AREAS
Tall Firethorn Corkwood

# VELVET BUSHWILLOW

*Combretum molle*

## BUSHWILLOW FAMILY
## COMBRETACEAE

**SA Tree Number 537**

**AFRIKAANS** Fluweelboswilg, Basterrooibos  **N. SOTHO** Mokgwethe  **SISWATI** inKukutwane  **TSONGA** Xikhukhutsane  **TSWANA** Modubatshipi, Moduba  **VENDA** Mugwiti  **ZULU** umBondwe omhlophe

The species name **molle** means 'soft', referring to the soft, velvety leaves.

## Where you'll find this tree easily

The Velvet Bushwillow grows singly among other tree species.

- 🔴 It is easiest to find in Rocky Areas on the North- or West-facing Slopes of all Ecozones.
- 🟢 It can also be found on South- or East-facing Slopes of the Mixed Bushveld (M), Northern Mountains (N) and Sour Bushveld (S); and on Rocky Areas of the Plains of the Mixed Bushveld (M).

## Ecozones where this tree occurs

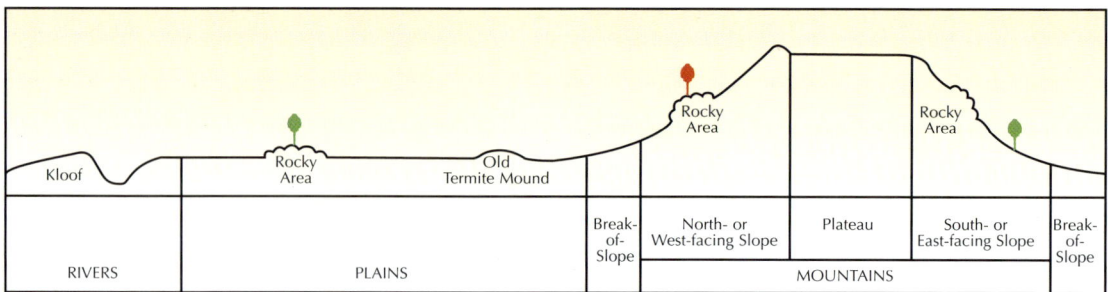

## Striking features

- This is a single-trunked tree, with a dark, crooked trunk that branches fairly high into meandering branches, branchlets and twigs.
- **The irregular, dark green canopy stands out among the surrounding vegetation.**
- **The leaves are large and distinctly oval to rounded, and are easy to see individually even from 30 metres.**
- **The leaves are velvety, with a distinct herringbone pattern of veins.**
- The bark is rough and dark grey, and breaks up into regular blocks on older trees.
- The tree has characteristic, four-winged Bushwillow pods (January to June).

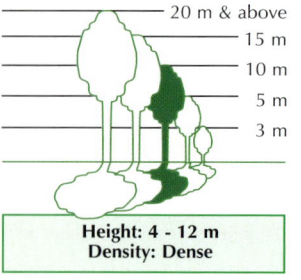

Height: 4 - 12 m
Density: Dense

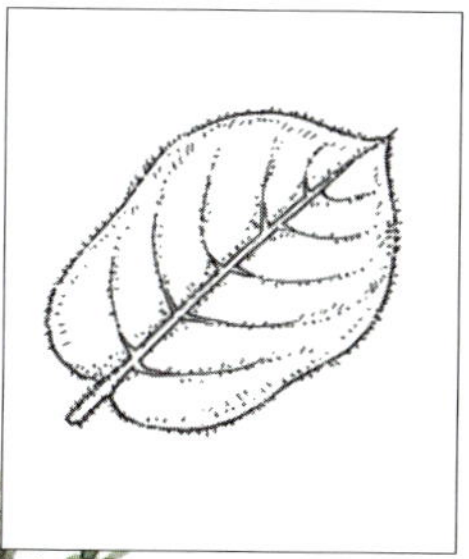

**ROCKY AREAS**
**Velvet Bushwillow**

**Largest tree currently registered**

**Diameter:** 0,49 m
**Girth:** 1,54 m
**Height:** 11 m

EA Galpin, 'Mosdene',
Zyferkraal, Dist. Potgietersrus

305

# VELVET BUSHWILLOW

*Combretum molle*

**Links with animals** The leaves are eaten by cattle and a wide variety of antelope. The caterpillars of 25 different species of butterfly eat the leaves.

**Human uses** The wood is used for fencing posts, implement handles, grain mortars, and bowls for grinding peanuts. Leaves are used as a red fabric-dye, and roots as a yellow-brown dye. The fresh or moistened dry leaves are used to dress wounds, and the root as an antidote to snakebite. Roots are used to induce abortion and to treat constipation.

**Gardening** This is an attractive garden tree, and when mature is frost-resistant. It grows easily from seed, and is suitable as a bonsai tree.

**Look-alike trees** See pages 74-75 for the comparison to other Bushwillows.

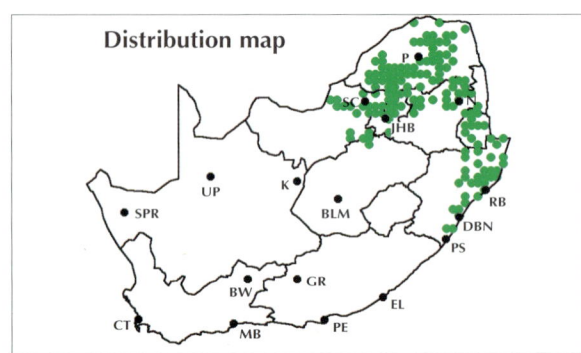

**Wood** The wood has a coarse texture with yellow-brown heartwood. It is termite-proof and brittle when dry.

*September; conspicuous flower-spikes and velvety new leaves*

# GROWTH DETAILS

This is a single-trunked tree with a crooked trunk that branches fairly high into meandering branches, branchlets and twigs. The moderate canopy is irregular and spreading.

**Leaves** Simple, opposite leaves are densely covered by velvety hairs when young, becoming smoother with age. The broadly elliptic leaf appears almost round, and has a smooth margin and a rounded point with a fine, hair-like tip. The central and side veins and even intermediary veins stand out clearly on the under-surface. They are often hairy, and may be covered with reddish scales. (Leaf: 60 - 100 x 40 - 60 mm)

**Pods** The abundant four-winged pods turn from yellow-green to golden red-brown when ripe from January to September. Pods may remain on the tree for the whole season. (13 - 23 mm)

*50% life-size*

**Flowers** Conspicuous, yellow-green spikes grow in the angles formed by the leaves. They are sweet-scented and appear before the leaves (September to November). (Spike: 40 - 90 mm; individual: 4 mm)

**Bark** The bark is grey-brown to black, and breaks up into regular, small blocks, to reveal a reddish-tinted under-bark. The bark of new branches, branchlets and twigs has a reticulate pattern, like elephant skin. Twigs are covered by reddish hairs.

## Seasonal changes
Deciduous. The leaves turn from copper to plum-red in autumn. The tree can be identified as long as the four-winged pods are present.

|  | Oct | Nov | Dec | Jan | Feb | Mar | Apr | May | Jun | Jul | Aug | Sep |
|---|---|---|---|---|---|---|---|---|---|---|---|---|
| Leaf | | | | | | | | | | | | |
| Flower | | | | | | | | | | | | |
| Fruit/Pod | | | | | | | | | | | | |

ROCKY AREAS
Velvet Bushwillow

307

# WHITE KIRKIA

*Kirkia acuminata*                                    White syringa; White Seringa

---

### TREE-OF-HEAVEN FAMILY
### SIMAROUBACEAE

SA Tree Number 267

**AFRIKAANS** Witsering   **N. SOTHO** Modumela   **PEDI** Modumela   **TSONGA** Mvumayila
**TSWANA** Modumêla   **VENDA** Mubvumela

The species name **acuminata** refers to the sharp, pointed leaflets.

## Where you'll find this tree easily

The White Kirkia grows in scattered groups.
- It is easiest to find in Rocky Areas on the North- or West-facing Slopes of the Northern Mountains (N).
- It can also be found in Rocky Areas on the Plains of the Northern Mountains (N), Sour Bushveld (S) and Mixed Bushveld (M).

## Ecozones where this tree occurs

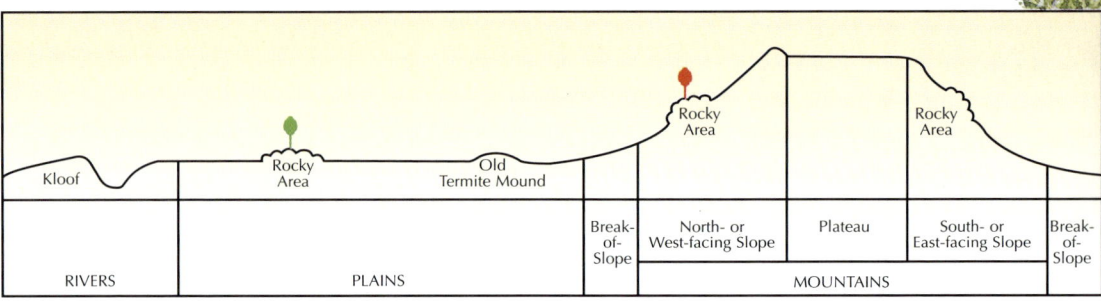

## Striking features

- It has a tall, straight, single trunk and a light green, feathery-looking, spreading canopy.
- The bark is light grey and smooth when young, and becomes flaky with corky knobs in older trees.
- The compound leaves are clustered at the ends of blunt-tipped branchlets.
- In April to May the brilliant yellow-to-red autumn colours are spectacular.

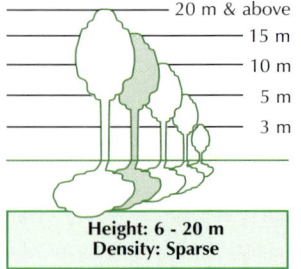

Height: 6 - 20 m
Density: Sparse

**ROCKY AREAS**
**White Kirkia**

309

# WHITE KIRKIA

*Kirkia acuminata*

**Links with animals** Game dig up the roots in times of drought.

**Human uses** Water-laden roots may be used as a source of drinking water. The wood is used for furniture and to make household goods such as bowls.

**Gardening** A very attractive tree, especially in autumn and spring when the leaves are very colourful. It will only grow well in well-drained soils, such as rocky outcrops in larger gardens. It is drought-resistant but not frost-resistant. It can be grown from seeds and cuttings, and is fairly fast-growing when well watered.

**Wood** The sapwood is light grey to whitish and the heartwood is narrow and dark coppery to greenish-brown with dark wavy markings.

**Look-alike trees** See page 69 for similar trees.

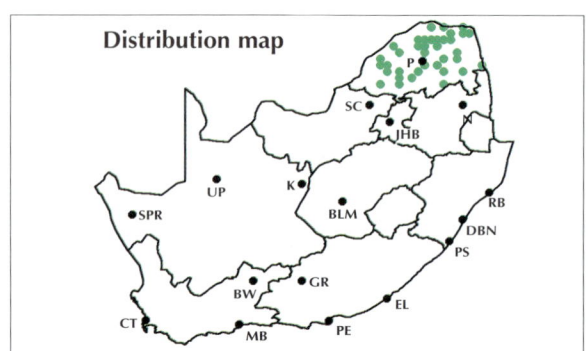

Distribution map

*May; Rocky Area, Plains, Mixed Bushveld*

# GROWTH DETAILS

It has a single, straight trunk with horizontal branches that form a sparse, spreading canopy.

**Leaves** The compound leaves are spirally arranged. They are clustered at the ends of bluntly-tipped branchlets, and have long leaf-stalks (50 - 100 mm). The leaf consists of 6 - 17 pairs of opposite or alternate leaflets, and a leaflet at the tip. The leaflets are elliptic, and have a narrowly tapering tip and a rounded base that is asymmetrically attached to the leaflet-stalk. The leaflets have a finely toothed margin, and are fresh green to dark green. The leaves turn to splendid golden and red colours in autumn. (Leaf: 200 - 450 mm long; leaflet: 20 - 83 x 10 - 29 mm)

**Flowers** The greenish-cream to creamy-white flowers grow in branched sprays at the ends of branchlets, or in the angles formed by the leaves (October to November). (Spray: up to 100 mm long)

*20% life-size*

**Fruit** The small, light brown woody capsule is divided into four sections (valves) and grows in bunches. When the capsule bursts open it releases one seed from each section. The capsules may remain on the tree for long periods, some until the next flowering season (January to September). (Fruit: 15 x 5 mm)

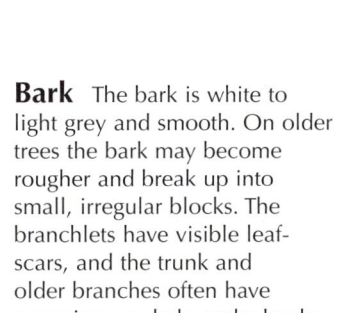

**Bark** The bark is white to light grey and smooth. On older trees the bark may become rougher and break up into small, irregular blocks. The branchlets have visible leaf-scars, and the trunk and older branches often have conspicuous dark, corky knobs.

## Seasonal changes
Deciduous. The leaves have brilliant yellow autumn colours. There is a long period without leaves in winter, when the tree is more difficult to identify. New reddish-green leaves appear in spring.

|  | Oct | Nov | Dec | Jan | Feb | Mar | Apr | May | Jun | Jul | Aug | Sep |
|---|---|---|---|---|---|---|---|---|---|---|---|---|
| Leaf | | | | | | | | | | | | |
| Flower | | | | | | | | | | | | |
| Fruit/Pod | | | | | | | | | | | | |

**ROCKY AREAS** — White Kirkia

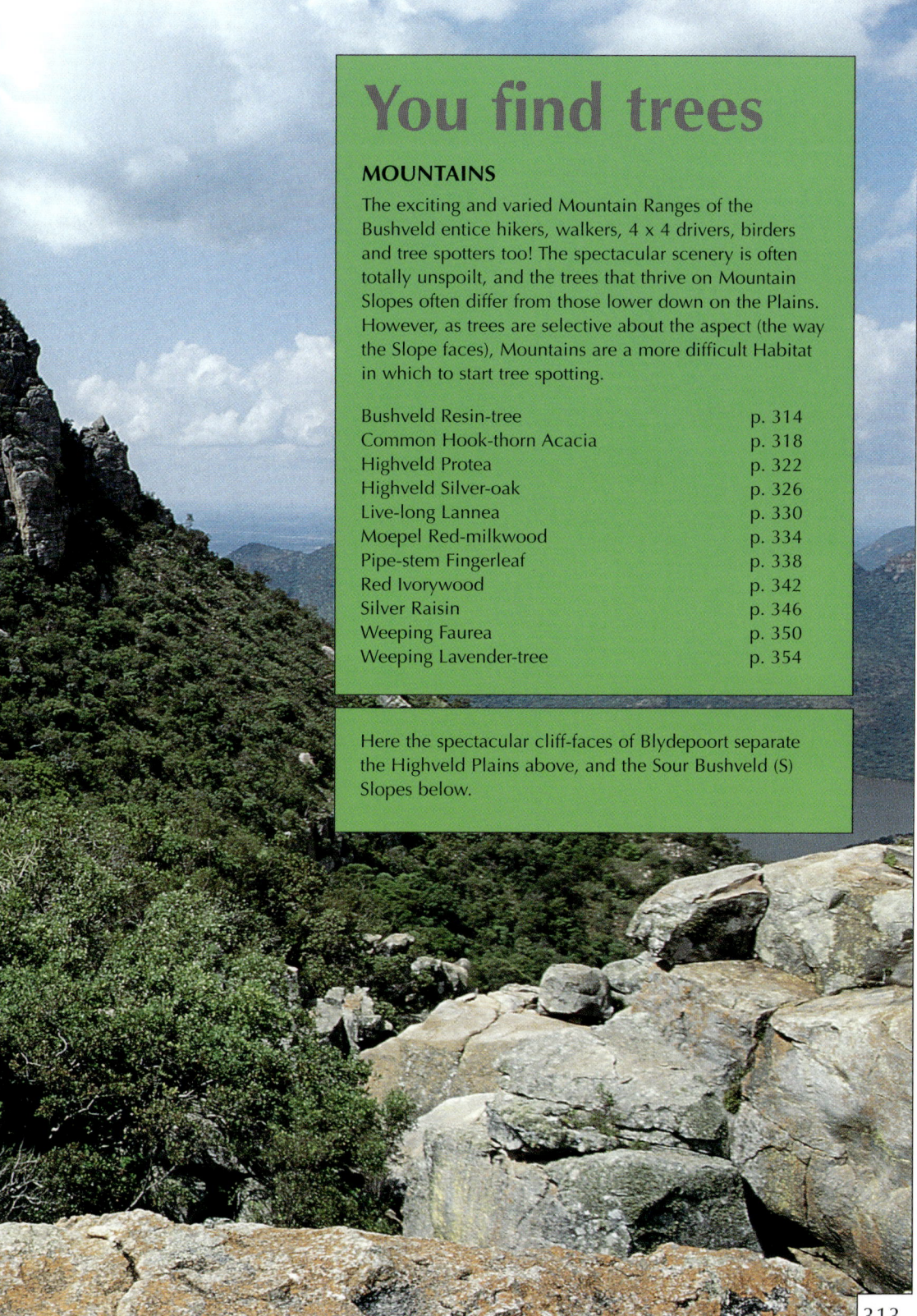

# You find trees

## MOUNTAINS

The exciting and varied Mountain Ranges of the Bushveld entice hikers, walkers, 4 x 4 drivers, birders and tree spotters too! The spectacular scenery is often totally unspoilt, and the trees that thrive on Mountain Slopes often differ from those lower down on the Plains. However, as trees are selective about the aspect (the way the Slope faces), Mountains are a more difficult Habitat in which to start tree spotting.

| | |
|---|---|
| Bushveld Resin-tree | p. 314 |
| Common Hook-thorn Acacia | p. 318 |
| Highveld Protea | p. 322 |
| Highveld Silver-oak | p. 326 |
| Live-long Lannea | p. 330 |
| Moepel Red-milkwood | p. 334 |
| Pipe-stem Fingerleaf | p. 338 |
| Red Ivorywood | p. 342 |
| Silver Raisin | p. 346 |
| Weeping Faurea | p. 350 |
| Weeping Lavender-tree | p. 354 |

Here the spectacular cliff-faces of Blydepoort separate the Highveld Plains above, and the Sour Bushveld (S) Slopes below.

# BUSHVELD RESIN-TREE

*Ozoroa paniculosa*  
Common resin tree; Bushveld Resin Tree

| **MANGO FAMILY**<br>**ANACARDIACEAE** | **SA Tree Number 375** |

**AFRIKAANS** Gewone Harpuisboom, Harsbessie  **N. SOTHO** Monoko  **TSONGA** Xinungumafi  **TSWANA** Monokane  **VENDA** Mubandulakhali, Mudumbula  **ZULU** isiFico

The species name **paniculosa** refers to the hanging bunches of flowers and fruit.

## Where you'll find this tree easily

The Bushveld Resin-tree grows singly among other species of trees.

- 🔴 It is easiest to find on the North- or West-facing Slopes of the Mixed Bushveld (M), the Central Mountains (C) and the Northern Mountains (N).
- 🟢 It can also be found on the South- or East-facing Slopes of the Mixed Bushveld (M); and on the Plains of the Central Mountains (C) and Northern Mountains (N).

### Ecozones where this tree occurs

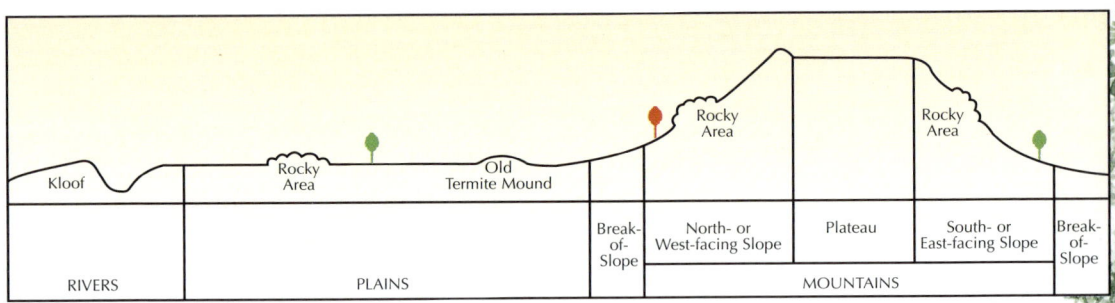

## Striking features

- This is a single-stemmed, silvery tree with meandering branches that tend to arch downwards, but twigs that grow upwards.
- The dark, reddish-tinged, branches contrast with the silver canopy.
- **The simple, alternate, long, elliptic leaves have a distinct, fine herringbone vein pattern.**
- The small, kidney-shaped fruit grows in sprays, and turns black when ripe from March to May.

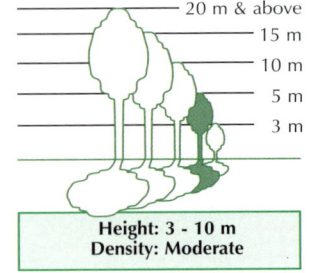

Height: 3 - 10 m  
Density: Moderate

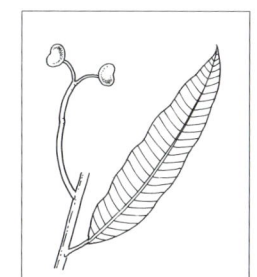

MOUNTAINS
Bushveld Resin-tree

# BUSHVELD RESIN-TREE

*Ozoroa paniculosa*

**Links with animals** The tree is sometimes browsed by Black Rhino and elephant. Birds enjoy the fruit.

**Human uses** The fruit is used for perfume, and as a dye for leather aprons, and the sap to mend cracks in pottery. Powdered bark is used to treat acute inflammation of the chest and dysentery, and as an enema.

**Gardening** This is an attractive garden tree that grows reasonably fast from fresh seed, although germination is usually poor. Birds are attracted to the fruit. It is reasonably frost-resistant and fairly drought-resistant.

**Look-alike tree** Currant Resin-tree (*Ozoroa sphaerocarpa*) has a very similar growth form, and is the most common Resin-tree of the Sour Bushveld. The main differences are that the leaves of Currant Resin-tree are dull green not silvery, and distinctly hairy below, and the fruit is round, not kidney-shaped.

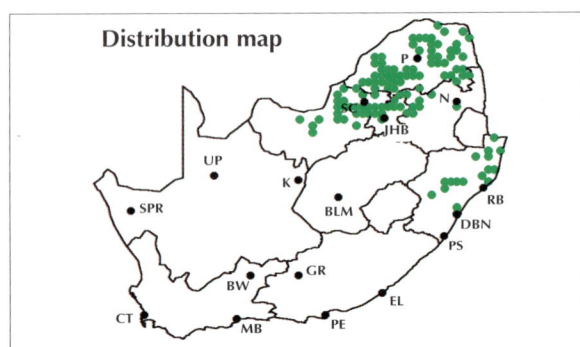

Distribution map

**Wood** The wood is reddish-brown, fine-grained and soft, but brittle and of poor quality.

*Summer; Plains of Pilanesberg*

# GROWTH DETAILS

This is a single or multi-stemmed tree that branches low down to form a moderate, spreading, irregular canopy. The meandering branches tend to arch downwards.

**Leaves** The simple leaves may be alternate or grow in whorls of three. The leaf-stalks are 2,5 - 12 mm, and leaves are narrowly elliptic with a smooth to wavy margin. The tip of the leaf is rounded with a short, spike-like point. The leaves are silvery-green, with a conspicuous herringbone vein pattern that stands out on the under-surface. (25 - 130 x 10 - 40 mm)

**Fruit** The small, kidney-shaped fruit grows on female trees in branched bunches at the ends of branchlets and twigs. It is initially shiny green with a few reddish-brown spots, becoming black and wrinkled when ripe (March to May). (7 x 10 mm)

**Flowers** The strong-scented, white, bell-shaped flowers grow in sprays at the ends of branchlets and twigs. Male and female flowers are similar but grow on separate trees (August to February). (Flower spray: up to 40 mm long)

*50% life-size*

**Bark** The bark is smooth and grey in young trees, becoming thick, rough and dark grey to brown in older trees. The branches have a brownish-red appearance. Young twigs have reddish hairs.

**MOUNTAINS — Bushveld Resin-tree**

## Seasonal changes
Deciduous. Difficult to identify when no leaves are present.

|  | Oct | Nov | Dec | Jan | Feb | Mar | Apr | May | Jun | Jul | Aug | Sep |
|---|---|---|---|---|---|---|---|---|---|---|---|---|
| Leaf |  |  |  |  |  |  |  |  |  |  |  |  |
| Flower |  |  |  |  |  |  |  |  |  |  |  |  |
| Fruit/Pod |  |  |  |  |  |  |  |  |  |  |  |  |

# COMMON HOOK-THORN ACACIA

*Acacia caffra*                                              Common hook-thorn

---

**THORN-TREE FAMILY**  
**MIMOSACEAE**                                              SA Tree Number 162

**AFRIKAANS** Gewone Haakdoring, Katdoring  **N. SOTHO** Motholo, Moroba-diêpe
**TSONGA** Mbvhinya-xihloka  **TSWANA** Morutlhare  **VENDA** Muvunda-mbado  **ZULU** umTholo

The species name **caffra** is from the Hebrew word 'kafri', meaning 'person living on the land'

## Where you'll find this tree easily

The Common Hook-thorn Acacia often grows in scattered groups.

- It is easiest to find on the South- or East-facing Slopes of all Ecozones.
- It can also be found along Rivers and Streams, and in Rocky Areas of all Ecozones; and on the Plains of the Sour Bushveld (S).

## Ecozones where this tree occurs

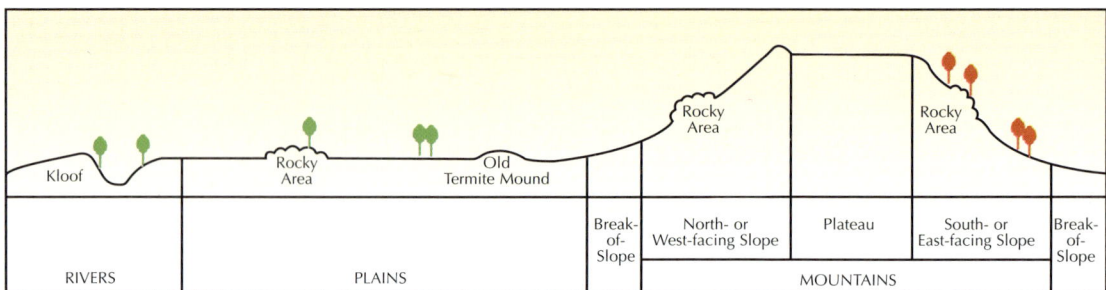

## Striking features

- It is a single-stemmed, V-shaped Thorn-tree, which branches low down, so that the leaves sometimes obscure the trunk.
- The long, fine, twice compound leaves droop to form an irregular, soft, feathery canopy.
- **The hooked thorns are paired, and successive pairs are at right angles to each other.**
- Early in spring the trees are covered by creamy-white flower-spikes.
- The chocolate-brown, flat bean pods have pointed tips, and grow in bunches.

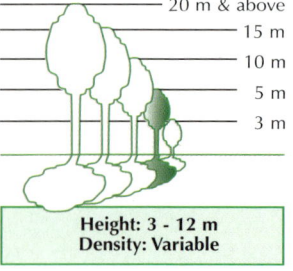

Height: 3 - 12 m
Density: Variable

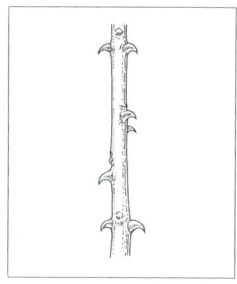

**MOUNTAINS
Common Hook-thorn Acacia**

# COMMON HOOK-THORN ACACIA

*Acacia caffra*

**Links with animals** This is a good fodder tree, on which the new leaves are particularly palatable.

**Human uses** The wood is hard, and makes good fence posts. It is also used to make tobacco pipes. The bark was used for tanning, and the bark, leaves and roots were believed to have magical properties. It was used to cleanse blood and to treat abdominal disorders in infants. The tree is still used in traditional medicine today.

**Gardening** The Common Hook-thorn Acacia is easy to grow. It is an attractive tree that is frost- and drought-resistant, but grows slowly from seed. The seeds should be soaked in hot water before planting.

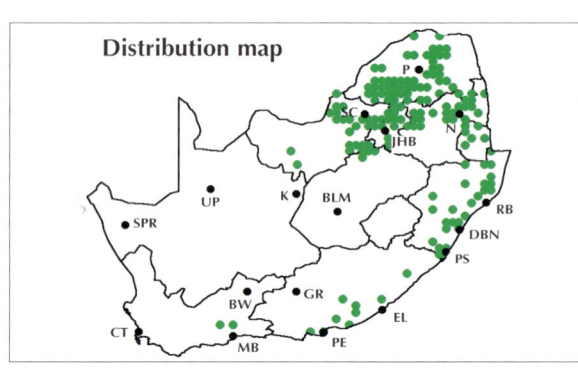

Distribution map

**Wood** The wood is hard and makes good fence posts. It is also used to make tobacco pipes.

**Look-alike trees** This tree may be confused with Flame-pod Acacia (*Acacia ataxacantha*), page 116, which is a more scrambling tree, with scattered, hooked thorns in no specific pattern, and purple-red pods.

African Weeping-wattle (*Peltophorum africanum*), page 214, has larger, rounder leaflets, no thorns, and pale, winged pods.

*Spring; buds, flowers and new leaves*

# GROWTH DETAILS

This is a single-stemmed tree, often with a crooked trunk, that branches low down to form a V-shaped, irregular canopy. In areas of lower rainfall, the canopy is less dense than in areas where rainfall is high. The dark branches are usually obvious between the leaves. The long, drooping, twice compound leaves give the canopy a soft, feathery appearance.

**Leaves**  The large, twice compound, feathery leaves grow on thin, pale, reddish-brown twigs. There are 8 - 24 feather pairs, with 13 - 30 pairs of very small leaflets. The leaf-stalk has small, hooked thorns. (Leaf: 60 - 230 mm; leaflet: 6 x 1,5 mm)

**Flowers**  The distinctive cream to pale-yellow, sweet-scented flower-spikes grow in bunches of 3 - 5, before the leaves appear (September to November). (60 - 140 mm)

**Pods**  The flat bean pods have a pointed tip, and grow in chocolate-brown bunches. Ripe pods split open on the tree from December to March. (70 - 160 x 10 - 13 mm)

*80% life-size*

**Thorns**  The short, hooked thorns grow in pairs at right angles to the next pair. Generally this is the least thorny of the Thorn-trees in South Africa, although younger trees and branches tend to have more thorns. (5 mm)

*80% life-size*

**Bark**  The bark is dark grey-brown to black. It is rough and loosely peeling in places, showing light brown, streaky under-bark. New branches, branchlets and twigs are red-brown.

## Seasonal changes
Deciduous. It is one of the first trees to come out in fresh green foliage in spring, and the leaves turn yellow and drop early in autumn. It is difficult to identify when leafless, but its thorns will help.

|  | Oct | Nov | Dec | Jan | Feb | Mar | Apr | May | Jun | Jul | Aug | Sep |
|---|---|---|---|---|---|---|---|---|---|---|---|---|
| Leaf | | | | | | | | | | | | |
| Flower | | | | | | | | | | | | |
| Fruit/Pod | | | | | | | | | | | | |

**MOUNTAINS — Common Hook-thorn Acacia**

# HIGHVELD PROTEA

*Protea caffra*                                   Common Sugarbush; Natal Protea

---

### PROTEA FAMILY
### PROTEACEAE
### SA Tree Number 87

**AFRIKAANS** Gewone Suikerbos  **NORTH SOTHO** Segwapi, Mogalagala  **SOUTH SOTHO** Sekila
**VENDA** Tshidzungu  **XHOSA** isAdlunge, isiQwane  **ZULU** isiQalaba

The species name **caffra** is from the Hebrew 'kafri' meaning 'person living on the land'.

## Where you'll find this tree easily

The Highveld Protea grows in scattered groups.
- It is easiest to find on South- or East-facing Slopes of the Central Mountains (C).
- It can also be found on South- or East-facing Slopes and on the Plateaus of the Mixed Bushveld (M), Northern Mountains (N) and Sour Bushveld (S).

## Ecozones where this tree occurs

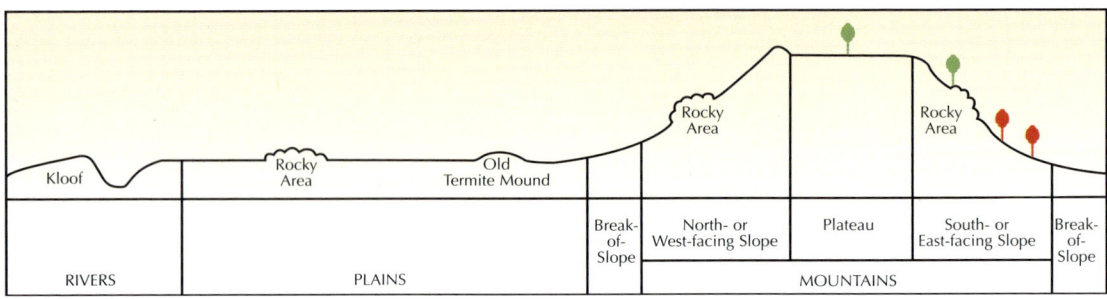

## Striking features

- **This is a sturdy, low-branching tree with dark bark and an irregular canopy.**
- The leaves, which grow directly off stout branchlets and twigs, with almost no leaf-stalk, are smooth and feel like thick leather.
- The leaves are blue-green, with almost no leaf-stalk.
- **The characteristic, sweet-scented Protea flowers have large, open cones the shape of deep saucers, flowering from October to March.**
- Old seed-heads, that are wider than those of the Silver Sugarbush, are usually visible on the tree all year round.

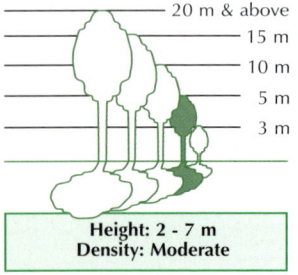

Height: 2 - 7 m
Density: Moderate

**MOUNTAINS
Highveld Protea**

# HIGHVELD PROTEA

*Protea caffra*

**Links with animals** The flowers attract many insects, especially beetles, as well as elegant sugarbirds such as Gurney's, and colourful sunbirds including the Malachite.

**Human uses** The flower was depicted on the South African threepenny (ticky) and sixpenny coins in the middle of the 20th Century. The bark contains tannins, and was used for tanning leather. Root-bark infusions were used to treat bleeding stomach ulcers in humans, and to treat calves with bloody diarrhoea.

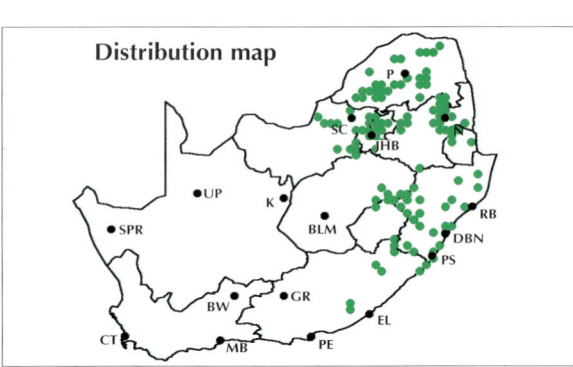
Distribution map

**Wood** The wood is very heavy, and pale brown with reddish flecks and has a moderate, even texture. It has a straight grain, saws and turns well, takes varnish well, and is suitable for making small pieces of fine, decorative work.

**Gardening** This can be an attractive addition to the large informal garden. It is frost-resistant and can be grown from seed, but is slow-growing.

**Look-alike trees** This tree can be confused with African Protea (*Protea gaguedi*), a winter-flowering Protea. The flower-head cones of African Protea are larger. The bracts surrounding the flower-head are covered by dense silver hairs, and the individual flowers stand out well above them.

Silver Protea (*Protea roupelliae*), page 58, has silver hairs on the new leaves, and its flower-heads are more cup-like and surrounded by silvery-pink petals (bracts).

*August; South-facing Slope; Pilanesberg*

# GROWTH DETAILS

This is a single- or multi-stemmed, low-branching, sturdy, gnarled tree with a crooked trunk and spreading branches, forming a moderate, irregular canopy. Leaves grow on thick, stubby twigs and branchlets, with large branches and branchlets visible in the canopy. Leaf scars are visible along the older branches.

**Leaves**  Simple, alternate leaves are crowded towards the ends of the branchlets and twigs. Leaves are closely packed, and have almost no leaf-stalks. The margins of the leathery, elliptic leaves are smooth, and the central vein is obviously yellow on both sides. New crimson leaves form rosettes at the tips of branchlets and twigs. These turn bright light green before maturing to the characteristic dull blue-green. (Leaf: 80 - 140 x 15 - 25 mm)

**Flowers**  This is a summer-flowering Protea. The conspicuous, sweet-scented Protea flower-heads are characteristic. Each velvety 'thread' in the woody cone is an individual flower. These flowers are surrounded by brown, woody outside bracts (petals), while the inner bracts are pink. (October to March) (50 - 80 x 50 mm)

70% life-size

life-size

**Fruit**  A small, hairy nutlet is formed at the base of each flower thread. These are blown out by the wind when the cone opens, often only after a fire. The woody cones remain on the tree for long periods and are  usually present throughout the year. (Width: 2 mm)

**Bark**  The bark is dark brown to black, rough, and broken into uneven, corky blocks. Young branchlets and twigs are smooth and pinkish.

|  | Oct | Nov | Dec | Jan | Feb | Mar | Apr | May | Jun | Jul | Aug | Sep |
|---|---|---|---|---|---|---|---|---|---|---|---|---|
| Leaf | | | | | | | | | | | | |
| Flower | | | | | | | | | | | | |
| Fruit/Pod | | | | | | | | | | | | |

## Seasonal changes
Evergreen. The tree is easy to identify throughout the year.

# HIGHVELD SILVER-OAK

*Brachylaena rotundata*                                     Mountain Silver Oak

### DAISY FAMILY
### ASTERACEAE

SA Tree Number 730

**AFRIKAANS** Bergvaalbos    **TSWANA** Moswane

The species name **rotundata** refers to the roundish form of the leaves.

## Where you'll find this tree easily

The Highveld Silver-oak grows singly among other tree species, but where one is found, there will usually be others in the vicinity.

- It is easiest to find on South- or East-facing Slopes of the Mixed Bushveld (M).
- It can also be found in Rocky Areas of both the Plains and North- or West-facing Slopes, and along Rivers of the Central Mountains (C).

## Ecozones where this tree occurs

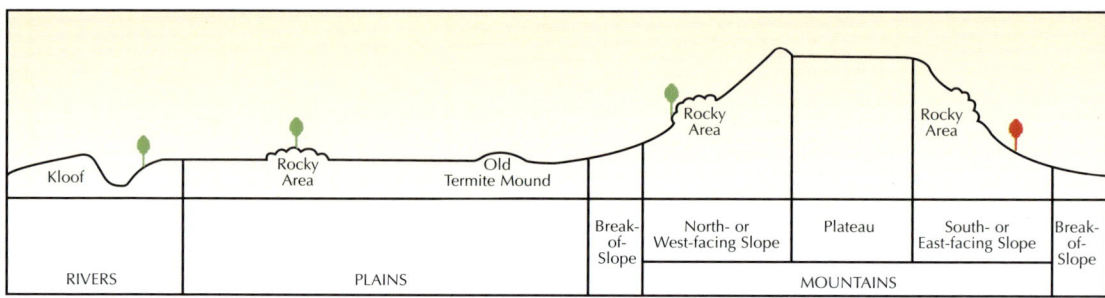

## Striking features

- **This single-stemmed tree has an irregular, blue-grey to silvery canopy that forms a strong contrast with the dark bark and surrounding vegetation.**
- **The bark is deeply fissured lengthways, showing pinkish under-bark.**
- The bicoloured leaves are broad and elliptic, and have an irregularly toothed margin.
- The simple alternate leaves are crowded towards the ends of twigs, forming rosettes.
- New leaves have a distinct pink-to-coppery tinge.

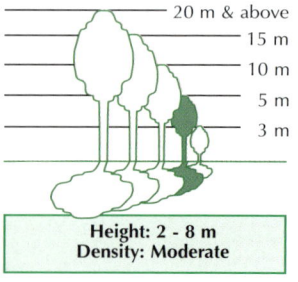

Height: 2 - 8 m
Density: Moderate

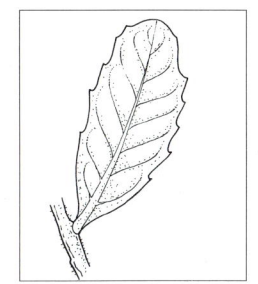

MOUNTAINS
Highveld Silver-oak

327

# HIGHVELD SILVER-OAK

*Brachylaena rotundata*

**Links with animals** It is seldom used as a fodder tree.

**Human uses** There is no record of this species being used for medicinal purposes, but trees of the same genus are used to treat various ailments, such as diabetes and kidney problems.

**Gardening** This can be an attractive tree in a well-watered garden. It is frost-resistant.

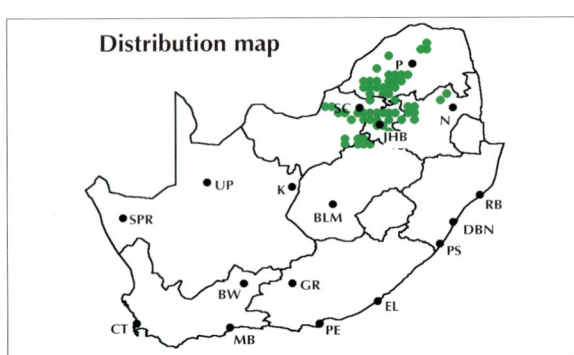
Distribution map

**Wood** This is a coarse wood with brown heartwood and a yellowing tint in the centre, and creamy sapwood.

**Look-alike trees** Forest Silver-oak (*Brachylaena discolor* subsp. *transvaalensis*) is found in the eastern part of the Bushveld. It is a very similar tree, in both growth form and general appearance but is evergreen. The leaves of Forest Silver-oak are 75 x 35 mm. They are also broadly elliptic, distinctly bicoloured and covered by thick, white, felt-like hairs on the under-surface. However they are dark green on the upper-surface, with the tip tapering to an almost rounded, rather than blunt, end.

Lowveld Silver-oak (*Brachylaena huillensis*) is usually a smaller tree, with narrower leaves (80 x 25 mm), and the tip tapering to a sharp point.

Lowveld Silver-oak

Highveld Silver-oak

Forest Silver-oak

# GROWTH DETAILS

This single-stemmed tree has a crooked trunk and branches that grow upwards. Large branches are visible in the canopy. The leaves grow in dense clusters, on slender, drooping twigs, forming a moderate, irregular canopy. New stems and twigs are covered by velvet hairs.

**Leaves** Simple, alternate leaves are crowded towards the ends of the branchlets, forming rosettes. The leaf-margins are mostly toothed, but may be smooth. The broadly elliptic, bicoloured leaves have a blunt tip, and are dull grey-green above, and paler, covered by whitish hairs below. Leaves are smooth, leathery and rigid when mature. Young leaves are velvety, covered by dense white hairs, and have a pink coppery tinge. (Leaf: 25 - 150 x 20 - 25 mm)

**Flowers** Conspicuous, pale yellow, star-like flowers appear before the leaves in spring. Male and female flowers are on separate trees, and are more noticeable on the male trees. They grow in sprays at the ends of twigs, with 7 - 50 flowers per spray (August to September). (10 mm)

45% life-size

60% life-size

**Fruit** The small, tufted fruit ripens from September, and may stay on the tree for long periods. (5 mm)

**Bark** The bark is dark and rough. It is deeply fissured lengthways, forming dark ribs with pink-grey under-bark in between.

MOUNTAINS
Highveld Silver-oak

## Seasonal changes
Deciduous. It is difficult to identify this tree in winter when it has no leaves.

|  | Oct | Nov | Dec | Jan | Feb | Mar | Apr | May | Jun | Jul | Aug | Sep |
|---|---|---|---|---|---|---|---|---|---|---|---|---|
| Leaf |  |  |  |  |  |  |  |  |  |  |  |  |
| Flower |  |  |  |  |  |  |  |  |  |  |  |  |
| Fruit/Pod |  |  |  |  |  |  |  |  |  |  |  |  |

329

# LIVE-LONG LANNEA

*Lannea discolor*  
Live-long; Tree Grape

| MANGO FAMILY ANACARDIACEAE | SA Tree Number 362 |

**AFRIKAANS** Dikbas, Bakhout  **N. SOTHO** Morula-môpšane, Mokgôkgôthwane  **TSONGA** Ximupyane  **TSWANA** Moôjwane  **VENDA** Muvhumbu  **ZULU** isiGanganyane

The species name **discolor** refers to the bicoloured leaves. **Live-long** refers to the fact that even when poles are made from the tree, they often grow again – the tree thus never dies.

## Where you'll find this tree easily

The Live-long Lannea grows singly, but where one is found, there are likely to be others in the vicinity.

- It is easiest to find on the North- or West-facing Slopes of the Northern Mountains (N) and the Central Mountains (C).
- It can also be found in Rocky Areas, and on many of the South- or East-facing Slopes of the other Ecozones.

## Ecozones where this tree occurs

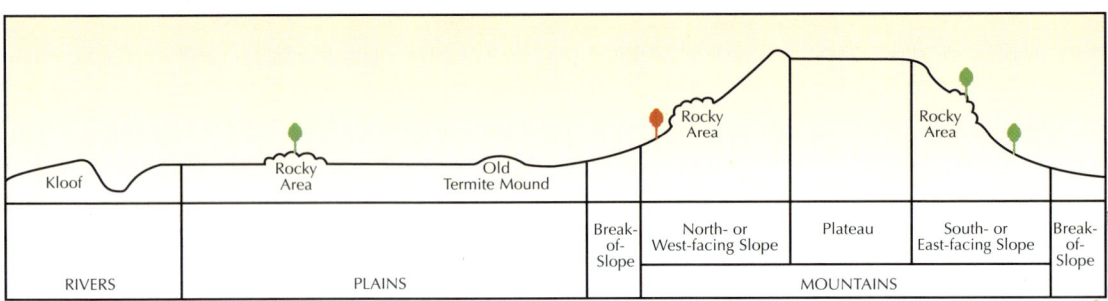

## Striking features

- This is a single-trunked tree that branches into a few thick, bare branches that spread to form a sparse, irregular canopy.
- **The compound leaves, with a leaflet at the tip, cluster at the ends of very thick, wrinkled twigs that are usually short and stubby.**
- **The bicoloured leaflets are dark grey-green above and velvety grey-white beneath.**
- The green leaf-stalks are fairly rigid, and hold the leaf in a relatively uniform plane.
- The bark is grey and smooth on larger branches and young trunks.
- The shiny, grape-like fruit has four horn-like projections at the tip (December to January).

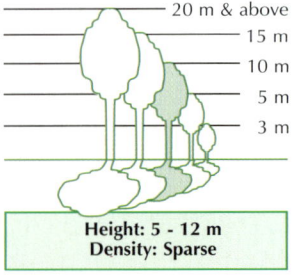

Height: 5 - 12 m  
Density: Sparse

MOUNTAINS
Live-long Lannea

# LIVE-LONG LANNEA

*Lannea discolor*

**Links with animals** Leaves are browsed by game, particularly giraffe, kudu and elephant. The fruit is eaten by monkeys, birds and baboons, and fallen fruit by bushpigs and warthogs. Rodents eat the seeds. Elephant and bushpigs eat the bark and the roots.

**Human uses** The wood is used to make pounding blocks, bowls, spoons and plates. The bark of young branchlets is used to make rope, and children use the bark to make popguns. The fruit is edible. Diarrhoea is treated with infusions from the root bark, and leaf infusions are sometimes used to treat sore eyes, boils and abscesses.

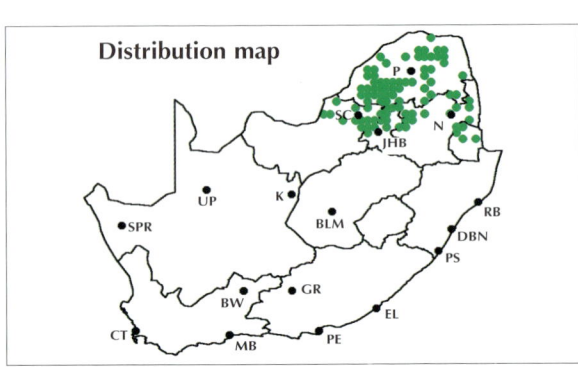
Distribution map

*Scattered trees; Northern Slope, Central Mountains*

**Wood** The wood is soft and light, without heartwood, and pale brown when dry. Despite its rough texture, it works off smoothly and polishes well.

**Gardening** The tree is an attractive addition to a larger garden, and in warm areas grows quickly and easily from both seeds and cuttings. It is not frost-resistant but is drought-resistant. See comparisons of these leaf arrangements on page 69.

**Look-alike trees** This is a distinctive tree in Rocky Areas. On lower slopes it can be confused with Marula (*Sclerocarya birrea*), page 230, and Burkea (*Burkea africana*), page 236, both of which have a similar leaf arrangement. Compared with the green of Live-long Lannea, the Marula has reddish leaflet- and leaf-stalks, and the Burkea has yellowish leaflet- and leaf-stalks. Live-long Lannea is usually a smaller tree than either of the others.

# GROWTH DETAILS

This is a single-trunked tree that branches into a few thick, bare branches that spread to form a sparse, irregular, spreading canopy. The leaves are spirally arranged on the ends of thick, wrinkled twigs.

**Leaves** The compound leaves cluster at the tips of thick, wrinkled, short, stubby twigs. The leaf consists of 3 - 5 opposite to sub-opposite leaflet pairs and a leaflet at the tip. The leaflet-stalks are fairly rigid, holding the leaf in a uniform plane. The leaflet at the tip has a long, greenish leaf-stalk of up to 20 mm, whereas the side-leaflets have short leaf-stalks. The elliptic leaflets have smooth margins, and the central vein is obvious. They are dark grey-green above, and greyish-white, covered in fine whitish hairs with conspicuous dark veins, on the under-surface. New leaves are a velvety pinkish-brown. (Leaf: up to 300 mm; leaflet: 30 - 105 x 15 - 55 mm)

20% life-size

**Fruit** The shiny, grape-like fruit grows in bunches at the ends of branchlets and twigs. There are four horn-like projections at the tip of the fruit. The fruit is reddish to purple when ripe (December to January). (Fruit: 10 x 7 mm)

7% life-size

**Flowers** The sweet-scented, cream-to-yellow flower-spikes are found in sprays at the ends of branchlets and twigs, and appear before the leaves. The male and female flowers are on separate trees (August to October). (Flower spikes: up to 230 mm long)

**Bark** The grey to dark grey bark is initially smooth, becoming rougher with age.

### Seasonal changes
Deciduous. The tree can be identified throughout the year by the short, stubby twigs, and general growth form.

|  | Oct | Nov | Dec | Jan | Feb | Mar | Apr | May | Jun | Jul | Aug | Sep |
|---|---|---|---|---|---|---|---|---|---|---|---|---|
| Leaf | ■ | ■ | ■ | ■ | ■ | ■ | ■ |  |  |  |  | ■ |
| Flower | ■ |  |  |  |  |  |  |  |  |  |  | ■ |
| Fruit/Pod |  | ■ | ■ | ■ |  |  |  |  |  |  |  |  |

333

# MOEPEL RED-MILKWOOD

*Mimusops zeyheri*           Moepel; Transvaal Red Milkwood

## MILKWOOD FAMILY
## SAPOTACEAE
**SA Tree Number 585**

**AFRIKAANS** Moepel, Transvaal Melkhout   **N. SOTHO** Mmupudu   **TSONGA** Nhlantswa, Mpfuxane
**TSWANA** Mmupudu   **VENDA** Mububulu, Mutaladzi   **ZULU** umPhushane

The term **zeyheri** refers to CLP Zeyher (a German botanist and plant collector, 1799-1858) after whom the tree was named.

## Where you'll find this tree easily

This tree grows singly, often in close association with rocks.

- It is easiest to find in Rocky Areas on the South- or East-facing Slopes of the Northern Mountains (N) and Sour Bushveld (S).
- It can also be found on some Rocky Areas of the Plains and North- or West-facing Slopes, and on Old Termite Mounds of all Ecozones except Thorny Bushveld (C, N, S, M).

## Ecozones where this tree occurs

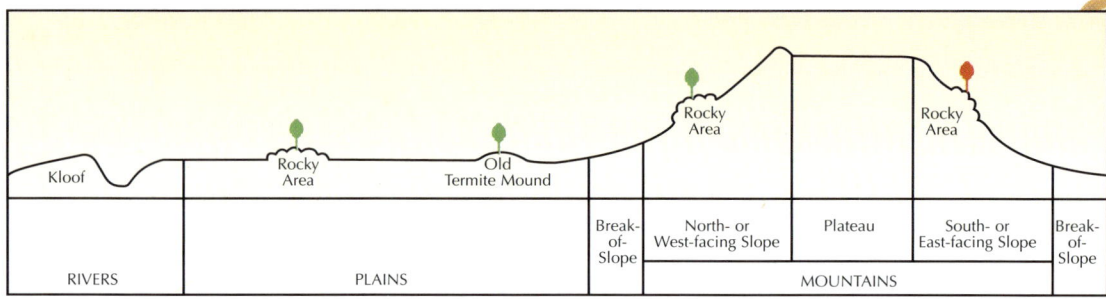

## Striking features

- This is a fig-like tree, with a dense, round canopy.
- **The simple leaves are glossy, dark lime-green and leathery, with a conspicuous creamy-yellow central vein.**
- All parts of the tree contain small quantities of milky latex.
- Tips of new twigs and young leaves are covered by rusty-brown hairs, sometimes giving the canopy a rusty tinge.
- **The smooth, fleshy, plum-like fruit turns orange-yellow when ripe (April to October).**

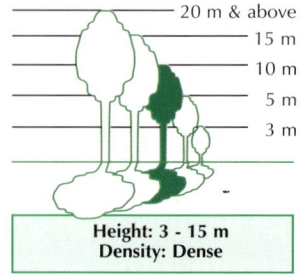

Height: 3 - 15 m
Density: Dense

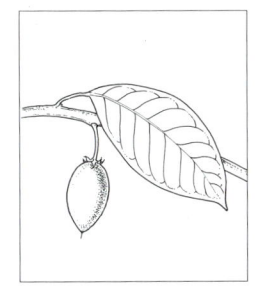

MOUNTAINS
Moepel Red-milkwood

# MOEPEL RED-MILKWOOD

*Mimusops zeyheri*

**Links with animals** Elephants and various game species eat the leaves and branches. Baboons, and Samango and Vervet Monkeys, as well as Green and Rameron Pigeons and other fruit-eating birds, eat the fruit, while dropped fruit is relished by kudu, nyala, duiker and bushpig. Caterpillars of the Pied False Acraea butterfly (*Pseudacraea lucretia tarquinia*) eat the leaves.

**Human uses** The wood is used to make various farm implements. The green wood contains an irritant that causes sneezing when it is worked. Edible fruit contains Vitamin C.

**Gardening** This tree is an attractive addition to the garden, grows fairly fast, and can be grown from fresh seed. It is fairly frost-resistant and can withstand drought. It makes an attractive container- and houseplant, though it requires sufficient airflow in the house. It is also a favourite with bonsai growers.

**Wood** The wood is pinkish-green, drying to light brown. It is medium-hard and fairly light, with wavy grain. It works easily and becomes smooth when sandpapered.

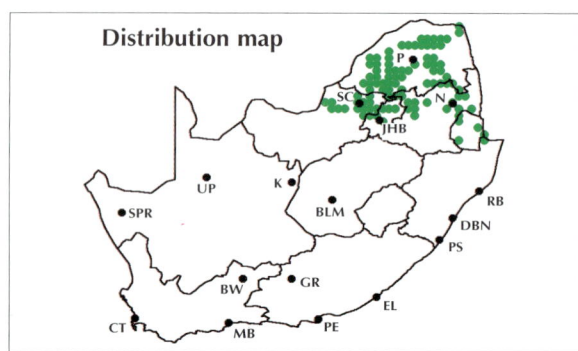

Distribution map

**Look-alike tree** Moepel Red-milkwood looks like a fig-tree, and can be confused with Common Wild Fig (*Ficus burkei*), page 196. Fig trees produce a large amount of latex as soon as the leaf is picked, while the latex seeps out slowly from Red-milkwood leaves. The fruit of this fig is rough-skinned and small, with no stalk, and the leaves have a rounded, not pointed, tip with a fine network of veins. Aerial roots may often be seen on older branches of Common Wild Fig, which also has a wide-spreading, semi-circular canopy that is not as round as that of Moepel Red-milkwood.

*Ideal Habitat next to ancient volcanic boulder, Pilanesberg*

# GROWTH DETAILS

This is a medium-large, single- or multi-trunked tree. It normally branches low down to form a spreading moderate-to-dense, patchy, round-to-irregular canopy. All parts of the tree contain some milky latex.

**Leaves** The simple, alternate or spiral leaves are elliptic, with a broadly tapering tip and a tapering base. The leaves are thickish and leathery, with long, sometimes reddish leaf-stalks of up to 35 mm. The leaves are shiny, dark lime-green. The creamy-yellow central vein is clearly visible, especially on the under-surface where it is raised. New leaves are covered in rusty-brown hairs, particularly on the under-surface. (40 - 110 x 20 - 50 mm)

**Fruit** The characteristic, smooth-skinned, fleshy, plum-like fruit is orange-yellow when ripe, and grows in the angles formed by the leaves. t may have a bristle-like tip (April to October). (30 x 25 mm)

*70% life-size*

**Flowers** The strong-smelling, creamy-white, star-shaped flowers have long flower-stalks, and grow in bunches in the angles formed by the leaves. The bottom part of the flower and the flower-stalks are reddish and hairy (October to March). (Individual flower: 10 mm diameter)

**Bark** The bark is grey and smooth when young, becoming dark brown, rougher, deeply grooved and cracked with age. Young branchlets are often covered in fine, rusty-brown hairs. The twigs are characteristically knobbly.

MOUNTAINS
Moepel Red-milkwood

## Seasonal changes
Evergreen. The tree can be recognised throughout the year.

|  | Oct | Nov | Dec | Jan | Feb | Mar | Apr | May | Jun | Jul | Aug | Sep |
|---|---|---|---|---|---|---|---|---|---|---|---|---|
| Leaf | | | | | | | | | | | | |
| Flower | | | | | | | | | | | | |
| Fruit/Pod | | | | | | | | | | | | |

337

# PIPE-STEM FINGERLEAF

*Vitex rehmannii*                                                                 Pipe-stem tree

### VERBENA FAMILY
### VERBENACEAE

SA Tree number 664

**AFRIKAANS** Pypsteelboom   **N. SOTHO** Mokgale   **TSWANA** Mokgale   **VENDA** Munyongatshifumbu
**ZULU** umDuli

The species name **rehmannii** refers to Anton Rehmann, a Polish traveller and collector in South Africa in the late 19th Century.

## Where you'll find this tree easily

This tree grows in loose groups on cool, moist, often rocky or sandy slopes.

- It is easiest to find on the South- or East-facing Slopes of the Northern Mountains (N).
- It can also be found on the South- or East-facing Slopes of the Mixed Bushveld (M) and the Central Mountains (C); and on the higher Plains and Rocky Areas of the Central Mountains (C).

## Ecozones where this tree occurs

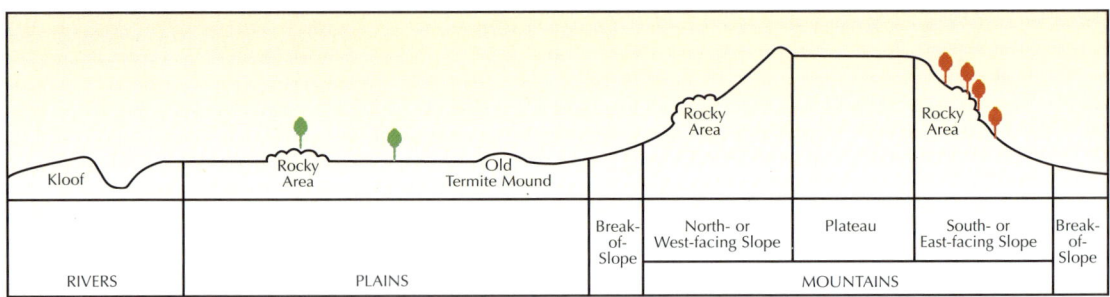

## Striking features

- This is a small, slender tree with branches that droop towards their ends to form a moderate, yellow-green canopy.
- **The compound hand-shaped leaves grow on thin twigs and tend to droop down.**
- Each hand-shaped, compound leaf has 3 - 5 long, narrow, elliptic leaflets.
- **The light purple flowers grow in branched sprays in the angle formed by the leaf (November to January).**
- Small, brownish fruit has five papery, flower-like lobes, and grows in hanging bunches (February to April).

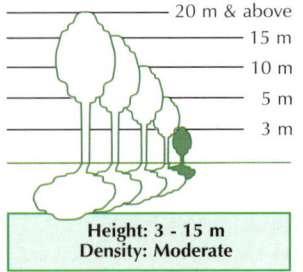

Height: 3 - 15 m
Density: Moderate

MOUNTAINS
Pipe-stem Fingerleaf

# PIPE-STEM FINGERLEAF

## *Vitex rehmannii*

**Links with animals** There are no records of animals or insects making use of this tree. Carpenter Bees use flowers of some other *Vitex* species.

**Human uses** Stools and hammer handles are made from the wood. The hollow stems are used for tobacco pipes. A leaf extract is used as a purgative, to treat body pains in children, and as a tonic. Bark extracts are used as a prophylactic when a member of the kraal is dying. Parts of the tree are sold widely by Zulu herbalists as a medicine to treat fits of hysteria.

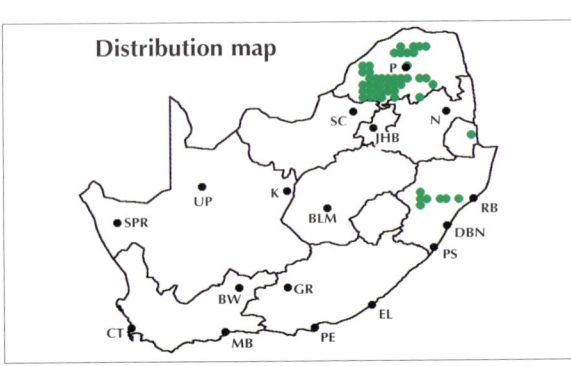

Distribution map

**Wood** The wood is yellow-grey, medium-hard, strong and straight-grained. It works easily, and produces a good finish when properly seasoned. It is resistant to termites.

**Gardening** This is an attractive shrub for cooler areas.

**Look-alike trees** The leaves of Rock Karree-rhus (*Rhus leptodictya*) page 76 and Karree (*Rhus lancea*), page 368, look similar at a distance, but they have three leaflets only, not five, and bunches of small grape-like fruit.

*December; scattered trees; high plains, Northern Mountains*

# GROWTH DETAILS

This is a small, slender, single- or multi-stemmed tree with straight stems. Low down it divides into slender branches that form a moderate canopy. The branches and branchlets tend to droop towards their ends.

**Leaves** The opposite, compound, hand-shaped leaves have long leaf-stalks (35 mm) and consist of five leaflets (occasionally three or four leaflets). The leaflets taper onto leaflet-stalks, and the leaflet-stalks attach at the same point. The three middle leaflets are usually larger. The leaflets are long and narrowly elliptic, and have a smooth or wavy margin. Leaflets are dull green and slightly hairy on the under-surface, which also has a clearly visible and prominent pale central vein. The leaves have a pleasant, herby smell when crushed. (Leaf: 80 - 130 mm; leaflet: 20 - 110 x 5 - 15 mm)

**Flowers** The conspicuous flowers have long flower-stalks, and grow in branched sprays in the angles formed by the leaves. The petals are white and tinged with pale purple or pink (November to January). (Individual flower: 8 mm in length)

*50% life-size*

**MOUNTAINS**
**Pipe-stem Fingerleaf**

**Fruit** Each small, dry fruit has five green to brown, flower-like, papery lobes, which are the old sepals. They grow in bunches that tend to hang down. The fruit itself turns dark brown when ripe (February to April). (6 mm long)

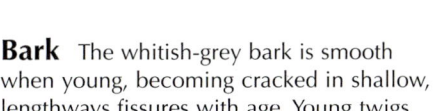

*65% life-size*

**Bark** The whitish-grey bark is smooth when young, becoming cracked in shallow, lengthways fissures with age. Young twigs and leaf-stalks are covered in fine, soft hairs.

**Seasonal changes**
Deciduous. The tree will be difficult to find when there are no leaves present.

|  | Oct | Nov | Dec | Jan | Feb | Mar | Apr | May | Jun | Jul | Aug | Sep |
|---|---|---|---|---|---|---|---|---|---|---|---|---|
| Leaf | ■ | ■ | ■ | ■ | ■ | ■ | ■ | ■ |  |  |  | ■ |
| Flower |  | ■ | ■ | ■ |  |  |  |  |  |  |  |  |
| Fruit/Pod |  |  |  | ■ | ■ | ■ | ■ |  |  |  |  |  |

# RED IVORYWOOD

*Berchemia zeyheri*

Red ivory; Purple Ivory; Pink Ivory

| DOGWOOD FAMILY RHAMNACEAE | SA Tree Number 450 |

**AFRIKAANS** Rooi-ivoor, Rooihout  **N. SOTHO** Monee  **SISWATI** umNeyi  **TSONGA** Xiniyani, Nyiyani  **TSWANA** Moye  **VENDA** Munia-niane, Muniane  **XHOSA** umNini  **ZULU** umNcaka, umNini

The species name **zeyheri** is after CLP Zeyher, a famous German botanist.

## Where you'll find this tree easily

This tree normally grows singly in dense groups of other trees.

- It is easiest to find on South- or East-facing Slopes of the Northern Mountains (N), Central Mountains (C), Mixed Bushveld (M) and Sour Bushveld (S).
- It can also be found along Rivers and Streams, and on Rocky Areas and Old Termite Mounds of the Plains of Mixed Bushveld (M) and Sour Bushveld (S).

## Ecozones where this tree occurs

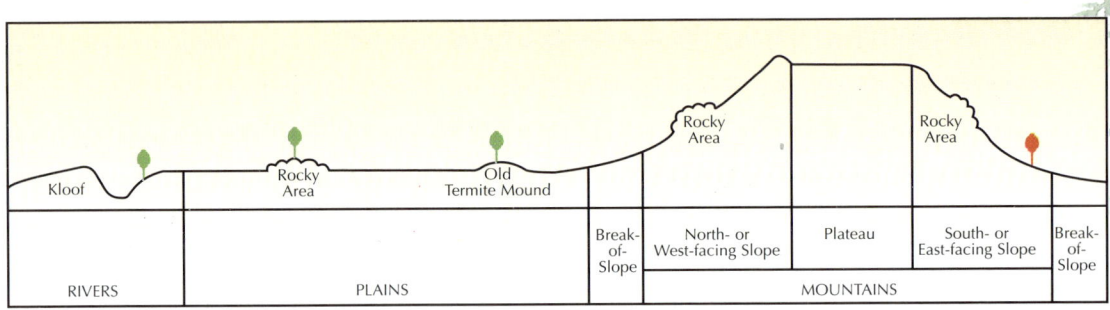

## Striking features

- It is a single-stemmed tree that branches fairly high up to form a dense, irregular canopy, shaped by the surrounding vegetation, or a rounded canopy when growing singly.
- **The broadly-elliptic leaves are shiny, dark green and stand out among other leaves.**
- **The side veins are arranged in a herringbone pattern. They curl in slightly at the margin, and are very distinct on the under-surface.**
- The leaf-stalks are often reddish.

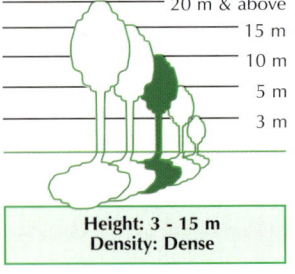

Height: 3 - 15 m
Density: Dense

MOUNTAINS
Red Ivorywood

# RED IVORYWOOD

*Berchemia zeyheri*

**Links with animals** Vervet Monkeys, baboons, bushbabies and goats eat the succulent fruit, as do many fruit-eating birds such as Black-eyed Bulbuls, Crested, Pied and Black-collared Barbets, Red-winged Starlings, Grey and Purple-crested Louries, Rameron and Green Pigeons, doves and mousebirds. Meyer's Parrots also eat the fruit, probably for the seeds. Leaves are browsed by Blue Wildebeest, giraffe, eland, kudu, nyala, bushbuck and impala. Porcupine eat the bark.

**Human uses** The wood is much sought after for carving, mainly of ornamental work, wooden bowls and walking sticks, which are sold as curios. It is a good furniture wood. The fleshy fruit is edible. The bark is used as a dye for fibre and woven material, giving it a purplish colour. The powdered root was smoked as a headache cure. An extract of the inner bark was used to relieve back pain, for enemas and to cure dysentery. In parts of Zululand it was considered a royal tree, the chief alone carrying knobkieries made from it.

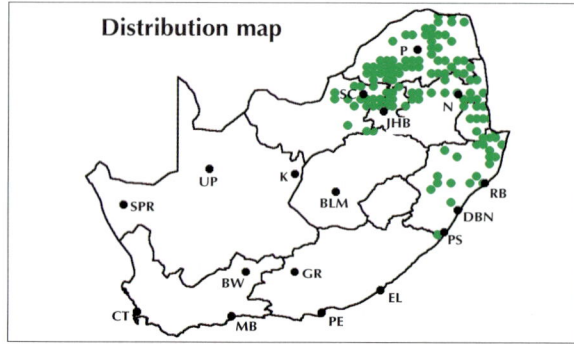

Distribution map

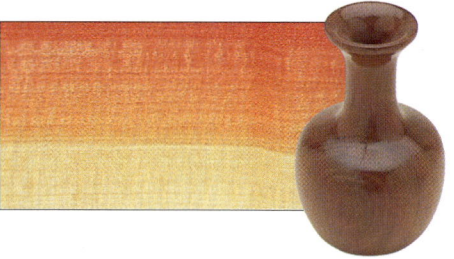

**Wood** The wood has a fine, even texture that is suitable for jewellery, carving and inlay work. The heartwood is pinkish-red and the sapwood is yellow. It is very durable, and takes paint and varnish well.

**Gardening** This is an attractive tree, and is one of the best trees to plant to attract birds. It is an ideal container-plant. The tree is drought-resistant and can take a little frost. Seedlings take slowly, but grow fast once they are established.

**Look-alike tree** Brown Ivorywood (*Berchemia discolor*) looks very similar, but the leaves are larger, and dark green above and distinctly paler below, with a more tapering tip and green leaf-stalk.

*January; herringbone-veined leaves, flowers and young fruit*

# GROWTH DETAILS

This is a single-stemmed tree with a straight trunk and spreading branches forming a dense, irregular canopy when growing among other trees, but rounded when growing singly.

**Leaves** The simple, opposite to sub-opposite leaves have short, reddish leaf-stalks. The broadly elliptic leaf has a rounded base and tip, and a smooth margin. The upper-surface is shiny blue-green, with the under-surface paler. The leaves have distinct herringbone veins that curl in slightly at the margin. Leaves turn golden-yellow in autumn, and new young leaves are bright green. (Leaf: 25 - 60 x 15 - 35 mm)

**Fruit** The oval, berry-like fruit is fleshy, and grows on long stalks. It is yellow-orange to deep red when ripe. (January to April) (6 - 13 x 5 mm)

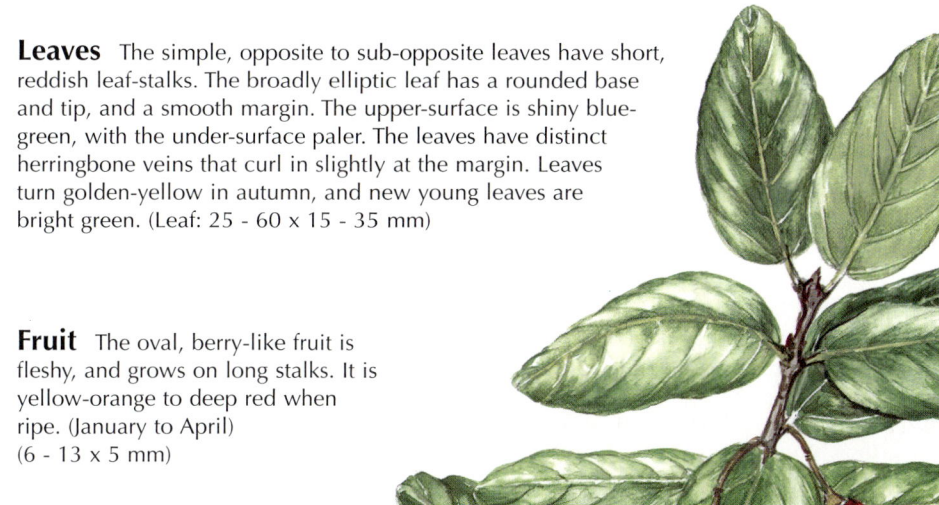

*90% life-size*

**Flowers** Inconspicuous, greenish-white, star-like flowers grow in small clusters on long stalks in the angles formed by the leaves. (September to December) (10 - 13 mm)

**Bark** The bark is grey-brown, and smooth in younger trees and branches, but coarse and splitting into neat rows of irregular blocks in older trees.

## Seasonal changes

Deciduous, but may be evergreen under very favourable circumstances. The tree is difficult to identify in winter.

|  | Oct | Nov | Dec | Jan | Feb | Mar | Apr | May | Jun | Jul | Aug | Sep |
|---|---|---|---|---|---|---|---|---|---|---|---|---|
| Leaf | | | | | | | | | | | | |
| Flower | | | | | | | | | | | | |
| Fruit/Pod | | | | | | | | | | | | |

MOUNTAINS
Red Ivorywood

# SILVER RAISIN

*Grewia monticola*

**LINDEN FAMILY
TILIACEAE**

**SA Tree Number 462**

**AFRIKAANS** Vaalrosyntjie  **TSONGA** Nsihana  **TSWANA** Mogwanakgômo
**ZULU** umLalampunzi, umDliwampunzi

The species name **monticola** refers to the preference of this species for mountainous areas.

## Where you'll find this tree easily

The Silver Raisin grows singly, often among other species of trees.

- It is easiest to find on the North- or West-facing Slopes of the Mixed Bushveld (M).
- It can also be found in Rocky Areas and on the North- or West-facing Slopes of Northern Mountains (N) and the Sour Bushveld (S); and on Old Termite Mounds, on the Plains and along Rivers and Streams of the Mixed Bushveld (M).

## Ecozones where this tree occurs

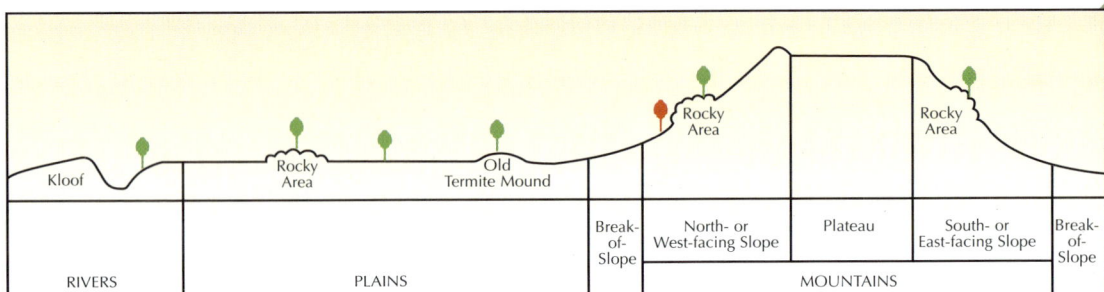

## Striking features

- This is a low-branching small tree or shrub with branches forming delicate arches that often hang down low.
- **The simple, leathery leaves are three-veined from the base, and have a distinctly asymmetrical base and toothed margin.**
- **Leaves are bicoloured, being dark, dull green on the upper-surface and greyish to almost white below.**
- The yellow, star-shaped flowers appear from October to January.
- The branchlets and twigs grow very long and straight for the size of the tree.
- Leaves have a very short leaf-stalk and are alternate. Growing on the same flat plane they look like very long compound leaves or fern fronds.

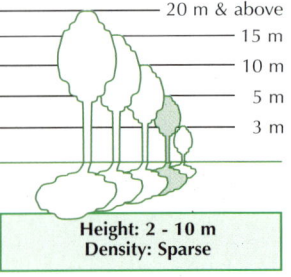

Height: 2 - 10 m
Density: Sparse

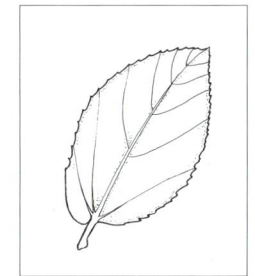

# MOUNTAINS
## Silver Raisin

347

# SILVER RAISIN

*Grewia monticola*

**Links with animals** The fruit is eaten by birds, baboons and monkeys. The leaves are browsed by game and stock, and elephant eat the bark. Green twigs are used by the Red-headed Weaver for nest-building.

**Human uses** The wood is very hard, strong and borer- and termite-resistant. The wood is used to make knobkieries, assegai handles and whips, and for building huts. The fruit is edible, and the leaves are sometimes used to make tea. The bark is used to weave baskets together.

**Gardening** This attractive little tree grows slowly from seed, and is not frost-resistant.

**Look-alike tree** Giant Raisin (*Grewia hexamita*), page 60, also has simple, alternate leaves, but they are strikingly shiny on the upper-surface in comparison to the dull upper-surface of leaves of Silver Raisin. It is also usually a much larger tree, with larger leaves than Silver Raisin. In the Sour Bushveld, Giant Raisin is more common than Silver Raisin.

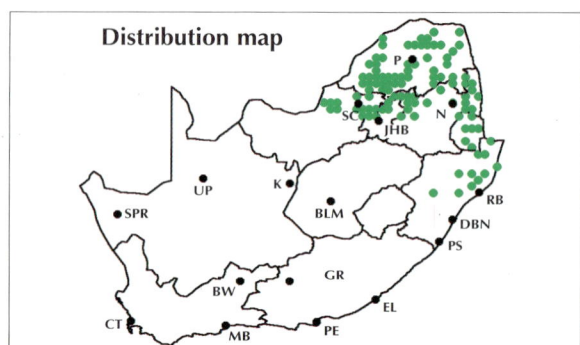

Distribution map

**Wood** The contrast between the light brown sapwood and the dark brown heartwood makes the wood attractive. It has very fine grain, which results in a smooth product that polishes well.

*May; Branches blowing in wind show bicoloured leaves; Plains, Mixed Bushveld*

# GROWTH DETAILS

This is a small, low-branching, single- or multi-stemmed tree with a sparse canopy. The main stems are short and crooked. Branchlets form delicate arches that look like fern fronds, and tend to droop and hang down low.

**Leaves** The simple, alternate, leathery leaves have three veins from the base, a short leaf-stalk and toothed margin. They are broadly elliptic with a tapering-to-rounded tip and a distinctly asymmetrical base. The conspicuously bicoloured leaves are dark, dull green above and greyish to almost white below. There are fine hairs on the upper-surface, while the under-surface is densely covered in grey-white hairs. (25 - 90 x 10 - 50 mm)

**Fruit** Small berries grow in clusters on short individual stalks. Each berry may be deeply two-lobed, looking like two fused berries. They are green, and sparsely covered with hairs when young, and yellowish or reddish-brown when ripe (October to January). (8 mm diameter)

*70% life-size*

**Flowers** The conspicuous, yellow, star-shaped flowers grow in clusters of 2 - 3 on short stalks, mostly in the angles formed by the leaves (October to January). (Individual flower: 8 - 20 mm diameter)

**Bark** The bark is rough, and dark brown or grey. Young branchlets and twigs are densely covered in creamy or rusty hairs.

**MOUNTAINS** 
**Silver Raisin**

### Seasonal changes
Deciduous. The tree will be difficult to identify without leaves.

|  | Oct | Nov | Dec | Jan | Feb | Mar | Apr | May | Jun | Jul | Aug | Sep |
|---|---|---|---|---|---|---|---|---|---|---|---|---|
| Leaf |  |  |  |  |  |  |  |  |  |  |  |  |
| Flower |  |  |  |  |  |  |  |  |  |  |  |  |
| Fruit/Pod |  |  |  |  |  |  |  |  |  |  |  |  |

349

# WEEPING FAUREA

*Faurea saligna*                                          Beechwood; Boekenhout

## PROTEA FAMILY
## PROTEACEAE

**SA Tree Number 75**

**AFRIKAANS** Transvaalboekenhout, Rooiboekenhout   **N. SOTHO** Mohlakô, Mongêna
**TSONGA** N'wamidzumba   **TSWANA** Monyena, Mofufu   **VENDA** Muṱango   **XHOSA** iSafo   **ZULU** isiSefo

The species name **saligna** refers to the resemblance between this species and the Willow Tree.

## Where you'll find this tree easily

The Weeping Faurea grows in loosely scattered groups.

- It is easiest to find on the lower, South- or East-facing Slopes of the Central Mountains (C).
- It can also be found on the South- or East-facing Slopes with a few on the North- or West-facing Slopes of the Mixed Bushveld (M), the Northern Mountains (N) and the Sour Bushveld (S); and on Plateaus of the Central Mountains (C) and Northern Mountains (N).

## Ecozones where this tree occurs

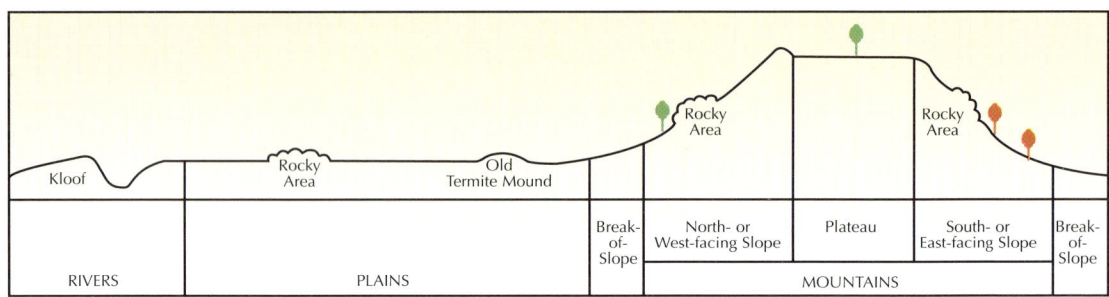

## Striking features

- This is a single-trunked tree with only a few main branches that grow directly upwards to form a narrow, irregular canopy.
- The bark is dark greyish-brown to black, and is blocky and rough, and deeply fissured lengthways.
- **The leaves are long, simple, narrow and willow-like, hanging down at the tips of thin twigs that move easily in the wind.**
- **The flowers and fruit both grow on slender spikes, and both resemble large, hairy caterpillars.**
- The leaves turn red in autumn, and the young leaves and leaf-stalks are pinkish throughout the year.

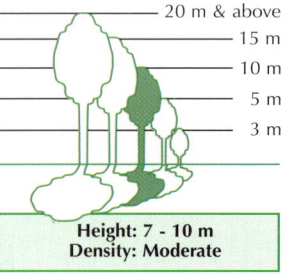

Height: 7 - 10 m
Density: Moderate

MOUNTAINS
Weeping Faurea

351

# WEEPING FAUREA

*Faurea saligna*

**Links with animals** Elephants sometimes browse on the tree.

**Human uses** To farmers, this tree is an indication of an area where grass is less palatable or 'sour', with a rainfall of over about 500 mm per year. This tree is often found in what is generally known as a sour veld area. The wood is generally useful, especially for furniture and doors. It has also been used for poles, wagons and waterwheels. What is probably the first butter churn made in the Transvaal was made of this wood, as were most of the first telephone poles between the old Transvaal and Natal. A red dye is obtained from the wood soaked in water, and the bark is sometimes used for tanning. The root is used in a steam bath for the relief of menstrual pains. An extract from the root and leaf are used to treat earache.

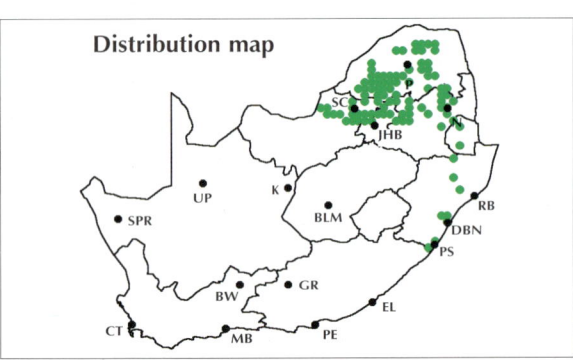

Distribution map

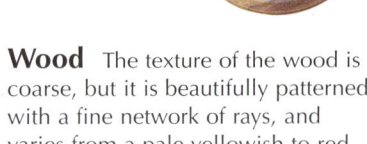

**Wood** The texture of the wood is coarse, but it is beautifully patterned with a fine network of rays, and varies from a pale yellowish to red.

**Gardening** This is an attractive and ornamental garden tree. It grows slowly from seed, and is frost- and fairly drought-resistant.

**Look-alike trees** This tree can be confused with exotic Willow and Bluegum trees. Bluegums grow much taller, and have a bark that peels in large strips to reveal smooth, pale under-bark. Willows are found only near water, are spreading, and have many thin, drooping branches and twigs.

*Group of trees; West-facing Slope, Mixed Bushveld*

# GROWTH DETAILS

This is a single-trunked, often low-branching, slender tree with branches that grow directly upwards to form a moderate, narrow or irregular-shaped canopy. The trunk is fairly straight, and the main branches are visible in the canopy.

**Leaves** The simple, alternate leaves are spirally arranged, and have long leaf-stalks that are pinkish when young. The leaves are leathery with a smooth or slightly wavy margin, and are long and narrowly elliptic. Young leaves are pinkish or red, maturing to shiny green, and turning red in autumn. (Leaf 100 - 150 mm x 20 - 30 mm)

**Flowers** The flower-spikes contain numerous, conspicuous, honey-scented, pink to creamy-white flowers with long stamens, that stand out on long, slender spikes that resemble hairy caterpillars. They grow at the ends of twigs, and produce a lot of nectar (October to January). (Flower-spike: 120 - 150 mm x 20 - 30 mm)

*60% life-size*

**Fruit** The small, nut-like fruit grows in slender spikes, similar in shape to the flower-spikes. The fruit is pinkish, and covered in long silvery hairs, and the fruiting spike resembles a hairy caterpillar (December to February). (Fruit spike: 120 - 150 mm x 20 - 30 mm)

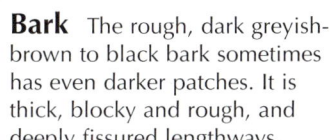

**Bark** The rough, dark greyish-brown to black bark sometimes has even darker patches. It is thick, blocky and rough, and deeply fissured lengthways.

**MOUNTAINS Weeping Faurea**

## Seasonal changes
Deciduous. The leaves turn red in autumn. The tree can be identified throughout the year by its growth form and bark.

|  | Oct | Nov | Dec | Jan | Feb | Mar | Apr | May | Jun | Jul | Aug | Sep |
|---|---|---|---|---|---|---|---|---|---|---|---|---|
| Leaf | | | | | | | | | | | | |
| Flower | | | | | | | | | | | | |
| Fruit/Pod | | | | | | | | | | | | |

353

# WEEPING LAVENDER-TREE

*Heteropyxis natalensis*                                   **Lavender tree**

### MYRTLE FAMILY
### MYRTACEAE (HETEROPYXIDACEAE)                SA Tree Number 455

**AFRIKAANS** Laventelboom, Wildelaventel  **N. SOTHO** Masepha, Mmasepha  **TSONGA** Thathasani
**VENDA** Mudedede  **ZULU** inKhuzwa, umKhuze

The species name **natalensis** refers to the Kwazulu-Natal province.

## Where you'll find this tree easily

The Weeping Lavender-tree grows singly, occasionally forming small, close groups; where one is found, there are likely to be others in the vicinity.

- It is easiest to find on the South- or East-facing Slopes of the Northern Mountains (N) and Central Mountains (C).
- It can also be found along Rivers of the Northern Mountains (N) and Central Mountains (C); and on all Slopes of the Sour Bushveld (S).

### Ecozones where this tree occurs

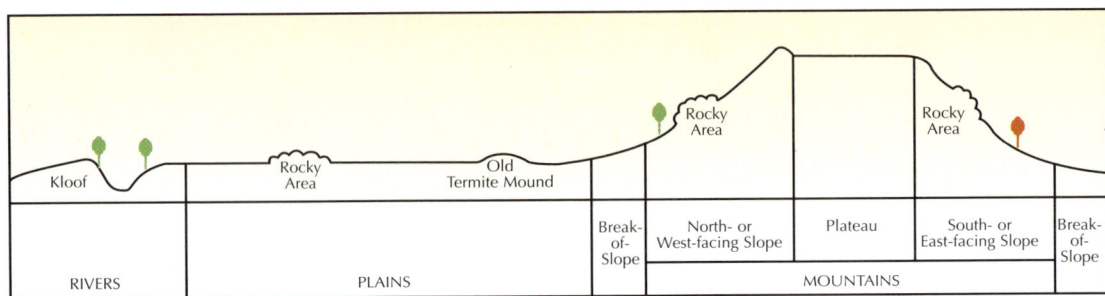

## Striking features

- This is a single-stemmed tree. It branches low down, and then the bare main branches grow upwards to form an elegant, neat canopy.
- **The very distinctive bark is smooth and pale grey with dark grey patches. It breaks off in large scales to expose paler grey under-bark, often scarred in circular rings.**
- Leaves spiral on relatively short, rigid twigs that are thin and crooked.
- The glossy, narrowly elliptic leaves have long, sometimes reddish leaf-stalks, and grow at the edge of the canopy, creating droopy rosettes.
- **The leaves have a strong scent, reminiscent of lavender, when crushed.**

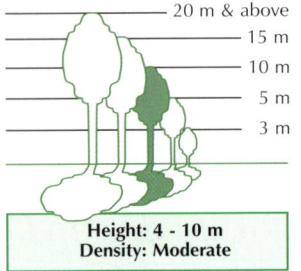

Height: 4 - 10 m
Density: Moderate

MOUNTAINS
Weeping Lavender-tree

# WEEPING LAVENDER-TREE

*Heteropyxis natalensis*

**Links with animals** The flowers attract bees, butterflies and wasps. The bark and leaves are eaten by the Black Rhino and some antelope.

**Human uses** The timber is used for fence posts, fencing kraals and charcoal. Steaming vapour from an extraction of the roots helps treat bleeding gums and noses. Powdered leaves are administered to cattle to kill intestinal worms. The leaves are used as tobacco and as a perfume.

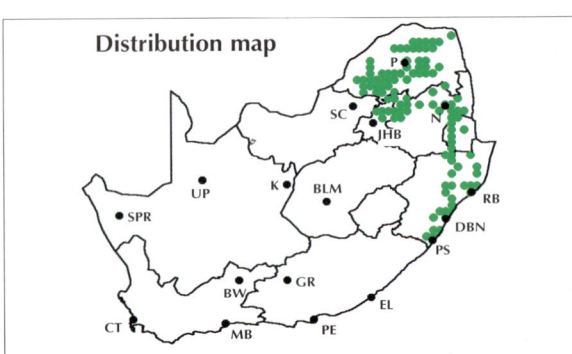

Distribution map

**Wood** The wood is relatively heavy, hard and tough. The heartwood is darker than the sapwood. The wood is pale brown with a purple or pale red shade. It has a particularly fine grain, and polishes well.

**Gardening** This is an attractive garden tree that grows fast from fresh seed. It makes a good container plant, and is a favourite for bonsai. These trees prefer full sun, but grow well in semi-shade. Young trees must be protected from frost for the first few years.

**Look-alike trees**
The Forest Lavender-tree (*Heteropyxis canescens*), page xii, is a spectacular tree of the Sour Bushveld Kloofs. Its leaves are large and hairy on the under-surface, and the under-bark is peachy-brown. See page xii.

*Small, close group; South-facing Slopes, Northern Mountains*

# GROWTH DETAILS

This is a single- or multi-stemmed tree that branches low down to form a neat, moderate canopy. The leaves grow near the ends of thin twigs. Old trees may have a crooked trunk that is sometimes fluted.

**Leaves** The simple leaves are alternate or spiral, and are crowded towards the ends of branchlets and twigs. They are curved, with the tips hanging down. They have long leaf-stalks, (8 - 25 mm), creating droopy rosettes. Some leaf-stalks are reddish towards the base. The narrowly elliptic leaves have smooth margins and a very tapering tip and base. The leaves are shiny pale to dark green above, and dull below, and turn yellow and red in autumn. When crushed, the leaves have a strong smell, reminiscent of lavender. (30 - 140 mm x 10 - 40 mm)

*70% life-size*

**Flowers** The individual flowers are minute, sweet-scented, creamy-yellow and star-shaped, with long stamens. They are tightly clustered in branched sprays that grow at the tips of the twigs (September to March). (Spray: 30 - 40 mm long; individual: 3 mm diameter)

**Fruit** The minute berry-like capsules are shiny brown, and grow in bunched sprays. Each capsule splits into two or three parts to release the seed (March to May). (4 x 25 mm)

*70% life-size*

**Bark** The bark is smooth and pale grey, with dark grey patches. It breaks off in large scales to expose paler grey under-bark, often scarred in circular rings.

## Seasonal changes
Deciduous. The tree can be identified by its bark throughout the year.

|  | Oct | Nov | Dec | Jan | Feb | Mar | Apr | May | Jun | Jul | Aug | Sep |
|---|---|---|---|---|---|---|---|---|---|---|---|---|
| Leaf | | | | | | | | | | | | |
| Flower | | | | | | | | | | | | |
| Fruit/Pod | | | | | | | | | | | | |

**MOUNTAINS** — Weeping Lavender-tree

357

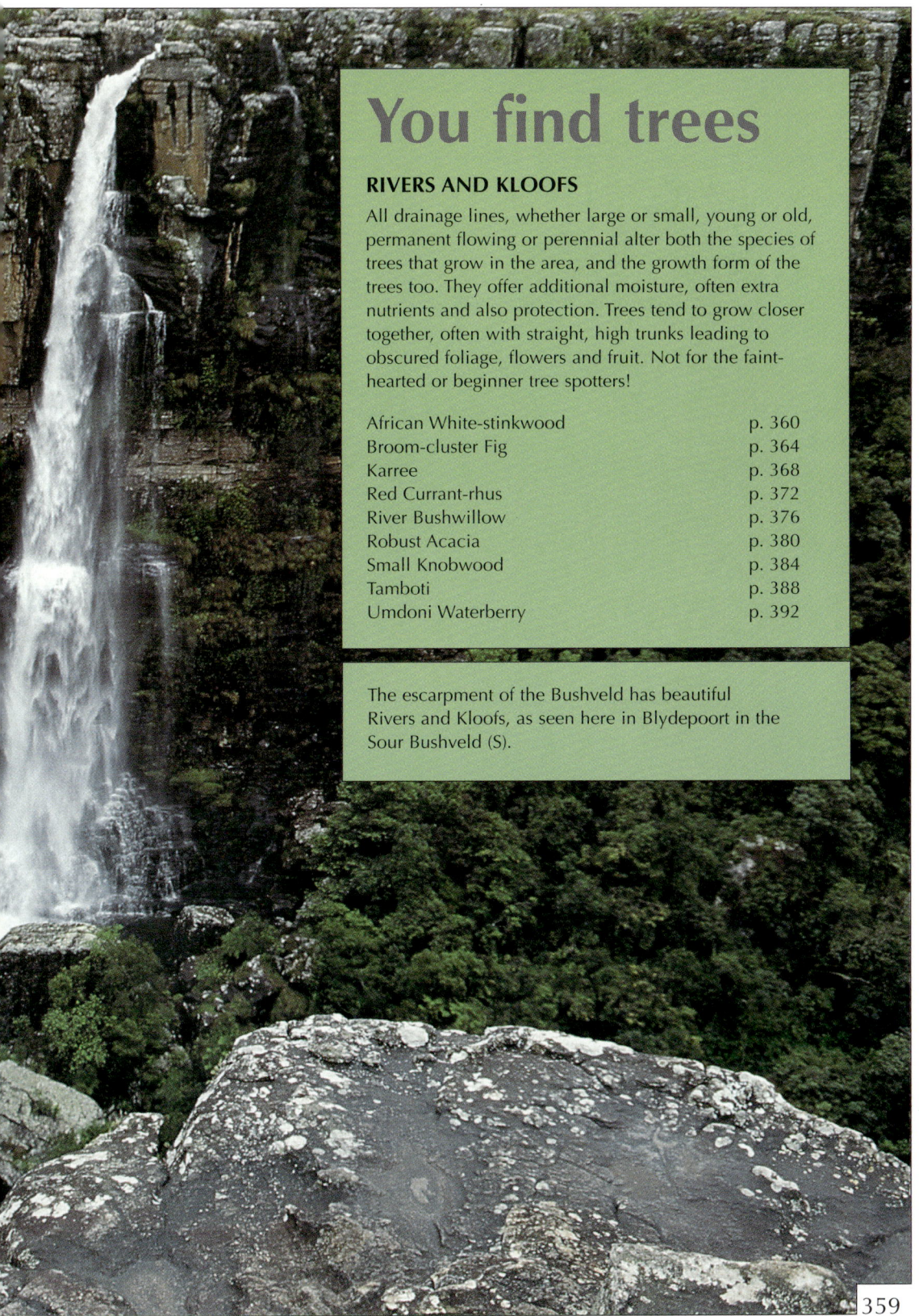

# You find trees

## RIVERS AND KLOOFS

All drainage lines, whether large or small, young or old, permanent flowing or perennial alter both the species of trees that grow in the area, and the growth form of the trees too. They offer additional moisture, often extra nutrients and also protection. Trees tend to grow closer together, often with straight, high trunks leading to obscured foliage, flowers and fruit. Not for the faint-hearted or beginner tree spotters!

| | |
|---|---|
| African White-stinkwood | p. 360 |
| Broom-cluster Fig | p. 364 |
| Karree | p. 368 |
| Red Currant-rhus | p. 372 |
| River Bushwillow | p. 376 |
| Robust Acacia | p. 380 |
| Small Knobwood | p. 384 |
| Tamboti | p. 388 |
| Umdoni Waterberry | p. 392 |

The escarpment of the Bushveld has beautiful Rivers and Kloofs, as seen here in Blydepoort in the Sour Bushveld (S).

# AFRICAN WHITE-STINKWOOD

*Celtis africana*   White Stinkwood; Camdeboo Stinkwood

### ELM FAMILY
### ULMACEAE

**SA Tree Number 39**

**AFRIKAANS** Witstinkhout   **N. SOTHO** Mothibadifate, Mogatakgomo   **S. SOTHO** Lesika
**TSONGA** Mbholovisi, Muyilakaya   **TSWANA** Modutu   **VENDA** Mumvumvu   **XHOSA** umVumvu
**ZULU** umVumvu, inDwandwazane

The species name **africana** refers to Africa.

## Where you'll find this tree easily

This tree grows singly among other tree species, but others will often be found in the vicinity.

- It is easiest to find in densely wooded areas and Kloofs along permanent Rivers and Streams in all Ecozones.
- It can also be found on South- or East-facing Slopes of the Central Mountains (C) and the Sour Bushveld (S).

## Ecozones where this tree occurs

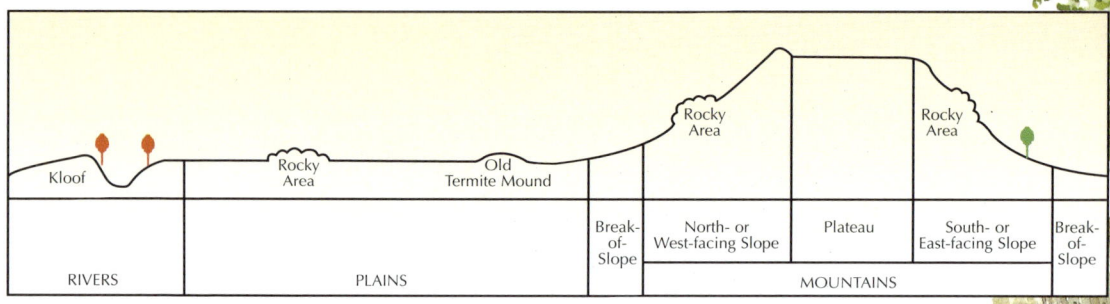

## Striking features

- This often huge, distinctive tree has a single, straight trunk that branches to form a dense, semi-circular canopy.
- **The bark is smooth and pale grey.**
- **The bright green, triangular leaves have three distinct veins from the base.**
- **Leaves have toothed margins along the top two-thirds of the leaf only.**
- Leaves tend to be held in a flat plane towards the light.

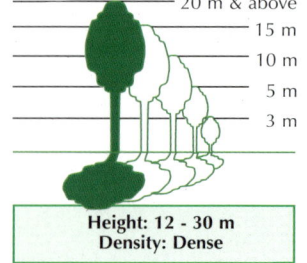

Height: 12 - 30 m
Density: Dense

**RIVERS AND KLOOFS**
*African White-stinkwood*

**Largest tree currently registered**

**Diameter:** 1,47 m
**Girth:** 4,62 m
**Height:** 39 m

Lotzaba Forests
Forest Hill, Dist. Letaba

361

# AFRICAN WHITE-STINKWOOD

*Celtis africana*

**Links with animals** Leaves and young shoots are eaten by cattle and goats. Birds like the Black-eyed Bulbul, the Red Crested Barbet and mousebirds are fond of the fruit. The fruit is also eaten by monkeys and baboons. The flowers are pollinated by bees.

**Human uses** The wood is white and has an unpleasant smell when cut – hence the common name. It can be used to make yokes, planks and tent bows as well as household articles. The wood is believed to have protective, magical properties; for example, mixed with crocodile fat it is used as a charm against lightning.

**Gardening** This is a very attractive garden tree. It is frost-resistant, and grows fast and easily from seed. The fruit attracts birds such as Rameron Pigeons, Thick-billed Weavers and Willow Warblers. It is excellent as a bonsai tree.

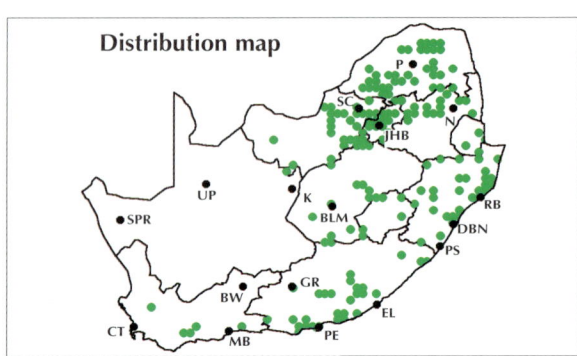

**Wood** The wood is dull white, sometimes tinged with green, and has an unpleasant smell when cut. It is a useful medium-weight timber with long grain and woolly texture.

**Look-alike tree** This tree can be confused with Pigeonwood (*Trema orientalis*), page 66. Pigeonwood is normally a shrub or small tree, often growing in previously disturbed areas. The leaves of Pigeonwood are longer and more triangular, with one prominent central vein only. The whole leaf-edge is toothed.

*July; Historical homestead site, Pilanesberg; East-facing Slope, near River*

# GROWTH DETAILS

This is a single-trunked tree with a straight trunk that branches to form a dense, semi-circular, spreading canopy. The growth form varies according to rainfall, trees being much smaller in areas of lower rainfall. The grey branches are usually obscured by the leaves, which hang from thin twigs and move easily in the wind.

**Leaves** Simple, alternate leaves grow on thin twigs. The triangular leaves have a toothed margin in the top two-thirds of the leaf only, while the lower third is smooth. There are three parallel veins from the base of the leaf, and the base is distinctively asymmetrical. The upper-surface of the fresh new leaves is bright green and hairy, becoming darker green and smoother as they mature. (Leaf: 15 - 100 x 10 - 50 mm)

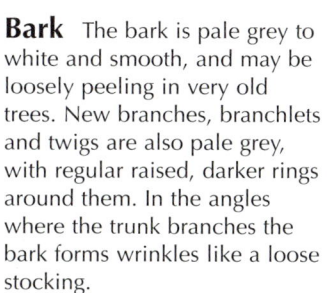

*80% life-size*

**Fruit** The small, berry-like fruit grows on a long stalk of about 13 mm. It turns yellow-brown to black when ripe, from October to February. (6 - 13 mm)

*life-size*

**Bark** The bark is pale grey to white and smooth, and may be loosely peeling in very old trees. New branches, branchlets and twigs are also pale grey, with regular raised, darker rings around them. In the angles where the trunk branches the bark forms wrinkles like a loose stocking.

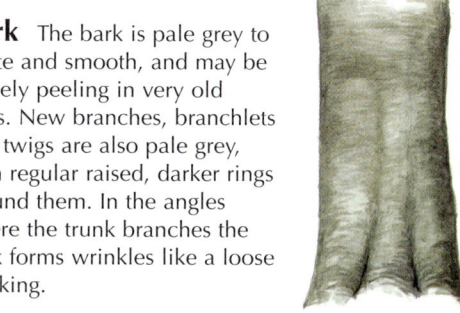

**Flowers** Inconspicuous, greenish, star-like flowers appear from August to October, with separate male and female flowers on the same tree. (3 mm)

## Seasonal changes
Deciduous. The smooth, grey bark and distinctive growth form are characteristic, and should help with identification throughout the year.

|  | Oct | Nov | Dec | Jan | Feb | Mar | Apr | May | Jun | Jul | Aug | Sep |
|---|---|---|---|---|---|---|---|---|---|---|---|---|
| Leaf | ■ | ■ | ■ | ■ | ■ | ■ | ■ | ■ | ■ |  |  | ■ |
| Flower |  |  |  |  |  |  |  |  |  |  | ■ | ■ |
| Fruit/Pod | ■ | ■ | ■ | ■ | ■ |  |  |  |  |  |  | ■ |

**RIVERS AND KLOOFS — African White-stinkwood**

# BROOM-CLUSTER FIG

*Ficus sur*                                                                 Broom Cluster Fig

### MULBERRY FAMILY
### MORACEAE
**SA Tree Number 50**

**AFRIKAANS** Besemtrosvy, Koeman  **N. SOTHO** Mogo  **TSONGA** Nkuwa, Xinkuwana
**VENDA** Muhuyu-ngala  **XHOSA** umKhiwane  **ZULU** umKhiwane

The species name **sur** refers to an area in Ethiopia.

## Where you'll find this tree easily

The Broom-cluster Fig usually grows singly among other species.

- It is easiest to find along permanent Rivers and Streams of the Central Mountains (C), Northern Mountains (N) and Sour Bushveld (S).
- It can also be found on the South- or East-facing Slopes of the Northern Mountains (N) and Sour Bushveld (S).

## Ecozones where this tree occurs

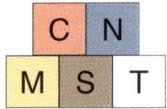

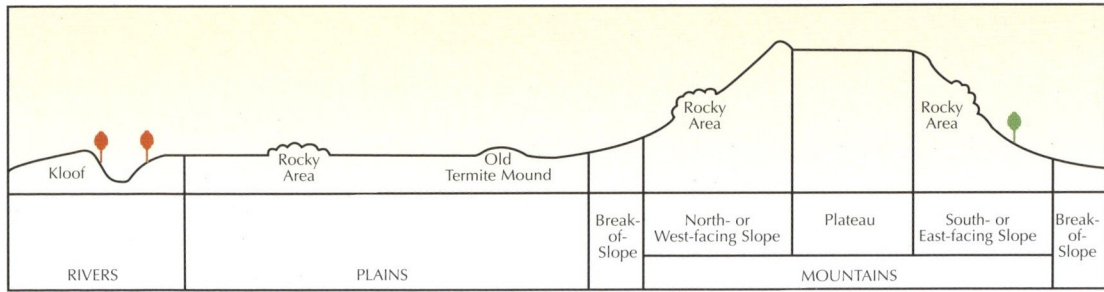

## Striking features

- This is a huge, single-stemmed tree that branches low down to form a dense canopy.
- The bark is smooth and grey, and the thick trunk is often conspicuously buttressed.
- **The plum-sized, fleshy figs grow in large, leafless, long-stemmed, broom-like clusters that hang from the trunk and main branches, and turn red when ripe, from June to January.**
- The simple, large, grey-green to green elliptic leaves have toothed margins, and new leaves can gleam copper-red on twig tips.

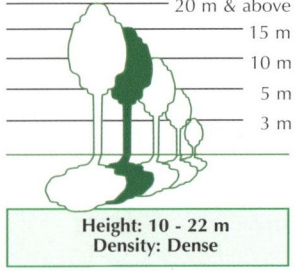

Height: 10 - 22 m
Density: Dense

**RIVERS AND KLOOFS**
Broom-cluster Fig

**Largest tree currently registered**

**Diameter:** 1,25 m
**Girth:** 3,92 m
**Height:** 24 m

Buffelskloof Nature Reserve,
Kalmoesfontein,
Dist. Lydenburg

# BROOM-CLUSTER FIG

*Ficus sur*

**Links with animals** Caterpillars of the Fig Tree butterfly and the African Map butterfly feed on the leaves. The fruit is a favourite with Vervet and Samango Monkeys, baboons, fruit bats and fruit-eating birds. Fallen fruit is eaten eagerly by Bushpigs. Leaves are eaten by Blue Duiker, elephant, kudu, nyala and cattle.

**Human uses** The ripe figs are edible. Mortars for grinding flour, and the major part of drums, are made from this wood. Dry pieces of wood were used as the base wood when making fire with sticks by friction. Rope was made from the inner bark. Many medicinal uses are recorded: the milky latex to treat burns, septic conjunctivitis and sore eyes; bark infusions to stimulate milk production; bark as a powder for rashes; and stems and twigs for dysentery, leprosy, epilepsy, rickets, oedema and poisoning. Certain trees have been regarded as sacred shrines and symbolic of Earth and Forest, the two great divinities of productivity.

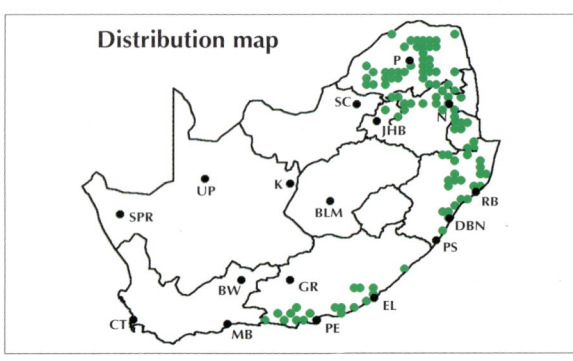

**Wood** The wood is soft and porous with yellow-brown heartwood and grey sapwood. It is not suitable for turning, but varnishes and stains well.

**Gardening** This is a very attractive garden tree, attracting fruit-eating birds, but it has an invasive root system. It is fast-growing, and easiest to grow from cuttings. It is not resistant to cold and frost.

**Look-alike tree** Red-leaved Fig (*Ficus ingens*), page 288, also has reddish young leaves, but the leaf-margins are smooth. The figs are fleshy, and grow on short stalks in the leaf angles. They turn red when ripe (June to January). See page 77 for a comparison with other figs.

*Fruit in clusters on broom-like stalks; River bank, Sour Bushveld*

# GROWTH DETAILS

This is a huge, single-stemmed tree with a thick trunk that is often buttressed, with shallow, spreading roots. The branches grow upwards to form a dense canopy, with large branches visible between the leaves.

**Leaves** The simple, alternate leaves have a characteristically toothed margin. They are broadly elliptic with a tapering point and rounded base. They are grey-green to green and hairless, and new leaves can gleam copper-red from midwinter. They grow on a long leaf-stalk (60 mm) that is furrowed and may be slightly pink. The veins are wide apart and clearly visible, and stand out on the under-surface. (Leaf: 80 - 200 x 25 - 90 mm)

**Flowers** As in all figs, the flowers are not visible, as they grow inside the fruit.

**Fruit** The round, smooth, fleshy, plum-like fruit hangs from large, thick stalks that divide many times to form a broom-like structure. Some figs may hang on main branches on short stalks. The figs may be smooth or slightly hairy, and turn deep wine-red when ripe (June to January). (Cluster: 1 m; individual: 20 - 40 mm)

*life-size*

**Bark** The bark is smooth and white when young, but becomes darker grey and rougher with age.

## Seasonal changes
Evergreen, but the tree may lose its leaves under dry conditions. It is easy to recognise by its leaves and fruit throughout the year.

|  | Oct | Nov | Dec | Jan | Feb | Mar | Apr | May | Jun | Jul | Aug | Sep |
|---|---|---|---|---|---|---|---|---|---|---|---|---|
| Leaf |  |  |  |  |  |  |  |  |  |  |  |  |
| Flower |  |  |  |  |  |  |  |  |  |  |  |  |
| Fruit/Pod |  |  |  |  |  |  |  |  |  |  |  |  |

RIVERS AND KLOOFS
Broom-cluster Fig

367

# KARREE

*Rhus lancea*                                                    Karoo-tree; Bastard Willow

---

**MANGO FAMILY**
**ANACARDIACEAE**                                                SA Tree Number 386

**AFRIKAANS** Karee, Rooikaree  **N. SOTHO** Motšhakhutšhakhu, Monhlohlo
**SISWATI** iNhlangutshane  **S. SOTHO** Mosilabele, Mosinabele  **TSWANA** Mošabêlê, Mosilabêlê
**VENDA** Mushakaladza  **XHOSA** umHlakotshane

The species name **lancea** refers to the lance-shaped leaflets.

## Where you'll find this tree easily

The Karree may be found singly in dry grassland, but normally groups of these trees are found along water courses.

- It is easiest to find along Rivers and Streams of the Mixed Bushveld (M).
- It can also be found along Rivers and Streams of the Central Mountains (C); and on the Plateau and South- or East-facing Slopes of the Mixed Bushveld (M).

## Ecozones where this tree occurs

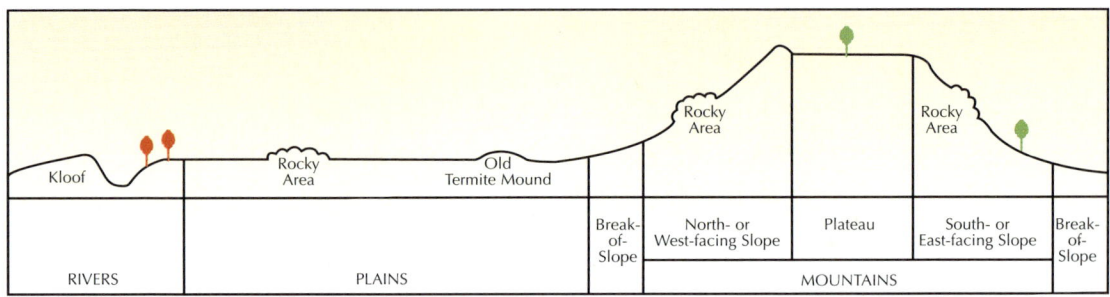

## Striking features

- This is usually a single-stemmed, low-branching tree with a dense, soft, round canopy.
- The bark is coarse and dark brown.
- **The branches divide into many thin branchlets and twigs, giving the tree a soft, drooping, willow-like appearance, with leaves and twigs moving easily in the wind.**
- The three-leaflet compound leaves are long and willow-like, and the leaflets join the leaf-stalk at an acute angle.
- Crushed leaves have a characteristic aromatic smell.

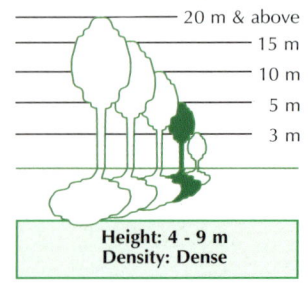

Height: 4 - 9 m
Density: Dense

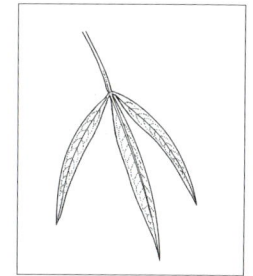

RIVERS AND KLOOFS
Karree

369

# KARREE

*Rhus lancea*

**Links with animals** The leaves contain tannins, and are therefore only eaten by game or cattle during dry periods. Bulbuls, guineafowl and francolins eat the ripe fruit.

**Human uses** It was used extensively for fence posts, as well as for pick handles and parts of wagons. In some areas it was used to make bowls for tobacco pipes, and the Khoisan used the soft branches for bows.

**Gardening** This is an attractive shade tree for any garden. It is frost- and drought-resistant, and grows fast from seed or cuttings. It is suitable as a bonsai tree.

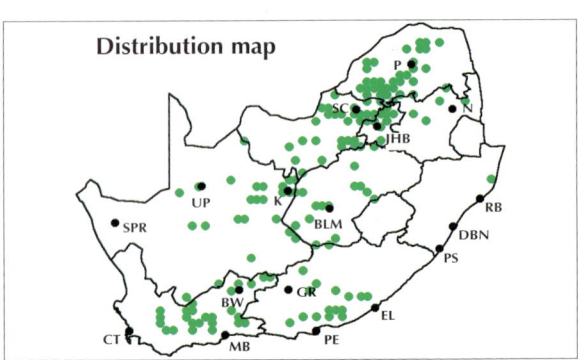

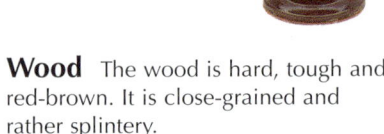

**Wood** The wood is hard, tough and red-brown. It is close-grained and rather splintery.

**Look-alike tree** The tree can be confused with Rock Karree-rhus (*Rhus leptodictya*), page 76, which is most common in Rocky Areas and is seldom found along rivers. Rock Karree-rhus is generally a smaller tree, and the leaves are lighter green, broader, and toothed along the whole margin. The leaflets of Rock Karree-rhus are attached to the leaf-stalk at right angles, and the fine vein pattern is clearly visible on the under-surface of the leaf. See page 67 and 76 for other three-leaflet compound leaves.

*A single tree near a River in Pilanesberg*

# GROWTH DETAILS

This is a single- or multi-stemmed, low-branching, dark green tree with a round, dense canopy. The branches divide into many thin branchlets and twigs, which give the tree a soft, drooping, willow-like appearance. Leaves and twigs move easily in the wind.

**Leaves** Three-leaflet compound leaves grow on very long leaf-stalks (50 mm). The three slender leaflets form an acute angle where they meet the leaf-stalk (like the toes of a chicken's foot). The dark green to olive-coloured leaflets are stiff, the margins are smooth, and the central vein stands out on both sides. The under-surface of the leaflet is slightly paler than that of the upper-surface. (Leaf: 150 - 190 mm; central leaflet: 90 - 120 x 6 - 15 mm)

**Fruit** The small, grape-like fruit ripens to shiny yellow-brown from September to January. (4 - 5 mm)

*65% life-size*

**Flowers** The inconspicuous, pale yellow, star-shaped flowers grow in dense clusters at the ends of the twigs from April to July. Male and female flowers are usually on separate trees. (Spray: 60 x 60 mm; individual: 3 mm)

**Bark** The bark of the main branches and stems is coarse and dark grey to brown, whereas young branches and twigs are reddish-brown.

**Seasonal changes**
Evergreen. The tree can be identified throughout the year.

|  | Oct | Nov | Dec | Jan | Feb | Mar | Apr | May | Jun | Jul | Aug | Sep |
|---|---|---|---|---|---|---|---|---|---|---|---|---|
| Leaf | ■ | ■ | ■ | ■ | ■ | ■ | ■ | ■ | ■ | ■ | ■ | ■ |
| Flower |  |  |  |  |  |  | ■ | ■ | ■ |  |  |  |
| Fruit/Pod | ■ | ■ | ■ |  |  |  |  |  |  |  |  | ■ |

RIVERS AND KLOOFS
Karree

# RED CURRANT-RHUS

*Rhus chirindensis*

Red currant rhus; Forest Currant; Bush Currant

## MANGO FAMILY
## ANACARDIACEAE

SA Tree Number 380

**AFRIKAANS** Bostaaibos  **N. SOTHO** Motha-thaa, Mphata-kgogo  **VENDA** Muvhadela-phanga
**XHOSA** umHlakothi, iNtlokolotshane enkulu  **ZULU** inHlokoshiyane enkulu, umHlakothi

The species name **chirindensis** refers to the Chirinda Forest in Zimbabwe.

### Where you'll find this tree easily

This tree grows singly among other trees.

- It is easiest to find along Rivers and Streams of the Northern Mountains (N) and the Sour Bushveld (S).
- It can also be found on South- or East-facing Slopes of the Northern Mountains (N) and the Sour Bushveld (S).

### Ecozones where this tree occurs

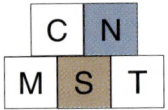

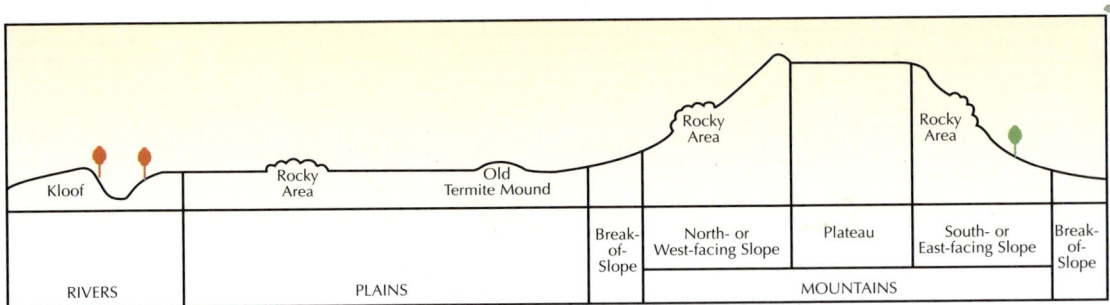

### Striking features

- This is a large, often crooked-trunked, low-branching tree with an irregular, spreading canopy.
- The drooping, compound leaves have three leaflets and a long, reddish leaf-stalk.
- The large elliptic leaflets have a wavy margin and a prominent central vein.
- The bark is dark and cracked lengthways, revealing deep red under-bark.

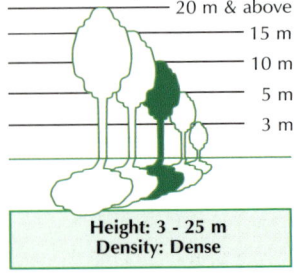

Height: 3 - 25 m
Density: Dense

RIVERS AND KLOOFS
Red Current-rhus

**Largest tree currently registered**

**Diameter:** 0,67 m
**Girth:** 2,10 m
**Height:** 20 m

State Forest, Hangklip,
Dist. Soutpansberg

# RED CURRANT-RHUS

*Rhus chirindensis*

**Links with animals** Leaves and bark are eaten by Black Rhino, and the leaves are eaten by Red Duiker, kudu, nyala, and bushbuck. The fruit attracts Vervet and Samango Monkeys, African Green Pigeons, Knysna and Purple-crested Louries, Black-eyed Bulbuls, Pied and Crested Barbets, Cape White-eyes and Cape Parrots.

**Human uses** The ripe fruit is edible, and has a sweet-sour taste. Zulu herbalists used the sap as medicine for treating heart complaints; the bark to strengthen the body, stimulate circulation and for rheumatism; and bark extracts for mental disturbances.

**Gardening** This is a very attractive garden tree, and does not have an aggressive root system. It grows easily and fast from cuttings, and is frost- and drought-resistant. It prefers well-drained soil.

**Look-alike trees** Having three-leaflet compound leaves, the Red Currant-rhus can be confused with the trees described on page 67 and 76.

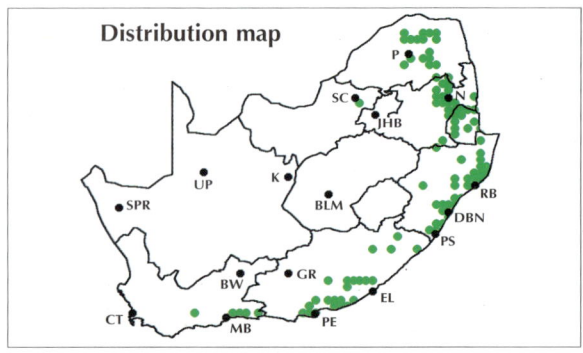

Distribution map

**Wood** The sapwood is yellowish and the heartwood red. It is heavy and strong, and makes attractive furniture with a lovely sheen.

*January; Blyde River Canyon; Kloof Forest, Sour Bushveld*

# GROWTH DETAILS

This can be a single- or multi-stemmed tree with a crooked trunk that branches to form a dense, irregular, spreading canopy. This is the largest of the Karree, Crowberry and Currant trees (*Rhus* species) in South Africa.

**Leaves** The three-leaflet compound leaves have broadly elliptic leaflets on short stalks that are attached at a single point to the long, often reddish leaf-stalk (70 mm). Leaflets are smooth and glossy, dark green above and slightly paler below. Young leaflets are reddish. Prominent central and side veins are often pinkish. The tips of the sharply tapering leaflets are hair-like, and the margins are wavy. (Leaf: 130 - 200 x 100 - 130 mm; central leaflet: 60 - 130 x 25 - 40 mm)

**Fruit** The small, round bunches of grape-like fruit can weigh down the branches. The fleshy fruit ripens to red-brown or pink (December to March). (4 - 7 mm)

*25% life-size*

**Flowers** Small, yellow-green, star-shaped flowers grow in long, delicate sprays at the ends of the branchlets and twigs (August to January). Male and female flowers are often a separate trees (Spray: 160 - 200 mm; individual: 3 mm)

**Bark** In mature trees the bark is dark and cracked lengthways, revealing deeper red under-bark. It is light brown to grey, and smooth when young. The stalks of young plants and new shoots may be spiny.

## Seasonal changes
Usually deciduous, but may be evergreen in the forest. This tree can be found as long as some leaves are present.

|  | Oct | Nov | Dec | Jan | Feb | Mar | Apr | May | Jun | Jul | Aug | Sep |
|---|---|---|---|---|---|---|---|---|---|---|---|---|
| Leaf | ■ | ■ | ■ | ■ | ■ | ■ | ■ | ■ |  |  | ■ | ■ |
| Flower | ■ | ■ | ■ | ■ |  |  |  |  |  |  | ■ | ■ |
| Fruit/Pod |  | ■ | ■ | ■ | ■ | ■ |  |  |  |  |  |  |

RIVERS AND KLOOFS
Red Currant-rhus

375

# RIVER BUSHWILLOW

*Combretum erythrophyllum*

| BUSHWILLOW FAMILY COMBRETACEAE | SA Tree Number 536 |

**AFRIKAANS** Riviervaderlandswilg, Vaderlandswilg  **N. SOTHO** Moduba-noka  **TSONGA** Mbvuva  **TSWANA** Modubu, Modubunoka  **VENDA** Muvuvhu  **XHOSA** umDubu, umDubi  **ZULU** umDubu wehlanze

The species name **erythrophyllum** refers to the red colour of the leaf in autumn.

## Where you'll find this tree easily

The River Bushwillow grows singly, but where one is found, there will often be others in the vicinity.

- It is found exclusively along the larger Rivers and Streams in all the Ecozones.

## Ecozones where this tree occurs

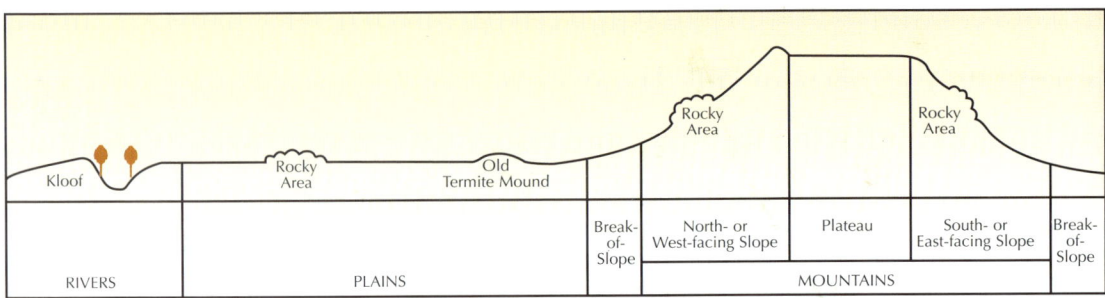

## Striking features

- It is usually a single-trunked, wide-spreading, densely leafed tree.
- **The trunk and larger branches tend to meander, and old stems are often bumpy with irregular swellings, like cellulite.**
- The bark is smooth, pale yellowish and grey-brown, and flakes in irregular patches to expose rich, apricot-coloured under-bark.
- It has typical four-winged Bushwillow pods.
- In the outer canopy new shoots are perpendicular. They carry pairs of simple, opposite leaves growing upright in a tight V-shape.

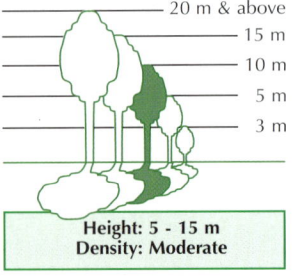

Height: 5 - 15 m
Density: Moderate

**RIVERS AND KLOOFS**
*River Bushwillow*

**Largest tree currently registered**

**Diameter:** 1,21 m
**Girth:** 3,80 m
**Height:** 16 m

WGF Neetling, Riverside Estate, Dist. Pretoria

# RIVER BUSHWILLOW

*Combretum erythrophyllum*

**Links with animals** Leaves are eaten by bushbuck. The fruit is eaten by Pied Barbets.

**Human uses** The wood is used to make cattle troughs. The root is used as a purgative and as a cure for venereal disease, but may be very poisonous. This tree is still used in traditional medicine today.

**Gardening** This is an attractive garden tree. Established trees are frost- and drought-resistant. The plant grows fast once established from seed. It is suitable as a bonsai tree.

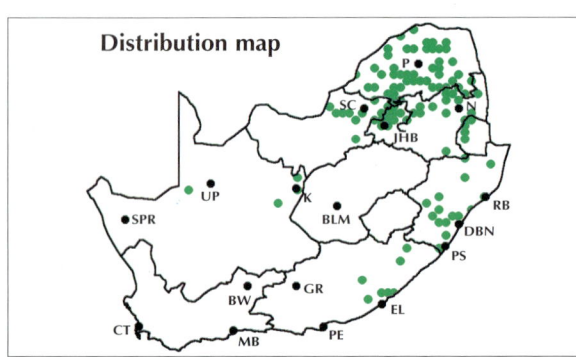
Distribution map

**Wood** The heartwood and sapwood are yellow. It has a straight grain, turns well and is suitable for carving.

**Look-alike trees** See the Bushwillow comparisons on pages 74 - 75.

*June; Autumn colour leaves; River bank, Pilanesberg*

# GROWTH DETAILS

This is a single-, sometimes multi-trunked, tree with a crooked trunk that branches low down to form a dense, spreading canopy. The trunk and larger branches of old trees are often bumpy with irregular swellings. Most older branchlets and twigs tend to hang down, but in the outer canopy new shoots are perpendicular.

**Leaves** New perpendicular shoots carry pairs of simple, opposite leaves growing upright in a tight V-shape. Simple, elliptic leaves are opposite on young twigs and tend to form whorls of three on older branches. They have a smooth margin, and the base and tip are tapering. The upper-surface of mature leaves is dark, shiny green, but young leaves are delicate green and often hairy. The under-surface of all leaves is slightly hairy. Leaves turn yellow and red in autumn. (Leaf: 50 - 130 x 20 - 65 mm)

**Flowers** Inconspicuous, cream to yellow-green, roundish flower-spikes appear just after the new leaves from August to November. (20 x 10 mm)

**Pods** The typical four-winged Bushwillow pods grow in abundance, and turn pale brown to camel when they mature from January. Pods often stay on the tree until the next flowers appear in August. (10 - 15 mm)

*60% life-size*

**Bark** The bark is yellowish, grey-brown and smooth, and peels irregularly to expose rich, apricot-coloured under-bark.

## Seasonal changes
Deciduous. The flaky bark and apricot under-bark, as well as the swellings on the trunk and the pods, are all characteristic, and should aid identification throughout the year.

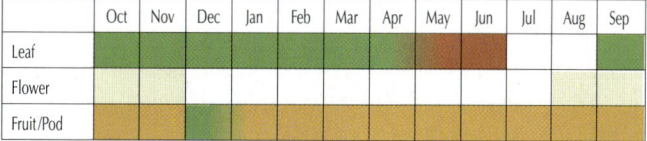

|  | Oct | Nov | Dec | Jan | Feb | Mar | Apr | May | Jun | Jul | Aug | Sep |
|---|---|---|---|---|---|---|---|---|---|---|---|---|
| Leaf | | | | | | | | | | | | |
| Flower | | | | | | | | | | | | |
| Fruit/Pod | | | | | | | | | | | | |

**RIVERS AND KLOOFS**
River Bushwillow

379

# ROBUST ACACIA

*Acacia robusta*                          Ankle Thorn

**THORN-TREE FAMILY**
**MIMOSACEAE**        SA Tree Numbers 183 & 183.1

**AFRIKAANS** Brakdoring, Enkeldoring   **NORTH SOTHO** Mooka
**TSONGA** Mungamazi, Mvumbangwenya   **TSWANA** Mokhu, Moga
**VENDA** Muvumba-ngwena   **XHOSA** umNgampunzi   **ZULU** umNgamanzi

The species name **robusta** refers to the robust growth form of the tree.

## Where you'll find this tree easily

The Robust Acacia is a large tree that normally grows singly among other species of trees.
- It is easiest to find along the larger Rivers and Streams of all Ecozones.
- It can also be found in Rocky Areas of the Plains and on all Slopes of the Mixed Bushveld (M).

## Ecozones where this tree occurs

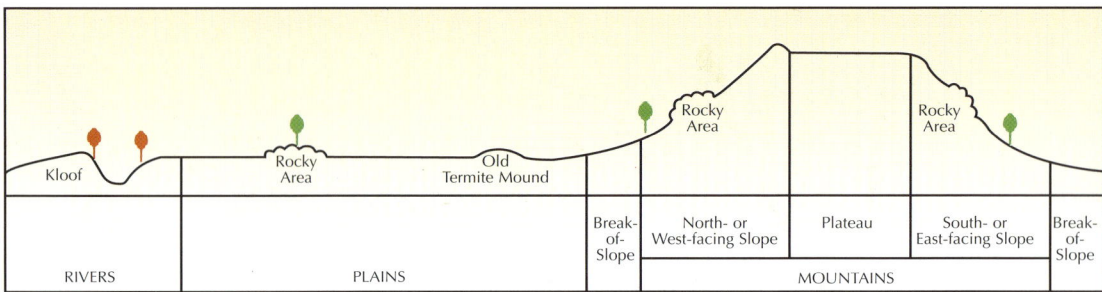

## Striking features

- This is an upright, often huge Thorn-tree with striking, dark green, feathery foliage.
- Branches stay thick, even towards their extremities.
- **The twice compound leaves tend to be very tightly arranged around the thick branchlets, forming a green sleeve.**
- **The conspicuous, prickly, cushion-like thickenings at the base of new thorns and leaves are characteristic.**
- The flower-balls are creamy-white, and can be seen very early in spring.
- The pods are thick and slightly sickle-shaped, and hang from the tree in large conspicuous bunches from January to August.

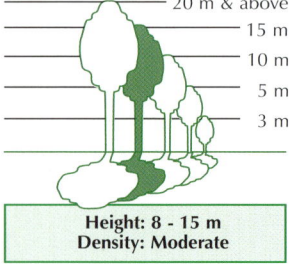

Height: 8 - 15 m
Density: Moderate

**RIVERS AND KLOOFS**
Robust Acacia

**Largest tree currently registered**

**Diameter:** 1,45 m
**Girth:** 4,55 m
**Height:** 16 m

Nwanedi Resort
Venda

381

# ROBUST ACACIA

*Acacia robusta*

**Links with animals** Leaves are browsed by kudu. Flowers attract bees and butterflies.

**Human uses** The wood can be used for yokes, and to make wedges to split other wood such as the Sickle-bush. The under-bark can be used to make twine, and the bark is used for tanning and to treat skin ailments. Steam from the boiled bark was inhaled to cure chest complaints. Edible wood-borer beetles are found in the wood. This tree is still important in traditional medicine.

**Gardening** This tree can be very attractive in a well-watered, warm garden in a position where the thorns do not pose a threat to small children. It grows fast from seed, and is suitable as a bonsai tree.

**Look-alike trees** This tree can be confused with the other Acacias. See pages 70 - 73 for comparisons.

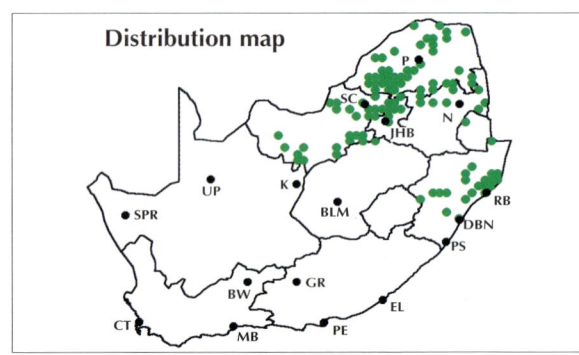

Distribution map

**Wood** The wood is light-coloured with a dark heart. It is very tough, but not good for timber.

*Characteristic, prickly, cushion-like swellings at the base of thorns and leaves*

# GROWTH DETAILS

This is a single-stemmed, fairly high-branching tree. The upper branches are almost erect, but the lower ones are more horizontal, forming a semi-circular canopy. Branches are thickened even towards their extremities, with thick branches clearly visible in the canopy, giving the tree a robust appearance.

**Leaves** The dark green leaves are twice compound, and are clumped on prickly 'cushions'. Leaflets grow at an acute angle, and tend to look half-closed. Leaves have 2 - 6 feather pairs, each consisting of 10 - 25 pairs of leaflets. (Leaf: 45 - 90 mm; leaflet: 7 - 12 x 3 - 4 mm)

**Thorns** The straight, white, paired thorns are joined at a base that may be swollen. Thorns are sometimes underdeveloped. (70 - 110 mm)

*45% life-size*

**Pods** The dark brown, slightly sickle-shaped pods are rounded at the tip. They grow in bunches and burst open on the tree when ripe. Pods ripen from January to August, and may be seen on the tree for long periods. (130 x 20 mm)

**Flowers** Conspicuous groups of up to 25 white flower-balls grow between the new green leaves in early spring (July to October). (15 - 20 mm)

**Bark** The bark is dark grey, but lighter on the younger branches. It is closely grooved lengthways.

**Seasonal changes**
Deciduous. The dark cushions remain on the branches after the leaves have dropped, making identification possible even in winter.

|  | Oct | Nov | Dec | Jan | Feb | Mar | Apr | May | Jun | Jul | Aug | Sep |
|---|---|---|---|---|---|---|---|---|---|---|---|---|
| Leaf | | | | | | | | | | | | |
| Flower | | | | | | | | | | | | |
| Fruit/Pod | | | | | | | | | | | | |

RIVERS AND KLOOFS
Robust Acacia

383

# SMALL KNOBWOOD

*Zanthoxylum capense*

### CITRUS / BUCHU FAMILY
### RUTACEAE

SA Tree Number 253

**AFRIKAANS** Kleinperdepram, Wildekardamon  **N. SOTHO** Senokomaropa, Monokwane
**SISWATI** umNungwane  **TSONGA** Manhungwana  **TSWANA** Monokomabêlê, Sekole
**VENDA** Munungu, Murandela  **XHOSA** umNungumabele, umLungumabele
**ZULU** umNungumabele, umNungwane omncane

The species name **capense** means 'of the Cape'.

## Where you'll find this tree easily

The Small Knobwood grows singly among other tree species.

- It is easiest to find in Rocky Areas on South- or East-facing Slopes of the Sour Bushveld (S).
- It can also be found in Rocky Areas and Kloofs on South- or East-facing Slopes of the Northern Mountains (N), Central Mountains (C) and Mixed Bushveld (M).

## Ecozones where this tree occurs

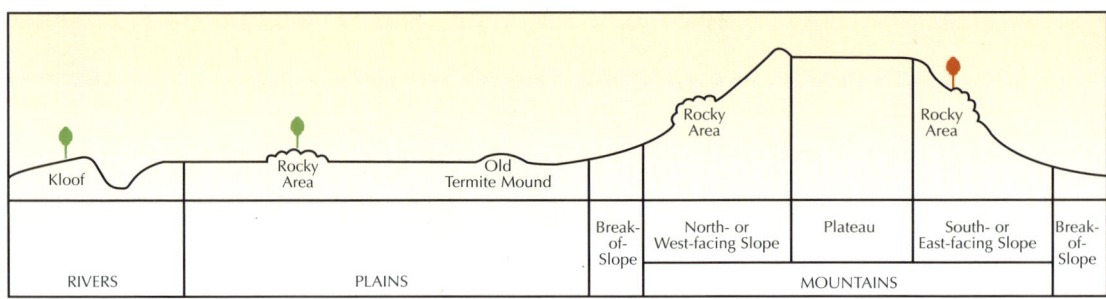

## Striking features

- This is a single-stemmed, low-branching tree that branches upwards to form a moderate, V-shaped canopy.
- **Prominent, knob-like swellings, ending in a rose-like thorn, cover the main stems and branches of mature trees.**
- **The shiny, compound leaves are spirally arranged towards the ends of twigs and branchlets.**
- The leaflets have a strong citrus smell when crushed.
- There are small, hooked thorns on the under-surface of the leaf-stalk.

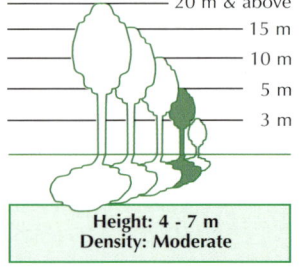

Height: 4 - 7 m
Density: Moderate

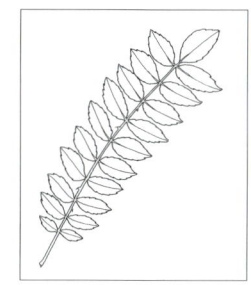

RIVERS AND KLOOFS
Small Knobwood

385

# SMALL KNOBWOOD

*Zanthoxylum capense*

**Links with animals** Some mammals browse the leaves. The flowers attract beetles. Birds such as mousebirds and barbets eat the fruit.

**Human uses** The wood can be used to make pick handles, knobkieries, planks and yokes. The seeds are used to make perfume. The tree is still used in traditional medicine today: the bark and roots to treat violent chronic coughs, pleurisy and tuberculosis; powdered bark rubbed into incisions along the sides of the body to treat paralysis; an infusion of the leaf for colic and gastro-intestinal disorders; the leaf to cure sores, and crushed leaves to cure colds, and for snakebite and toothache; and the plant itself to disinfect anthrax-infected meat.

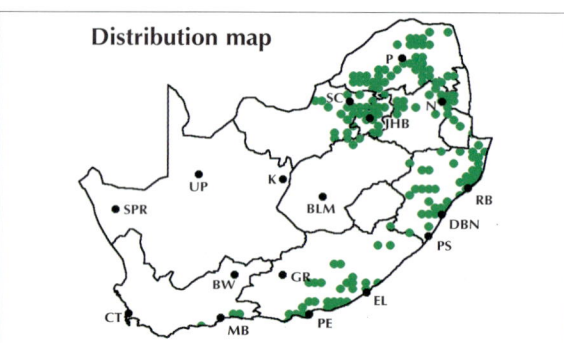
Distribution map

**Wood** The logs are lemon-yellow when freshly cut, with a darker heartwood. It has a wavy grain and turns well.

**Gardening** This is an attractive garden tree, but it is difficult to grow from seed. It is frost- and drought-resistant.

**Look-alike trees** Perdepis (*Clausena anisata*), page 68, has very similar leaves, but the tree is always slender and straggly. The leaflets of Perdepis are alternate (not opposite), the central vein is off-centre, and crushed leaves have a pungent aniseed (horse urine) smell.

False Perdepis (*Hippobromus pauciflorus*) is also a straggling tree of the forest, and is often multi-stemmed. It has alternate leaflets with the top of the leaflet deeply toothed. Crushed leaves have a resinous smell, and the leaf-stalk is winged on alternate sides.

*Characteristic trunks; Kloof, Central Mountains*

# GROWTH DETAILS

This is a single-stemmed tree with a straight trunk that branches upwards to form a V-shaped canopy. A few large branches are visible in the canopy, acutely branching into thin, delicate branchlets and twigs.

**Leaves** Compound leaves are spirally arranged towards the ends of twigs and branchlets, and their leaf-stalks may have small, hooked thorns on the under-surface. There are 3 - 10 pairs of leaflets with a single leaflet at the tip that may be absent or very small. Elliptic leaflets have sharply toothed margins, may be opposite or alternate, and do not have leaf-stalks. Leaflets have 8 pairs of side veins, and are shiny above and duller below. The leaves have a strong citrus smell when crushed. The scent comes from oil glands that are visible when the leaf is held against the light. (Leaf: 40 - 200 mm; leaflet: 1 - 4 x 1 - 2 mm)

*40% life-size*

**Fruit** Small, round, fleshy, berry-like fruit grows in clusters, and the skin is covered by tiny glands. The berries turn red to red-brown when ripe, and split open on the tree to reveal a single, black seed with an oily appendage (November to June). (5 - 13 mm)

**Flowers** Inconspicuous, greenish-white, sweet-scented flowers grow in sprays at the end of the twigs. Similar male and female flowers are on separate trees (October to February). (20 - 60 mm)

**Bark** The bark is grey and smooth with hooked, rose-like thorns on prominent, knob-like swellings on the main stems and branches of mature trees.

## Seasonal changes
Deciduous. Mature trees can be identified by their typical bark throughout the year.

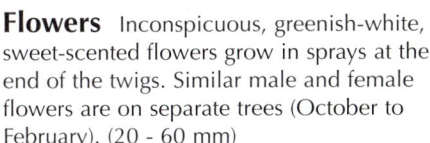

| | Oct | Nov | Dec | Jan | Feb | Mar | Apr | May | Jun | Jul | Aug | Sep |
|---|---|---|---|---|---|---|---|---|---|---|---|---|
| Leaf | | | | | | | | | | | | |
| Flower | | | | | | | | | | | | |
| Fruit/Pod | | | | | | | | | | | | |

RIVERS AND KLOOFS
Small Knobwood

# TAMBOTI

*Spirostachys africana*

| EUPHORBIA FAMILY  EUPHORBIACEAE | SA Tree Number 341 |
|---|---|

**AFRIKAANS** Tambotie, Sandelhout  **N. SOTHO** Morekuri  **SISWATI** umThombotsi, umThombothi
**TSONGA** Ndzopfori, Xilangamahlo  **TSWANA** Morukuru  **VENDA** Muonze  **ZULU** umThombothi

The species name **africana** means 'of Africa'.

## Where you'll find this tree easily

The Tamboti grows as a single tall tree, or in larger groups of smaller trees, forming groves. It prefers clay soils.

- It is easiest to find in groups on the clay banks of Rivers and Streams of the Mixed Bushveld (M).
- It can also be found on the Plains of the Mixed Bushveld (M) and the Sour Bushveld (S); and in Rocky Areas and on the South- or East-facing Slopes of the Mixed Bushveld (M).

## Ecozones where this tree occurs

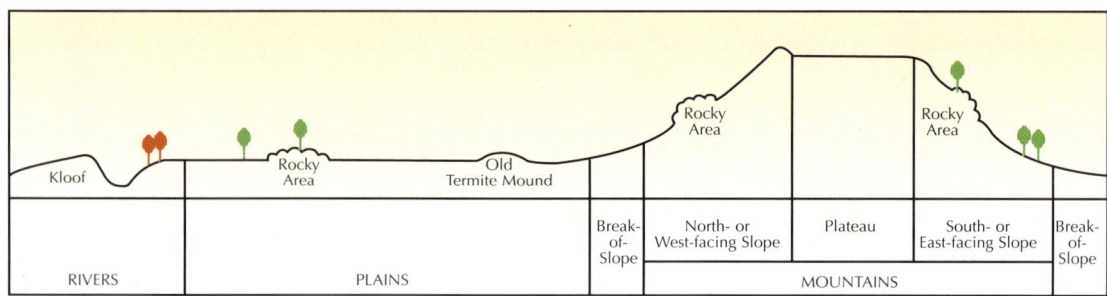

## Striking features

- This tree has a single, straight, high-branching trunk.
- The narrow canopy is dense, and usually has some red leaves among the green.
- **The bark is characteristic dark brown to black, thick, rough, and deeply cracked into relatively small, distinctive, very regular rectangles.**
- **The simple, alternate leaves have finely toothed margins, and produce a white, milky, irritant latex when broken off.**

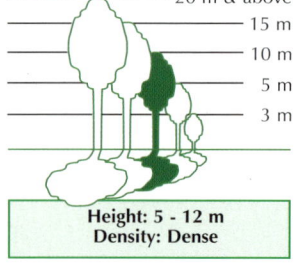

Height: 5 - 12 m
Density: Dense

RIVERS AND KLOOFS
Tamboti

**Largest tree currently registered**

**Diameter:** 1,85 m
**Girth:** 5,81 m
**Height:** 13 m

S van Schalkwyk, Diepkuil, Dist. Thabazimbi

# TAMBOTI

*Spirostachys africana*

**Links with animals** The fallen seeds are eaten by Crested Guineafowl, francolin and doves. Black Rhino eat the young branches. Giraffe eat leaves on the tree and dry fallen leaves are eaten by Vervet Monkeys, kudu, nyala and impala. The seeds are often infected with the caterpillars of the Knotthorn Moth (*Melanobasis*) which cause the seeds to jump when the caterpillars straighten themselves inside.

**Gardening** This tree can be very attractive in a large garden. It is fairly drought- and frost-resistant. It grows well from seed, but grows slowly.

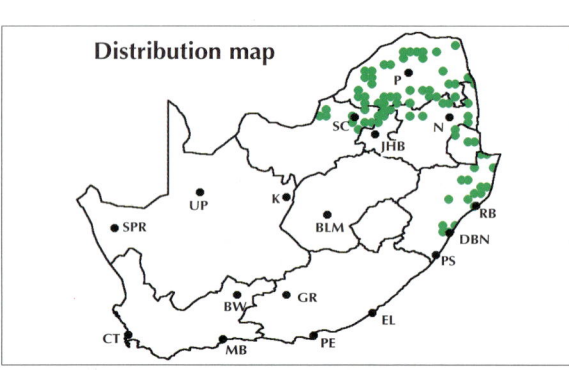

Distribution map

**Wood** The wood is hard and oily. It turns easily and must be planed in the direction of the grain. It is suitable for decorative veneer.

**Human uses** The milky latex is poisonous and extremely irritant. Toxic fumes from wood used as firewood, can cause severe illness. The latex was used to treat boils and toothache, and to stupefy fish, making them easier to catch. Extracts of the roots and bark were used as an eye-wash, to cure stomach ulcers, and for kidney ailments. The powdered bark was used as perfume, and pieces of the wood can be put among clothing act as an insect repellent.

*Dark, blocky bark is easy to recognise*

# GROWTH DETAILS

The single, straight trunk is usually high-branching, with main branches growing upwards. In Riverine Forests it forms a narrow, dense canopy. Young trees often have multiple stems. Young branchlets stand out above the canopy, with leaves spirally arranged along the entire length of the branchlet. Being a member of the Euphorbia family, it produces a small amount of poisonous and irritant, milky latex when any part of the tree is broken.

*80% life-size*

**Leaves**  Simple, alternate, dull green leaves are arranged in a spiral along the branchlets. They have finely toothed margins and a short leaf-stalk. Older red leaves are often visible among the mature green leaves. Leaves show striking yellow and red autumn colours. (30 - 80 mm)

**Spines**  Young trees often have conspicuous spines up to 150 mm, which make them look like a different species.

**Flowers**  In late winter, before the leaves appear, Tamboti trees have a distinct red sheen caused by the red-brown flower-spikes. (July to November). (15 - 30 mm)

*65% life-size*

**Fruit**  The dry, brown capsules are three-lobed. They open on hot summer days with an audible explosion. Seeds infected by Knotthorn caterpillars appear to jump, and are known as jumping beans (Mature September to November). (10 mm)

**Bark**  The bark is characteristically dark brown to black, thick, rough, and neatly cracked into relatively small, distinctive, very regular rectangles. In young trees the bark is smooth and grey, and often has white patches.

## Seasonal changes
Deciduous to evergreen, depending on Habitat. The bark makes identification possible all year.

|  | Oct | Nov | Dec | Jan | Feb | Mar | Apr | May | Jun | Jul | Aug | Sep |
|---|---|---|---|---|---|---|---|---|---|---|---|---|
| Leaf |  |  |  |  |  |  |  |  |  |  |  |  |
| Flower |  |  |  |  |  |  |  |  |  |  |  |  |
| Fruit/Pod |  |  |  |  |  |  |  |  |  |  |  |  |

**RIVERS AND KLOOFS** — Tamboti

# UMDONI WATERBERRY

*Syzygium cordatum*      Umdoni; Water Berry; Water Tree; Waterwood

### MYRTLE FAMILY
### MYRTACEAE

**SA Tree Number 555**

**AFRIKAANS** Waterbessie, Waterhout   **N. SOTHO** Monhlo, Montlho   **SISWATI** umCozi
**TSONGA** Muthwa, Muhlwa   **VENDA** Mutu   **XHOSA** umSwi, umJome   **ZULU** umDoni

The species name **cordatum** means 'heart-shaped', referring to the heart-shaped base of the leaves.

## Where you'll find this tree easily

The Umdoni Waterberry is a water-loving, fire-resistant tree. It grows singly among other tree species, but where one is found, others will be found in the vicinity.

- It is easiest to find on the South- or East-facing Slopes of the Sour Bushveld (S).
- It can also be found on the South- or East-facing Slopes of the Central Mountains (C); and along Rivers and Streams of the Central Mountains (C) and Sour Bushveld (S); as well as on North- or West-facing Slopes of the Sour Bushveld (S).

## Ecozones where this tree occurs

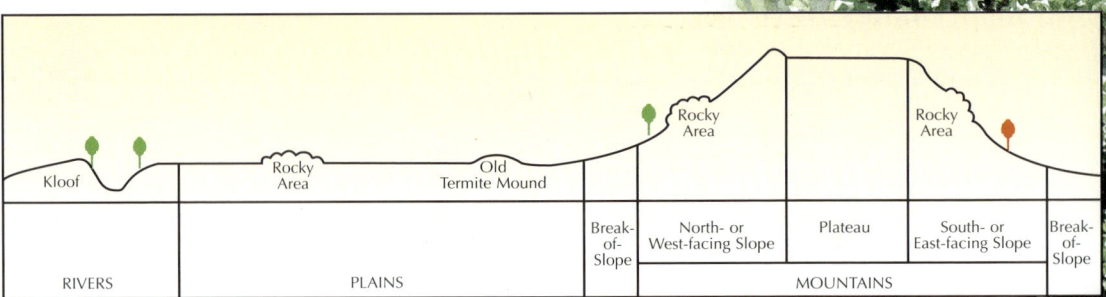

## Striking features

- This is a single-trunked, low-branching tree that branches to form a blue-green, dense, semi-circular canopy.
- **The stalkless leaves are round, and are clustered towards the ends of thick twigs, forming distinct rosettes.**
- The central vein is yellow and conspicuous.
- The characteristic pin-cushion flowers grow at the ends of the twigs, in the leaf-rosettes.
- **The succulent berries turn deep purple when ripe, and are conspicuous from October to May.**

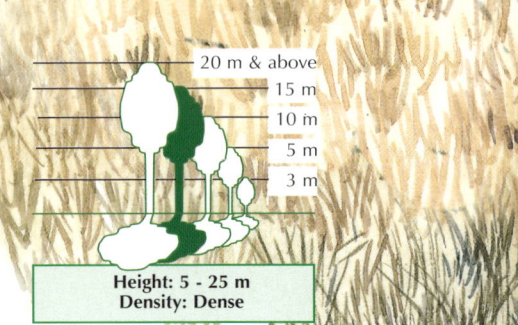

Height: 5 - 25 m
Density: Dense

RIVERS AND KLOOFS
Umdoni/Waterberry

# UMDONI WATERBERRY

*Syzygium cordatum*

**Links with animals** Caterpillars of two Charaxes and three Playboy butterflies feed on this tree. The Emperor Moth (*Micragone cana*) also feeds on it. Monkeys, baboons, bushpigs and bushbabies eat the fruit, as well as many birds, such as Tambourine Doves, African Green Pigeons, and both Purple-crested and Knysna Louries. Grey Duiker, kudu, nyala and bushbuck browse the foliage. Ball-like webs are made by the bright ginger Tailor Ant, which favours this tree.

**Human uses** The succulent berries are edible, and are sometimes used to make beer. The wood has a beautiful grain, and is used for furniture and canoes. The powdered bark is sometimes used as a fish poison. An extract of the leaves was used as a purgative, for treatment of diarrhoea, and to treat stomach and respiratory disorders such as tuberculosis, colds and fever. Bark and roots were used for headaches and wounds.

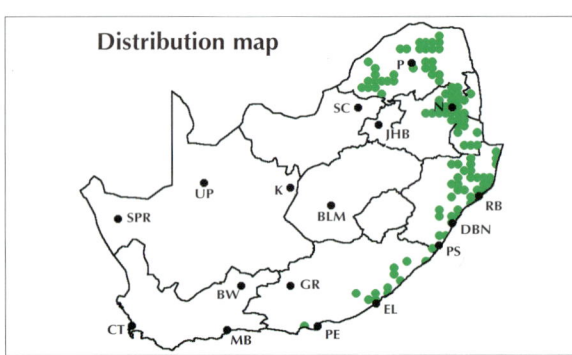
Distribution map

**Wood** This reddish-brown wood is fine and even-textured, durable and extremely resistant. It is easy to saw, planes well to a smooth, lustrous finish, turns well and can be used for both heavy and light construction material.

**Gardening** This is a very attractive garden tree, but must be planted near water. It has an aggressive root system, and grows well in a container. It grows fast from seed but will not withstand severe frost. It can withstand extended periods of waterlogging, and can be used to stabilise stream and river banks, or as a shade tree planted in swampy areas.

*Rosettes of leaves growing on the ends of branchlets and twigs.*

# GROWTH DETAILS

This is a single-trunked, often low-branching tree with branches growing upwards and outwards to form a dense, semi-circular, blue-green canopy. The round leaves are clustered towards the end of the thick twigs, forming distinct rosettes. Young twigs and branchlets are square.

**Leaves**  Simple, opposite leaves are blue-green, leathery and smooth, with a distinct yellow central vein. They are almost round, with a deeply notched base that clamps the twig. The margins are smooth. Leaves grow towards the ends of the branchlets and twigs, with successive pairs at right angles, forming rosettes. New leaves are bright red. (30 - 100 x 20 - 80 mm)

**Fruit**  The fleshy, berry-like fruit grows in bunches in the leaf-rosettes, resembling posies. The fruit turns deep purple when ripe (June to January). (13 - 20 x 10 mm)

*life-size*

**Flowers**  The sweet-smelling, pin-cushion flowers are creamy-white to pinkish, and are rich in nectar. They grow in bunches on the ends of branchlets and twigs in the leaf-rosettes (October to June). (Bunch: 100 mm; individual: 20 x 25 mm)

**Bark**  The bark is dark and coarse, and may even be corky in older trees. In young trees it is smooth and pale grey, with grey and white blotches.

**Seasonal changes**
Evergreen. The tree can be identified throughout the year.

|  | Oct | Nov | Dec | Jan | Feb | Mar | Apr | May | Jun | Jul | Aug | Sep |
|---|---|---|---|---|---|---|---|---|---|---|---|---|
| Leaf | | | | | | | | | | | | |
| Flower | | | | | | | | | | | | |
| Fruit/Pod | | | | | | | | | | | | |

**RIVERS AND KLOOFS**
Umdoni Waterberry

# References

## FAMILY FEATURES, GRIDS AND MAPS

All of these sections are designed to add to your knowledge base, rapidly and easily. They are also an inspirational centre, inviting you to travel to other places, check out other Habitats, and even try a few new hobbies!

| | |
|---|---|
| Enjoy tree spotting | p. 398 |
| Recommended English names | p. 399 |
| Record-breaking trees | p. 400 |
| Gardening | p. 401 |
| Places to tree spot | p. 404 |
| Map of Bushveld | p. 410 |
| Map of enlarged W Bushveld | p. 412 |
| Map of enlarged NE & SE Bushveld | p. 414 |
| Family features | p. 416 |
| Index | p. 421 |
| Book references | p. 428 |

The finale of a day – and the last section in a book about an adventure in tree spotting. Dramatic colours in the evening at Inyati Lodge shift the focus from the Big Five to the outlines of Sour Bushveld (S) trees, and the silhouette of the nearby Drakensberg Mountains. In this magnificent Reserve the Sour Bushveld meets the Lowveld, and trees of both areas are easy to find.

# Enjoy tree spotting

Tree spotting in the Bushveld is much more than just putting names to trees. It can be coming across the Sycamore Cluster-fig where a leopard has hidden its kill, or the large Marula that elephants are using to rub mud off their backs. It can be watching giraffe stripping the flower-buds of the Red Bushwillow, as eagerly as a child devours an ice-cream lolly! It can be noticing a tiny Pearl-spotted Owl in the early morning greyness, only because you know that a Sickle-bush does not normally have such a rounded, tuberous growth on its twigs.

Tree spotting can be the smell of lavender on the crumpled leaves of a Lavender Croton, or the sight of the Wild-pear Dombeya flowers. It is so often the fingertip thrill of feeling different textures – the incredible peeling barks of the Paperbark Albizia and its first cousin the Paperbark Acacia – the smoothness of the Peeling-bark Ochna – the concentric ridges of the Lavender Trees – the flaky paperness and synthetic wet shine of the Corkwoods – and the corkiness of the Ladies Cabbage-tree. It can be the taste of the Jacket-plum, the tartness of a Sourplum or the sweetness of Marula jam – or would you prefer the liqueur?

Above all it is the amazement at the diversity of leaves – the huge, wavy paddles of the Big-leaf Fever-tree; the shimmering decoration of compound leaves dangling on the White Kirkia, the dazzling yellow in autumn on the Mountain Kirkia; the stinging threats on the Rock Tree-nettle; and the incongruously small grey leaves on the swollen Eastern Sesame-bush.

Tree spotting can be part of so many other adventures. You can lie on a river bank fishing, and add to the interest of the day. You can change the whole value of a hike by not only recognising the trees, but learning from them about the ecosystem you are tramping through. It need cost you no more than the price of this book, or you can invest in a few modern toys and add a further dimension to your enjoyment. You could invest in a GPS, and use it to mark certain special trees for your own interest, or to help friends find them too. With a GPS you can mark the exact co-ordinates of the spot, return to the place at any time, and dream up a dozen entertaining games based on treasure hunts or orienteering. You can join a group of 4 x 4 enthusiasts, and find trees that are hidden away, off the hard track trails.

Binoculars do make a real difference, and a good pair, with at least a magnification of 8, is ideal for carrying around on a hike or in a vehicle. With the right binoculars you can see details at a distance, and not always have to be right next to the tree to see what it has to show you. Turn the binocs "back-to-front" and you have an ideal magnifying glass to look at hairs or veins, or the tiny creatures that eat the leaves.

Photographing animals and birds has become a popular hobby for thousands of enthusiasts. Photographing trees, and all their fascinating details and inhabitants, is a new challenge. It is only for those who can cope with the intricacies of really complex lighting contrasts, and, believe it or not, trees almost never stop moving in the wind! The right lenses, the right film, and obviously the right camera, will help you to capture spectacular memories that you can be proud of.

Tree spotting can be a drive or a walk, on the flat Plains of the Springbok Flats, the rocky koppies in the Mixed Bushveld, or the mountainous slopes of a dozen mountain ranges. It is not only South Africa's Cape that boasts stunning cliff faces and spectacular colours in the rocks. The Pilanesberg, Soutpansberg, Waterberg, Blouberge, and the northern stretches of the massive Drakensberg, offer sights and sounds, running water, bending branches, thick trunks, and leaves twinkling in the wind and sunshine.

White Kirkia (White Syringa), page 308

# Recommended English names

One of the main reasons for having any name is to "identify and remember" objects or organisms. Being able to put names to objects is part of a learning process, and having easy-to-remember, descriptive names makes the whole process a lot easier.

Southern Africa has approximately 1 600 named trees, many of them growing in a vast diversity of habitats and therefore forms. It is confusing for the uninitiated to learn their first trees, unless they have the advantage of an expert on hand – which is not always practical. If tree-spotting and indigenous gardening are to be promoted, which in turn will add to the number of people contributing in some way to conservation, it is imperative to have easy-to-use, say and remember names.

During the latter six months of 1999 the Sappi and Jeep Workgroup met regularly to follow the decisions taken at a day-long congress held at the Avis centre in Johannesberg in July. The central belief was that it is in Southern Africa's long-term interests to improve or co-ordinate the existing tree names, where necessary. In many instances a number of different English names had been used over the last 30 years, and the most recent name was not always accurate, or the best. In addition, with eco-tourism moving rapidly away from obsession with the Big Five mammals, it has become necessary to take into account at least our closest neighbours and their terminology. Birders are currently facing this crisis, and the number of "common name" users in Birding way outstrips the "common name' users amongst Tree spotters.

A list of principles was drawn up at the conference to guide decisions about these changes. In particular it was decided that tree names should be scientifically accurate, politically sensitive and should aid identification where possible. Conservatism was also the guiding principle, and many well-loved names were not changed even though they did not entirely meet the "new" requirements. In the majority of those names that were changed, some portion of their "old" name was retained. The Workgroup committed over 850 group hours, 380 secretarial hours and over 10 reams of precious paper to the endeavour, and they are justly proud of the new list.

**Members of the group were:**

Kevin Balkwill, Dept. Animal, Plant and Environmental Sciences, Wits University; Tree Society.

Richard Boon, Conservation Ecologist, KwaZulu-Natal.

Meg Coates Palgrave, botanist, author, tree expert and tour leader.

Hugh Glen, National Herbarium, National Botanical Institute; Tree Society.

Marie Jordaan, National Herbarium, National Botanical Institute.

Mervyn Lotter, Mpumalanga Parks Board, Mpumalanga; Mpumalanga Plant Specialist Group.

Ernst Schmidt, Mpumalanga Plant Specialist Group.

Val Thomas, co-author Sappi Tree Spotting Series.

**Sappi Tree Spotting Bushveld** is proud to be the first publication in Southern Africa to carry these new names. Many other significant authors are following suit and it is likely that 2000 will see a number of major works carrying these names.

**When using this book the following summary should be helpful in the transition from old to new names:**

- All trees have their botanical names listed as a source of further reference.

- For the main trees in the book, all names commonly used in English over the past 30 years are listed both in the introductory position of the name of that tree, and in the index.

- All trees with general descriptions, whether in the main body, the Introduction, or Distinctive Striking Features sections, have the 1999 S.A. National Botanical Tree Number next to their names.

Kiaat Bloodwood
(Wild Teak), page 166

# Record-breaking trees

## Do you know a record-breaking tree?

### Dendrological Society of South Africa

The Dendrological Society (page viii), compiles a register of exceptionally large trees country wide. This means that they record large trees of different species. A large Broom-cluster Fig reaches 22 metres and is huge in anyone's eyes. A massive Sickle-bush, however, will tower at only 6 metres, but is still an exceptional tree for its kind. One of the great delights of learning about trees is the vast variety of shapes, forms and sizes in which they grow.

In some cases more than one large tree of a species is on the register. Jacana has chosen one tree per species from this register, and you will find their height, diameter and girth details, as well as the area where they grow, on the pages listed on the right. You can compare the more "normal" Bushveld size of each tree in its height block.

Readers should contact the Dendrological Society to obtain a form for registering very large trees. The Society publish their information in their journal the *Dendron*.

| Largest trees currently registered | |
|---|---|
| African Olive | p. 184 |
| African White-stinkwood | p. 360 |
| Big-leaf Fever-tree | p. 162 |
| Black-monkey Acacia | p. 218 |
| Broom-cluster Fig | p. 364 |
| Buffalo-thorn Jujube | p. 188 |
| Knob-thorn Acacia | p. 222 |
| Large-fruited Bushwillow | p. 128 |
| Leadwood | p. 226 |
| Marula | p. 230 |
| Mobola-plum | p. 170 |
| Paperbark Acacia | p. 174 |
| Peeling-bark Ochna | p. 136 |
| Red Currant-rhus | p. 372 |
| Red-leaved Fig | p. 288 |
| River Bushwillow | p. 376 |
| Sickle-bush | p. 258 |
| Splendid Acacia | p. 384 |
| Sweet-thorn Acacia | p. 208 |
| Tamboti | p. 388 |
| Umbrella Acacia | p. 262 |
| Velvet Bushwillow | p. 304 |

### Jacana

Jacana is keen to start a register which will record trees that have any historical or geographical significance within Southern Africa. You are invited to contact Jacana at (011) 648-1157 to discuss any trees of interest that might be included in a future publication.

### Sangiro's Camel-thorn Acacia

*Acacia erioloba*
Here, and on page 29, is a photograph of a Camel-thorn Acacia which grows near Brits, alongside the ruins of the house of Sangiro, the famous Afrikaans author. His well-loved "Op Oerwoud en Vlakte" has been a setwork in South African schools for years. It is said that he sat next to this tree when writing. The tree itself is of interest because it was struck by lightning and fell over with some roots still functional. It then grew four new major trunks which appear to be independent trees.

See also pages 240 - 243 for more information on this species.

# Gardening

Indigenous trees are ideally suited for gardens as they require minimum care, and attract birds and butterflies. The following information has been summarised to help you decide which trees will give you the most pleasure in your garden. The most important considerations before choosing a tree are how large the tree will be when grown, and whether it loses its leaves in winter or not. After that, it is a matter of choice as to the function of the tree in providing shade, acting as a hedge, or offering you the thrill of showy flowers or fruit in certain seasons.

Jacket-plum, page 272

## NURSERIES

The following nurseries in the Bushveld stock indigenous trees, and will help you with detailed planting instructions.

Any nursery that would like to be included in this list, should contact Jacana (011) 648-1157.

| BUSHVELD NURSERIES | |
|---|---|
| **Cullinan** | |
| Bergsig Kwekery | (012) 732-0128 |
| **Honeydew** | |
| Princess Groot Bome | (011) 795-3675 |
| Random Harvest Nursery | (011) 957-2758 |
| **Pretoria** | |
| Malanseuns | (012) 549-2128 |
| Geoffs Garden Centre | (012) 46-3264 |
| Tip Top Wholesale Nursery | (012) 54-22103 |
| **Britz** | |
| Bark Enterprises | (012) 252-7582 |
| Grass Roots Nursery | (012) 252-7235 |
| **Hartebeespoort** | |
| Rosendal Farms | (012) 253-0442 |
| Bristle Cone Nursery | (012) 207-1041 |
| **Schagen** | |
| Fishwick's Nursery | (013) 733-4270 |
| **Hoedspruit** | |
| Eden Nursery | (015) 793-2266 |
| **Gravelotte** | |
| Green Gables Nursery | 082 808 9187 |
| **Mtunzini** | |
| Indigenous Tree Nursery | (0353) 40-2530 |
| **Ellisras** | |
| Connies Nursery | (014) 763-3423 |
| **Louis Trichardt** | |
| Capricorn Garden Centre | (015) 516-3827 |
| **Midrand** | |
| Eco-scapes | 082 892 8860 |

## BONSAI

Some trees are ideal to grow as bonsai from seeds or cuttings, while others are not successful. Most people start with a full-grown tree bought from an expert and develop the hobby thereafter. Below is a list of trees that are covered in this book. A useful contact in the Highveld is Bonsai Friend, Randfontein (011) 698-3002. They will tell you of a distributor near you in the Bushveld.

| BONSAI TREE LIST | |
|---|---|
| African Olive | p. 184 |
| African White-stinkwood | p. 360 |
| Baobab | p. 86 |
| Big-leaf Fever-tree | p. 162 |
| Black-monkey Acacia | p. 218 |
| Black-thorn Acacia | p. 250 |
| Brittlewood Nuxia | p. 108 |
| Buffalo-thorn | p. 188 |
| Camel-thorn Acacia | p. 240 |
| Common Wild Fig | p. 196 |
| Jacket-plum | p. 272 |
| Karree | p. 368 |
| Knob-thorn Acacia | p. 222 |
| Large-leaved Rock Fig | p. 276 |
| Moepel Red-milkwood | p. 334 |
| Paperbark Acacia | p. 174 |
| Red Ivorywood | p. 342 |
| Red-leaved Fig | p. 288 |
| River Bushwillow | p. 376 |
| Robust Acacia | p. 384 |
| Sacred Coral-tree | p. 148 |
| Sickle-bush | p. 258 |
| Sweet-thorn Acacia | p. 208 |
| Tamboti | p. 388 |
| Umbrella Acacia | p. 262 |
| Velvet Bushwillow | p. 304 |
| Weeping Lavender-tree | p. 354 |
| Wild-pear Dombeya | p. 156 |

# CHOOSING THE RIGHT TREES

## TALL TREES CAN GROW OVER 10 METRES

| | Height | Showy flower | Showy fruit/pod | Ornamental | Deciduous | Evergreen | Provide shade | Seed or cutting | Frost/Drought res. | Fast-growing | Invasive roots |
|---|---|---|---|---|---|---|---|---|---|---|---|
| African White-stinkwood | 12 - 30 m | | | | • | | • | S | F | • | |
| Baobab | 10 - 25 m | Oct - Nov | Jan - May | • | • | | | S | D | | |
| Big-leaf Fever-tree | 6 - 30 m | | | | • | | | S | | | |
| Broom-cluster Fig | 10 - 22 m | | Jun - Jan | | | • | | C | | • | • |
| Burkea | 8 - 10 m | | | | • | | • | S | D | | |
| Camel-thorn Acacia | 4 - 16 m | Jul - Nov | Dec - Mar | | • | | • | S | D/F | | |
| Common Wild fig | 10 - 20 m | | Aug - Dec | | • | | | S/C | D/F | • | • |
| Flame-pod Acacia | 3 - 12 m | Sep - Feb | Dec - Jun | | • | | | | | | |
| Kiaat Bloodwood | 5 - 15 m | | Feb - Aug | | • | | • | C | | | |
| Knob-thorn Acacia | 5 - 20 m | Jul - Sep | | | • | | • | S | D | | |
| Leadwood | 15 m | | | | • | | • | S | D | | |
| Marula | 5 - 17 m | | | | • | | • | S | D | | |
| Robust Acacia | 8 - 15 m | Jul - Oct | | | • | | | S | | • | |
| Sacred Coral-tree | 4 - 12 m | Jun - Oct | Sep - Feb | • | • | | • | S | D/F | • | |
| Umdoni Waterberry | 5 - 25 m | Oct - Jun | Jun - Jan | | | • | • | S | | • | |
| White Kirkia | 6 - 20 m | | | | • | | • | S/C | D | | |

## MEDIUM TREES OFTEN GROW UP TO 10 METRES

| | Height | Showy flower | Showy fruit/pod | Ornamental | Deciduous | Evergreen | Provide shade | Seed or cutting | Frost/Drought res. | Fast-growing | Invasive roots |
|---|---|---|---|---|---|---|---|---|---|---|---|
| African Olive | 4 - 10 m | | | | | • | • | | D/F | | |
| African Weeping-wattle | 5 - 10 m | Sep - Feb | Feb - May | | • | | • | S | D | • | |
| Black-monkey Acacia | 4 - 12 m | Oct - Jan | | | | • | | S | | | • |
| Brittlewood Nuxia | 2 - 20 m | Mar - Jul | | | | • | • | | | | |
| Buffalo-thorn Jujube | 3 - 12 m | | | | • | | | S | D/F | • | |
| Bushveld Bead-Bean | 5 - 10 m | Jul - Oct | Sep - Apr | | • | | | S | D/F | • | |
| Forest Karree | 3 - 25 m | | | | | • | | C | D/F | | |
| Ladies Cabbage-tree | 4 - 10 m | | Oct - Dec | • | | • | | | | • | |
| Lavender Tree | 4 - 10 m | | | | | • | | S | | | |
| Live-long Lannea | 5 - 12 m | | | • | • | | • | S/C | D | • | |
| Mobola-plum | 3 - 24 m | | | | | • | • | S | | • | |
| Moepel Red-milkwood | 3 - 15 m | | | | | • | • | S | D/F | • | |
| Mountain Kirkia | 5 - 10 m | | | | • | | • | S/C | F | | |
| Naboom Euphorbia | 7 - 15 m | | | • | | • | | S/C | D | | |
| Paperbark Acacia | 7 - 15 m | Oct - Dec | | | • | | • | | | • | |
| Paperbark Albizia | 8 - 15 m | Aug - Nov | Sep - Dec | | • | | | S | D | • | • |
| Red Ivorywood | 3 - 15 m | | | | | • | • | S | D/F | • | |
| River Bushwillow | 5 - 15 m | | | | | • | • | S | D/F | • | |
| Silver Cluster-leaf | 6 - 20 m | | Jan - Jun | | • | | | | D/F | | |
| Sweet-thorn Acacia | 4 - 15 m | Oct - Apr | | | • | | | S | D/F | • | |
| Tamboti | 5 - 12 m | | | | • | | | S | D/F | | |
| Umbrella Acacia | 5 - 15 m | Oct - Feb | Dec - Jun | • | • | | • | S | D/F | | |
| Velvet Bushwillow | 4 - 12 m | | Jan - Sep | | • | | | S | F | | |
| Weeping Faurea | 7 - 10 m | Oct - Jan | Dec - Feb | • | | • | | S | D/F | | |
| Wild-pear Dombeya | 3 - 9 m | Jul - Oct | | | • | | | S | D/F | | |

## SHORT TREES AVERAGE GROWTH UP TO 5 METRES

| | Height | Showy flower | Showy fruit/pod | Ornamental | Deciduous | Evergreen | Provide shade | Seed or cutting | Frost/Drought res. | Fast-growing | Invasive roots |
|---|---|---|---|---|---|---|---|---|---|---|---|
| Black-thorn Acacia | 3 - 9 m | Aug - Nov | | | • | | | S | D | | |
| Bushveld Resin-tree | 3 - 10 m | | | | • | | | S | D/F | • | |
| Bushveld Shepherds-tree | 3 - 7 m | | | • | | • | | | | | |
| Common Hook-thorn Acacia | 3 - 12 m | Sep - Nov | | | • | | • | S | D/F | | |
| Eastern Sesame-bush | 3 - 6 m | Nov - Feb | Dec - Apr | • | • | | | | | | |
| Hairy-leaved Monkey-orange | 3 - 8 m | | Mar - Aug | | • | | | S | | • | |
| Highveld Protea | 2 - 7 m | Oct - Mar | All year | • | | • | | S | F | | |
| Highveld Silver-oak | 2 - 8 m | | | • | • | | | | F | | |
| Hornpod-tree | 4 - 10 m | | Mar - Aug | | • | | | S | | • | |
| Jacket-plum | 4 - 10 m | | Dec - Jul | | • | | • | S | D | | |
| Karree | 4 - 9 m | | | | | • | • | S/C | D/F | • | |
| Kooboo-berry | 3 - 15 m | | Jan - Jun | | • | | | | D/F | | |
| Large-fruited Bushwillow | 5 - 15 m | | Feb - Oct | • | | | | S | | | |
| Large-leaved Rock Fig | up to 6 m | | | | • | | | C | D | | • |
| Large Sourplum | 1 - 6 m | | Nov - Jan | | • | | | S | D/F | | |
| Lavender Croton | 3 - 8 m | | Dec - Jun | | • | | | | D/F | | |
| Peeling-bark Ochna | 3 - 7 m | Aug - Nov | Oct - Jan | | • | | | | D | | |
| Pipe-stem Fingerleaf | 3 - 15 m | | | | • | | | | | | |
| Red Bushwillow | 4 - 7 m | | Jan - May | | • | | | | D/F | | |
| Red-leaved Fig | 3 - 13 m | | | | • | | | S/C | D/F | • | • |
| Rock Tree-nettle | 3 - 7 m | | | | • | | | S/C | | | |
| Russet Bushwillow | 3 - 5 m | | Dec - Jul | | • | | | S | D/F | • | |
| Scented-pod Acacia | 4 - 7 m | Sep - May | Mar - Sep | | • | | | S | D/F | | |
| Shepherds-tree | 3 - 8 m | | | • | | • | | S/C | D | | |
| Sickle-bush | 2 - 6 m | Oct - Jan | May - Sep | | • | | | S/C | D | | |
| Silver Raisin | 2 - 10 m | Oct - Jan | | | • | | | S | | | |
| Small Knobwood | 4 - 7 m | | Nov - Jun | | • | | | | D/F | | |
| Small-leaved Guarri | 3 - 6 m | | | | | • | | | D/F | | |
| Squat Star-chestnut | 3 - 6 m | | Aug - Mar | • | • | | | | | | |
| Stamvrug Milkplum | 2 - 10 m | | Dec - Feb | | | • | | S/C | D/F | • | |
| Tall Firethorn Corkwood | 2 - 6 m | | | • | • | | | S/C | D/F | • | |
| White Cats-whiskers | 2 - 15 m | Nov - Apr | | | • | | | S/C | | • | |

**Seed or cutting (S/C)** indicates how you can propagate this tree.

**Frost/Drought res. (F/D)** indicates trees that are frost- and/or drought-resistant.

**Height** indicates the normal range of the mature tree in a habitat that suits it in the wild.

Sacred Coral-tree, page 148

# Places to tree spot

The destinations listed on the following six pages cross-correlate with both the five Ecozones and the Maps on pages 410 - 415. Information that will enable you contact them is combined with data to help you decide where you would like to tree spot. Jacana has contacted every venue listed here, but not visited them all. They have been included because they appear to be the best tree spotting venues of the Bushveld. Those with actual lists of indigenous trees on their property have bullets in the column "Tree List".

## Central Mountains Destinations

|  | TEL. NO. | LOCATION | AUTHORITY | Accommodation | Shop on site | Restaurant |
|---|---|---|---|:---:|:---:|:---:|
| D'Nyala Nature Reserve & Mokolo Dam | (014) 763-5148 | Ellisras | Prov | • | | |
| Doorndraai Dam Nature Reserve | (014) 743-1911 | Potgietersrus | Prov | | | |
| Entabeni Nature Reserve | (014) 743-1131 | Naboomspruit | P | • | | • |
| Kransberg Walks and Hikes | (014) 777-1745 | Thabazimbi | P | | | |
| Inkwe Valley Game Reserve | (014) 743-1891 | Naboomspruit | P | • | | |
| Inyathi Nature Reserve | (011) 880-5907 | Skukuza | P | • | • | |
| Keta Nature Reserve | (014) 765-0264 | Marken | P | • | | • |
| Kololo Game Reserve | (014) 721-0920 | Vaalwater | P | • | • | |
| Lapalala Wilderness | (011) 453-7645 | Melkrivier | P | • | | |
| Lindani Game Farm | 083 631 5579 | Vaalwater | P | • | | |
| Mabalingwe Nature Reserve | (014) 736-2334 | Warmbaths | P | • | • | • |
| Madikela Game Reserve | 083 759 0088 | Vaalwater | P | • | | |
| Marakele National Park | (014) 773-7145 | Mafikeng | Prov | • | | |
| Mokolo Nature Reserve | (014) 755-4221 | Ellisras | Prov | | | |
| Rhenosterpoort Bush Camp | (012) 662-1140 | Nylstroom | P | • | | |
| Sambane Game Lodge | (014) 743-0572 | Naboomspruit | P | • | • | • |
| Shingwedzi Game Ranch | (014) 734-1735 | Nylstroom | P | • | | |
| Spreeuwal Game Farm | (014) 763-3011 | Ellisras | P | • | | |
| Thabaphaswa Trails | (015) 491-4882 | Potgietersrus | P | • | | |
| Tibani Lodge | (015) 491-5609 | Potgietersrus | P | • | • | • |
| Touchstone Game Ranch | (014) 765-0230 | Marken | P | • | | • |
| Yellow Wood Game Lodge | (011) 432-3812 | Nylstroom | P | • | | • |
| Waterberg Game Reserve | 083 630 3615 | Vaalwater | P | • | • | • |

## Northern Mountains Destinations

|  | TEL. NO. | LOCATION | AUTHORITY | Accommodation | Shop on site | Restaurant |
|---|---|---|---|:---:|:---:|:---:|
| Aventura Eco - Tshipise | (015) 539-0651 | Tshipise | P | • | • | • |
| Bergpan Eco | (015) 593-0127 | Louis Trichardt | P | • | • | |
| Blouberg Nature Reserve | (015) 593-0702 | Vivo | Prov | • | | |
| Camp Mangwele | (015) 583-0356 | Louis Trichardt | Tribal (Venda) | | | |
| Goro Game Reserve | (015) 575-1445 | Louis Trichardt | P | • | | |
| Greater Kuduland Safaris | (015) 539-0720 | Tshipise | P | • | | |
| Lesheba Wilderness | (015) 593-0076 | Louis Trichardt | P | • | | |
| Medike Mountain Reserve | (015) 516-0481 | Louis Trichardt | P | • | | |
| Northwich Game Reserve | (015) 517-7185 | Louis Trichardt | P | • | • | |
| Nwanedi National Park | (015) 539-0703 | Tshipise | Prov | • | • | |
| Schoemansdal Enviro Education Centre | (015) 516-4273 | Louis Trichardt | Prov | • | • | |
| Wallers Camp | (015) 963-3802 | Masisi | M | | | |

Authority key: Prov = Provincial; P = Private; M = Municipal

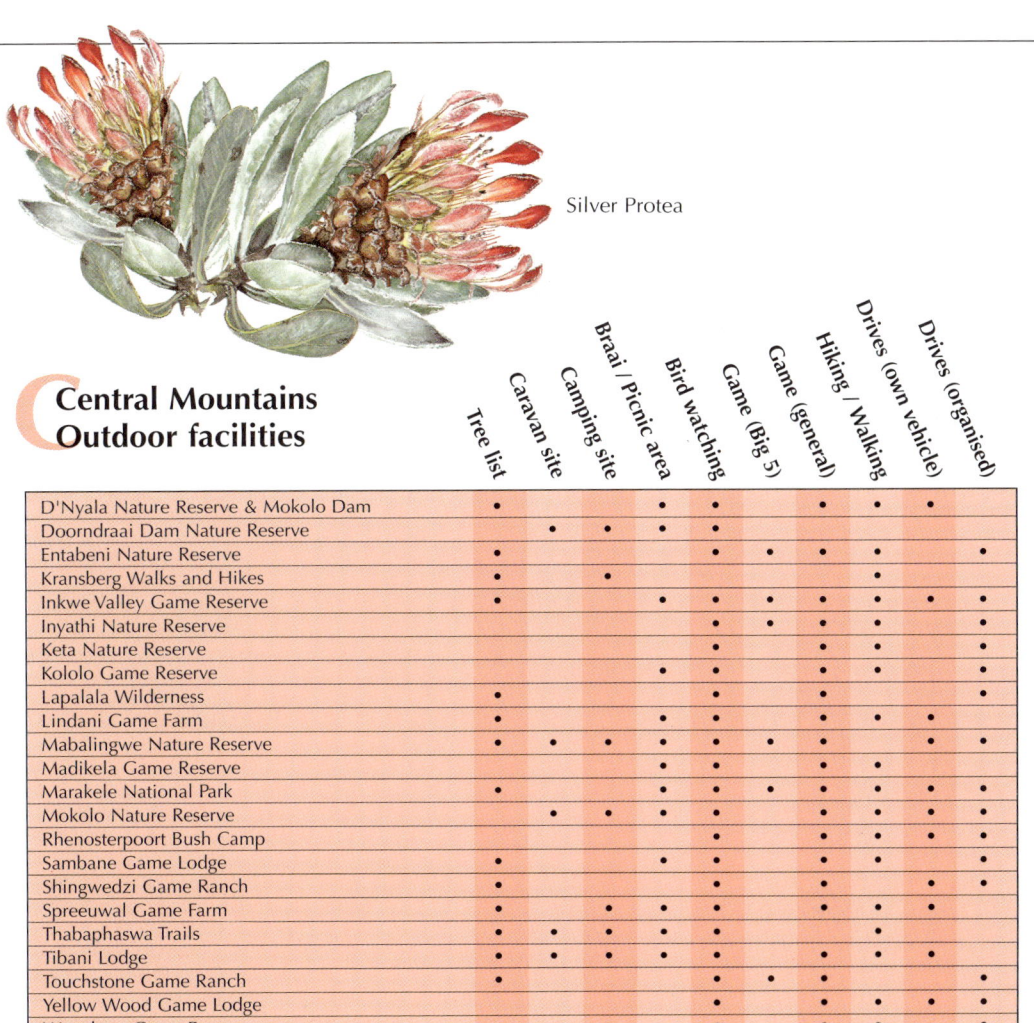

Silver Protea

## Central Mountains Outdoor facilities

| | Tree list | Caravan site | Camping site | Braai / Picnic area | Bird watching | Game (Big 5) | Game (general) | Hiking / Walking | Drives (own vehicle) | Drives (organised) |
|---|---|---|---|---|---|---|---|---|---|---|
| D'Nyala Nature Reserve & Mokolo Dam | • | | | • | • | | • | • | • | |
| Doorndraai Dam Nature Reserve | | • | • | • | • | | | | | |
| Entabeni Nature Reserve | • | | | | | • | • | • | • | • |
| Kransberg Walks and Hikes | • | | • | | | | | | | |
| Inkwe Valley Game Reserve | • | | | | • | • | • | • | • | • |
| Inyathi Nature Reserve | | | | | | • | • | • | • | • |
| Keta Nature Reserve | | | | | | | • | • | • | • |
| Kololo Game Reserve | | | | | • | | • | • | • | • |
| Lapalala Wilderness | • | | | | | | • | • | | • |
| Lindani Game Farm | • | | | | • | | • | • | • | • |
| Mabalingwe Nature Reserve | • | • | • | • | • | • | • | • | • | • |
| Madikela Game Reserve | | | | | • | | • | • | | • |
| Marakele National Park | • | | | | • | • | • | • | • | • |
| Mokolo Nature Reserve | | • | • | • | • | | • | • | • | • |
| Rhenosterpoort Bush Camp | | | | | | | • | • | • | • |
| Sambane Game Lodge | • | | | | • | | • | | • | • |
| Shingwedzi Game Ranch | • | | | | | | • | • | • | • |
| Spreeuwal Game Farm | • | | • | • | • | | • | | • | |
| Thabaphaswa Trails | • | • | • | • | • | | | | • | |
| Tibani Lodge | • | • | • | • | • | | | • | • | |
| Touchstone Game Ranch | • | | | | | • | • | | | • |
| Yellow Wood Game Lodge | | | | | | • | • | • | • | • |
| Waterberg Game Reserve | • | | | | | • | | • | • | • |

## Northern Mountains Outdoor facilities

| | Tree list | Caravan site | Camping site | Braai / Picnic area | Bird watching | Game (Big 5) | Game (general) | Hiking / Walking | Drives (own vehicle) | Drives (organised) |
|---|---|---|---|---|---|---|---|---|---|---|
| Aventura Eco - Tshipise | | • | • | • | • | | | • | • | • |
| Bergpan Eco | | • | • | • | • | | | • | • | • |
| Blouberg Nature Reserve | • | | | | • | • | • | • | • | |
| Camp Mangwele | • | | | • | • | | • | • | • | |
| Goro Game Reserve | • | | | | • | • | • | • | | • |
| Greater Kuduland Safaris | • | | | • | • | • | • | • | | • |
| Lesheba Wilderness | • | | | | • | | • | • | • | • |
| Medike Mountain Reserve | • | | • | | • | | • | • | • | • |
| Northwich Game Reserve | | | • | | • | | • | • | • | • |
| Nwanedi National Park | • | • | • | • | • | | • | • | • | |
| Schoemansdal Environmental Education Centre | • | | | • | • | | • | • | • | • |
| Wallers Camp | • | | | | • | | • | • | • | • |

# Mixed Bushveld Destinations

| | TEL. NO. | LOCATION | AUTHORITY | Accommodation | Shop on site | Restaurant |
|---|---|---|---|:---:|:---:|:---:|
| Aventura Eco - Loskopdam | (013) 262-3077 | Middleberg | P | • | • | • |
| Ben Albert's Nature Reserve | (014) 777-1670 | Thabazimbi | P | • | • | |
| Ben Lavin Nature Reserve | (015) 516-4534 | Louis Trichardt | P | • | • | • |
| Carpidiem Game Lodge | (013) 262-2426 | Groblersdal | P | • | | • |
| Cosa Nostra Hunting Lodge | (015) 575-1091 | Alldays | P | • | | • |
| Dikhololo Nature Reserve | (012) 277-1200 | Brits | P | • | • | • |
| Gethlane Lodge | (013) 231-7316 | Burghersfort | P | • | | • |
| Goedgedacht Game Lodge | (013) 262-2119 | Groblersdal | P | • | | |
| Golden Leopard Resorts - Mankwe | 0800 60 1092 | Sun City | Prov | • | | |
| Golden Leopard Resorts - Metswedi | 0800 60 1092 | Sun City | Prov | • | | |
| Golden Leopard Resorts - Moretele | 0800 60 1092 | Assen | Prov | | | |
| Golden Leopard Resorts - Phundufudu | 0800 60 1092 | Assen | Prov | • | | |
| Golden Leopard Resorts - Pitjane | 0800 60 1092 | Assen | Prov | | | |
| Golden Leopard Resorts -Borakalalo | (014) 555-6135 | Assen | S | • | • | • |
| Golden Leopard Resorts Bakgatla | (014) 555-6135 | Sun City | Prov | • | • | • |
| Golden Leopart Resorts - Manyane | (014) 555-6135 | Sun City | Prov | • | • | • |
| Hannah Lodge | (013) 238-0483 | Ohrigstad | P | • | | • |
| Hartbeeshoek Nature Reserve | (012) 251-0992 | Britz | P | • | • | |
| Hartebeespoortdam Nature Reserves | – | Cosmos | Prov | | | |
| Hoogland Hydro | (012) 370-3322 | Pretoria (Erafmia) | P | • | | |
| Ingwe Bush Camp | 082 449 9075 | Magaliesberg | P | • | | |
| Khumula Game Lodge | (013) 231-7122 | Burgersfort | P | • | | • |
| Klein Maricopoort Game Farm | (018) 646-0146 | Groot Marico | Prov | • | • | |
| Kleine Scheidegg | (014) 577-1733 | Magaliesberg | P | • | | |
| Kruisrivier Nature Reserve | (013) 262-2297 | Groblersdal | P | • | | • |
| Kudu Canyon Nature Reserve | (011) 884-3662 | Vaalwater | P | • | | |
| Kwa Maritane Game Lodge | (014) 552-1820 | Sun City | P | • | | • |
| Langjan Nature Reserve | 083 771 8730 | Sabie | P | • | | |
| Legalameetse Nature Reserve | (015) 383-0015 | Trichardtsdal | Prov | • | | |
| Loskop Dam Nature Reserve | (013) 363-4184 | Groblersdal | P | | | |
| Mabula Lodge | (014) 734-0000 | Warmbaths | P | • | • | • |
| Madikwe Game Reserve | (018) 3672 x2411 | Zeerust | Prov | • | | |
| Manyane Game Lodge | (018) 381-6021 | Mafikeng | P | • | • | • |
| Mokolo Nature Reserve | (014) 763-5447 | Ellisras | Prov | | | |
| Montane Log Cabins | 082 893 4208 | Thabazimbi | P | • | | |
| Motlhware Game Lodge | (018) 642-1994 | Zeerust | P | • | | |
| Mountain Sanctuary Park | (014) 534-0114 | Kroondal | P | • | | |
| Nylsvley Nature Reserve | (014) 743-1074 | Nylstroom | Prov | • | | |
| Percy Fyfe Nature Reserve | (015) 491-5678 | Potgietersrus | Prov | • | | |
| Pietersburg Game Reserve | (015) 290-2331 | Pietersburg | M | • | • | |
| Pilanesberg National Park | (014) 555-6135 | Sun City | Prov | • | • | • |
| Potlake Nature Reserve | (015) 615-6009 | Pietersburg | Prov | | | |
| Pretoria Botanical Gardens | (012) 804-3200 | Pretoria | | | | |
| Pretty Place | (014) 577-1733 | Magaliesberg | P | • | | |
| Rhino Bushveld Eco-Park | (014) 773-1403 | Thabazimbi | P | • | | |
| Rra Ditau | (014) 772-2716 | Thabazimbi | P | • | | |
| Rustenburg Nature Reserve | (014) 533-2050 | Rustenburg | Prov | • | | |
| Syferfontein Game Lodge | (013) 261-1238 | Marble Hall | P | • | | |
| Schuindraai Nature Reserve | (013) 261-1607 | Marble Hall | Prov | • | | |
| Tau Game Lodge | (018) 365-9027 | Zeerust | P | • | • | |
| Tibani Lodge | (015) 491-4882 | Potgietersrus | P | • | • | • |
| Tilodi Wilderness | (014) 735-0603 | Warmbaths | M | • | • | |
| Vaalkop Dam Nature Reserve | (014) 555-5351 | Mogwase | Prov | | | |

Weeping Faurea, page 350

## Mixed Bushveld Outdoor facilities

| | Tree list | Caravan site | Camping site | Braai / Picnic area | Bird watching | Game (Big 5) | Game (general) | Hiking / Walking | Drives (own vehicle) | Drives (organised) |
|---|---|---|---|---|---|---|---|---|---|---|
| Aventura Eco - Loskopdam | • | • | • | • | • | | • | • | • | • |
| Ben Albert's Nature Reserve | | • | • | • | | | • | • | • | • |
| Ben Lavin Nature Reserve | • | • | • | • | | | • | • | • | • |
| Carpidiem Game Lodge | | | | | | • | • | • | | • |
| Cosa Nostra Hunting Lodge | • | | • | • | • | | • | • | • | • |
| Dikhololo Nature Reserve | • | | | • | • | | • | • | • | • |
| Gethlane Lodge | • | | | | | | • | • | • | • |
| Goedgedacht Game Lodge | | | | | | | • | • | • | • |
| Golden Leopard Resorts - Mankwe | • | | | | | • | • | • | • | • |
| Golden Leopard Resorts - Metswedi | • | | | • | • | | • | • | • | • |
| Golden Leopard Resorts - Moretele | • | | • | • | | | • | • | • | • |
| Golden Leopard Resorts - Phundufudu | | | | | • | | • | • | • | • |
| Golden Leopard Resorts - Pitjane | • | | | • | • | | • | • | • | • |
| Golden Leopard Resorts -Borakalalo National Park | • | • | • | • | | • | • | • | • | • |
| Golden Leopard Resorts Bakgatla | | • | • | • | | | • | • | • | • |
| Golden Leopart Resorts - Manyane | • | • | • | • | | | • | • | • | • |
| Hannah Lodge | | | | | • | • | | • | • | • |
| Hartbeeshoek Nature Reserve | • | • | • | • | • | | • | • | • | |
| Hartebeespoortdam Nature Reserves | | | | | | | | | | |
| Hoogland Hydro | • | | | | | | • | • | | • |
| Ingwe Bush Camp | | | | • | • | | • | • | • | • |
| Khumula Game Lodge | • | | | | | | • | • | | • |
| Klein Maricopoort Game Farm | • | | • | • | • | | • | • | • | |
| Kleine Scheidegg | | | | • | • | | • | • | | |
| Kruisrivier Nature Reserve | • | | | | | • | • | • | • | • |
| Kudu Canyon Nature Reserve | | | | • | • | | • | • | • | |
| Kwa Maritane Game Lodge | | | | | | • | • | • | • | • |
| Langjan Nature Reserve | • | | | • | • | | • | • | | |
| Legalameetse Nature Reserve | • | | | | | | | | | |
| Loskop Dam Nature Reserve | | | | | | | • | • | • | • |
| Mabula Lodge | • | | | | | • | • | • | • | • |
| Madikwe Game Reserve | | | • | | | • | • | • | | |
| Mahushe Shongwe Nature Reserve | | | | | | | • | • | • | • |
| Manyane Game Lodge | • | | | • | • | | • | • | • | |
| Mokolo Nature Reserve | • | • | • | • | | | • | | | |
| Montane Log Cabins | • | | | | | | • | • | • | |
| Motlhware Game Lodge | • | | | • | • | | • | • | | • |
| Mountain Sanctuary Park | • | • | • | • | • | | • | • | | |
| Nylsvley Nature Reserve | • | • | • | • | • | | • | • | • | |
| Percy Fyfe Nature Reserve | • | • | • | • | • | | • | • | | |
| Pietersburg Game Reserve | • | • | • | • | • | | • | • | • | • |
| Pilanesberg National Park | • | • | • | • | • | • | • | • | • | • |
| Potlake Nature Reserve | • | • | • | • | | | • | • | | |
| Pretoria Botanical Gardens | • | | | | • | | | • | | |
| Pretty Place | • | | | | • | | • | • | • | |
| Rhino Bushveld Eco-Park | • | | • | | | | • | • | • | |
| Rra Ditau | • | | | | | | • | • | • | • |
| Rustenburg Nature Reserve | • | • | • | • | • | | • | • | • | |
| Syferfontein Game Lodge | | | | • | • | | • | • | | |
| Schuindraai Nature Reserve | | | • | • | • | | • | | | |
| Tau Game Lodge | • | | | | | • | • | • | • | • |
| Tibani Lodge | | • | | • | • | | • | • | • | |
| Tilodi Wilderness | • | | | | | | • | • | • | • |
| Vaalkop Dam Nature Reserve | • | | | | • | | • | • | • | |

# Sour Bushveld Destinations

| | TEL. NO. | LOCATION | AUTHORITY | Accommodation | Shop on site | Restaurant |
|---|---|---|---|---|---|---|
| Assupol Lodge | (015) 793-3195 | Hoedspruit | P | • | | |
| Aventura Eco - Swadini | (015) 795-5141 | Hoedspruit | P | • | • | • |
| Barber Trails | (013) 712-2121 | Barberton | M | | | |
| Barberton Nature Reserve | (013) 712-2121 | Barberton | M | | | |
| Best Western Premier Lodge | (013) 741-4222 | Nelspruit | P | • | | • |
| Blyde River Canyon Nature Reserve | (013) 769-6019 | Graskop | Prov | • | • | |
| Casa Do Sol | (013) 737-8111 | Sabie | P | • | | |
| Cheetah Inn | (015) 793-1200 | Hoedspruit | P | • | | • |
| Ekutheleni | (015) 793-1211 | Hoedspruit | P | • | • | |
| Entabeni Game Lodge | (014) 743-1131 | Potgietersrus | P | • | • | • |
| Khoka Moya Safari Lodge | (015) 793-1729 | Hoedspruit | P | • | • | • |
| Kwanyoni Lodge | (013) 733-3096 | Nelspruit | P | • | | |
| Lowveld Botanical Garden | (013) 752-5531 | Nelspruit | Prov | | | • |
| Makalali Private Game Reserve | (011) 883-5786 | Hoedspruit | P | • | | |
| Modjadji Cycad Nature Reserve | (015) 232-5221 | Duiwelskloof | P | • | • | • |
| Nelspruit Nature Reserve | (013) 759-9111 | Nelspruit | M | | | |
| Ntshengane Lodge | (017) 844-1233 | Badplaas | P | • | | |
| Rose Sands | (011) 453-6525 | Machadodorp | P | • | | |
| Shiluvari Lakeside Lodge | (015) 556-3406 | Louis Trichardt | P | • | | • |
| Songimvelo Nature Reserve | (017) 883-0390 | Badplaas | Prov | • | | |
| Sudwala Caves | (013) 733-4152 | Waterval Boven | P | • | • | |
| Thornybush | (015) 793-2771 | Hoedspruit | P | • | | |
| Tom Jac Hu Bush Lodge | 082 704 4804 | Nelspruit | P | • | | |

Sweet-thorn Acacia, page 208

# Thorny Bushveld Destinations

| | TEL. NO. | LOCATION | AUTHORITY | Accommodation | Shop on site | Restaurant |
|---|---|---|---|---|---|---|
| Aventura Eco - Warmbaths | (014) 736-2200 | Warmbaths | P | • | • | • |
| Bonwa Phala Game Lodge | (014) 736-4101 | Warmbaths | P | • | | |
| Lyon Safaris | (014) 772-2935 | Thabazimbi | P | • | • | • |
| Madikwe Game Reserve | (018) 365-9027 | Thabazimbi | P | • | • | • |
| Roodeplaat Nature Reserve | (012) 808-1164 | Magaliesberg | P | • | | |
| Sondéla Nature Reserve | (014) 736-4304 | Warmbaths | P | • | • | |
| Vogelfontein Safari Lodge | (015) 667-0222 | Marble Hall | P | • | | |

# Sour Bushveld
## Outdoor facilities

| | Tree list | Caravan site | Camping site | Braai / Picnic area | Bird watching | Game (Big 5) | Game (general) | Hiking / Walking | Drives (own vehicle) | Drives (organised) |
|---|---|---|---|---|---|---|---|---|---|---|
| Assupol Lodge | | | | | • | | • | • | • | • |
| Aventura Eco - Swadini | • | • | • | • | • | | • | • | • | • |
| Barber Trails | • | | | | | | • | | • | |
| Barberton Nature Reserve | | | | | | | | | | |
| Best Western Premier Lodge | • | | | | • | | • | | • | • |
| Blyde River Canyon Nature Reserve | • | | | | • | | • | | • | |
| Casa Do Sol | • | | | | | | • | | | |
| Cheetah Inn | • | | | | | | • | | • | |
| Ekutheleni | • | • | | | | | | | | • |
| Entabeni Game Lodge | • | | | | • | • | • | • | • | • |
| Khoka Moya Safari Lodge | • | | | | | • | • | | | • |
| Kwanyoni Lodge | | | | • | | | • | | | |
| Lowveld Botanical Garden | • | | | • | • | | | • | | |
| Makalali Private Game Reserve | • | | | | | • | • | • | • | • |
| Modjadji Cycad Nature Reserve | • | • | • | • | • | | • | • | • | |
| Nelspruit Nature Reserve | | | | | | | | | | |
| Ntshengane Lodge | • | | | | • | | • | | • | • |
| Rose Sands | | | | | | | • | | | • |
| Shiluvari Lakeside Lodge | | | | | | | | | | |
| Songimvelo Nature Reserve | • | | | | • | | • | • | • | • |
| Sudwala Caves | | • | • | • | • | | • | • | • | • |
| Thornybush | • | | | | | • | | • | • | • |
| Tom Jac Hu Bush Lodge | • | | | | • | | • | | • | • |

# Thorny Bushveld
## Outdoor facilities

| | Tree list | Caravan site | Camping site | Braai / Picnic area | Bird watching | Game (Big 5) | Game (general) | Hiking / Walking | Drives (own vehicle) | Drives (organised) |
|---|---|---|---|---|---|---|---|---|---|---|
| Aventura Eco - Warmbaths | | • | • | • | • | | • | | • | |
| Bonwa Phala Game Lodge | | • | | | • | • | | • | | • |
| Lyon Safaris | | • | | | • | • | • | | • | • |
| Madikwe Game Reserve | | | • | • | | • | • | | | • |
| Roodeplaat Nature Reserve | | • | | | | | | • | • | |
| Sondéla Nature Reserve | | • | | | | | • | • | • | • |
| Vogelfontein Safari Lodge | | • | • | • | • | | | • | | • |

Common Hook-thorn Acacia, page 318

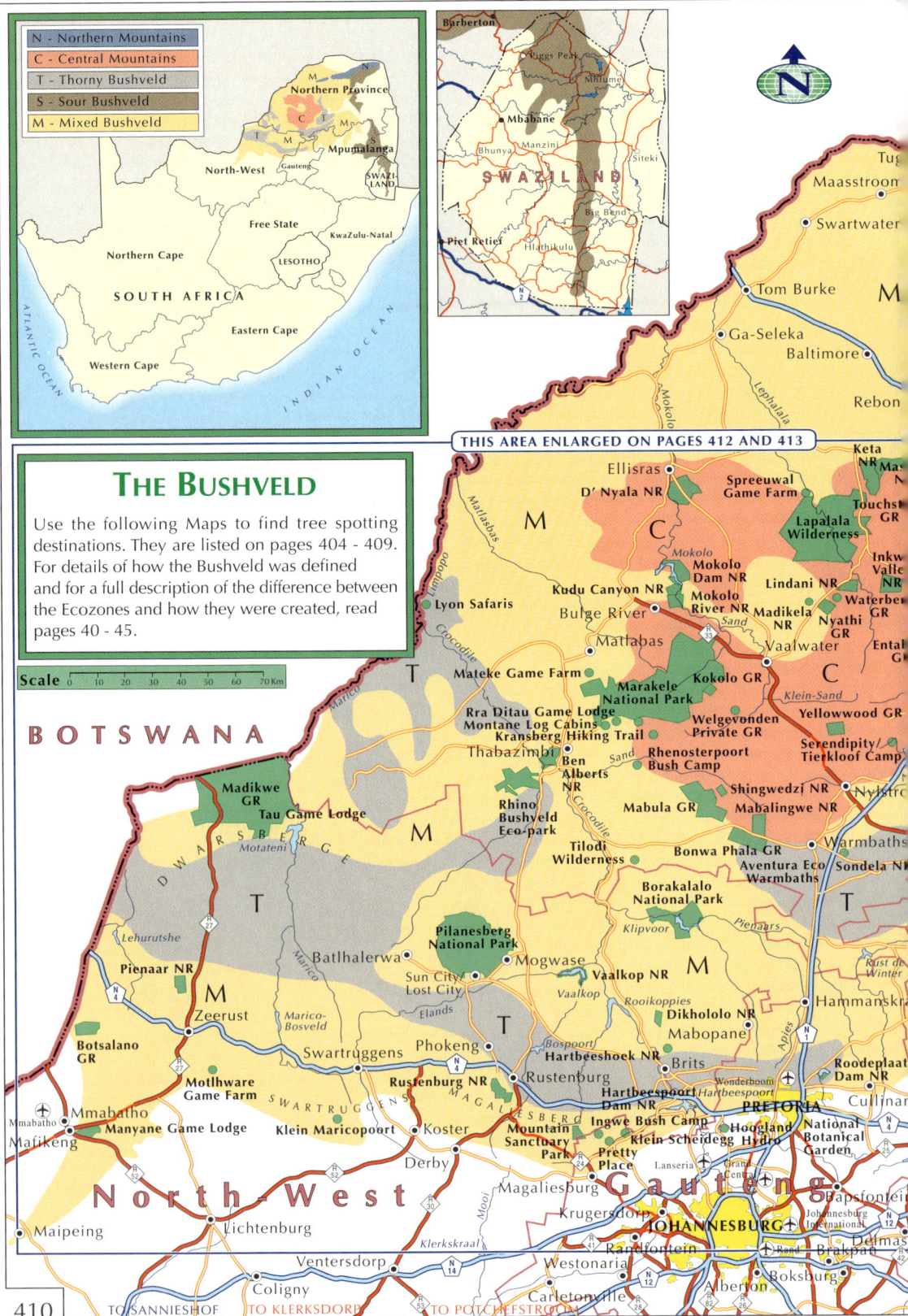

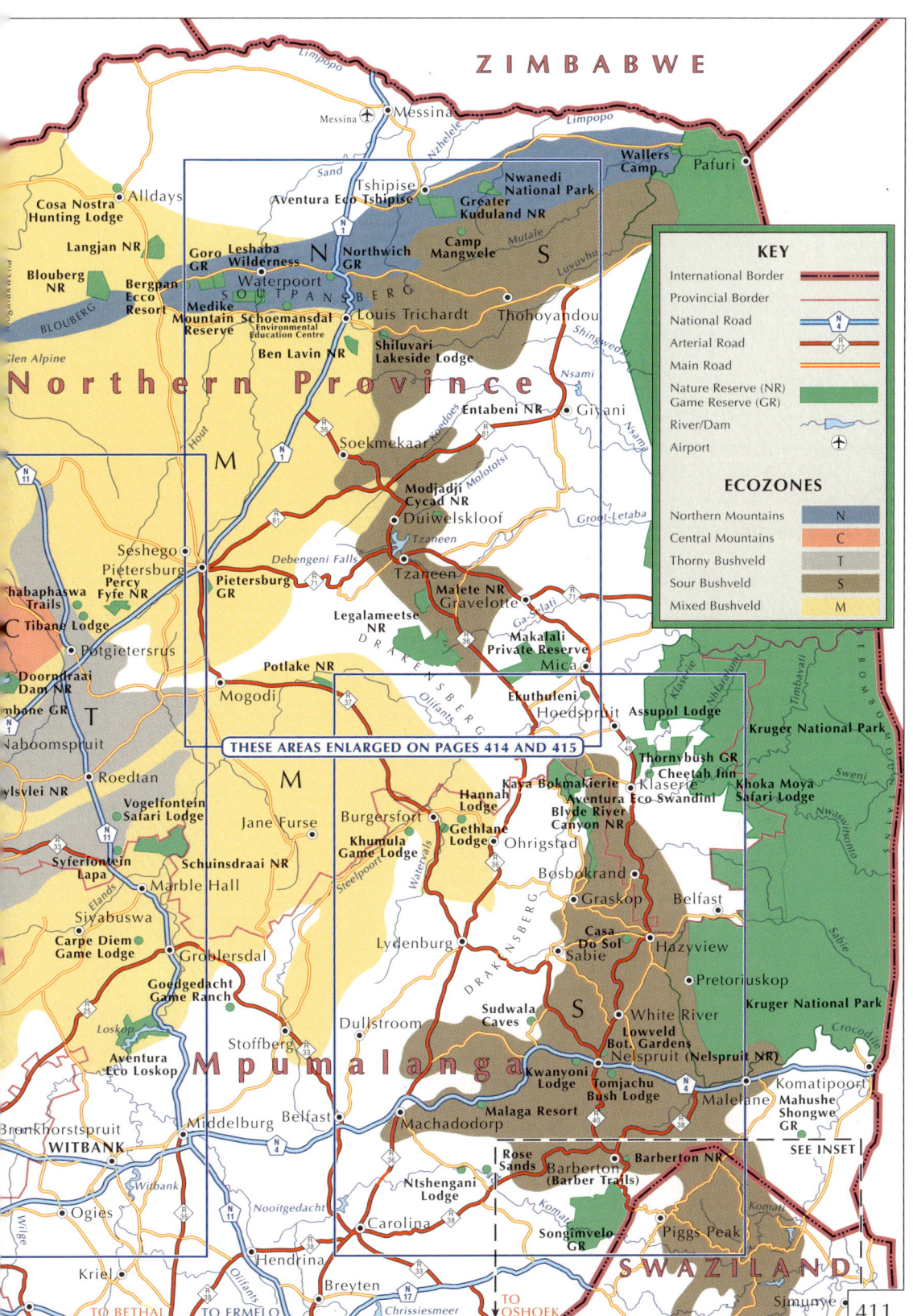

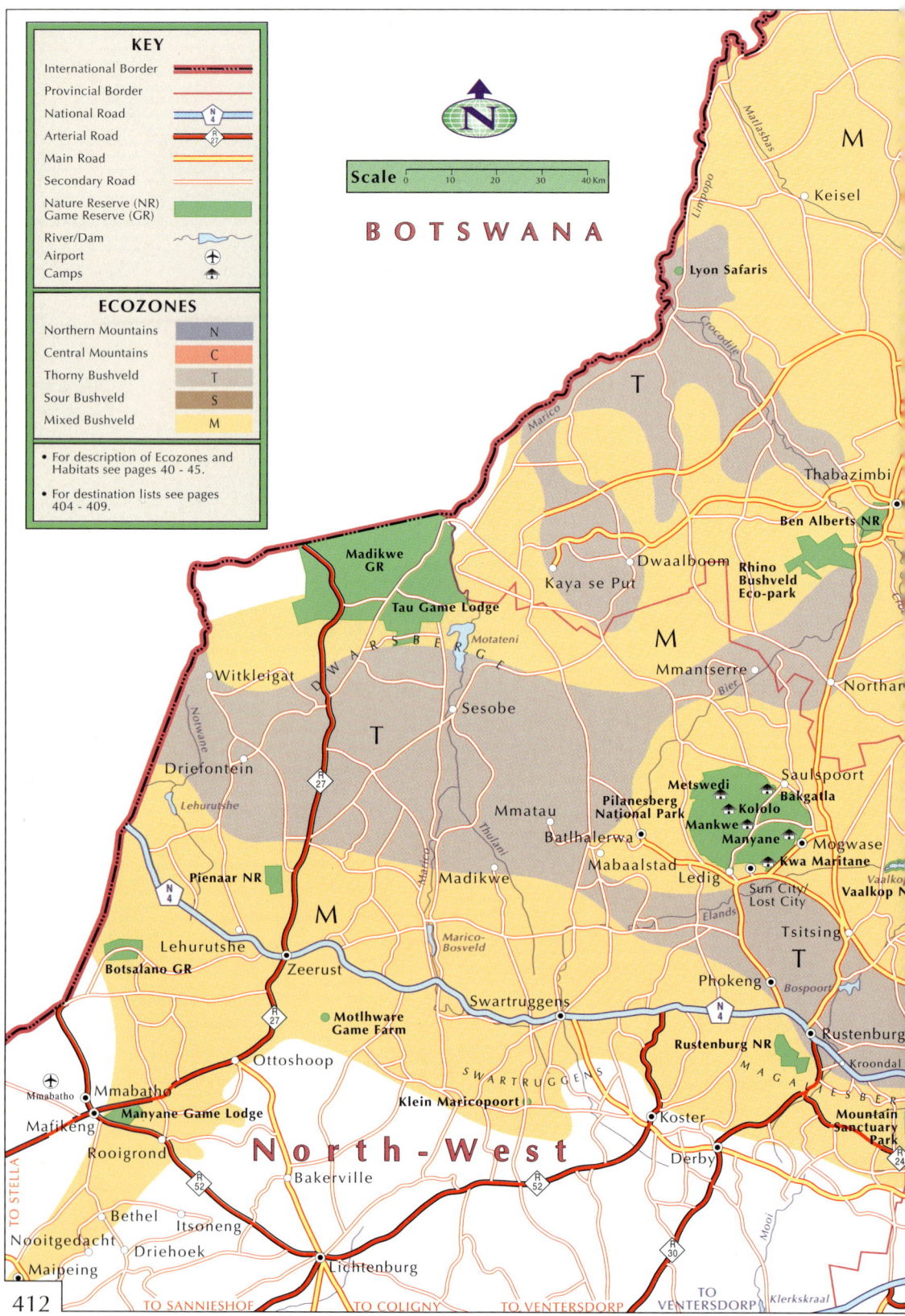

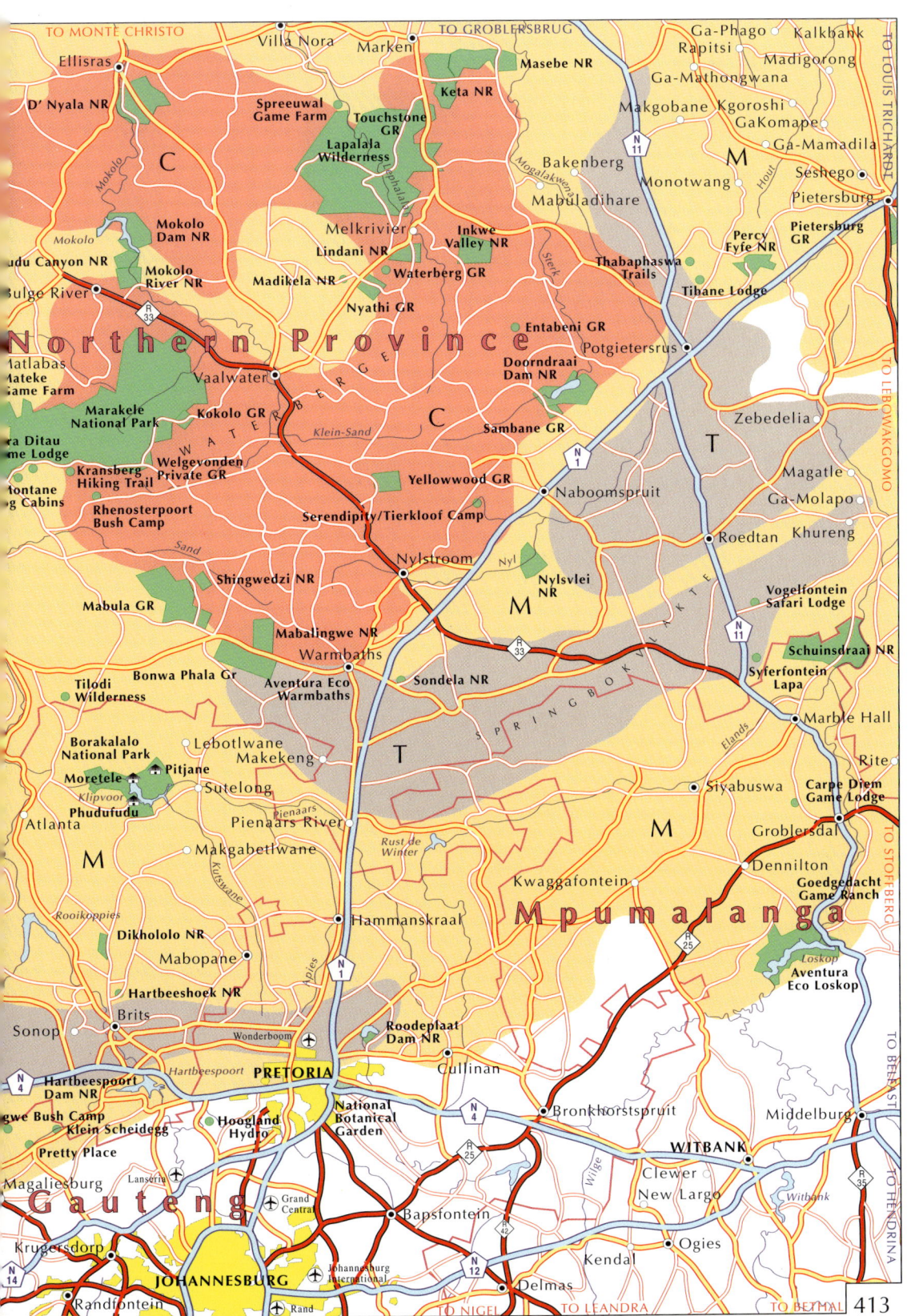

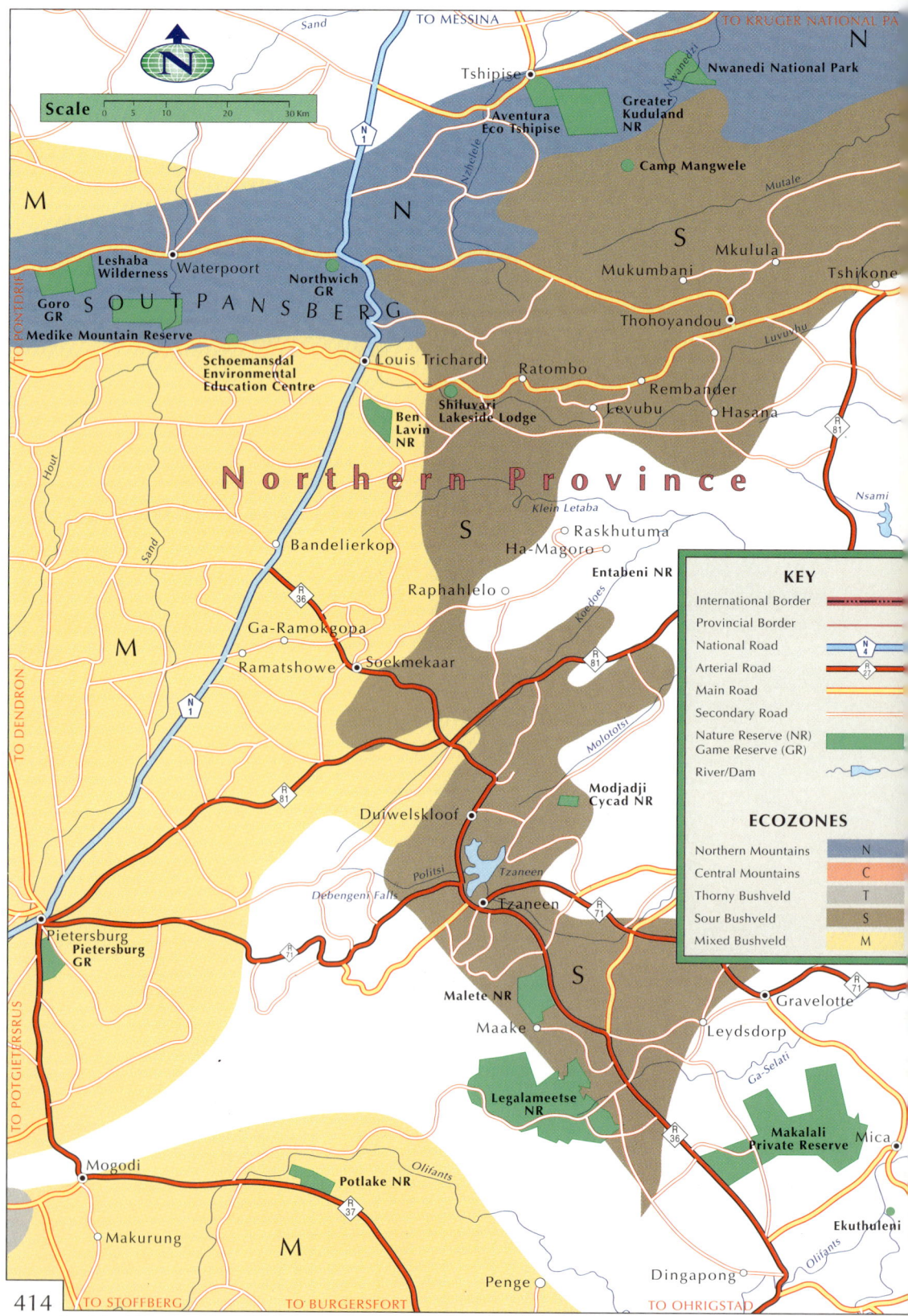

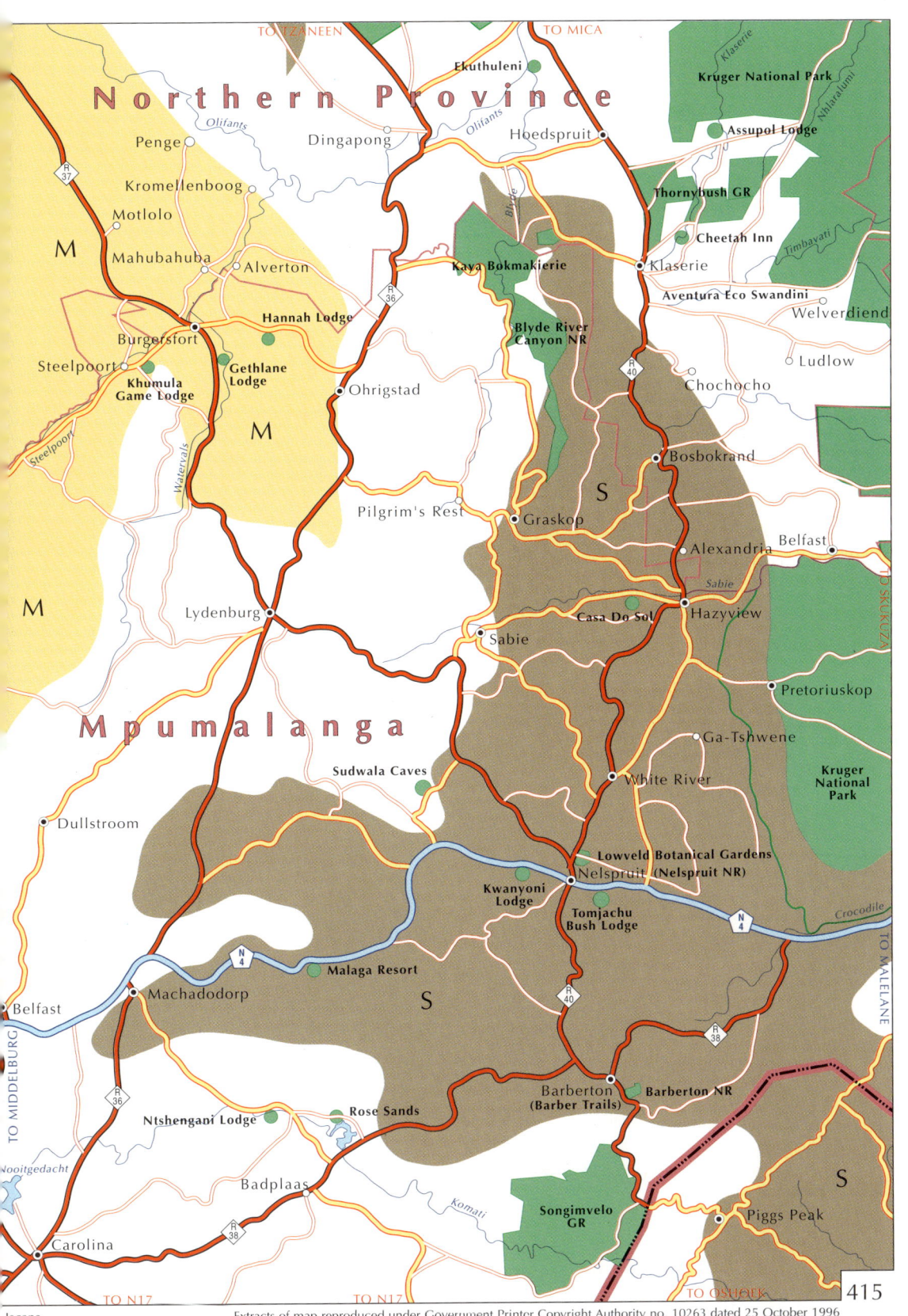

# Family features

All living things have relatives that share certain distinctive features. In plants this can be similar growth form, seed dispersal mechanism, or leaf, flower, fruit or pod structure. Scientists classify plants by their flower features which can be minute details, hardly visible to the naked eye.

As a pleasure-seeking tree spotter you will find that knowing some visible similarities between family members will help you build up methods of recognising new trees wherever you go in Africa or further afield.

The scientific classifications tend to change quite regularly, so these statistics of world and South African distribution are simply there to give you an idea of the family size and distribution.

The information includes the Ecozones where you are most likely to find each family member. This is shown by the letter C, N, M, S or T in brackets. With this information you can look for related trees in one area. Remember to check their Habitat distribution on the Ecozone Tree Lists, pages 46 - 55.

### BUSHWILLOW Combretaceae
Worldwide – 60 genera, 400 species; South Africa – well represented with 5 genera, 41 tree species.
**Family Features**
- Leaves – simple
- Flowers – spiked
- Seeds – four-winged

**Trees in this book**
Forest Bushwillow (N, M, S) p 74; Large-fruited Bushwillow (C, N, M, S, T) p 128; Leadwood (C, N, M, S) p 226; Purple-pod Cluster-leaf (N, M, S) p 30; Red Bushwillow (C, N, M, S, T) p 140; River Bushwillow (C, N, M, S, T) p 376; Russet Bushwillow (C, M, S, T) p 144; Silver Cluster-leaf (C, N, M, S, T) p 244; Velvet Bushwillow (C, N, M, S, T) p 304; Weeping Collina Bushwillow (N, S) p 75

### CABBAGE TREE Araliaceae
Worldwide – 54 genera, 650 species; South Africa – 15 tree species. Ivy family member; widely grown in gardens.
**Family Features**
- Leaves – conspicuous, large, palm-like

**Trees in this book**
African Schefflera (N, M, S) p 67; Highveld Cabbage-tree (C, M, T) p 96; Ladies Cabbage-tree (C, N, M, S, T) p 94; Silver Cabbage Tree (C, N, M, S) p 96; Simple-leaved Cabbage-tree (C, N, M, S) p 96

### CAPE MYRTLE Myrsinaceae
Worldwide – 32 genera, 1 000 species, tropical and subtropical areas; South Africa – 5 shrub or tree species.
**Family Features**
- Leaves – simple, usually alternate, gland-dotted

**Trees in this book**
Eastern Rapanea (C, N, M, S) p 32

### CAPER Capparaceae
Worldwide – 46 genera and about 700 species; South Africa – 40 species.
**Family Features**
- Leaves - variable
- Flowers - 4 free petals, numerous long stamens

**Trees in this book**
Bushveld Bead-bean (C, N, M, S, T) p 112; Bushveld Shepherds-tree (C, N, M, T) p 192; Shepherds-tree (C, N, M, S, T) p 200

### CHEESEWOOD Pittosporaceae
Worldwide – 300 species; South Africa – 1 species.
**Family Features**
- Leaves – resinous smell of liquorice when crushed
- Flowers – indistinct
- Fruit – indistinct

**Trees in this book**
Lover's Cheesewood (C, N, M, S) p 1

### CITRUS/BUCHU Rutaceae
Worldwide – 100 genera, 800 species, warm temperate areas; South Africa – 8 genera, 26 species. Some have medicinal properties.
**Family Features**
- Leaves – strong-scented, gland-dotted

**Trees in this book**
Perdepis (C, N, S, T) p 68; Small Knobwood (C, N, M, S) p 384

Large-fruited Bushwillow, page 128

**COCO PLUM** Chrysobalanaceae
Worldwide – 120 genera, about 3 000 species; South Africa – about 8 tree species, 12 genera.
**Family Features**
- Leaves – alternate, simple or compound usually with toothed margins
- Leaf-like scales (stipules) present and often conspicuous
- Flowers – showy with 5 short-stalked petals
- Fruit – many of the common fruit trees such as plum, apricot and peach belong to this family

**Trees in this book**
Mobola-plum (S) p 170; Ouhout (C, N, M, S) p 34

**DAISY** Asteraceae
Worldwide – 200 genera, 2 000 species; South Africa – about 40 shrub and/or tree species.
**Family Features**
- Flowers – dense, clustered heads resemble single flower; attractive blooms in some species

**Trees in this book**
Forest Silver-oak (N, S) p 328; Highveld Silver-oak (C, M) p 326; Lowveld Silver-oak (C, N, M, S) p 328

**DOGWOOD / BLINKBLAAR** Rhamnaceae
Worldwide – 51 genera, 600 species; South Africa – 7 genera, 20 tree species.
**Family Features**
- Leaves – shiny, simple, alternate
- Flowers – small, inconspicuous, nectar-rich

**Trees in this book**
Brown Ivorywood (N, S) p 344; Buffalo-thorn Jujube (C, N, M, S, T) p 188; Red Ivorywood (C, N, M, S) p 342

**EBONY** Ebenaceae
Worldwide – 2 genera, 485 species, mostly tropical regions; South Africa – 2 genera, 35 tree species. Wood traded by ancient merchants.
**Family Features**
- Very variable
- Leaves – simple, smooth margin

**Trees in this book**
River Guarri (S) p 186; Small-leaved Guarri (C, N, M, T) p 204

Pride-of-De Kaap Bauhinia, page 27

**ELM** Ulmaceae
Worldwide – 16 genera, over 1 000 species, tropical and temperate regions, mostly in Northern Hemisphere; South Africa – 2 genera, 5 tree or shrub species.
**Family Features**
- Leaves – simple, alternate
- Flowers – small, greenish stamen appears opposite each petal-like sepal

**Trees in this book**
African White-stinkwood (C, N, M, S, T) p 360; Pigeonwood (C, N, M, S) p 66

**EUPHORBIA** Euphorbiaceae
Worldwide – 2 000 species; South Africa – 100 species. 2nd largest woody family.
**Family Features**
- Latex – milky or watery, often poisonous
- Leaves – simple, usually alternate, toothed margin
- Fruit – small, 3-lobed capsule

**Trees in this book**
Deadliest Euphorbia (C, N, M, S) p 100; Fever Croton (C, N, M, S, T) p 44; Lavender Croton (C, N, M, S, T) p 280; Lebombo Euphorbia (N, S) p 100; Naboom Euphorbia (C, N, M, S, T) p 98; Rubber Hedge Euphorbia (C, N, M, S, T) p 100; Tamboti (C, N, M, S, T) p 388; Velvet-leaved Sweetberry (N, M, S, T) p 26

**FLAMBOYANT** Caesalpiniaceae
Worldwide - 162 genera, 2 000 species, mainly tropics; South Africa – 50 species. One of the largest woody families.
**Family Features**
- Leaves – compound, alternate, paired leaflets at tip, swelling at base of leaf-stalk
- Flowers – large, showy, 5 symmetrical petals
- Seeds – usually more pod-encased, usually more than one seed

**Trees in this book**
African Weeping-wattle (C, N, M, S, T) p 214; Burkea (C, N, M, T) p 236; Mopane (N, S) p 28; Pride-of-De Kaap Bauhinia (N, M, S) p 27; Weeping Boer-bean (C, N, M, S) p 31

**KAPOK** Bombacaceae
Worldwide – about 21 genera and 150 species. This is the only tree of this family in Africa.
**Family Features**
- Trunks - swollen, bottle-shaped or barrel-shaped
- Leaves – alternate, often palmately compound
- Flowers – large with 5 free petals and numerous stamens
- Fruit – capsule or nut

**Trees in this book**
Baobab (C, N, M, S) p 86

**LINDEN** Tiliaceae
Worldwide – 44 genera, 500 species; South Africa – 30 tree and shrub species.
**Family Features**
- Leaves - simple, alternate, 3-veined from base, toothed margin, star-shaped hairs

**Trees in this book**
Giant Raisin (N, M, S) p 60; Silver Raisin (C, N, M, S) p 346

**LITCHI** Sapindaceae
Worldwide – 120 genera, about 1 000 species; South Africa – about 30 species.
**Family Features**
- Leaves – variable
- Flowers – small and inconspicuous in local species
- Fruit – small, fleshy parts (arils) of many species are edible

**Trees in this book**
Bushveld Red-balloon (M) p 37; False Perdepis (C, N, S) p 382; Jacket-plum (C, N, M, S, T) p 272

**MANGO** Anacardiaceae
Worldwide – 60 genera; South Africa – 10 genera, 80 species
**Family Features**
- Trees have a watery latex
- Leaves – three leaflets (Karree members only)
- Flowers – separate male and female flowers, on separate trees
- Fruit – edible in most species
- Bark – rich in resin

**Trees in this book**
Bushveld Resin-tree (C, N, M, S, T) p 314; Common Currant-rhus (C, N, M, S, T) p 76; Crowberry Currant-rhus (C, N, M, S) p 76; Currant Resin-tree (C, M, S, T) p 316; False-marula Lannea (N, M, S) p 82; Karree (C, N, M, S) p 368; Live-long Lannea (C, N, M, S, T) p 330; Marula (C, N, M, S, T) p 230; Red Currant-rhus (N, S) p 372; Rock Karree-rhus (C, N, M, S, T) p 76

**MILKWOOD** Sapotaceae
Worldwide – 40 genera, 600 species; South Africa – 7 genera, 22 species. Chewing gum made from rubber-like juice of one species.
**Family Features**
- Leaves – young leaves, rusty colour
- Latex – milky
- Fruit – fleshy

**Trees in this book**
Moepel Red-milkwood (C, N, M, S, T) p 334;

Moepel Red-milkwood, page 334

**MULBERRY** Moraceae
Worldwide – tropical and sub-tropical areas, 1 000 species; South Africa – *Ficus* genus, 35 species.
**Family Features**
- Leaves – alternate, rounded leaf-buds
- Latex – milky

**Trees in this book**
Broom-cluster Fig (C, N, M, S) p 364; Common Wild Fig (C, N, M, S) p 196; Golden-haired Rock Fig (C, N, M, S) p 35; Large-leaved Rock Fig (C, N, M, S, T) p 276; Natal Fig (S) p 198; Red-leaved Fig (C, N, M, S, T) p 288; Sycomore Fig (C, N, M, S) p 77; Wonderboom Fig (C, N, M, S) p 278

**MYRTLE** Myrtaceae
Worldwide – large tropical and sub-tropical family, 2 000 species; South Africa – 25 species.
**Family Features**
- Leaves – simple, opposite, smooth margin
- Flowers – many stamens
- Fruit – tipped with remains of flower

**Trees in this book**
Forest Lavender-tree (S) p xii; Umdoni Waterberry (C, N, S) p 392; Weeping Lavender-tree (C, N, M, S) p 354

**MYRRH** Burseraceae
Worldwide – 200 species, mainly Africa and Arabia; South Africa – 26 species. Linked to biblical times; produced frankincense and myrrh from resin.
**Family Features**
- Latex – milky
- Leaves – compound, aromatic
- Bark – thin, papery, flaky (some species)

**Trees in this book**
Firethorn Corkwood (C, N, M, S) p 78; Glossy-leaved Corkwood (C, N, M, S) p 67; Paperbark Corkwood (N) p 79; Poison-grub Corkwood (C, N, M, S, T) p 298; Sand Corkwood (M) p 78; Tall Firethorn Corkwood (C, N, M, S, T) p 300; Velvet Corkwood (C, N, M, S, T) p 68; Zebra-bark Corkwood (N) p 302

**NETTLE** Urticaceae
Worldwide – 42 genera and over 500 species; South Africa – about 4 indigenous species.
**Family Features**
- Trees have a watery latex, and tough fibrous bark
- Leaves – alternate, simple 3-veined from the base, covered in coarse stinging hairs
- Flowers – small and inconspicuous in local species

**Trees in this book**
Rock Tree-nettle (C, N, M, S, T) p 292

**OLEANDER** Apocynaceae
Worldwide – large family; South Africa – 14 genera, 40 tree species, Some species medicinal properties, others extremely poisonous.
**Family Features**
- Flowers – attractive
- Latex – milky or watery

**Trees in this book**
Hornpod-tree (C, N, M, S, T) p 268

**OLIVE** Oleaceae
Worldwide – 40 genera, 300 species; South Africa – 5 genera, 15 species. Associated with humans since 3 000 BC.
**Family Features**
- Leaves – opposite, smooth margin
- Branchlets – raised, white dots

**Trees in this book**
African Olive (C, N, M, S, T) p 184

**PEA** Fabaceae
Worldwide – 437 genera, 11 300 species; South Africa – 2 genera, 35 tree species.
**Family Features**
- Flowers – pea-like, broad, erect upper petal, 2 narrower wings on both sides, 2 lowest petals joined (boat-like keel)
- Seeds - encased in pods usually covering more than one seed

**Trees in this book**
Apple-leaf (N, M, S) p 45; Broad-leaved Coral-tree (S) p 67; Kiaat Bloodwood (M, N, S) p 166; Round-leaved Bloodwood (C, N, M, S) p 29; Sacred Coral-tree (C, N, M, S) p 148; Thorny-rope Flat-bean (C,N, M, S) p 42

**PROTEA** Proteaceae
Worldwide – 60 genera and about 1 300 species; South Africa 14 genera with over 300 species, and more than 60 species may be considered trees.
**Family Features**
- Leaves – simple, alternate, entire, leathery and without stipules
- Flowers – very characteristic, showy heads or spikes. Each has 4 petal-like sepals and 4 stamens which are opposite and fused to the sepals
- Fruit – nut, drupe or capsule formed at the base of each flower

**Tree in this book**
African Protea (N, M, S) p 324; Highveld Protea (C, N, M, S) p 322; Silver Protea (C, N, M, S) p 58; Weeping Faurea (C, N, M, S) p 350

**SESAME** Pedaliaceae
South Africa – about 8 genera, mainly annual or perennial, and only 3 tree species.
**Family Features**
- Leaves – simple
- Flowers – irregular, tubular with 5 united petals
- Fruit – often winged or armed with hooks or spines
- Spines – very spiny

**Trees in this book**
Eastern Sesame-bush (N, M, S) p 90

**SNEEZEWOOD** Ptaeroxylaceae
African family; South Africa – 1 species
**Family Features**
- Leaves – opposite, compound, single leaflet at tip

**Trees in this book**
Sneezewood (N, M, S) p 41

**SOURPLUM** Olacaceae
Worldwide – about 100 species; South Africa – only 2 species.
**Family Features**
- Leaves – simple, alternate, untoothed and without stipules
- Flowers – bisexual, born in leaf axils
- Fruit – often a drupe

**Trees in this book**
Blue Sourplum (C, N, M, S) p 134; Large Sourplum (C, N, M, S) p 132

**SPIKE-THORN** Celastraceae
Worldwide – 60 - 70 genera; South Africa – 60 tree species, widely distributed.
**Family Features**
- Very variable

**Trees in this book**
Common Spikethorn ( C, N, M, S, T) p xi; Kooboo-berry (C, N, M, S) p 124

**STAR-CHESTNUT** Sterculiaceae
Worldwide – 50 genera, 1 000 species; South Africa – 3 genera. Cocoa tree family member.
**Family Features**
- Leaves – star-shaped clumps of hairs (visible only with magnifying glass)

**Trees in this book**
Squat Star-chestnut (C, N, M, S,) p 102; Wild-pear Dombeya (C, N, M, S, T) p 156

Squat Star-chestnut, page 102

### THORN-TREE Mimosaceae
Worldwide – 58 genera, 3 100 species, mainly tropical regions; South Africa – 8 genera, 100 tree species (3rd largest woody family).
#### Family Features
- Leaves – twice compound, the leaves of certain species fold up at night
- Flowers – balls or spikes, protruding stamens
- Seeds – protected by palatable bean-like pods

#### Trees in this book
Black-monkey Acacia (C, N, M, S,T) p 218; Black-thorn Acacia (C, N, M, T) p 250; Blue Acacia (C, N, M, S) p 70; Broad-pod Elephant-root (C, N, M, S, T) p 61; Bushy Three-hook Acacia (N, M, S) p 62; Camel-thorn Acacia (C, N, M) p 240; Candle-pod Acacia (C, M, T) p 62; Common Hook-thorn Acacia (C, N, M, S, T) p 318; Flame-pod Acacia (C, N, M, S, T) p 116; Knob-thorn Acacia (C, N, M, S, T) p 222; Monkey Acacia (C, N, M, T) p 71; Paperbark Acacia (M, S) p 174; Paperbark Albizia (C, N) p 178; Red Acacia (M, S, T) p 43; Robust Acacia (C, N, M, S, T) p 380; Scented-pod Acacia (C, N, M, S, T) p 254; Sickle-bush (C, N, M, S, T) p 258; Sweet-thorn Acacia (C, N, M, S, T) p 208; Umbrella Acacia (C, N, M, S, T) p 262; Worm-cure Albizia (N, M, S) p 61

### TREE-OF-HEAVEN Simaroubaceae
Worldwide – 30 genera and over 100 species; South Africa – about 4 indigenous tree species.
#### Family Features
- Leaves – alternate, compound leaves with a leaflet at the tip, and toothed margins
- Flowers – some have separate male and female flowers
- Fruit – may be dry and woody, or fleshy

#### Trees in this book
Mountain Kirkia (C, N, M, S) p 284; White Kirkia (C, N, M, S, T) p 308

### VERBENA Verbenaceae
Worldwide – 73 genera, 2 000 species; South Africa – 22 species. Chinese Hat plant is popular garden exotic shrub; Tick Berry is noxious weed.
#### Family Features
- Leaves – aromatic when crushed
- Twigs – 4-angled

#### Trees in this book
Pipe-stem Fingerleaf (C, N, M) p 338; White Cats-whiskers (C, N, M, S, T) p 152

### WILD ELDER Loganiaceae
Worldwide – 5 genera, 21 species; South Africa – 20 species.
#### Family Features
- Very varied
- Leaves – simple, opposite or in threes
- Flowers – bisexual

#### Trees in this book
Big-leaf Fever-tree (M, N, S) p 162; Brittlewood Nuxia (C, N, M, S) p 108; Corky-bark Monkey-orange (C, N, M) p 79; Forest Nuxia (S) p 110; Hairy-leaved Monkey-orange (C, N, M, S) p 120; Olive Buddleja (M, S) p 39; Quilted Buddleja (C, N, M, S, T) p 38; Spine-leaved Monkey-orange (C, N, M) p 63; Spiny Monkey-orange (C, N, M, S) p 79

### WILD PLANE Ochnaceae
Worldwide – 30 genera and over 300 species; South Africa – 1 genus with over 20 tree species.
#### Family Features
- Leaves – alternate, simple, toothed or untoothed, narrow stipules, and many closely spaced parallel lateral veins
- Flowers – usually yellow
- Fruit – flower-like, 11 - 3 kidney-shaped carpels which ripen to black, surrounded by reddish enlarged sepals

#### Trees in this book
Peeling-bark Ochna (C, N, M, S, T) p 136; Showy Ochna (C, N, S) p 60

### YELLOWWOOD Podocarpaceae
Worldwide – these are cone-bearing trees with 7 genera; South Africa – about 4 indigenous species.
#### Family Features
- Leaves – simple, alternate, narrow, stiff and leathery with a distinct central vein
- Flowers – small and inconspicuous in local species

#### Trees in this book
Broad-leaved Yellowwood (C, N, M, S, T) p 33; Small-leaved Yellowwood (C, N, M, S) p 33

Showy Ochna, page 60

# Index

*Acacia ataxacantha* 116-119, 61, 71, 118, 320
*Acacia burkei* 218-221, 61, 70, 176
*Acacia caffra* 318-321, 118, 60, 71
*Acacia erioloba* 240-243, 62, 70, 82
*Acacia erubescens* 70, 81
*Acacia galpinii* 70, 176, 220
*Acacia gerrardii* 43, 72
*Acacia hebeclada* 62, 71
*Acacia karroo* 208-211, 60, 72
*Acacia mellifera* 250-253, 70
*Acacia nigrescens* 222-225, 71, 83, 220
*Acacia nilotica* 254-257, 61, 72
*Acacia robusta* 380-383, 72
*Acacia senegal* 62, 70
*Acacia sieberiana* 174-177, 72, 81
*Acacia tortilis* 262-265, 62, 72
Acacias 43, 70-73, 116, 174, 176, 178, 208, 218, 220, 222, 240, 250, 254, 262, 318, 384
*Adansonia digitata* 86-89, 58, 63, 67, 104
African Olive 184-187
African Protea 324
African Schefflera 59, 67, 96
African Wattle 214
African Weeping-wattle 214-217, 59, 61, 73
African White-stinkwood 360-363, 66, 80
*Albizia anthelmintica* 58, 61, 73
*Albizia tanganyicensis* 178-181, 58, 61, 73, 81
Albizias 73, 178
amaBulwa 170
amaNgwe amhlophe 244
Anacardiaceae 76, 82, 230, 314, 316, 330, 368, 372, 418
Ankle Thorn 380
*Anthocleista grandiflora* 162-165, 58, 63, 65
Apiesdoring 218
Apocynaceae 268
Apple-leaf 45, 59, 61, 67
Araliaceae 67, 94, 96, 416
Asteraceae 326, 328, 417

Bakhout 330
Baobab 86-89, 58, 63, 67, 104
Bastard Pepper Tree 284
Bastard Willow 368
Basterrooibos 304
*Bauhinia galpinii* 27, 58, 61, 65
Bead-bean Tree 112
Beechwood 350
*Berchemia discolor* 64, 344
*Berchemia zeyheri* 342-345, 64, 66
Bergboegoe 280

Bergbrandnetel 292
Bergsering 284
Bergvaalbos 326
Besemtrosvy 364
Big-leaf Fever-tree 162-165, 58, 63, 65
Big-leaf Tree 162
Black Monkey Orange 120
Black Monkey Thorn 218
Black Thorn 250, 254
Black-barked Camel Thorn 240
Black-monkey Acacia 218-221, 61, 70, 176
Black-thorn Acacia 250-253, 70
Blinkbaar-wag-'n-bietjie 188
Blinkblaar Family 188, 342, 344, 417
Bloedhout 166
Bloodwood 166
Blossom tree 156
Blue Acacia 70, 81
Blue Sourplum 134
Bluegum 352
Boekenhout 350
Bombacaceae 86, 417
Bosappel 170
*Boscia albitrunca* 200-203, 80, 194
*Boscia foetida* 192-195, 202
Boskoorsboom 162
Bostaaibos 372
Botterklapper 120
*Brachylaena transvaalensis* 328
*Brachylaena huillensis* 328
*Brachylaena rotundata* 326-329, 65, 83
Brakdoring 380
*Bridelia mollis* 26, 66
Brittlewood 108
Brittlewood Nuxia 108-111, 59
Broad-leaved Coral-tree 58, 67, 150
Broad-leaved Yellowwood 33, 83
Broad-pod Elephant-root 61, 73
Broom-cluster Fig 364-367, 77
Broshout 108
Brown Ivorywood 64, 344
Bruinhaakdoring 250
Buchu Family 68, 384, 416
*Buddleja saligna* 39, 59, 186
*Buddleja salviifolia* 38, 59, 65
Buffalo-thorn 188
Buffalo-thorn Jujube 188-191, 64, 66
Burkea 236-239, 61, 69, 232, 332
*Burkea africana* 236-239, 61, 69, 232, 332
Burseraceae 67, 68, 78, 79, 298, 300, 302, 418
Bush Currant 372
Bushveld Bead-bean 112-115, 58, 61
Bushveld Cherry 124

Bushveld Red-balloon 37, 63
Bushveld Resin Tree 314
Bushveld Resin-tree 314-317, 64, 66
Bushveld Shepherds-tree 192-195, 202
Bushwillow Family 30, 74, 75, 128, 140, 144, 226, 244, 376, 304, 416
Bushwillows 74, 75, 107, 128, 130, 140, 144, 226, 304, 376
Bushy Three-hook Acacia 62, 70

Cabbage tree 94
Cabbage Tree Family 67, 94, 96, 416
Cactus euphorbia 98
Caesalpiniaceae 27, 28, 31, 214, 236, 417
Camdeboo Stinkwood 360
Camel thorn 240
Camel-thorn Acacia 240-243, 62, 70, 82
Candelabra Tree 98
Candle-pod Acacia 62, 71
Cape Cherry 124
Cape Myrtle Family 32, 416
Cape Thorn Tree 208
Caper Family 112, 192, 200, 416
Capparaceae 112, 192, 200, 416
*Cassine aethiopica* 124-127, 64
Celastraceae xi, 124, 419
*Celtis africana* 360-363, 66, 80
Cheesewood Family 1, 416
Chrysobalanceae 34, 170, 417
Citrus Family 68, 384, 416
*Clausena anisata* 68, 382
*Clerodendrum glabrum* 152-155, 59, 63
Coco Plum Family 34, 170, 417
Coffee-tree 200
*Colophospermum mopane* 28, 62, 67
Combretaceae 30, 74, 75, 128, 140, 144, 226, 244, 376, 304, 416
*Combretum apiculatum* 140-143, 74
*Combretum collinum suluense* 75, 130
*Combretum erythrophyllum* 376-379, 74, 83
*Combretum hereroense* 144-147
*Combretum imberbe* 226-229, 74, 82
*Combretum kraussii* 74, 107
*Combretum molle* 304-307, 66, 75, 82
*Combretum zeyheri* 128-131, 62, 74
Combretums 74, 75, 107, 128, 130, 140, 144, 226, 304, 376
*Commiphora africana* 302
*Commiphora angolensis* 78, 302
*Commiphora glandulosa* 300-303, 78

421

*Commiphora marlothii* 79, 302
*Commiphora mollis* 68, 78, 302
*Commiphora pyracanthoides* 78
*Commiphora schimperi* 67, 78, 302
*Commiphora viminea* 78, 302
Commiphoras 78, 79, 300, 302
Common Cabbage Tree 94
Common Coral Tree 148
Common Currant-rhus 76
Common Guarri 204
Common hook-thorn 318
Common Hook-thorn Acacia 318-321, 60, 71, 118
Common resin tree 314
Common Spikethorn xi
Common star-chestnut 102
Common Sugarbush 322
Common Tree Euphorbia 98
Common Wild Elder 108
Common Wild Fig 196-199, 77, 336
Common Wild Pear 156
Cork Tree 170
Corkwoods 78, 79, 300, 302
Corky-bark Monkey-orange 79, 122, 82
*Croton gratissimus* 280-283, 65
*Croton megalobotrys* 42, 64, 65, 66
Crowberry Currant-rhus 76
Currant Resin-tree 316
*Cussonia natalensis* 96
*Cussonia paniculata* 96
*Cussonia spicata* 94-97, 58, 63, 72
*Cussonia transvaalensis* 96

**D**aisy Family 326, 328, 417
*Dalbergia armata* 44, 61, 83
Deadliest Euphorbia 100
*Dichrostachys cinerea* 258-261, 60, 62, 73
Dikbas 330
*Diplorhynchus condylocarpon* 268-271, 62, 66, 80
Dogwood Family 188, 342, 344, 417
*Dombeya rotundifolia* 156-159, 60, 62, 66, 82
Doppruim 272
Drolpeer 156
Dzuvudzuvu 178

**E**astern Rapanea 32, 64, 80
Eastern Sesame-bush 90-93, 58, 62, 81
Ebenaceae 186, 204, 417
Ebony Family 186, 204, 417
*Elephantorrhiza burkei* 61, 73
Elm Family 66, 360, 417
*Englerophytum magalismontanum* 296-299, 64, 65

Enkeldoring 380
*Erythrina latissima* 58, 67, 150
*Erythrina lysistemon* 148-151, 58, 61, 67, 80
*Erythrophysa transvaalensis* 37, 63
*Euclea schimperii* 186
*Euclea undulata* 204-207
*Euphorbia confinalis* 100
*Euphorbia cooperi* 100
Euphorbia Family 26, 44, 98, 100, 280, 388, 417
*Euphorbia ingens* 98-101
*Euphorbia tirucalli* 100
Euphorbiaceae 26, 44, 98, 100, 280, 388, 417

**F**abaceae 29, 42, 45, 67, 148, 166, 419
False Perdepis 382
False-marula Lannea 69, 82, 232
*Faurea saligna* 350-353, 60, 63, 82
Fever Croton 42, 64-66, 280
*Ficus abutilifolia* 276-279, 65, 67
*Ficus burkei* 196-199, 77, 336
*Ficus cordata* 77, 278, 290
*Ficus glumosa* 35, 77, 278
*Ficus ingens* 288-291, 64, 77, 278, 366
*Ficus natalensis* 198
*Ficus salicifolia* 77, 278, 290
*Ficus sur* 364-367, 77
*Ficus sycomorus* 77
*Ficus thonningii* 196-199, 77, 336
Figs 77, 196, 276, 278, 288, 364
Firethorn Corkwood 78
Flamboyant Family 27, 28, 31, 214, 236, 417
Flame-pod Acacia 116-119, 61, 71, 320
Fluweelsboswilg 304
Forest Bushwillow 74, 107
Forest Currant 372
Forest Fever Tree 162
Forest Lavender-tree xii, 81, 356
Forest Nuxia 59, 110
Forest Silver-oak 328
Fynblaarwitgat 192

**G**aludzu 162
Gewone Drolpeer 156
Gewone Ghwarrie 204
Gewone Haakdoring 318
Gewone Harpuisboom 314
Gewone Koraalboom 148
Gewone Naboom 98
Gewone Sterkastaiing 102
Gewone Suikerbos 322
Gewone Wildevlier 108
Gewone Wildevy 196

Giant Raisin 60, 69, 348
Giraffe Tree 240
Glossy-leaved Corkwood 67, 78, 302
Golden-haired Rock Fig 35, 77, 278
*Grewia hexamita* 60, 69, 348
*Grewia monticola* 346-349, 60, 64
Groot Gewone Kanniedood 300
Grootblaarrotsvy 276
Grootdoring 240
Grootsuurpruim 132
Grysappel 170
Gulaswimbi 272
*Gymnosporia buxifolia* xi

**H**aak-en-steek 262
Haak-en-steek-wag-'n-bietjie 188
Hairy-leaved Monkey-orange 120-123, 79
Hardekool 226
Harsbessie 314
Heteropyxidaceae xii, 354, 392, 418
*Heteropyxis canescens* xii, 81, 356
*Heteropyxis natalensis* 354-357, 59, 81
Highveld Cabbage-tree 96
Highveld Protea 322-325, 58, 65
Highveld Silver-oak 326-329, 65, 83
*Hippobromus paucif lorus* 382
Hissing tree 170
Horingpeultjieboom 268
Horn-pod tree 268
Hornpod-tree 268-271, 62, 66, 80
Huilboom 214
Hwele 132

**I**liTye 272
imBati 292
iMinyela 300
imPayi 276
imPondondlovu 226
imPondozendhlovu 226
inDwandwazane 360
inGulutane 124
iNhlangutshane 368
inHlokoshiyane enkulu 372
inKhuphenkhuphe 102
inKhuzwa 354
inKukutu 140
inKukutwane 304
iNtlokolotshane enkulu 372
isAdlunge 322
iSafo 350
iShupa 98
isiFico 314
isiGanganyane 330
isiHlahlavane 144
isiKhabakhombe 214
isiLahla 188
isiLahlankosi 188

422

isiNga 208
isiQalaba 322
isiQwane 322
isiSefo 350
isiThwethwe 252, 262

**J**acket-plum 272-275, 64, 80

**K**ameeldoring 240
Kapok Family 86, 417
Karee 368
Karoo thorn 208
Karoo-tree 368
Karoodoring 208
Karree 368-371, 76, 340
Katdoring 318
Kiaat 166
Kiaat Bloodwood 166-169, 62, 68, 82
Kiepersol 94
Kierieklapper 144
*Kirkia acuminata* 308-311, 69, 286
*Kirkia wilmsii* 284-287, 69
Kleinperdepram 384
Klipvy 276
Knob Thorn 222
Knob-thorn Acacia 222-225, 71, 83, 220
Knoppiesboontjieboom 112
Knoppiesdoring 222
Koeboebessie 124
Koeman 364
Kooboo-berry 124-127, 64
Koorsboom 178
Kremetart 86

**L**adies Cabbage-tree 94-98, 58, 63, 82
Laeveldkiepersol 94
*Lannea discolor* 330-333, 64, 69, 232, 238
*Lannea schweinfurthii* 69, 82, 232
Large Sourplum 132-135, 64
Large-fruited Bushwillow 128-131, 62, 74
Large-leaved Rock Fig 276-279, 65, 77
Large-leaved Sickle Bush 258
Lavender Croton 280-283, 65
Lavender Fever-berry 280
Lavender tree 354
Laventelboom 354
Laventelkoorsbessie 280
Leadwood 226-229, 74, 82
Lebombo Euphorbia 100
Lekkerbreek 136
Lekkerruikpeul 254
Leoka 208
Lepelhout 124

Lesika 360
*Leucosidea sericea* 34, 68, 83
Linden Family 60, 346, 418
Litchi Family 37, 272, 382, 418
Live-long 330
Live-long Lannea 330-333, 64, 69, 232, 238
Loganiaceae 38, 39, 63, 79, 108, 110, 120, 162, 420
*Lonchocarpus capassa* 45, 59, 61, 67
Loodhout 226
Lover's Cheesewood 1, 59, 63
Lowveld Cabbage Tree 94
Lowveld Silver-oak 328
Lucky Bean Tree 148

**M**aerua angolensis 112-115, 58, 61
Mafambaborile 128
Mango Family 76, 82, 230, 314, 316, 330, 368, 372, 418
Manhungwana 384
Maroela 230
Marula 230-233, 64, 69, 82, 238, 332
Masepha 354
*Maytenus heterophylla* xi
Mbholovisi 360
Mbulwa 170
Mbvhinya-xihloka 318
Mbvuva 376
Melkbos 268
Milkwood Family 296, 334, 418
Mimosa Thorn 208
Mimosaceae 43, 61, 62, 70, 71, 116, 174, 178, 208, 218, 222, 240, 250, 254, 258, 262, 318, 380, 420
*Mimusops zeyheri* 334-337, 64
Mmabi 292
Mmalê 148
Mmasepha 354
Mmilo 166
Mmola 170
Mmotô 226
Mmupudu 334
Moboana 90
Mobola 170
Mobola Plum 170
Mobola-plum 170-173, 64, 66, 82
Moduba 128, 304
Moduba-noka 376
Moduba-tšhipi 128
Modubana 170
Modubatshipi 304
Modube 128
Modubu 376
Modubunoka 376
Modumela 284, 308
Modumêla 308

Modutu 360
Moepel 334
Moepel 334
Moepel Red-milkwood 334-337, 64
Mofudiri 140
Mofufu 350
Moga 380
Mogalagala 322
Mogaletlwa 116
Mogatakgomo 360
Mogo 364
Mogô-nônô 244
Mogodiri 140
Mogohlo 240, 254
Mogôkatau 116
Mogonono 244
Mogônônô 244
Mogorwagorwana 120
Mogôtlhô 240
Mogwagwa 120
Mogwanakgômo 346
Mohlakô 350
Mohlakola 204
Mohlatswa 296
Mohloaare 184
Mohloare 184
Mohlohlo-kgomo 98
Mohlokohloko 152
Mohlôpi 200
Mohlware 184
Mohwelere 140
Mohwelere-tšhipi 226
Mokabi 144
Mokakata 102
Mokala 222
Mokalabata 188
Mokata 144
Mokgale 338
Mokgalo 188
Mokgalô 188

Highveld Protea, page 58

Mokgalwa 188
Mokgoba 156
Mokgofa 156
Mokgôkgôthwane 330
Mokgoro 98
Mokgoto 98
Mokgwa 218
Mokgwakgwatha 102
Mokgwethe 304
Mokha 174
Mokhu 380
Mokhupye 148
Mokoba 222
Mokubu 244
Mokwa 166
Mokwêrêkwêrê 108
Moletša-ṅakana 244
Moleye 268
Mologa 116, 280
Momelantsweng 276
Monamane 136
Monatô 236
Mondzo 226
Monee 342
Mongana 250
Mongangatau 250
Mongêna 350
Monhlo 392
Monhlohlo 368
Monkey Acacia 71, 176, 220
Monkey Oranges 79, 120, 122
Monkgôpô 98
Monokane 276, 288, 314
Monoko 314
Monokomabêlê 384
Monokwane 384
Montlho 392
Monyêlênyêlê 136
Monyena 350
Moôjwane 330
Mooka 208, 254, 380
Mookana 208
Moologa 280
Moomane 112
Mopane 28, 62, 67
Mopennwêeng 272
Mophala 162
Mophêthê 148
Mopipi 192
Mopsinyugane 272
Moraceae 35, 77, 196, 198,
 276, 278, 288, 364, 418
Moralejwe 292
Morapa 120
Morêketli 112
Morekuri 388
Morêtologa wa podi 132
Morêtologane 132
Morêtsê 258

Moritidi 222
Moroba-diêpe 318
Morôka 300
Morôtô 166
Morukuru 388
Morula 230
Morula-môpšane 330
Morutlhare 318
Mošabêlê 368
Mosehla 214
Mosêlêsêlê 258
Mosese 214
Mosêtlha 214
Mosêtsê 94
Mošibihla 174
Mosilabele 368
Mosilabêlê 368
Mosinabele 368
Mošu 262
Mosu 240, 262
Mošwana 262
Moswane 326
Motha-thaa 372
Mothibadifate 360
Motholo 318
Motlhabakgosi 240
Motlhabare 108
Motlhakola 204
Motlhakwa 296
Motlhatlha 272
Motlhatsa 288
Motlhatswa 296
Motlhôpi 200
Motlhware 184
Motsha 254
Motšhakhutšhakhu 368
Motšhetšhe 94
Motšhidi 132
Motswiri 226
Motubane 156
Moumo 196
Mountain Kirkia 284-287, 69
Mountain Nettle 292
Mountain Seringa 284
Mountain Silver Oak 326
Mountain syringa 284
Mowana 86
Moye 342
Mpfuxane 334
Mphasamhala 188
Mphata-kgogo 372
Mphoka 174
Mpotsa 144
Mpulu 236
Mubandulakhali 314
Mubululu 334
Mubvumela 308
Mudedede 354
Mudumbula 314

Mudzwiri 226
Mueneene 162
Mufhatela 128
Mufhaṱela-ṱhunḓu
Mufhôrola 280
Mufhulu 236
Mufula 230
Mugavhi 144
Mugwiti 304
Muhiri 226
Muhlwa 392
Muhuyu-ngala 364
Mukakate 102
Mukhalu 188
Mukonde 98
Mukwakwa 120
Mulberry Family 35, 77, 196, 198,
 276, 278, 288, 364, 418
Mulelu 178
Muluwa 116
Mumvumvu 360
Munanga 222
Munembedzi 250
Munga 208
Mungamazi 380
Mungugunu 124
Muṋia-ṋiane 342
Muniane 342
Munombelo 296
Munukha-tshilongwe 152
Munungu 384
Munungufhefhe 178
Munyongatshifumbu 338
Muonze 388
Murambo 136
Murandela 384
Murenzhe 258
Murovha-ḓembe 292
Musaunga 174
Musenje 94
Musenzhe 94
Musese 214
Mushakaladza 368
Musingidzi 140
Musivhiṱha 240
Mususu 244
Muswu 262
Muṱaladzi 334
Muṱalu 300
Mutamba-na-mme 112
Muṱango 350
Muṱanzwa-dombo 132
Muteteneka 108
Muṱhanzwa 292
Muṱhobi 200
Muṱhowa 268
Muthwa 392
Mutlhwari 184
Mutondo 166

Mutshetshete 188
Mutshili 132
Muṯu 392
Muṯwari 184
Muumo 196
Muunga 208
Muunga-khanga 262
Muunga-ludzi 208
Muunga-luselo 174
Muvale 148
Muvhaḓela-phanga 372
Muvhale 148
Muvhula 170
Muvhumbu 330
Muvhuyu 86
Muvumba-ngweṋa 380
Muvunḓa-mbaḓo 318
Muvuvhu 376
Muyilakaya 360
Mvhangazi 166
Mvumayila 308
Mvumbangwenya 380
Myrrh Family 67, 68, 78, 79, 298, 300, 302, 418
Myrsinaceae 32, 416
Myrtaceae xii, 354, 392, 418
Myrtle Family xii, 354, 392, 418
*Mystroxylon aethiopicum* 124-127, 64

**N**'wamidzumba 350
Naboom Euphorbia 98-101
Natal Fig 198
Natal Protea 322
Ndzedze 214
Ndzenga 258
Ndzopfori 388
Nettle Family 292, 418
Nhlangula 204
Nhlantswa 334
Nkanyi 230
Nkasinga 218
Nkaya 222
Nkonde 98
Nkondze 98
Nkonola 244
Nkonono 244
Nkowankowa 174
Nkuwa 364
Nkuwamaribye 276, 288
Nkwakwa 120
Nombhela 296
Nqayi 124
Nsasani 262
Nsihana 346
Nsihaphukuma 156
Nsisimbana 148
Nsolodza 102
Ntadzwa 292

Ntsengele 132
Ntsengele-lowu-kulu 132
Ntsowa 268
Nuko 116
*Nuxia congesta* 108-111, 59
*Nuxia floribunda* 59, 110
Nxangwa 254
Nyasimbitane 280
Nyiyani 342
Nzololo 136

**O**betia tenax 292-295, 65
*Ochna natalitia* 60, 63, 138
*Ochna pulchra* 136-139, 60, 63, 81
Ochnaceae 60, 136, 420
Olacaceae 132, 134, 419
*Olea europeae* 184-187
Oleaceae 184, 419
Oleander Family 268, 419
Olienhout 184
Olive Buddleja 39, 59, 186
Olive Family 184, 419
Ouhout 34, 68, 83
*Ozoroa paniculosa* 314-317, 64, 66
*Ozoroa sphaerocarpa* 316

**P**alule 112
Paperbark Acacia 174-177, 72, 81
Paperbark Albizia 178-181, 58, 61, 73, 81
Paperbark Corkwood 79, 302
Paperbark False-thorn 178
Paperbark Thorn 174
Papierbasdoring 174
Papierbasvalsdoring 178
*Pappea capensis* 272-275, 64, 80
*Parinari curatellifolia* 170-173, 64, 66, 82
Pea Family 29, 42, 45, 67, 148, 166, 419
Pedaliaceae 90, 419
Peeling Plane 136
Peeling-bark Ochna 136-139, 60, 63, 81
*Peltophorum africanum* 214-217, 59, 61, 73
Perdepis 68, 382
Perdepram 222
Pigeonwood 66, 80, 362
Pink Ivory 342
Pipe-stem Fingerleaf 338-341, 60, 63, 67
Pipe-stem tree 338
Pittosporaceae 1, 416
*Pittosporum viridiflorum* 1, 59, 63
Podocarpaceae 33, 420
*Podocarpus falcatus* 33, 83
*Podocarpus latifolius* 33, 83
Poison-grub Corkwood 302

Pride-of-De Kaap Bauhinia 27, 58, 61, 65
*Protea caffra* 322-325, 58, 65
Protea Family 58, 322, 324, 350, 419
*Protea gaguedi* 324
*Protea roupelliae* 58, 324
Proteaceae 58, 322, 324, 350, 419
Ptaeroxylaceae 41, 419
*Ptaeroxylon obliquum* 41, 68
*Pterocarpus angolensis* 166-169, 62, 68, 82
*Pterocarpus rotundifolius* 29, 62, 66, 68
Purple Ivory 342
Purple-pod Cluster-leaf 30, 59, 62, 75
Pypsteelboom 338

**Q**uilted Buddleja 38, 59, 65

**R**aasbessie 204
Raasblaar 128
Rank-wag-'n-bietjie 116
*Rapanea melanophloeos* 32, 64, 80
Red Acacia 43, 72
Red Bushwillow 140-143, 74
Red Currant-rhus 372-375, 76, 82
Red ivory 342
Red Ivorywood 342-345, 64, 66
Red syringa 236
Red-heart Thorn Tree 254
Red-leaved Fig 288-291, 64, 77, 278, 366
Red-leaved Rock Fig 288
Resin-leaf 152
Rhamnaceae 188, 342, 344, 417
Rhodesian Wattle 214
*Rhus chirindensis* 372-375, 76, 82
*Rhus lancea* 368-371, 76, 340
*Rhus leptodictya* 76, 340, 370
*Rhus pentheri* 76
*Rhus pyroides* 76
Rhus' 76, 368, 370, 372

Spine-leaved Monkey-orange, page 79

425

River Bushwillow 376-379, 74, 83
River Guarri 186
Riviervaderlandswilg 376
Robust Acacia 380-383, 72
Rock Figs 77, 276, 278, 288
Rock Karree-rhus 76, 340, 370
Rock Tree-nettle 292-295, 65
Rooi-ivoor 342
Rooiblaarrotsvy 288
Rooiblaarvy 288
Rooiboekenhout 350
Rooiboswilg 140
Rooihout 342
Rooikaree 368
Rooikiaat 214
Round-leaved Bloodwood 29, 62, 66, 68
Rubber Hedge Euphorbia 100
Russet Bushwillow 144-147
Rutaceae 68, 384, 416

**S**acred Coral-tree 148-151, 58, 61, 67, 80
Samani 102
Sambreelboom 94
Sand Corkwood 78, 302
Sandelhout 388
Sandsering 236
Sandvaalbos 244
Sapindaceae 37, 272, 382, 418
Sapotaceae 296, 334, 418
Scented Thorn 254
Scented-pod Acacia 254-257, 61, 72
*Schefflera umbellifera* 59, 67, 96
*Schotia brachypetala* 31, 58, 61, 68, 69
*Sclerocarya birrea* 230-233, 64, 69, 82, 238, 332
Seboi 86
Segwapi 322
Sekelbos 258
Sekila 322
Sekole 384
Senokomaropa 384
Sesame Family 90, 419
*Sesamothamnus lugardii* 90-93, 58, 62, 81
Shepherd's tree 200
Shepherds-tree 200-203, 80, 194
Showy Ochna 60, 63, 138
Siboana 90
Sickle Bush 258
Sickle-bush 258-261, 60, 62, 73
Silver Cabbage-tree 96
Silver Cluster-leaf 244-247, 62, 75, 83
Silver Protea 58, 324
Silver Raisin 346-349, 60, 64
Silver terminalia 244

Simaroubaceae 284, 308, 420
Simple-leaved Cabbage-tree 96
Small Knobwood 384-387, 64, 68, 83
Small-leaved Guarri 204-207
Small-leaved Yellowwood 33, 83
Smelly shepherd's tree 192
Sneezewood 41, 68
Sneezewood Family 41, 68, 419
Soetdoring 208
Soetpeul 258
Sourplum 132, 149
Sourplum Family 132, 134
Spike-thorn Family xi, 124
Spine-leaved Monkey-orange 63, 79, 122
Spiny Monkey-orange 79, 122
*Spirostachys africana* 388-391, 82
Squat Star-chestnut 102-106, 63, 65, 81
Stamvrug 296
Stamvrug Milkplum 296-299, 64, 65
Star-chestnut Family 102, 156, 419
Stem-fruit Tree 296
*Sterculia rogersii* 102-106, 63, 65, 81
Sterculiaceae 102, 156, 419
Stink-bush 192
Stinkboom 152
Stinkleaf Tree 152
Stinkwitgat 192
*Strychnos cocculoides* 79, 82, 122
*Strychnos madagascariensis* 120-123, 79
*Strychnos pungens* 63, 79, 122
*Strychnos spinosa* 79, 122
Strychnos' 79, 120, 122
Swartapiesdoring 218
Swarthaak 250
Swartklapper 120
Swartolienhout 184
Swartsaadpeul 254
Sweet Thorn 208
Sweet-thorn Acacia 208-211, 60, 72
Sycomore Fig 77
*Syzygium cordatum* 392-395, 59, 64

**T**all Firethorn Corkwood 300-303, 78
Tamboti 388-391, 82
Tambotie 388
*Terminalia prunioides* 30, 59, 62, 75
*Terminalia sericea* 244-247, 62, 75, 83
Terminalias 75, 30, 244
Thathasani 354
Thorn-tree Family 43, 61, 62, 70, 71, 116, 174, 178, 208, 218, 222, 240, 250, 254, 258, 262, 318, 380, 420

Thorny-rope Flat-bean 44, 61, 83
Tiliaceae 60, 346, 418
Tinderwood 152
Tontelhout 152
Transvaal Melkhout 334
Transvaal Milkplum 296
Transvaal Red Milkwood 334
Transvaal Rubber Tree 268
Transvaal sesame bush 90
Transvaal Silver-leaf 244
Transvaal teak 166
Transvaalboekenhout 350
Transvaalse Sesambos 90
Tree Grape 330
Tree-of-heaven Family 284, 308, 420
*Trema orientalis* 66, 80, 362
Tshidzungu 322
Tshikavhavhe 272
Tshikululu 276, 288
Tshikwakwashi 272
Tshiluvhari 156
Tshiṯonzhe 90
Tshiṯangule 204
Tshiṯhoṯhonya 136

**u**Gagane 258
Ulmaceae 66, 360, 417
uluZi 196
uMahlabekufeni 280
umBabazane 292
umBikanyaka 156
umBilo 166
umBombe 196
umBondomyana 140
umBondwe omhlophe 304
umBondwe omnyama 140
umBondwe wasembudwini 128
Umbrella Acacia 262-265, 62, 72
Umbrella Thorn 262
umCozi 392
umDenda obomvu 288
umDliwampunzi 346
Umdoni 392
umDoni 392
Umdoni Waterberry 392-395, 59, 64
umDubi 376
umDubu 376
umDubu wehlanze 376
umDuli 338
umEnwayo 112
UmGana 230
umGanu 230
umGonswane 288
umGqalutye 272
umGqogqo 272
umGuluguza 120
umGunguluzane 124
umGwali 204
umGxube 124

umHlakothi 372
umHlakotshane 368
umHlalavane 144
umHlalhankosi 188
umHlonhlo 98
umHonono 244
umJome 392
umKhamba 174
umKhaya 222
umKhaya wehlalahlathi 218
umKhiwane 364
umKhobeza 108
umKhuze 354
umKwakwa 120
umLahlabantu 188, 272
umLalampunzi 346
umLungumabele 384
umMono 226
umNcaka 342
umNcawe 254
umNeyi 342
umNga 208
umNgamanzi 380
umNgampunzi 380
umNganduzi 174
umNini 342
umNqawe 254
umNquma 184
umNqumo 184
umNumbela 296
umNungumabele 384
umNungwane 384
umNungwane omncane 384
umPhafa 188
umPhapha 98
umPhushane 334
umQangazani 152
umQaqongo 152
umQwaqu 152
umSasane 262
umSehle 214
umSenga 94
umSenge 94
umShekisane 204
umSilazembe 258
umSinsi 148
umSintsi 148
umSisi 148
umSwi 392
umThathawe 116
umThezane 258
umTholo 318
umThombe 196, 288
umThombothi 388
umThombotsi 388
umThunduluka 132
umTshekisane 204
umuNga 208
umVangatsi 166

umVangazi 166
umVithi 192, 200
umVumvu 360
umWane 156
umWangati 166
uNhliziyonkulu 156
*Urera tenax* 292-295, 65
Urticaceae 292, 418

**V**aalboom 244
Vaalrosyntjie 346
Vaderlandswilg 376
Velvet Bushwillow 304-307, 66, 75, 82
Velvet Corkwood 68, 78, 302
Velvet-leaved Sweetberry 26, 66
Verbena Family 152, 338, 420
Verbenaceae 152, 338, 420
Verveldoring 174
*Vitex rehmannii* 338-341, 60, 63, 67
Vlamdoring 116

**W**ater Berry 392
Water Tree 392
Waterbessie 392
Waterhout 392
Waterwood 392
Weeping Boer-bean 31, 58, 61, 68, 69
Weeping Collina Bushwillow 75, 130
Weeping Faurea 350-353, 60, 63, 82
Weeping Lavender-tree 354-357, 59, 81
Weeping wattle 214
White cat's whiskers 152
White Cats-whiskers 152-155, 59, 63
White Kirkia 308-311, 69, 286
White Seringa 308
White Stinkwood 360
White syringa 308
White-stem Tree 200
Wild Elder Family 38, 39, 63, 79, 108, 110, 120, 162, 420
Wild Olive 184
Wild Pear 156
Wild Pepper Tree 284
Wild Plane Family 60, 136, 420
Wild Plum 296
Wild Seringa 236
Wild Teak 166
Wild Tobacco Tree 162
Wild-pear Dombeya 156-159, 60, 62, 66, 82
Wildekardamon 384
Wildelaventel 354
Wildepeperboom 284
Wildepruim 272

Wildesering 236
Wildetabakboom 162
Willow 352
Witgat 200
Withaakdoring 262
Witsalie 108
Witsering 308
Witstamboom 200
Witstinkhout 360
Wonderboom Fig 77, 278, 290
Worm-cure Albizia 58, 61, 73
Wurgvy 196

**X**ifati 300
Xikhukhutsane 304
Xikukutsi 140
Xikwakwaxu 272
Xilangamahlo 388
Xiluvarhi 156
*Ximenia americana* 134
*Ximenia caffra* 132-135, 64
Ximupyane 330
Ximuwu 86
Xinhun'welambeva 154
Xiniyani 342
Xinkuwana 364
Xinungumafi 314
Xirhomberhombe 196
Xukutsi 200

**Y**ellowwood Family 33, 420
Yellowwoods 33

**Z**anthoxylum capense 384-387, 64, 68, 83
Zebra-bark Corkwood 78, 302
*Ziziphus mucronata* 188-191, 64, 66

Quilted Buddleja,
page 38

427

# Book references

Acocks, JPH, 1988, *Veld Types of South Africa, No. 57, Botanical Research Institute, Pretoria.*

Carr, JD, 1976, *The South African Acacias,* Conservation Press Pty Ltd, Johannesburg.

Carr, JD, 1988, *Combretaceae in South Africa,* Tree Society of Southern Africa, Johannesburg.

Coates Palgrave, K, 1977, *Trees of Southern Africa,* 1st edition, C. Struik, Cape Town.

Coetzee, BJ, van Wyk, WPD, Gertenbach, WPD, Hall-Martin, A. & Joubert, SCJ, 1981, *'n Plantekologiese Verkenning van die Waterberggebied in die Noord-Transvaalse Bosveld,* Koedoe, 24: 1-23.

Deall, GB & Backer, AP, 1989. *The Vegetation Ecology of the Eastern Transvaal Escarpment in the Sabie Area,* 3, Annotated checklist, Bothalia, 19:91 - 110.

Deall, GB, Scheepers JC & CJ Schultz, 1989, *The Vegetation Ecology of the Eastern Transvaal Escarpment in the Sabie Area.* 3, Annotated checklist, Bothalia, 19:53 - 67.

Deall, GB, Theron, GK & Westfall, RH, 1989, *The Vegetation Ecology of the Eastern Transvaal Escarpment in the Sabie Area,* 3, Floristic classification, Bothalia, 19:69 - 89.

Hahn, N, *Tree List of the Soutpansberg,* Fantique Publishers, Hatfield, Pretoria.

Hutchings, A, Scott, AH, Lewis ,G & Cunningham, A B, 1996, *Zulu Medicinal Plants - An Inventory,* University of Natal Press, Pietermaritzburg.

Journal of Dendrology, 1991, *National Register of Big Trees.*

Low, AB & Rebelo, AG, (Eds), 1996, *Vegetation of South Africa, Lesotho and Swaziland* (with accompanied vegetation map), Department of Environment Affairs & Tourism, Pretoria.

Nel, PG, Bredenkamp GJ & van Rooyen N, 1993, *Ecological Status of Grass Species in the Red Turfveld of the Springbok Flats Turf Thronveld, Transvaal, South African Journal of Botany,* 59:45 - 49.

Palmer, E & Pitman, N, 1972 & 1973, *Trees of Southern Africa,* 3 Vols, AA Balkema, Cape Town.

Pooley, E, 1993, *The Complete Field Guide to Trees of Natal, Zululand & Transkei,* 1st edition, Natal Flora Publications Trust, Durban.

Schmidt, AG, Theron, GK & van Hoven, W, 1993, *The Phytosociology and Structure of Vegetation near Villa Nora, North-Western Transvaal, South Africa,* 59:500 - 510.

Shackleton, CM, 1993, Demography and Dynamics of the Woody Species in a Communal and Protected Area of the Eastern Transvaal Lowveld, *South African Journal of Botany,* 59: 569-574.

Steyn, Marthinus, 1996, *SA Ficus Identification Guide for Wild Figs in South Africa,* Promedia, Marks Street, Waltloo.

Trendler, R & Hes, L, 1994, *Attracting Birds to Your Garden in Southern Africa,* Hirt & Carter (Pty) Ltd, Cape Town.

Van Wyk, 1973, *Bome van die Nasionale Krugerwildtuin,* Perskor-Uitgewery, Johannesburg.

Van Wyk, B & Van Wyk, P, 1997, *Field Guide to Trees of Southern Africa,* Struik Publishers (Pty) Ltd, Cape Town.

Van Wyk, BE, Van Oudtshoorn, B & Gericke, N, 1997, *Medicinal Plants of South Africa,* 1st edition, Briza Publications, Pretoria.

Venter, F & JA, 1996, *Making the most of Indigenous Trees,* 1st edition, Briza Publications, Pretoria.

Von Breitenbach, F, 1995, *National List of Indigenous Trees,* 3rd edition, Dendrological Foundation, Pretoria.

Watt, JM & Breyer-Brandwijk, MG, 1962, *Medicinal and Poisonous Plants of Southern and Eastern Africa,* 2nd edition, E & S Livingstone Ltd, Edinburgh and London.

Bushveld Red-balloon, page 37